FAIRY TAIL

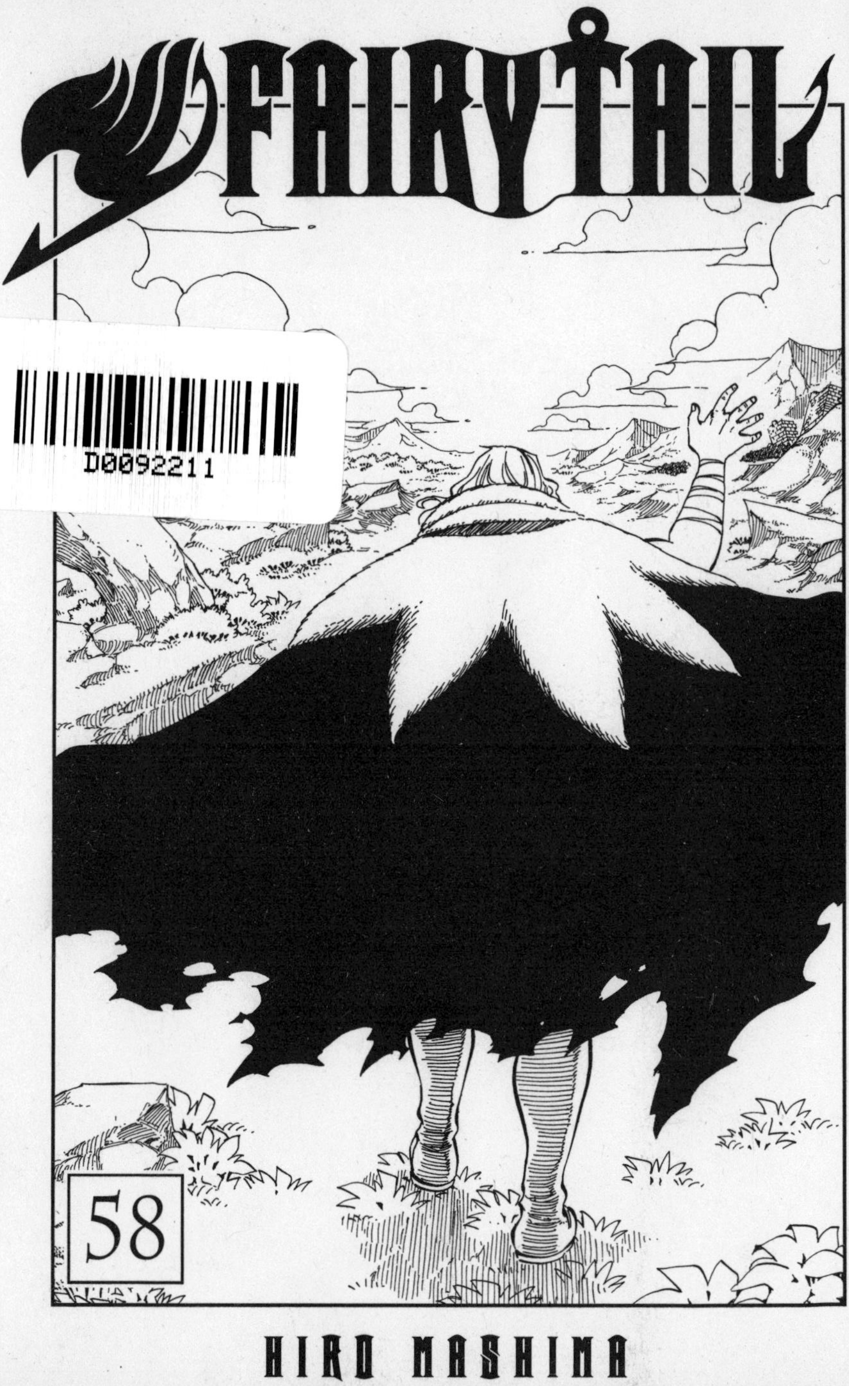

58

HIRO MASHIMA

FAIRY TAIL 58 CONTENTS

FAIRY TAIL

フェアリーテイル

Chapter 492: Older and Younger Sisters

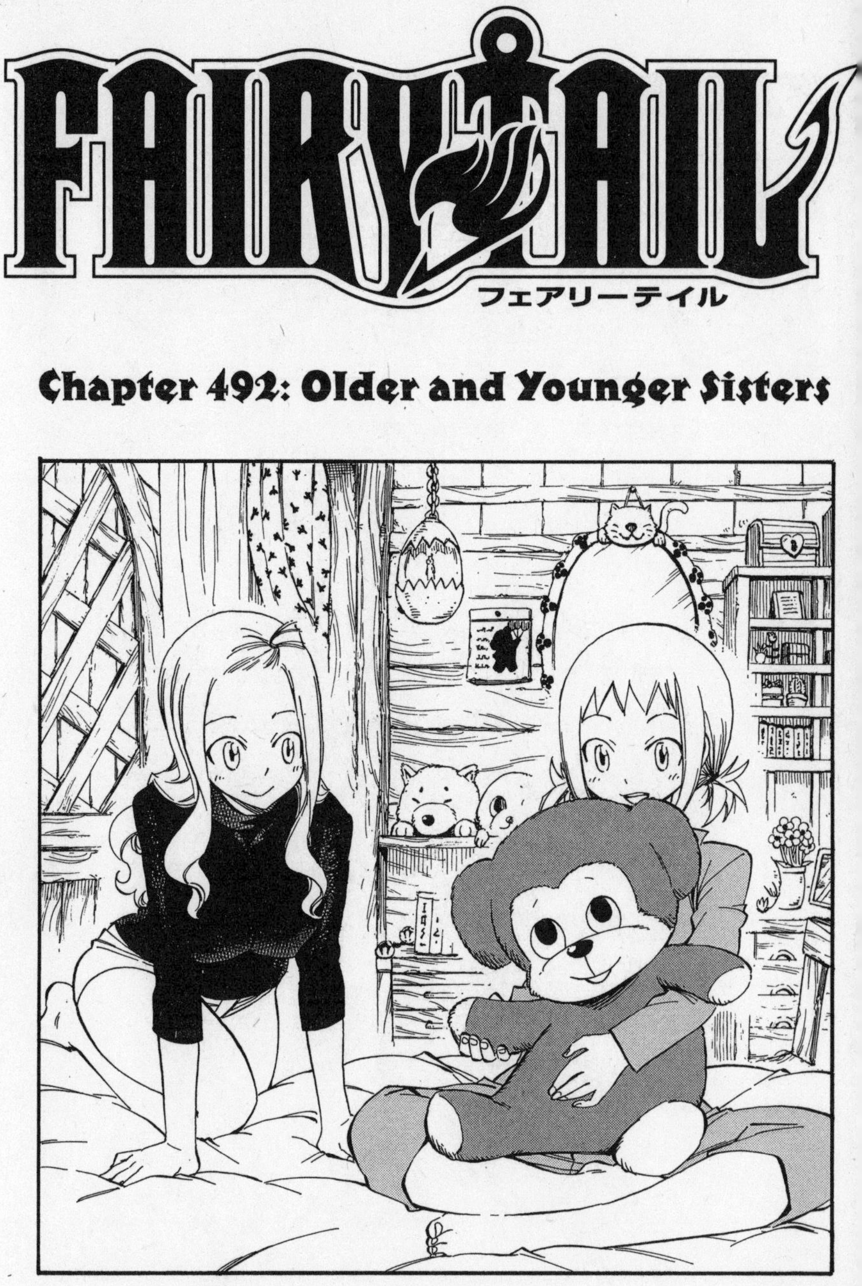

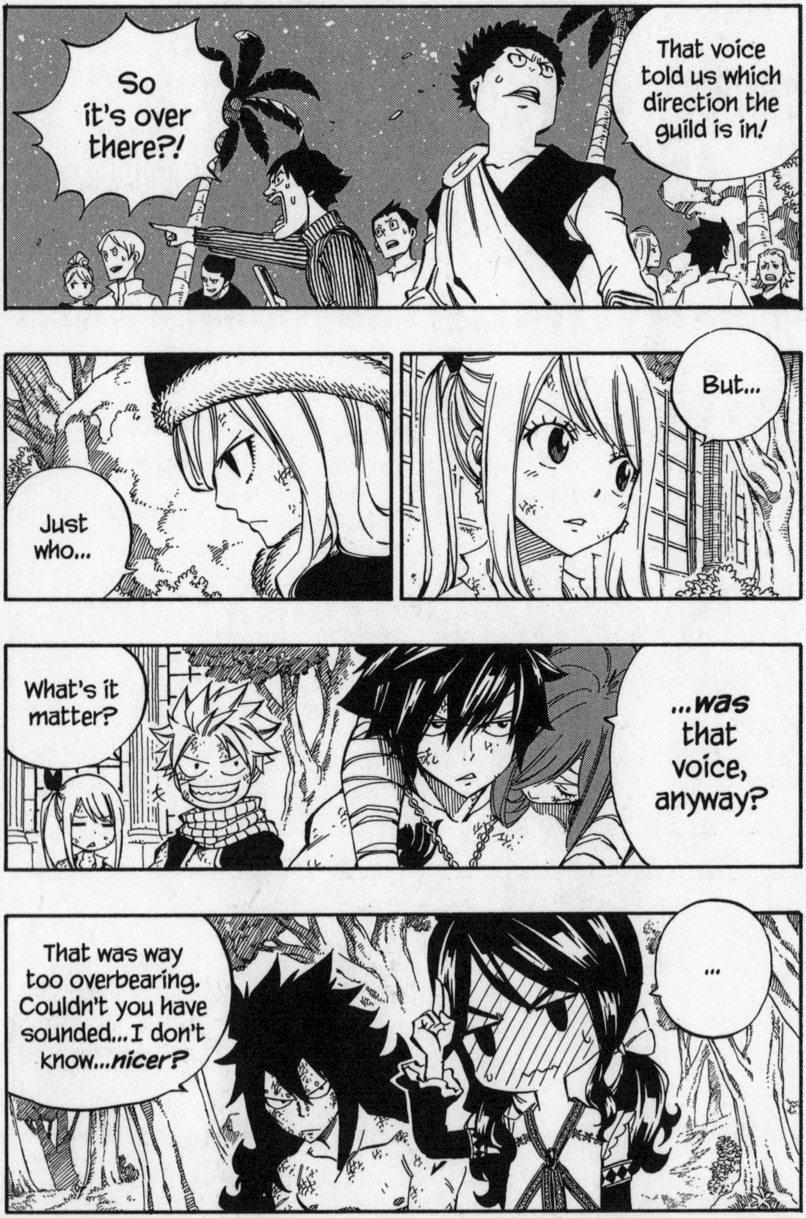
That voice told us which direction the guild is in!
So it's over there?!
But...
Just who...
...*was* that voice, anyway?
What's it matter?
...
That was way too overbearing. Couldn't you have sounded...I don't know...*nicer?*

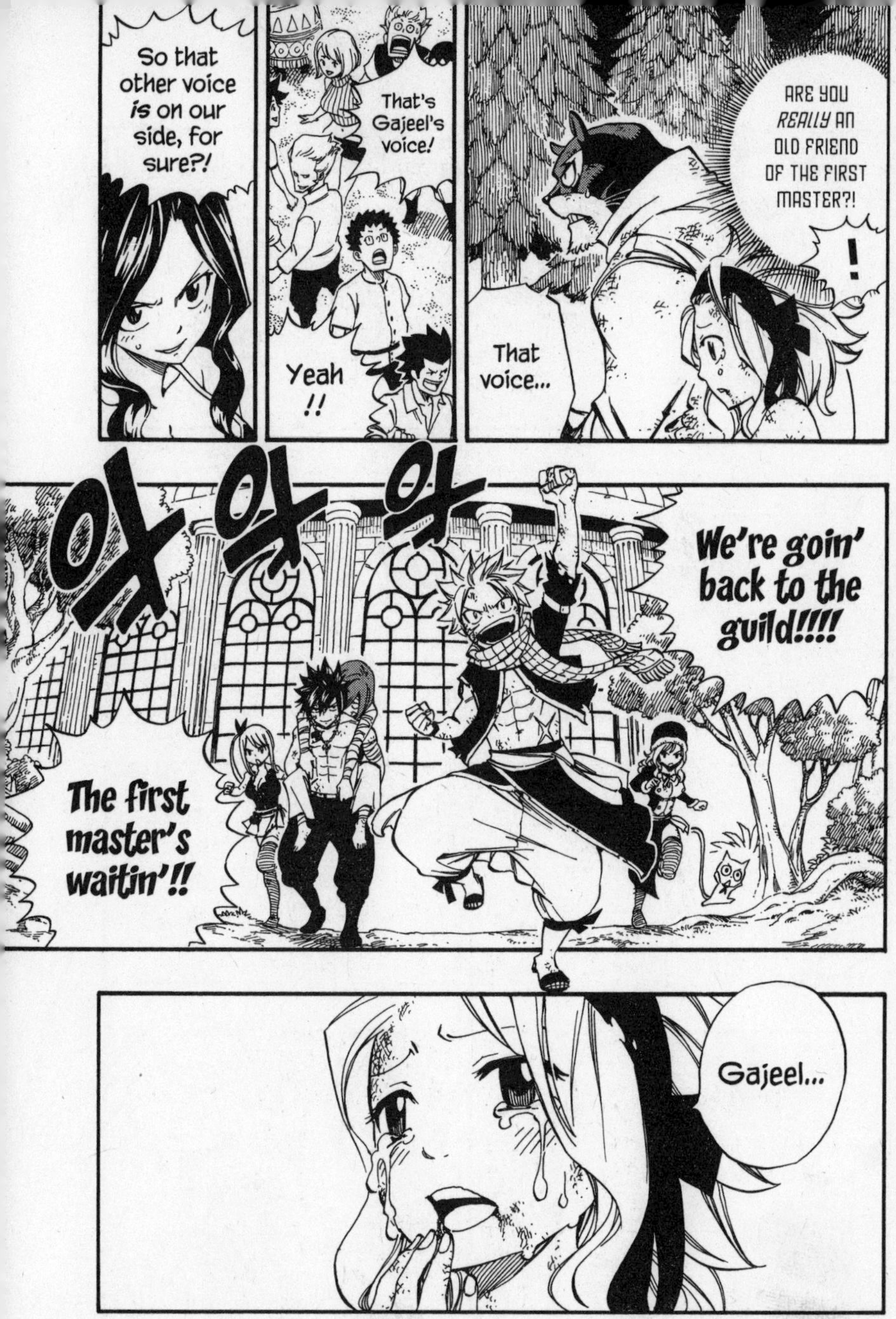
ARE YOU *REALLY* AN OLD FRIEND OF THE FIRST MASTER?!
!
That voice...
That's Gajeel's voice!
Yeah!!
So that other voice *is* on our side, for sure?!
We're goin' back to the guild!!!!
The first master's waitin'!!
Gajeel...

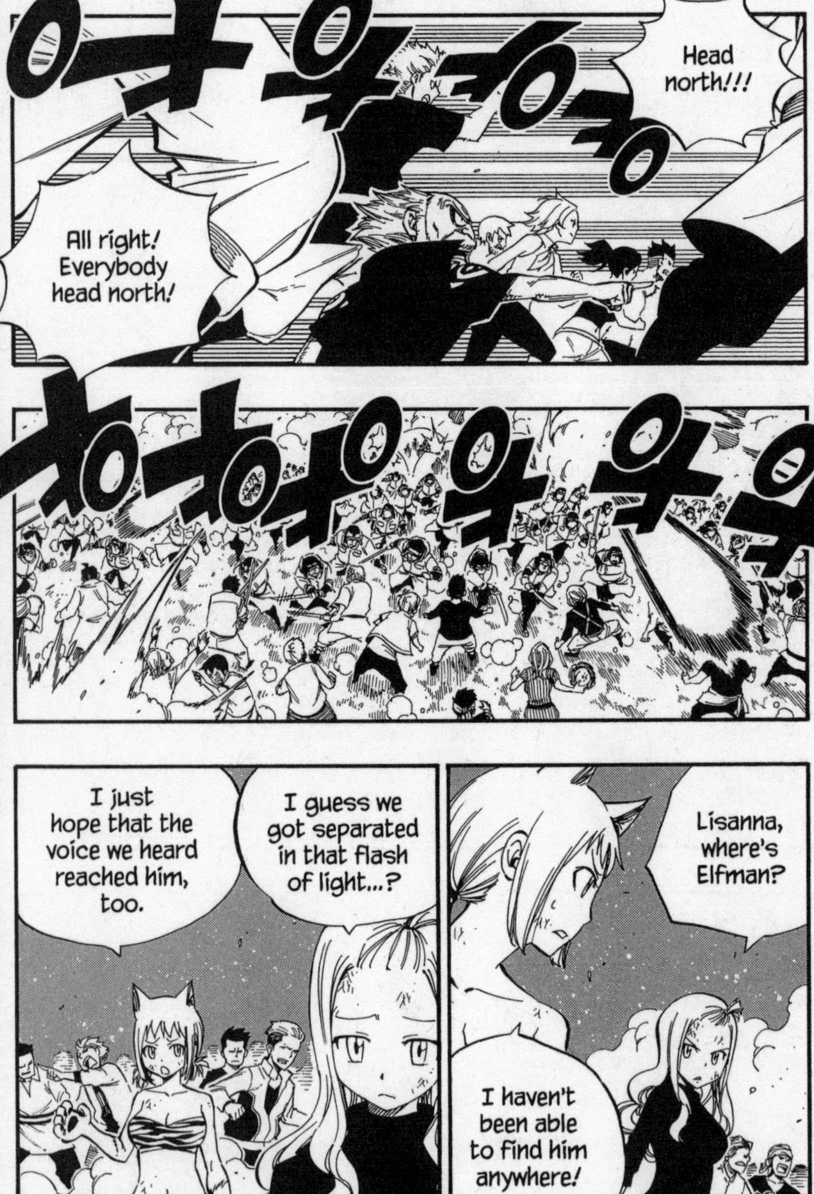
Head north!!!
All right! Everybody head north!
Lisanna, where's Elfman?
I haven't been able to find him anywhere!
I guess we got separated in that flash of light...?
I just hope that the voice we heard reached him, too.

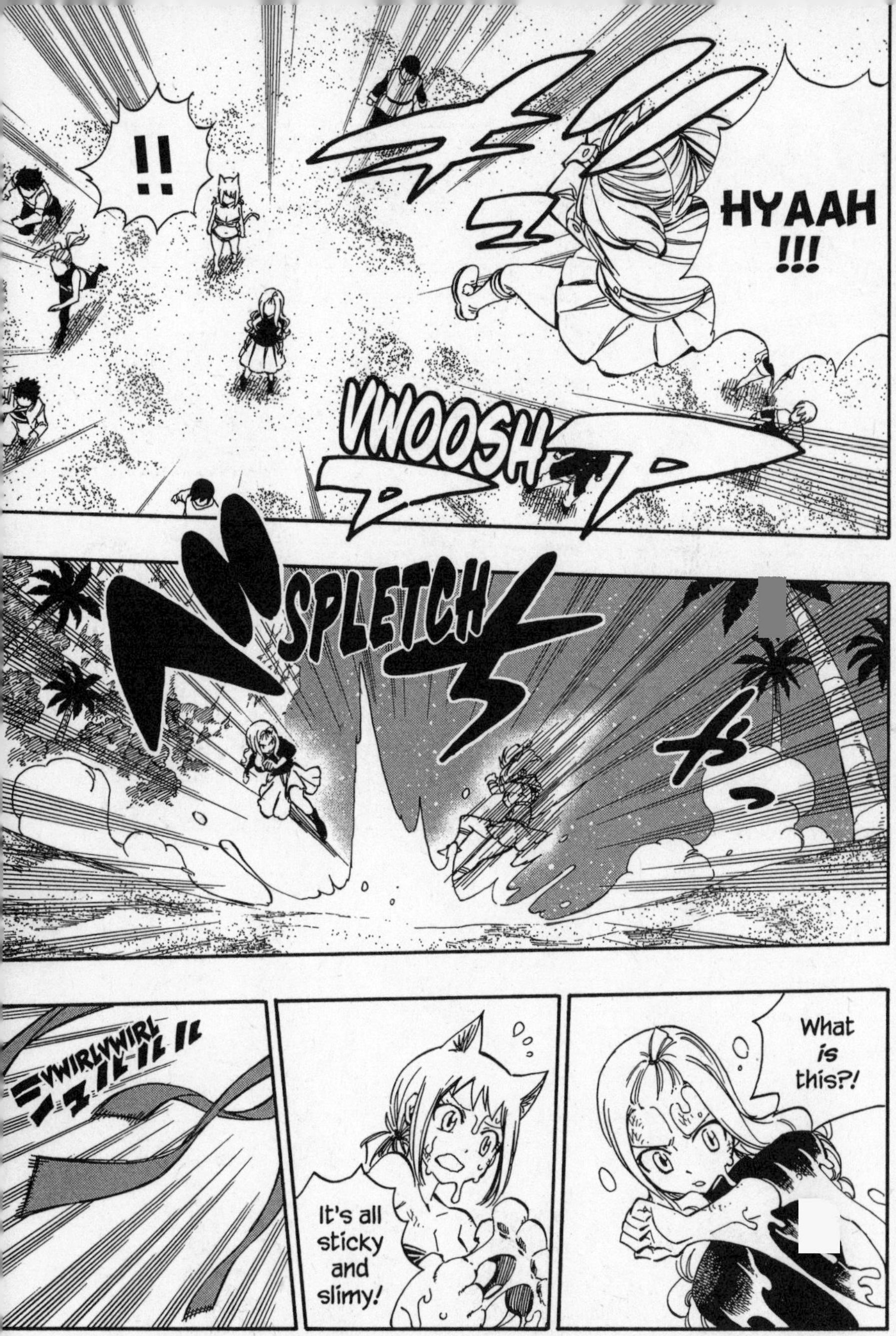
HYAAH !!!
!!
VWOOSH
SPLETCH
What is this?!
It's all sticky and slimy!
SWIRLWIRL
シュルルルル

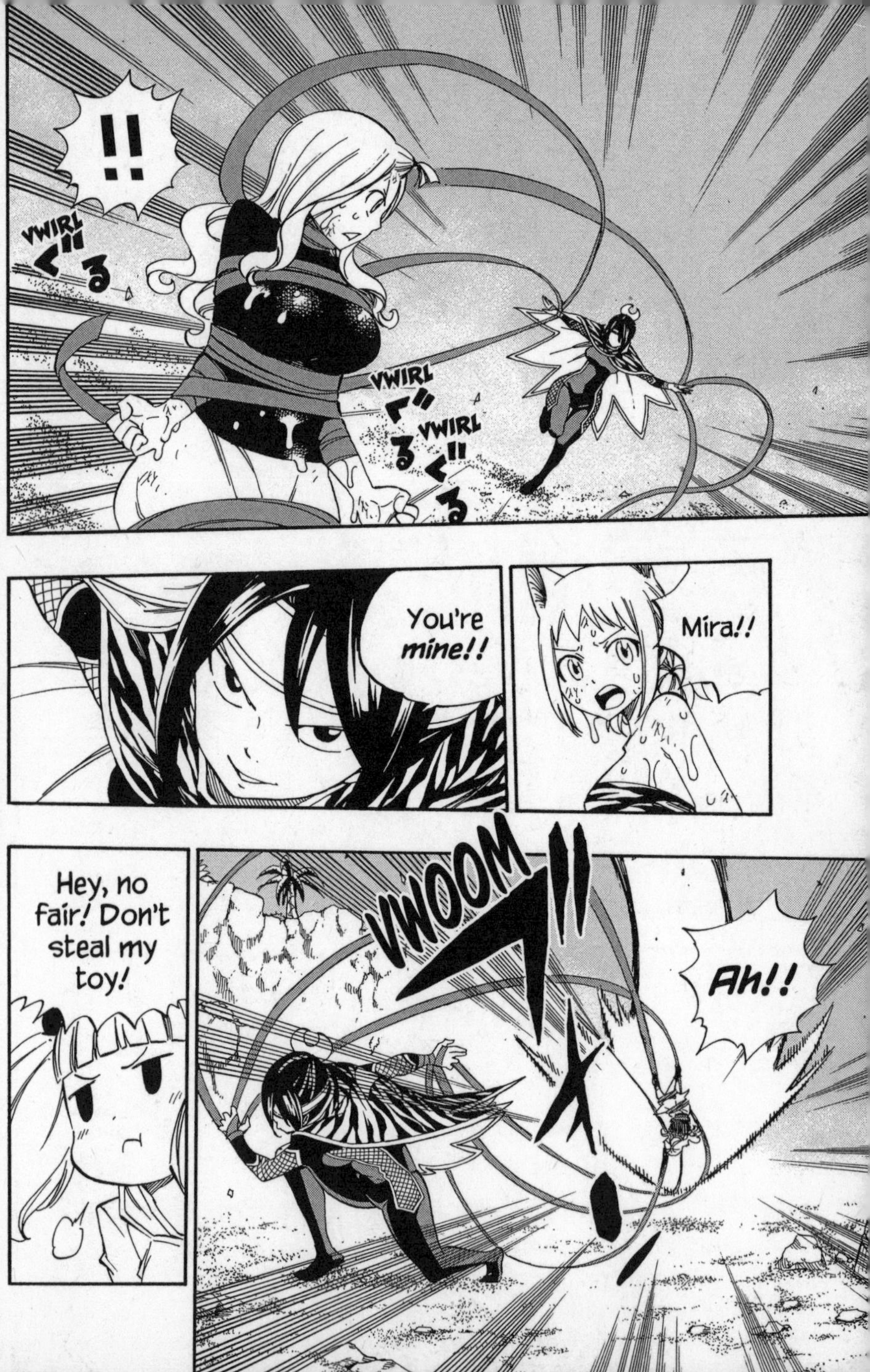
!!
VWIRL ぐる
VWIRL ぐる
VWIRL ぐる
Mira!!
You're mine!!
VWOOM!!
Ah!!
Hey, no fair! Don't steal my toy!

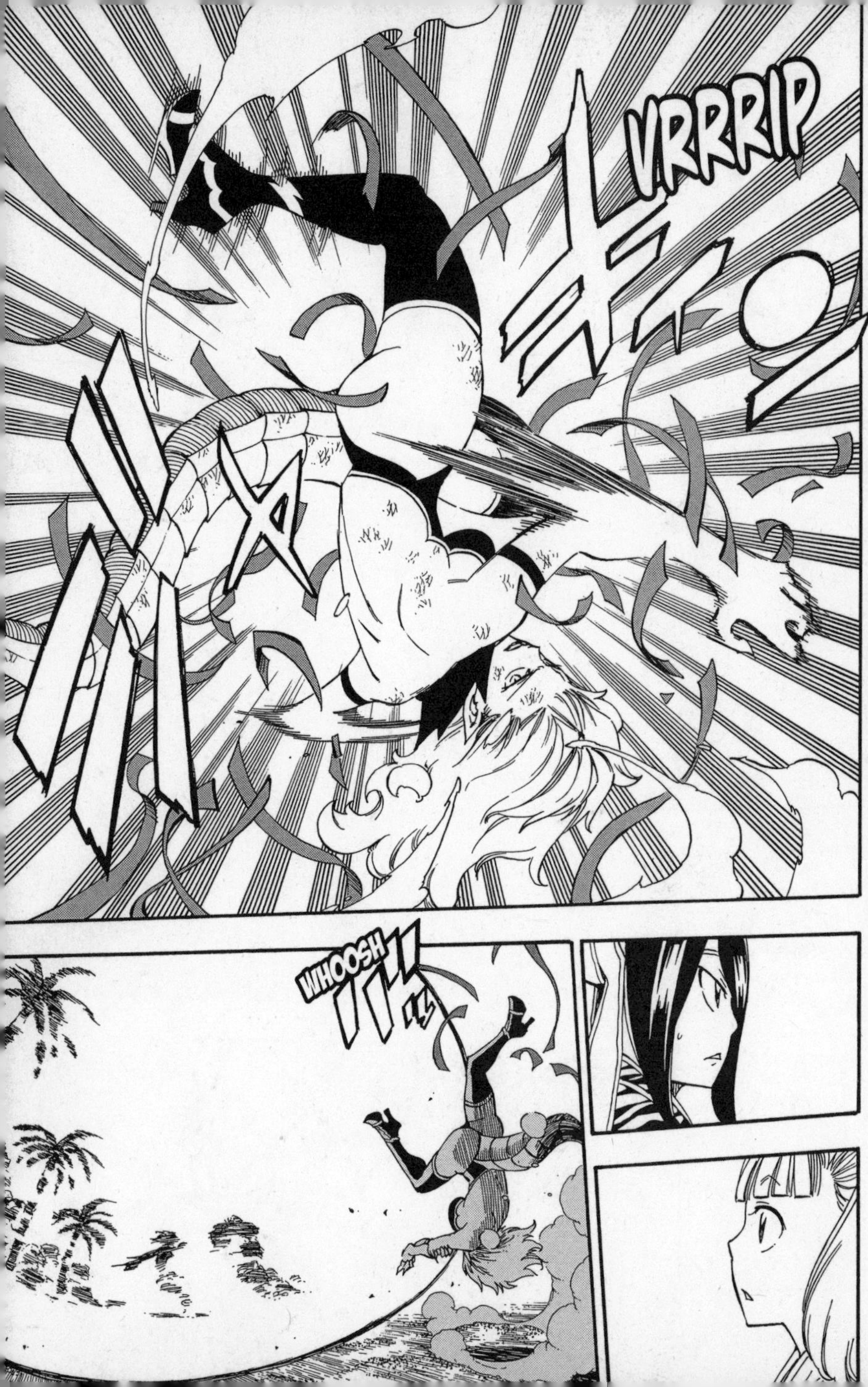
VRRRIP
WHOOSH

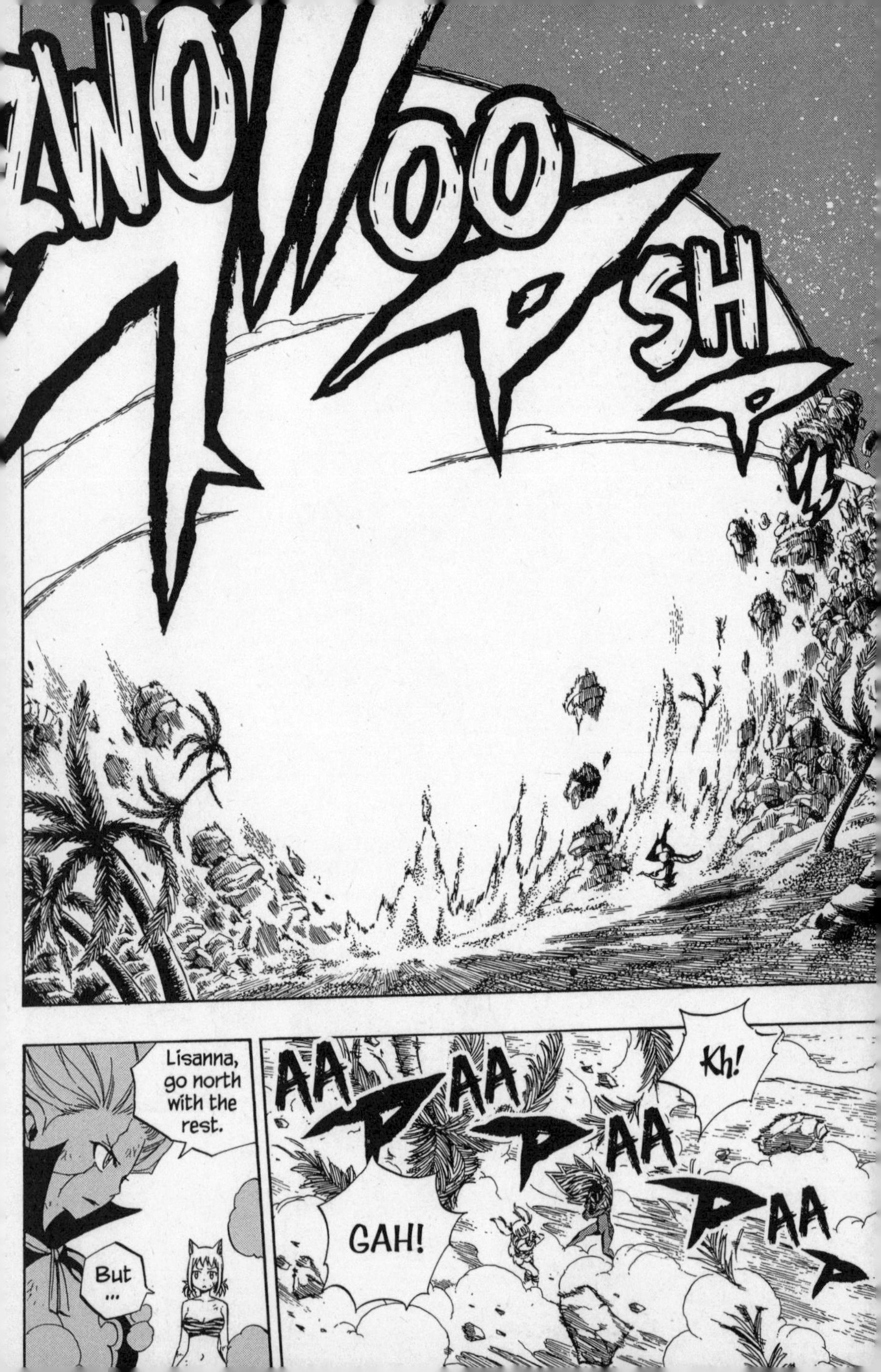
AAAAAAAAAAP
Kh!
GAH!
Lisanna, go north with the rest.
But ...

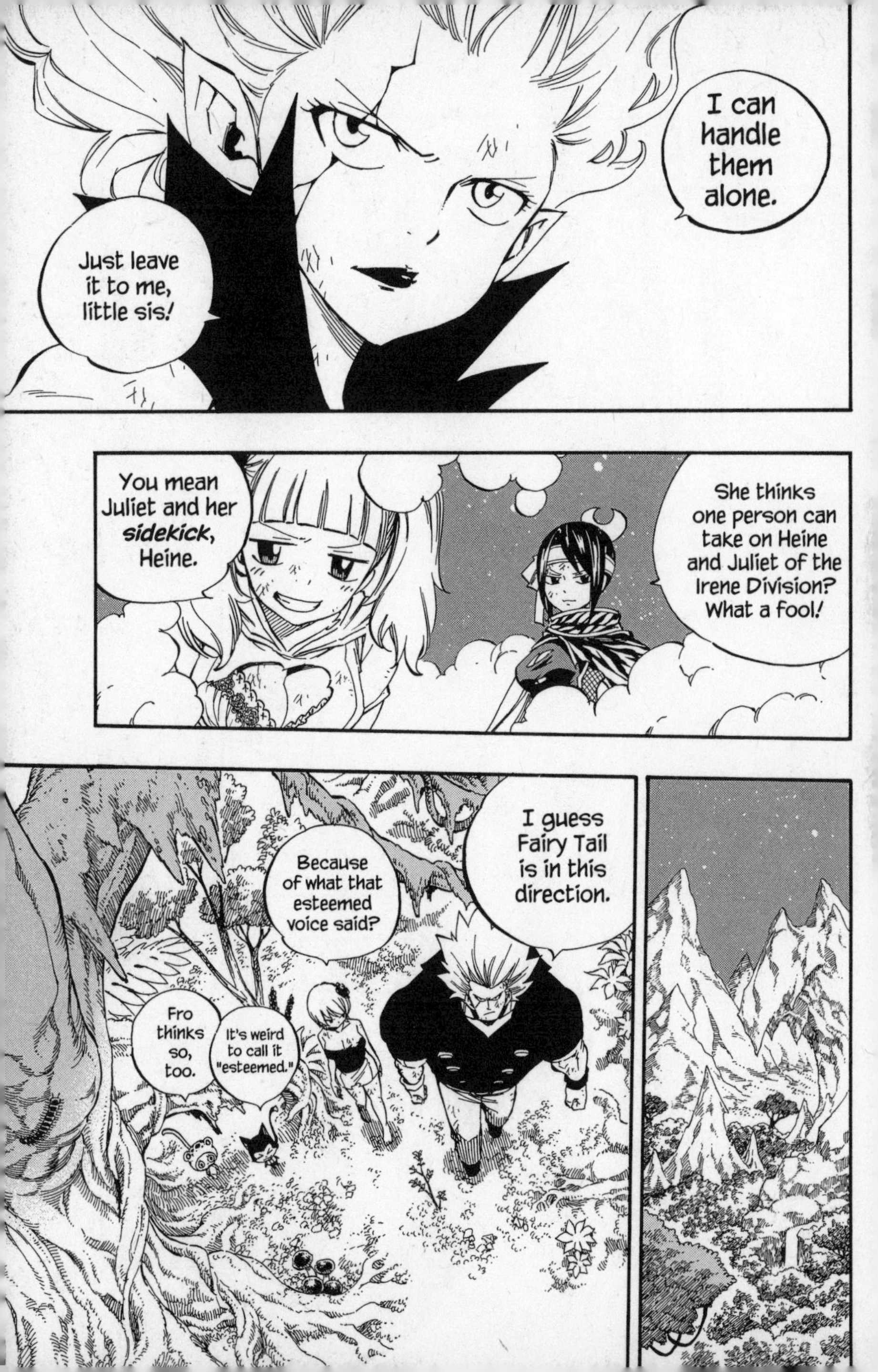
I can handle them alone.
Just leave it to me, little sis!
She thinks one person can take on Heine and Juliet of the Irene Division? What a fool!
You mean Juliet and her *sidekick*, Heine.
I guess Fairy Tail is in this direction.
Because of what that esteemed voice said?
It's weird to call it "esteemed."
Fro thinks so, too.

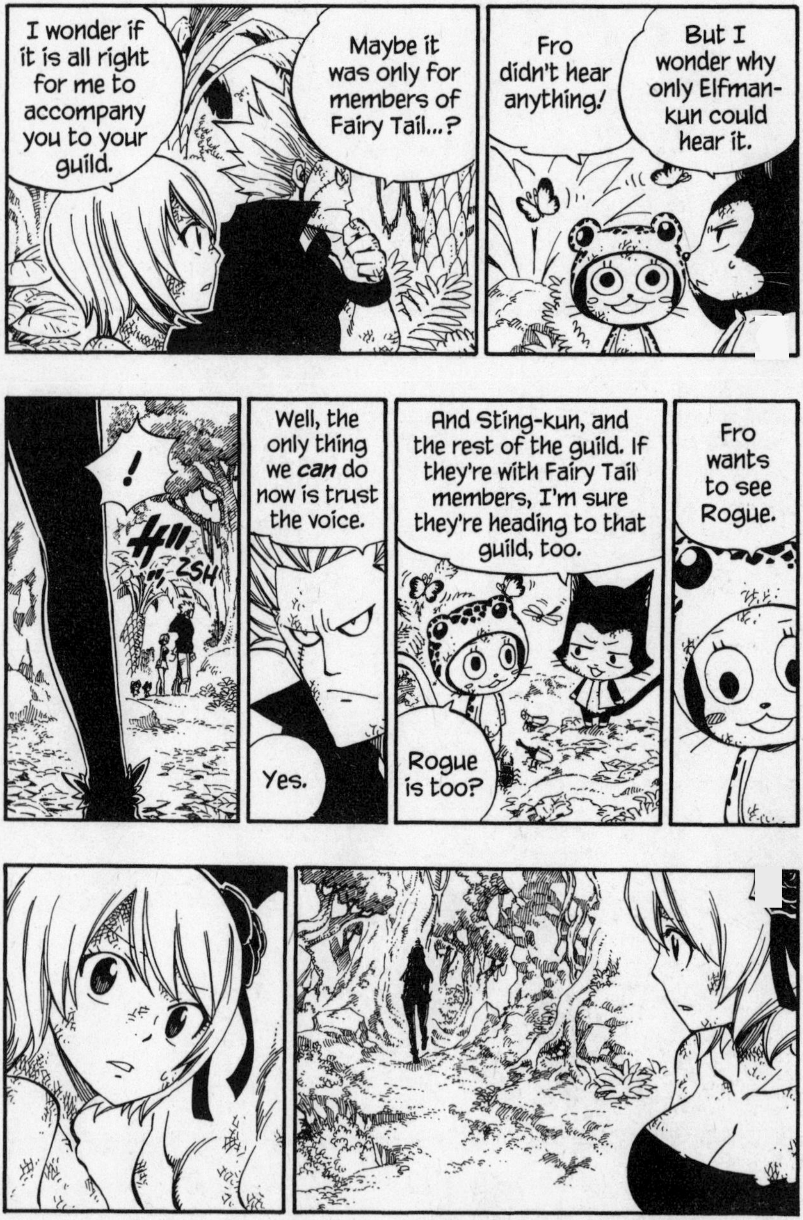

But I wonder why only Elfman-kun could hear it.
Fro didn't hear anything!
Maybe it was only for members of Fairy Tail...?
I wonder if it is all right for me to accompany you to your guild.
Fro wants to see Rogue.
And Sting-kun, and the rest of the guild. If they're with Fairy Tail members, I'm sure they're heading to that guild, too.
Rogue is too?
Well, the only thing we *can* do now is trust the voice.
Yes.
!
ZSH

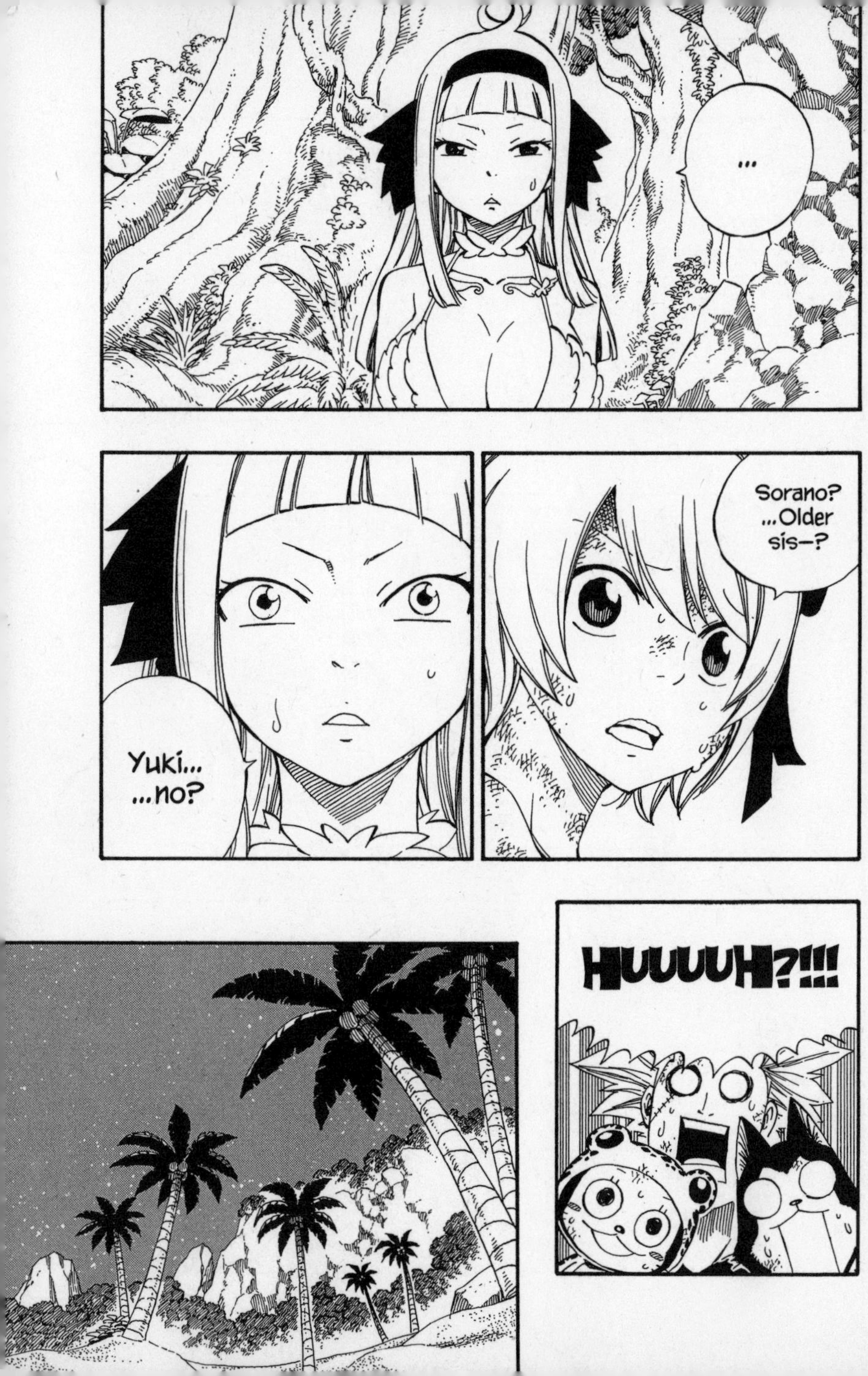
...
Sorano? ...Older sis–?
Yuki... ...no?
HUUUUH?!!!

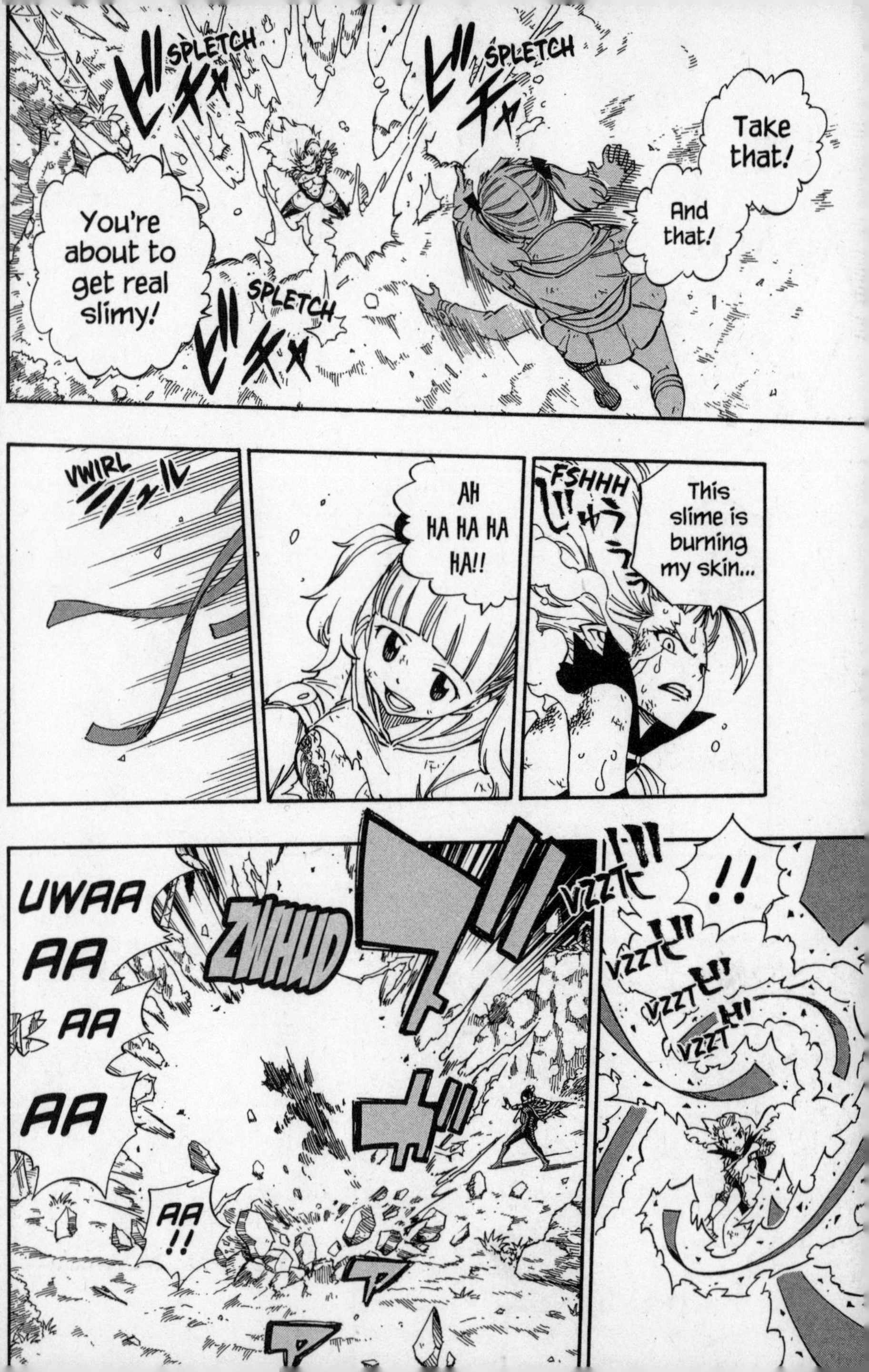
SPLETCH
Take that!
And that!
SPLETCH
You're about to get real slimy!
SPLETCH
This slime is burning my skin...
FSHHH
AH HA HA HA HA!!
VWIRL
!!
VZZT
VZZT
VZZT
VZZT
VZZT
UWAA AA AA AA
ZWHUD
AA !!

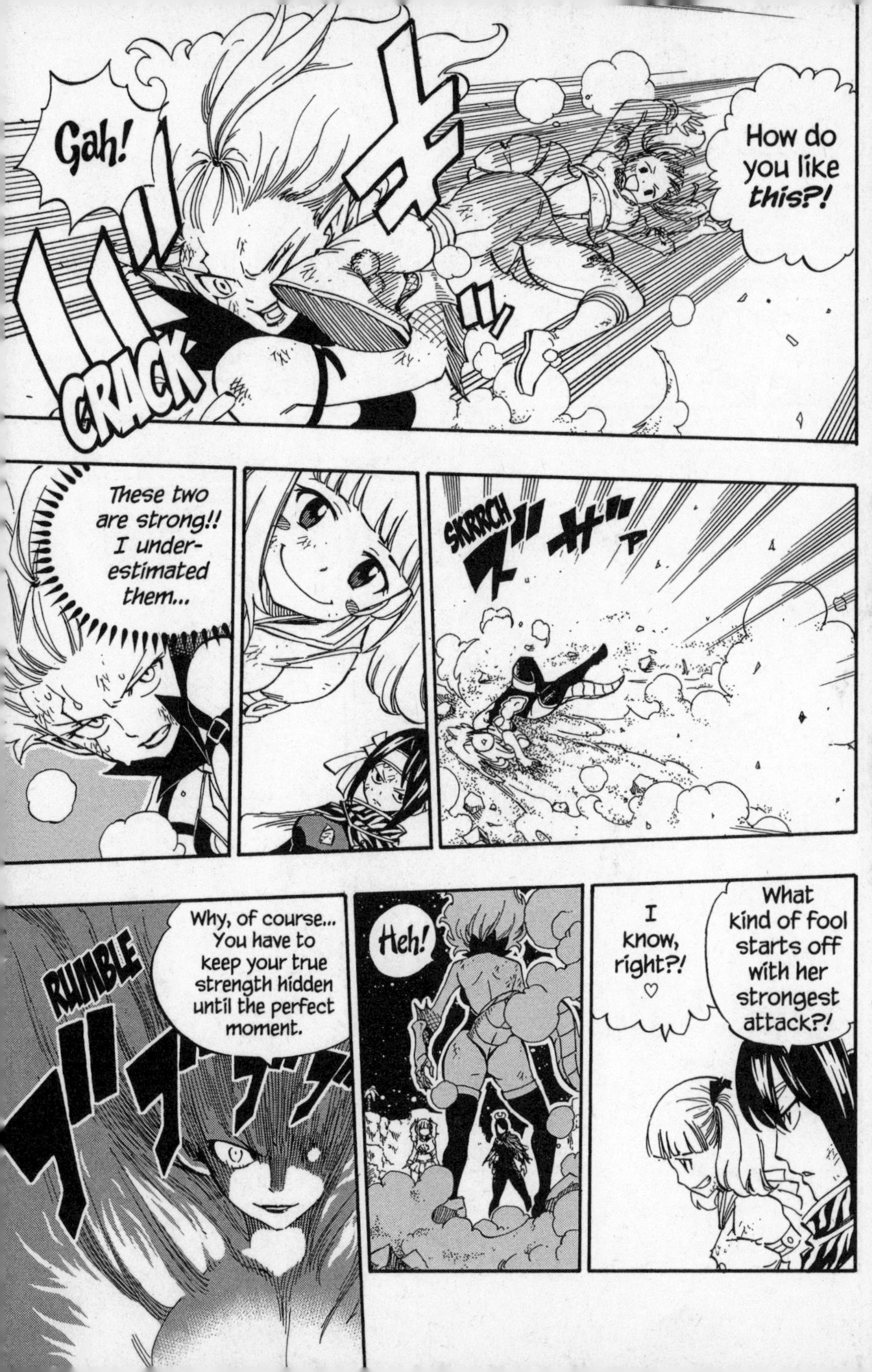
How do you like this?!
Gah!
CRACK
SKRRCH
These two are strong!! I under-estimated them...
What kind of fool starts off with her strongest attack?!
I know, right?! ♡
Heh!
Why, of course... You have to keep your true strength hidden until the perfect moment.
RUMBLE

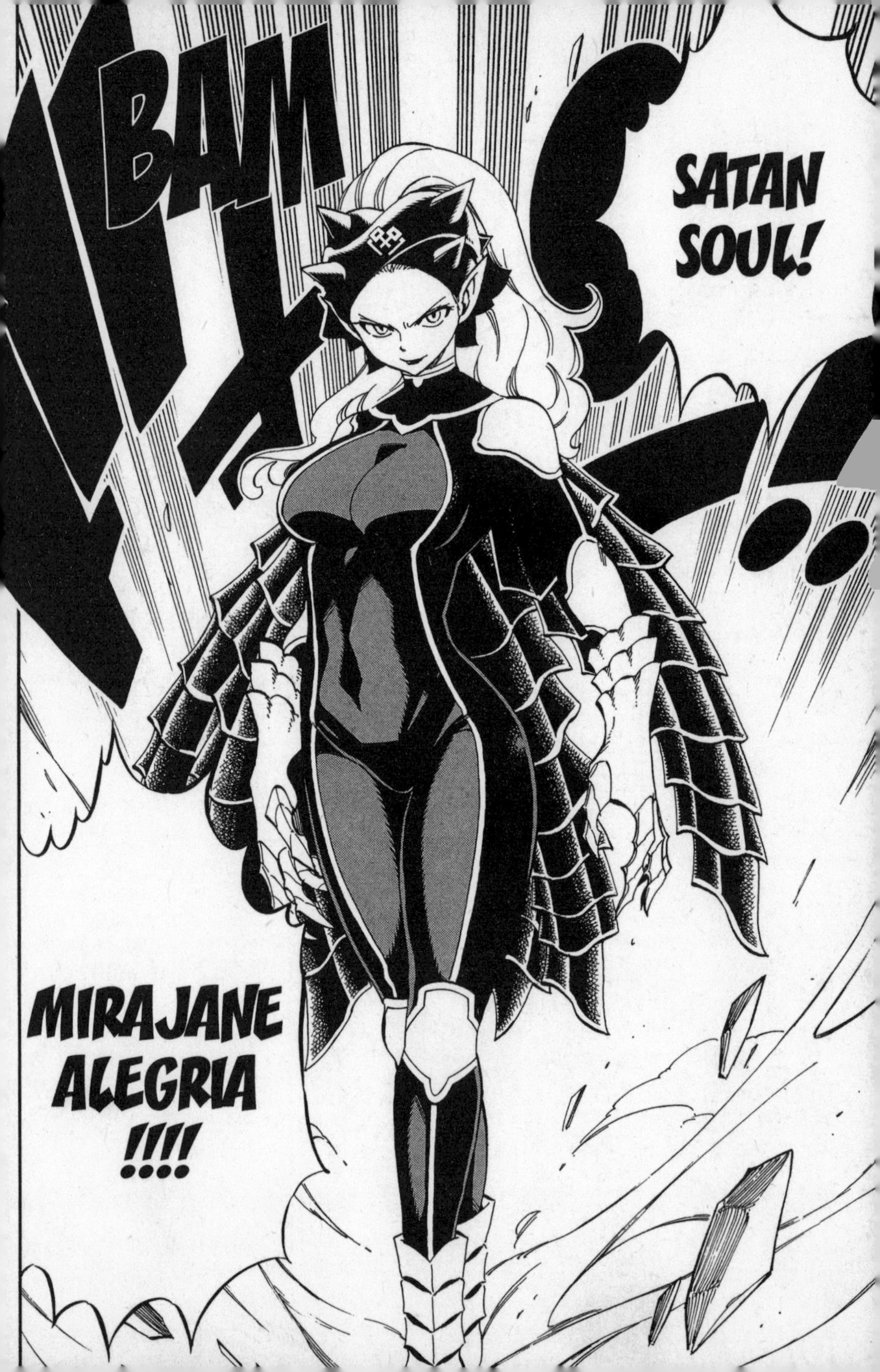
SATAN SOUL!
BAM
MIRAJANE ALEGRIA !!!!

Chapter 493: White Dragneel

*Good Fortune

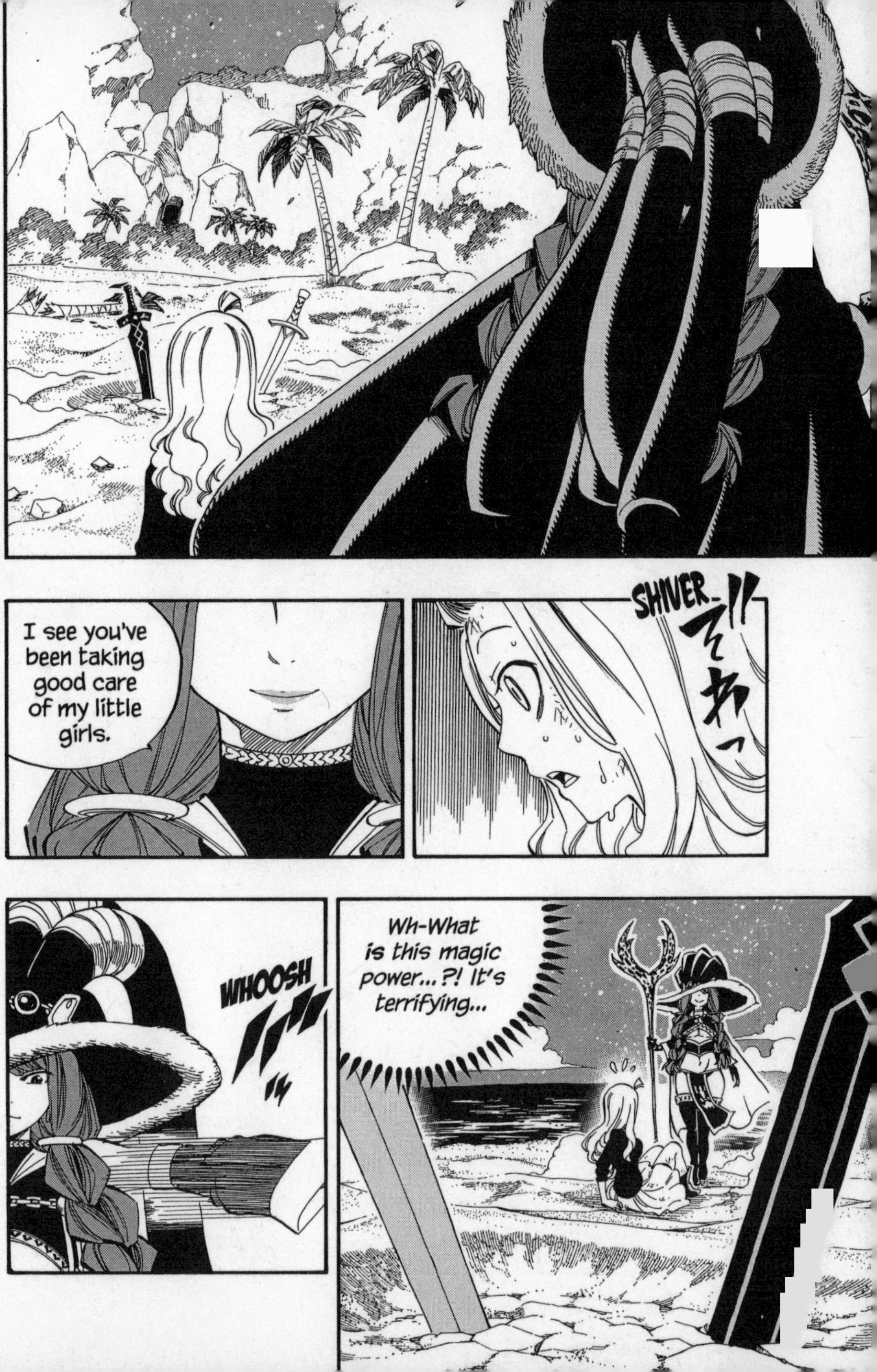
SHIVER
I see you've been taking good care of my little girls.
Wh-What is this magic power...?! It's terrifying...
WHOOSH

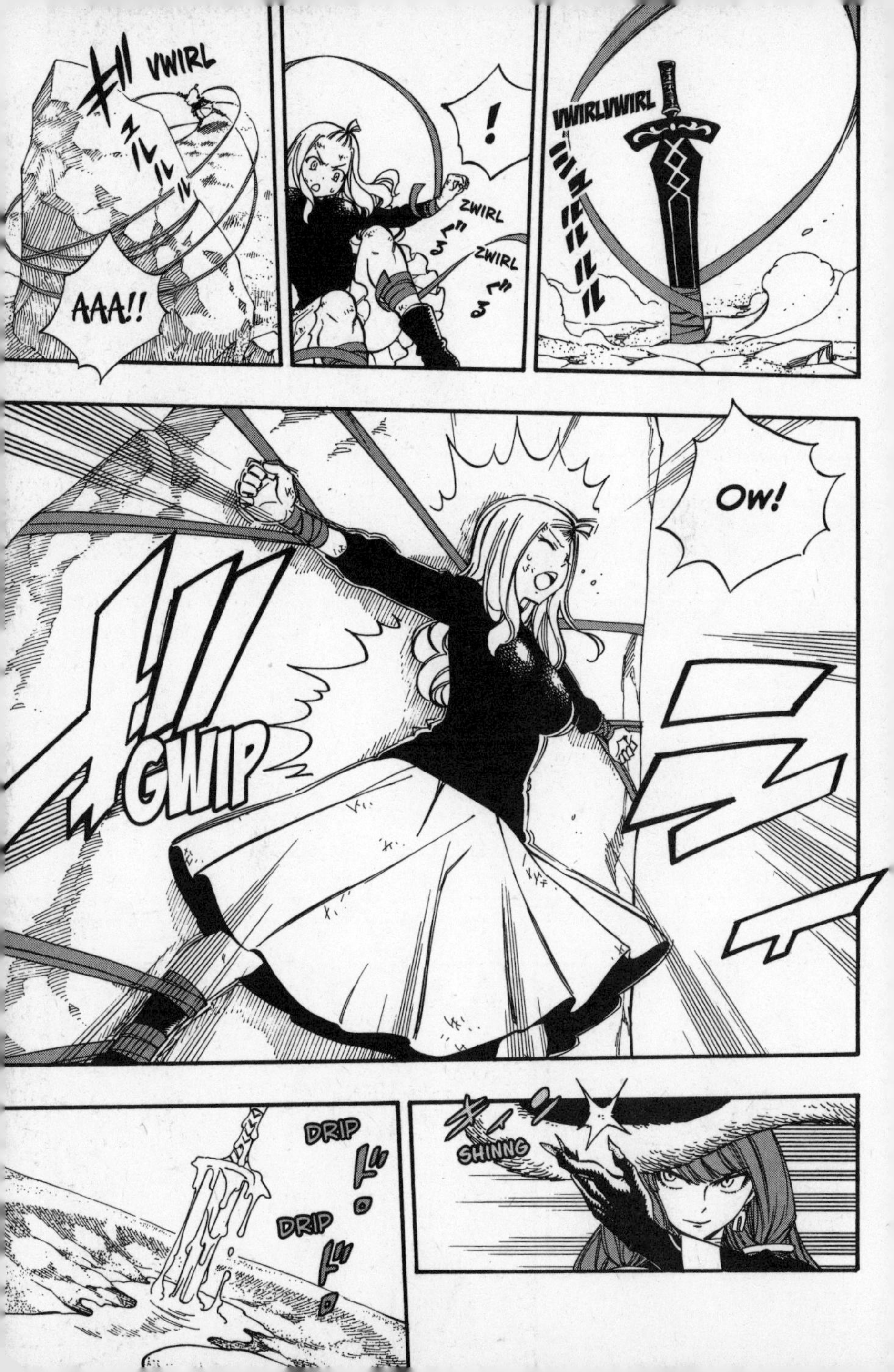

VWIRLVWIRL
!
ZWIRL
ZWIRL
VWIRL
AAA!!
OW!
GWIP
SHINNG
DRIP
DRIP

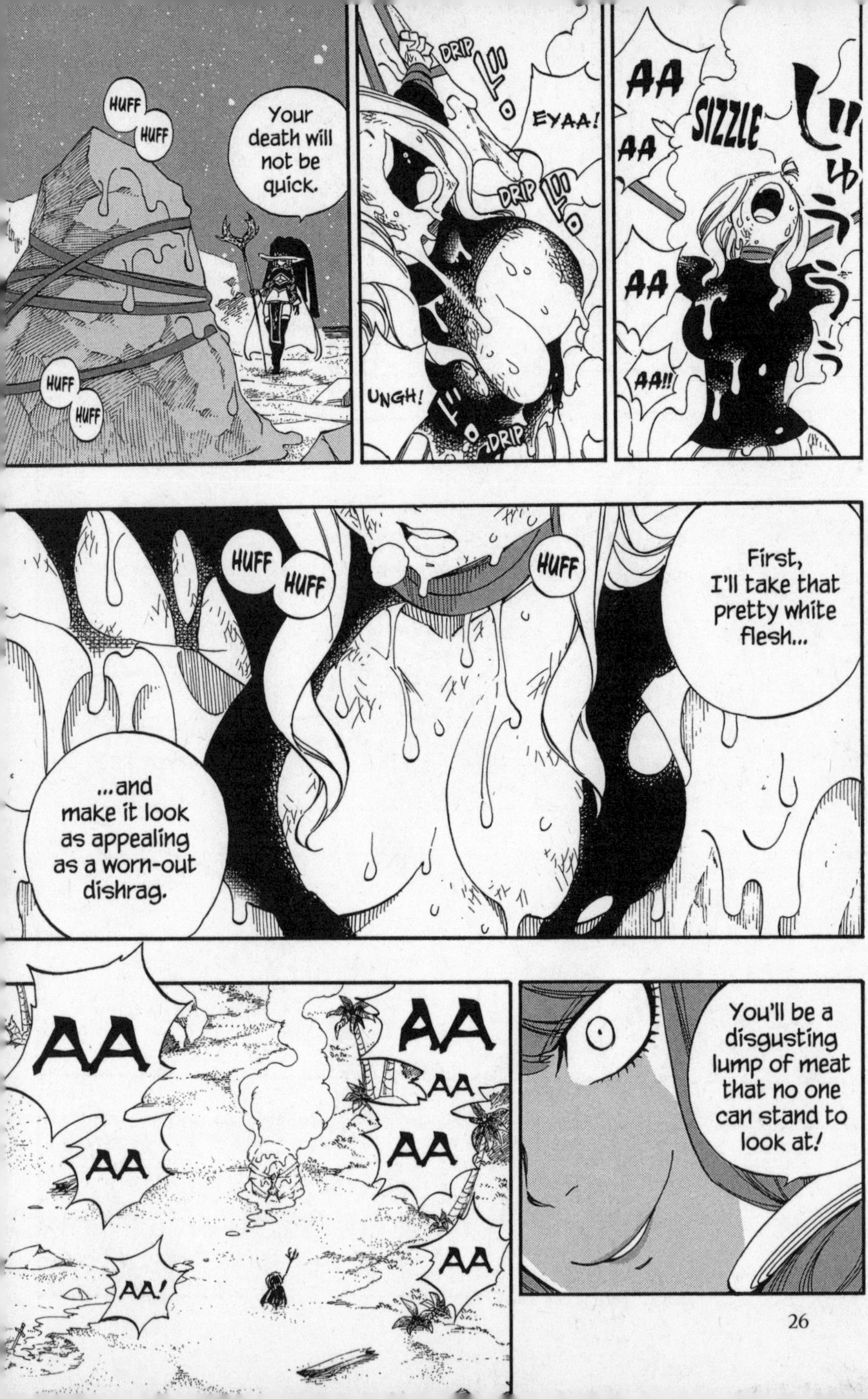
AA
SIZZLE
AA
AA
AA!!
DRIP
EYAA!
DRIP
UNGH!
DRIP
Your death will not be quick.
HUFF
HUFF
HUFF
HUFF
First, I'll take that pretty white flesh...
HUFF
HUFF
HUFF
...and make it look as appealing as a worn-out dishrag.
You'll be a disgusting lump of meat that no one can stand to look at!
AA
AA
AA
AA
AA
AA
AA!

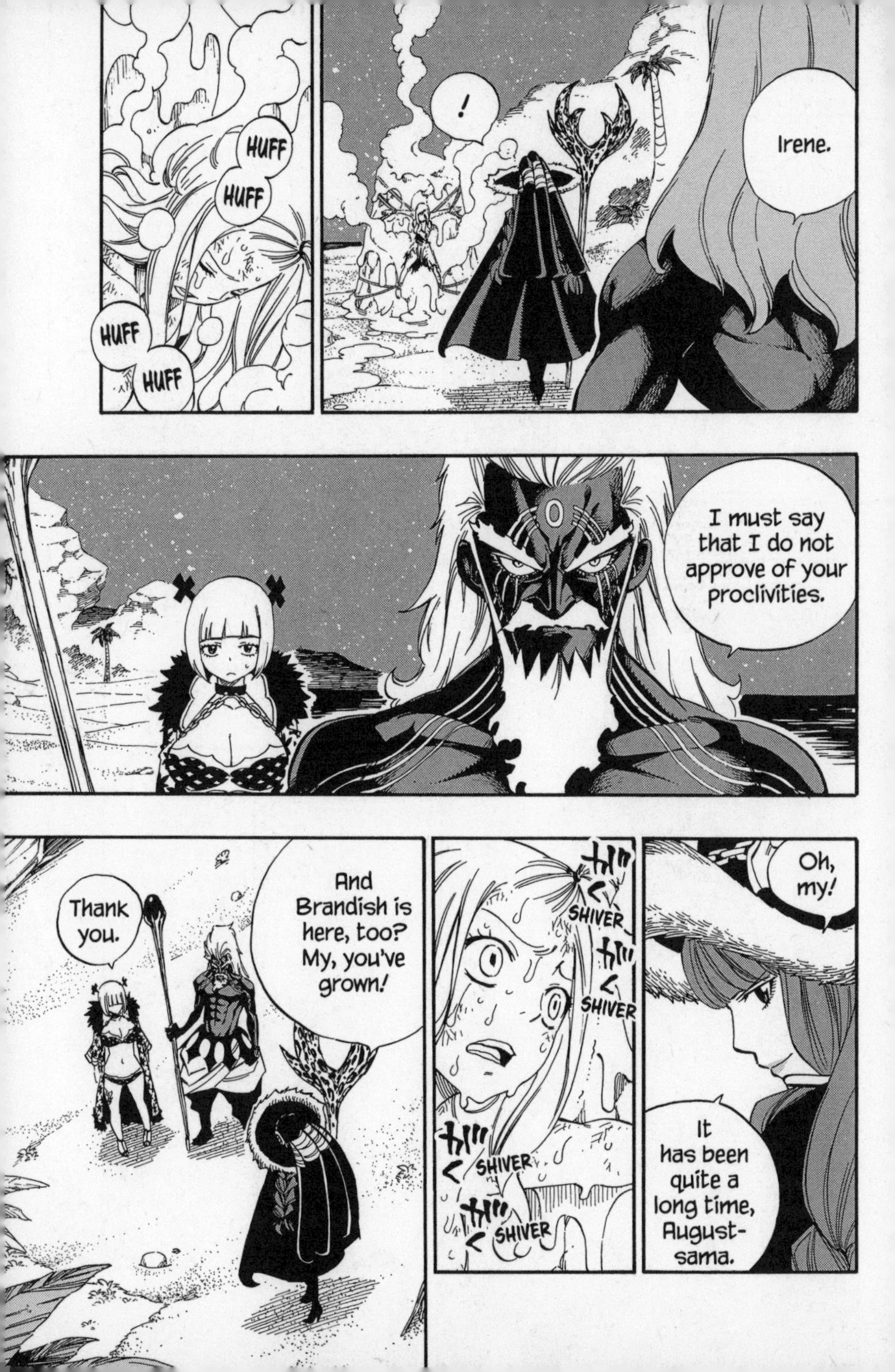
Irene.
!
HUFF
HUFF
HUFF
HUFF
I must say that I do not approve of your proclivities.
Oh, my!
It has been quite a long time, August-sama.
SHIVER
SHIVER
SHIVER
SHIVER
And Brandish is here, too? My, you've grown!
Thank you.

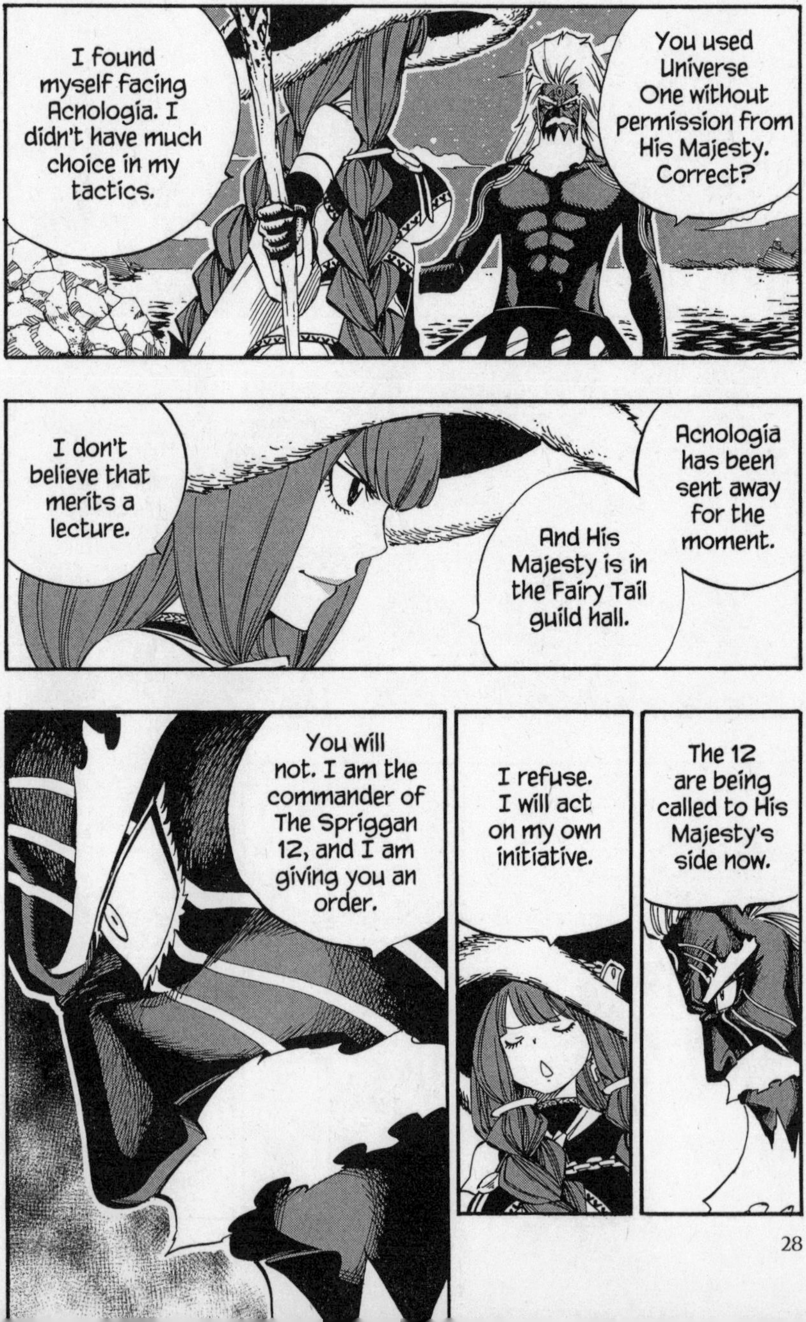
You used Universe One without permission from His Majesty. Correct?
I found myself facing Acnologia. I didn't have much choice in my tactics.
Acnologia has been sent away for the moment.
And His Majesty is in the Fairy Tail guild hall.
I don't believe that merits a lecture.
The 12 are being called to His Majesty's side now.
I refuse. I will act on my own initiative.
You will not. I am the commander of The Spriggan 12, and I am giving you an order.

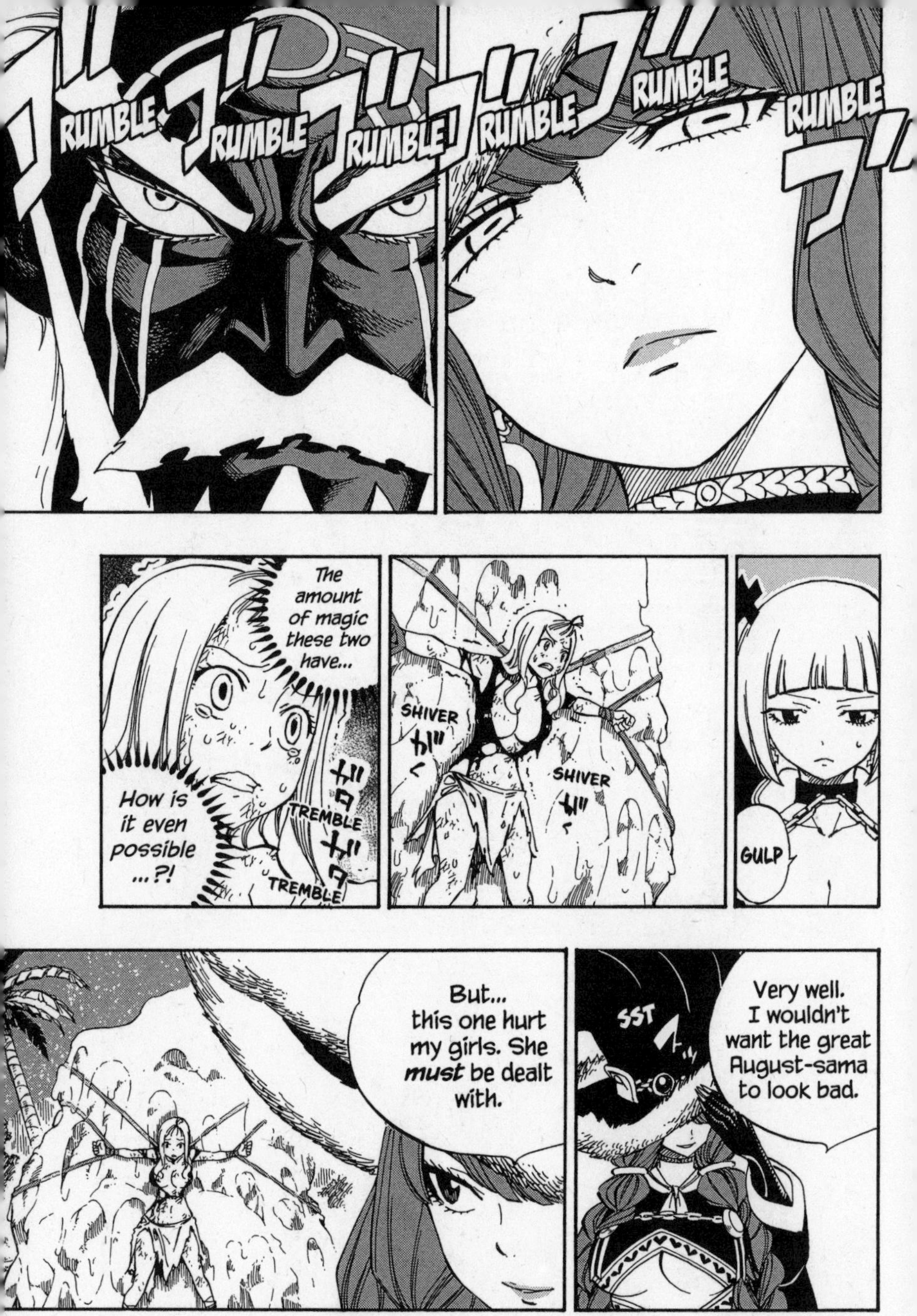
RUMBLE
RUMBLE
RUMBLE
RUMBLE
RUMBLE
RUMBLE
GULP
SHIVER
SHIVER
The amount of magic these two have...
How is it even possible ...?!
TREMBLE
TREMBLE
SST
Very well. I wouldn't want the great August-sama to look bad.
But... this one hurt my girls. She *must* be dealt with.

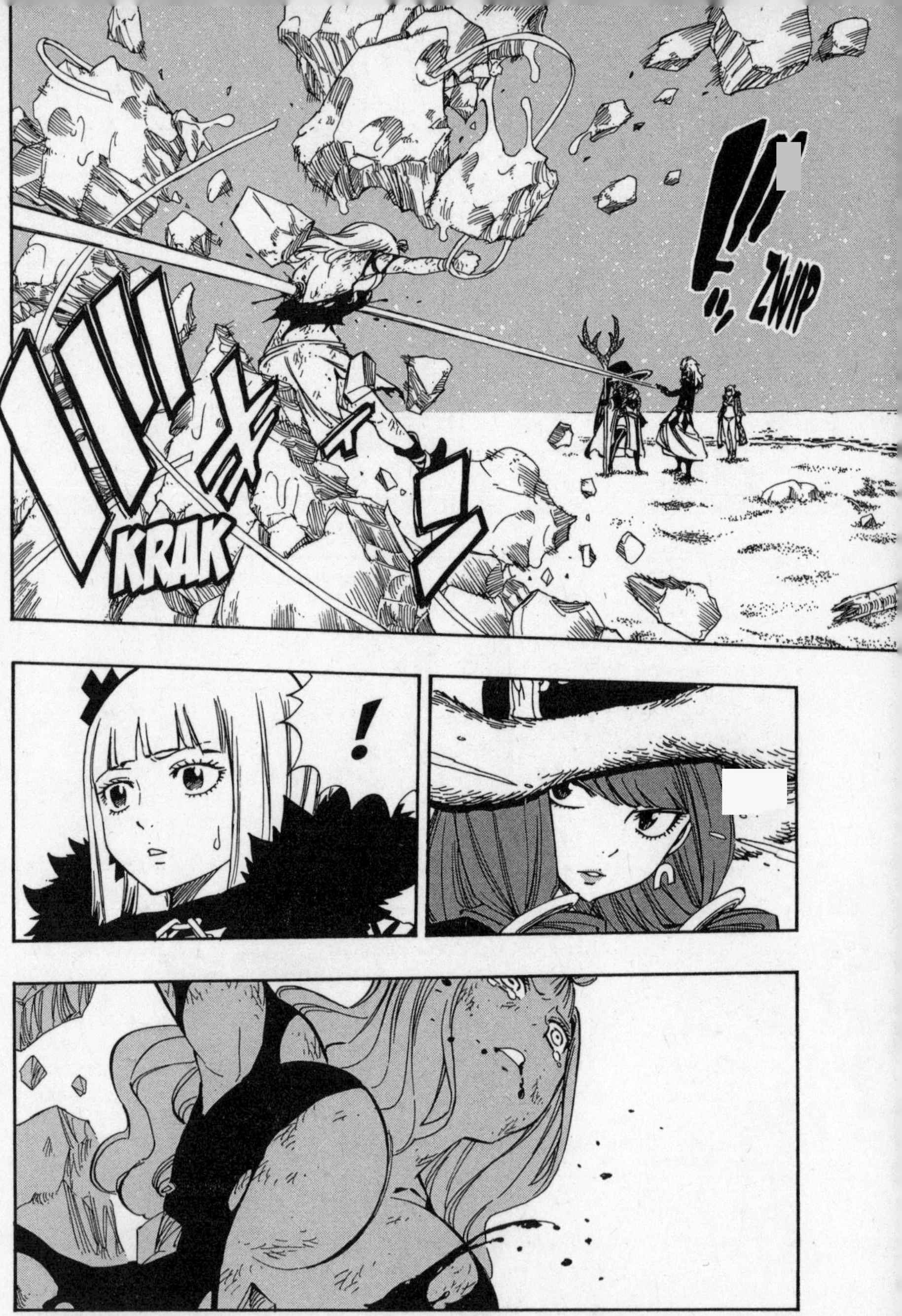
ZWIP
KRAK
!

Her heart's pierced.

Now, if you have no further objections...

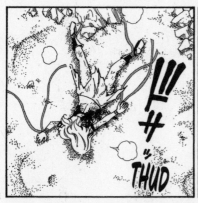

THUD

THUP

I wouldn't have suspected that August "the calamity" would be quite so...merciful.

No objections. Shall we proceed?

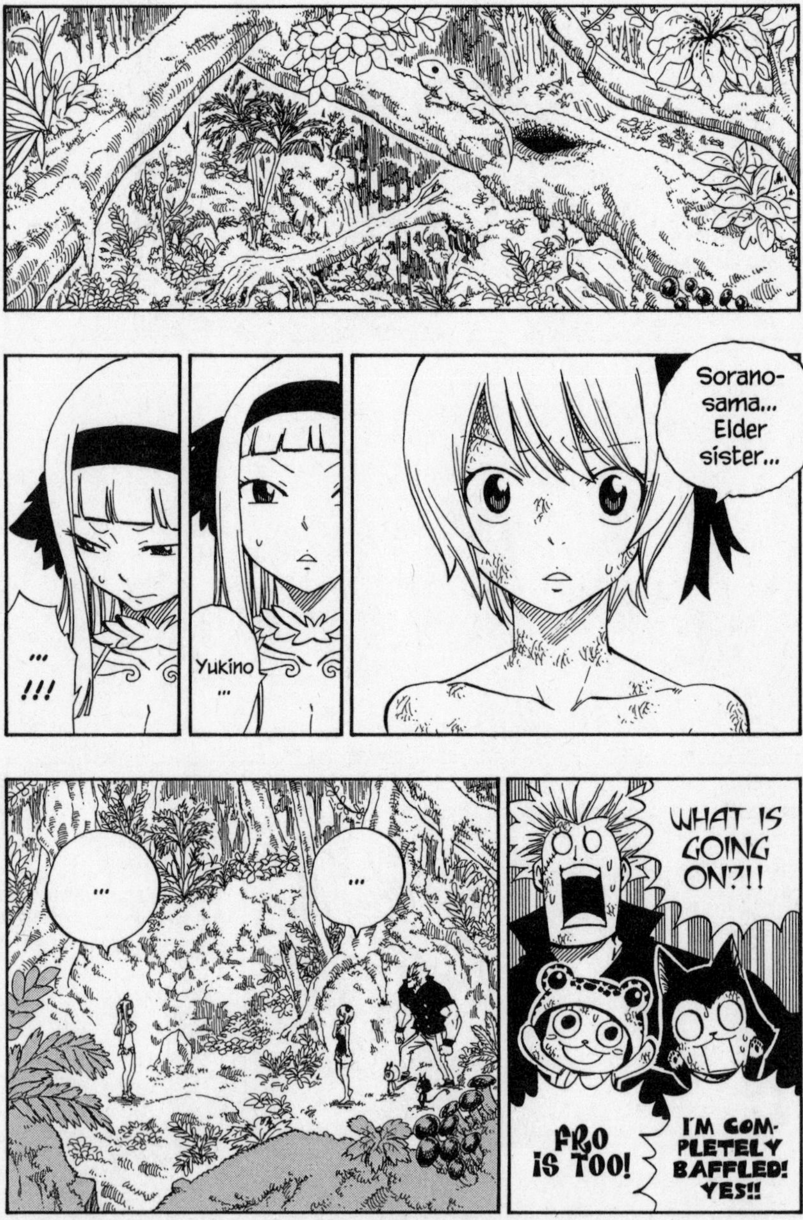
Sorano-sama... Elder sister...
Yukino ...
... !!!
WHAT IS GOING ON?!!
I'M COMPLETELY BAFFLED! YES!!
FRO IS TOO!
...
...

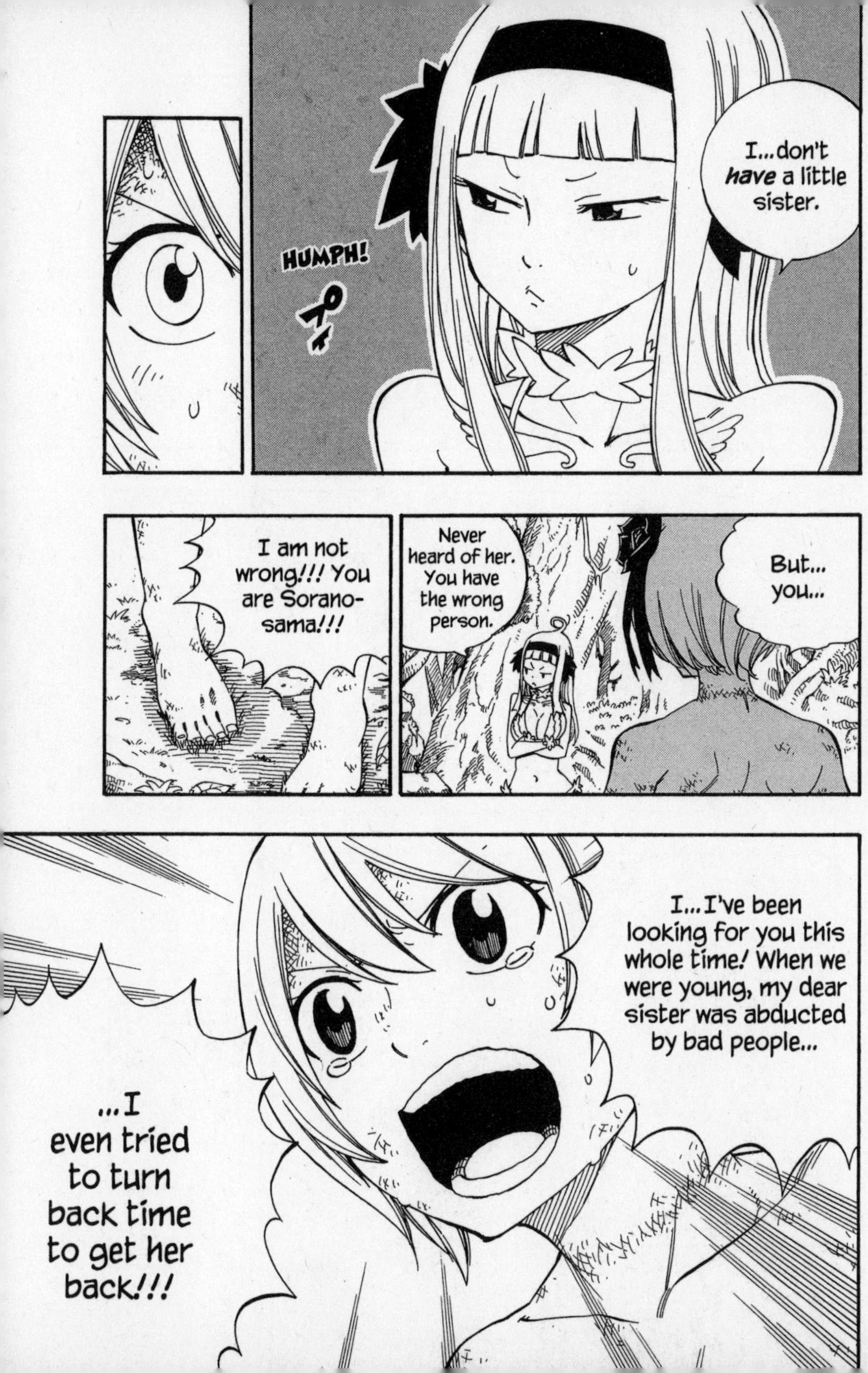
I...don't *have* a little sister.
HUMPH!
But... you...
Never heard of her. You have the wrong person.
I am not wrong!!! You are Sorano-sama!!!
I... I've been looking for you this whole time! When we were young, my dear sister was abducted by bad people...
...I even tried to turn back time to get her back!!!

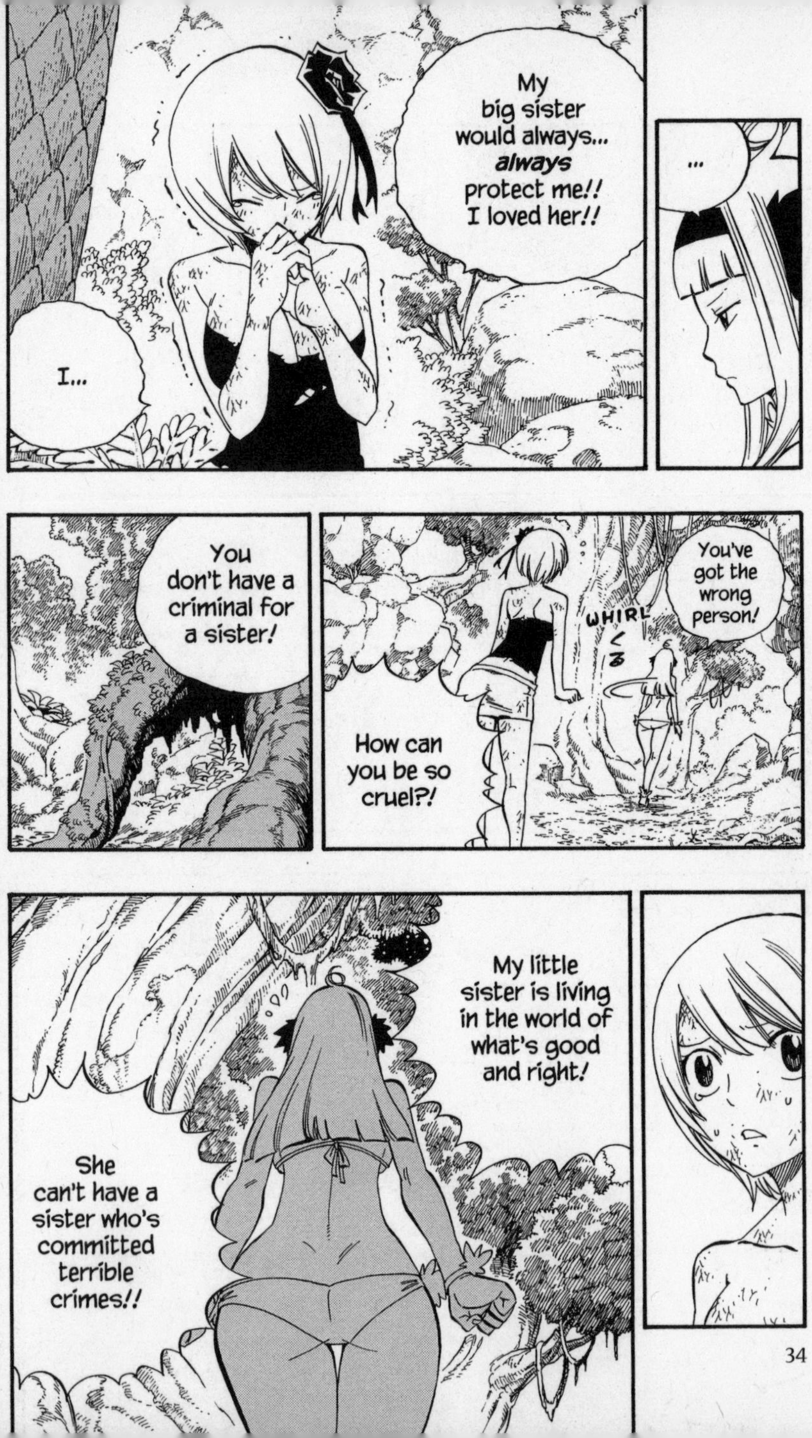
...
My big sister would always... *always* protect me!! I loved her!!
I...
You've got the wrong person!
WHIRL
How can you be so cruel?!
You don't have a criminal for a sister!
My little sister is living in the world of what's good and right!
She can't have a sister who's committed terrible crimes!!

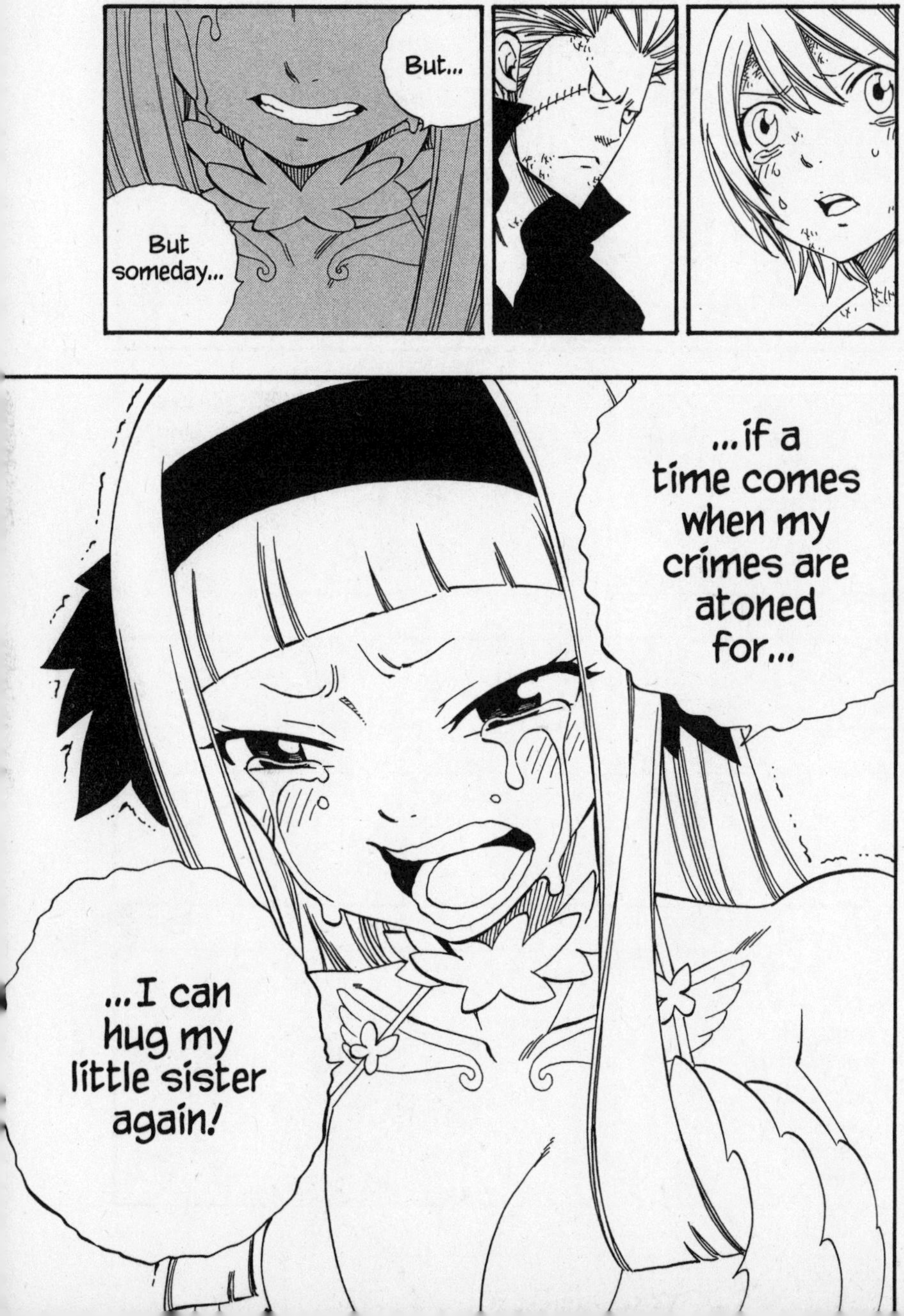
But...
But someday...
...if a time comes when my crimes are atoned for...
...I can hug my little sister again!

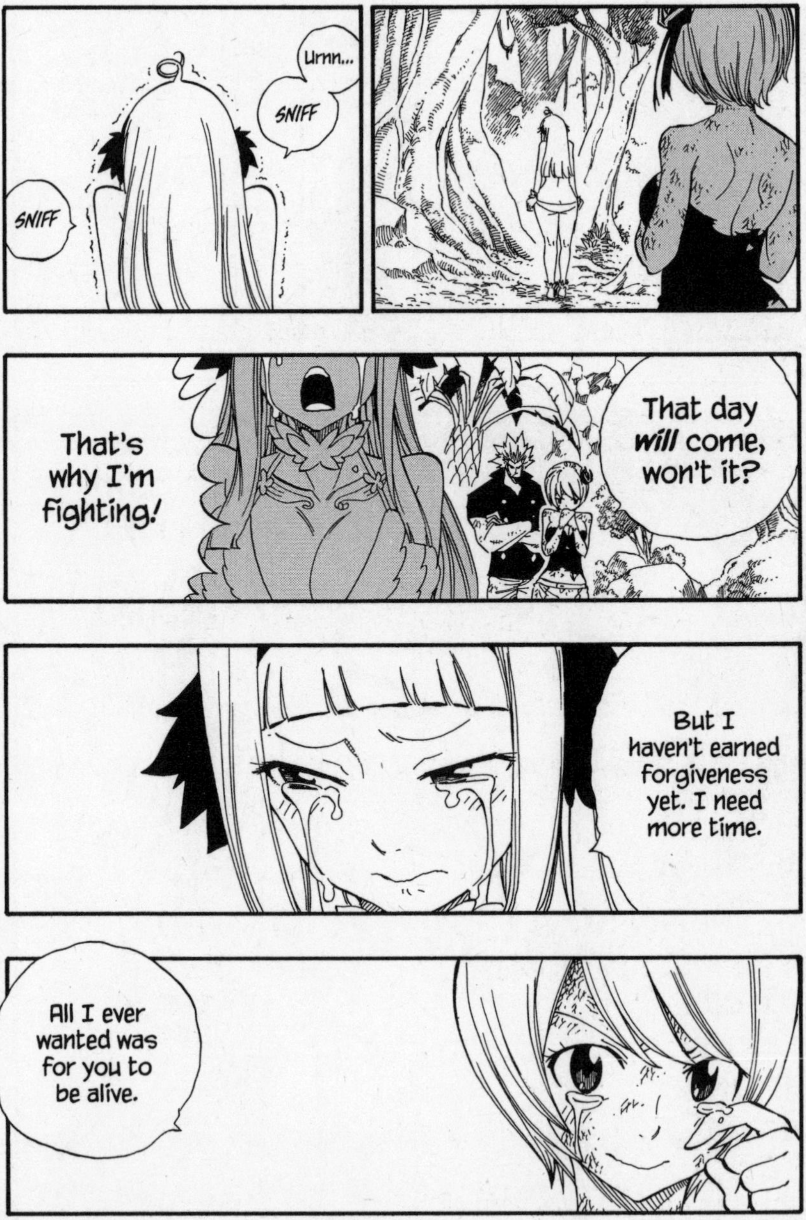

Urnn...
SNIFF
SNIFF
That day *will* come, won't it?
That's why I'm fighting!
But I haven't earned forgiveness yet. I need more time.
All I ever wanted was for you to be alive.

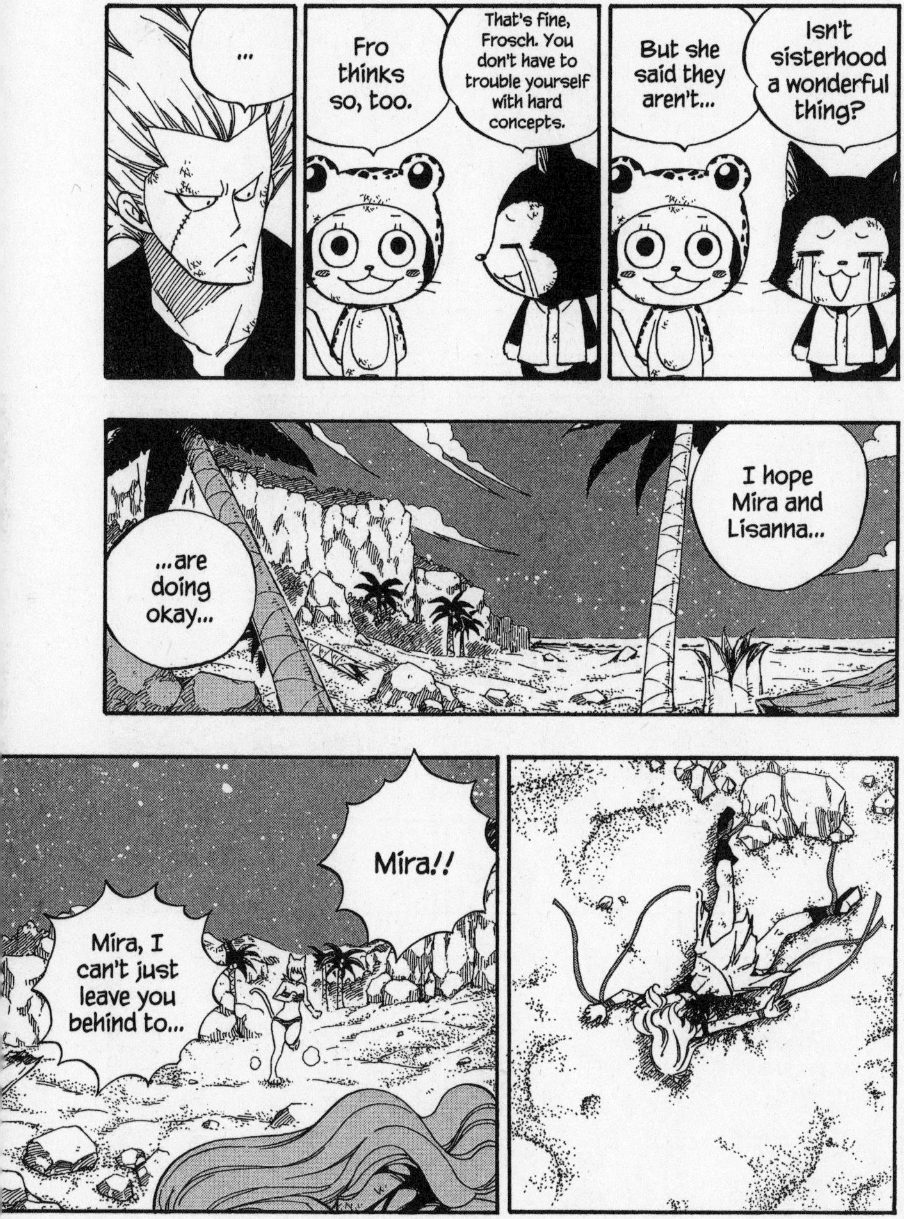
Isn't sisterhood a wonderful thing?
But she said they aren't...
That's fine, Frosch. You don't have to trouble yourself with hard concepts.
Fro thinks so, too.
...
I hope Mira and Lisanna...
...are doing okay...
Mira!!
Mira, I can't just leave you behind to...

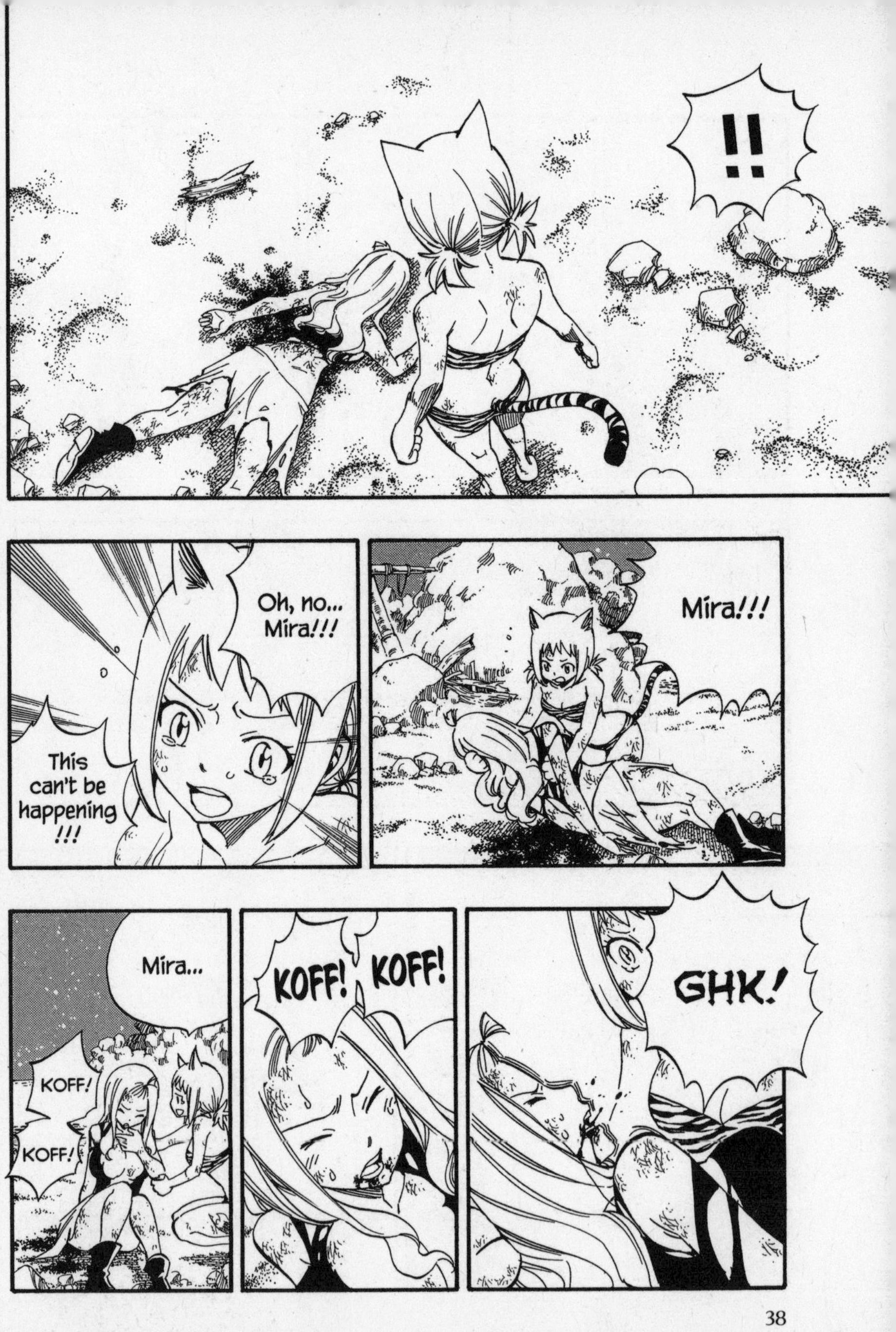
!!
Mira!!!
Oh, no... Mira!!!
This can't be happening!!!
GHK!
KOFF! KOFF!
Mira...
KOFF!
KOFF!

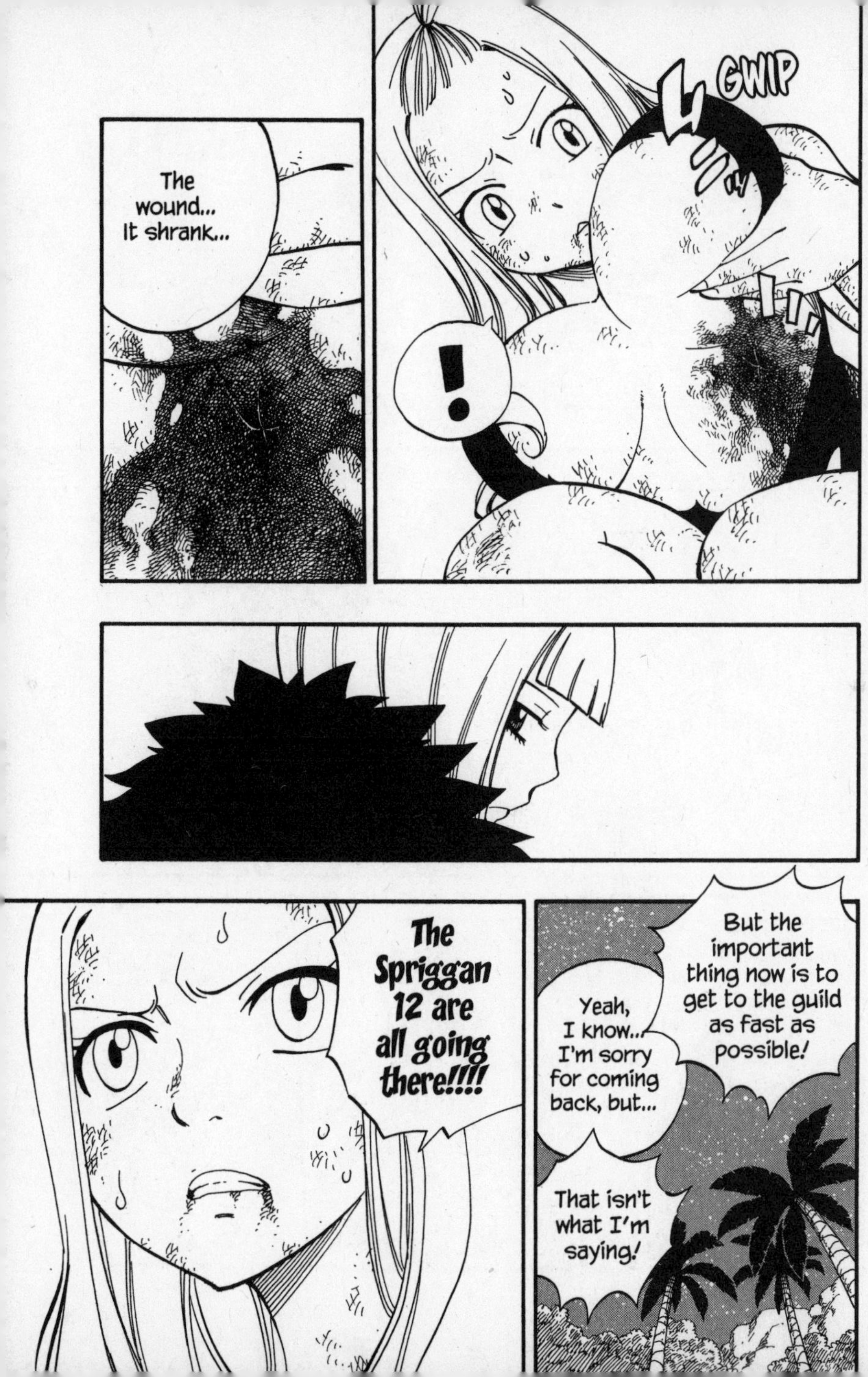
GWIP
!
The wound... It shrank...
But the important thing now is to get to the guild as fast as possible!
Yeah, I know... I'm sorry for coming back, but...
That isn't what I'm saying!
The Spriggan 12 are all going there!!!!

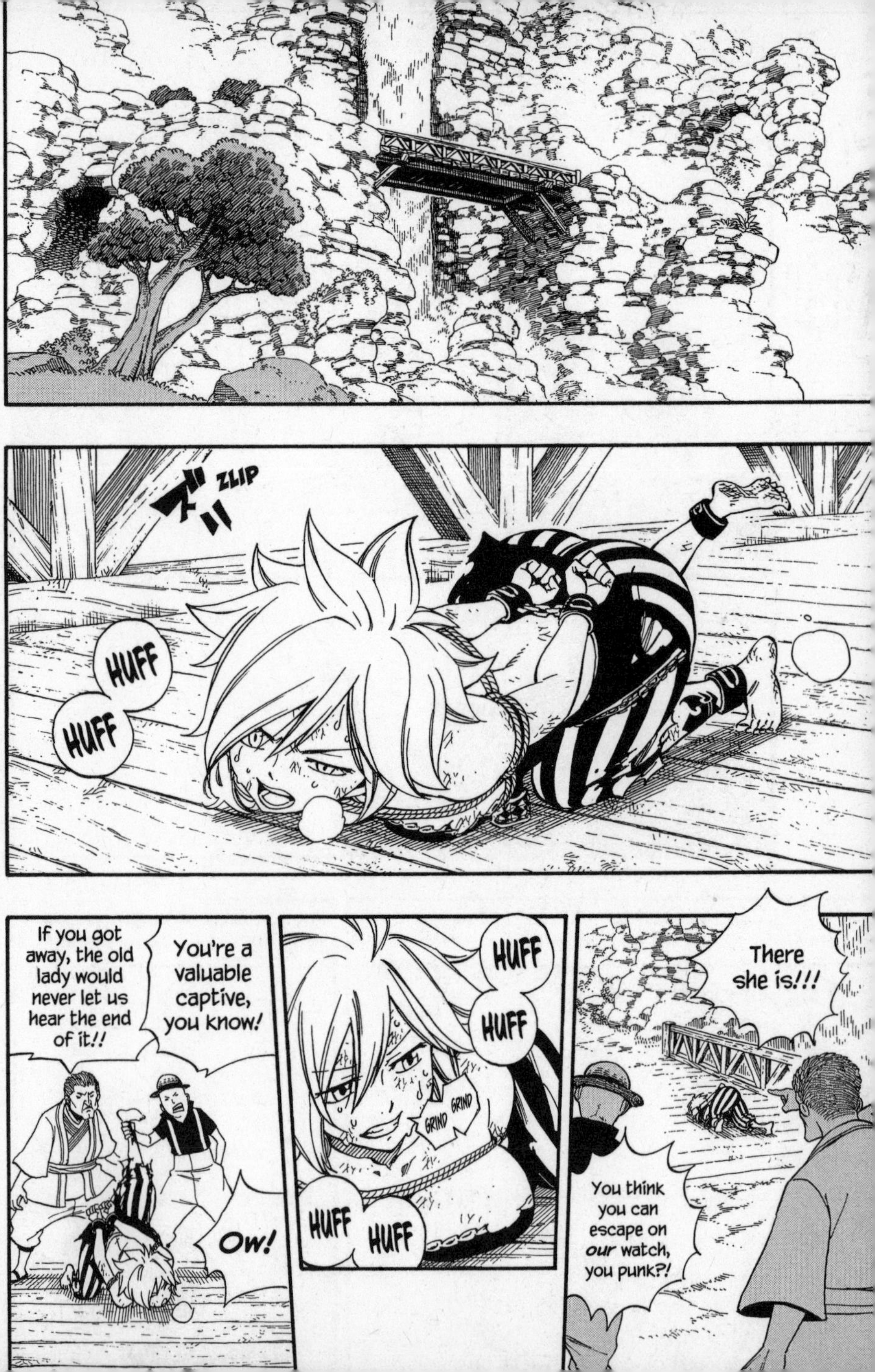
ZLIP
HUFF
HUFF
There she is!!!
You think you can escape on *our* watch, you punk?!
HUFF
HUFF
GRIND GRIND
HUFF
HUFF
You're a valuable captive, you know!
If you got away, the old lady would never let us hear the end of it!!
Ow!

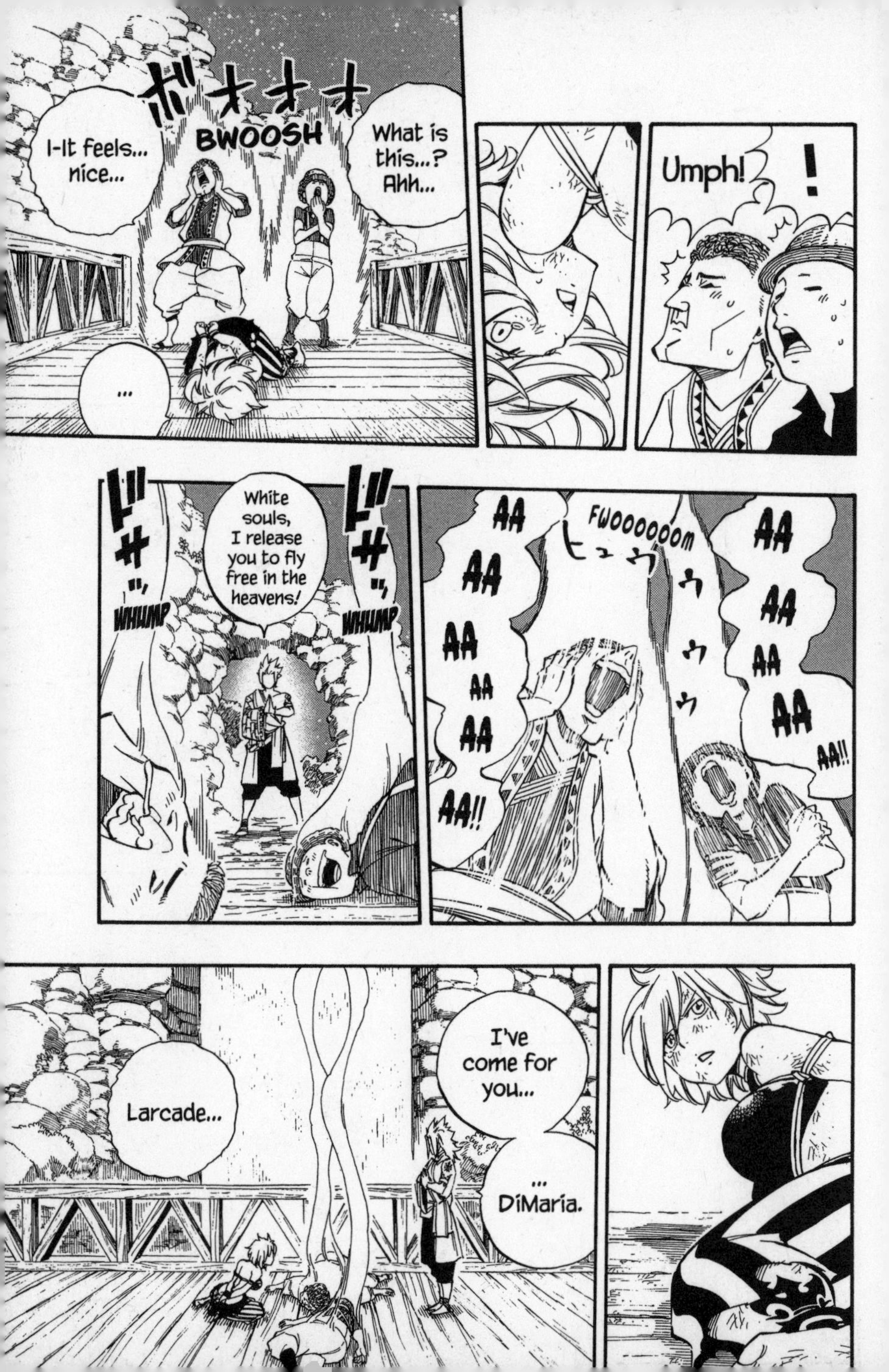
Umph!
!
What is this...? Ahh...
ボオオオ
BWOOSH
I-It feels... nice...
...
FWOOOOOOM
ヒュウウウ
AA AA AA AA AA AA!!
AA AA AA AA AA AA!!
ドサッ
WHUMP
White souls, I release you to fly free in the heavens!
ドサッ
WHUMP
I've come for you...
... DiMaria.
Larcade...

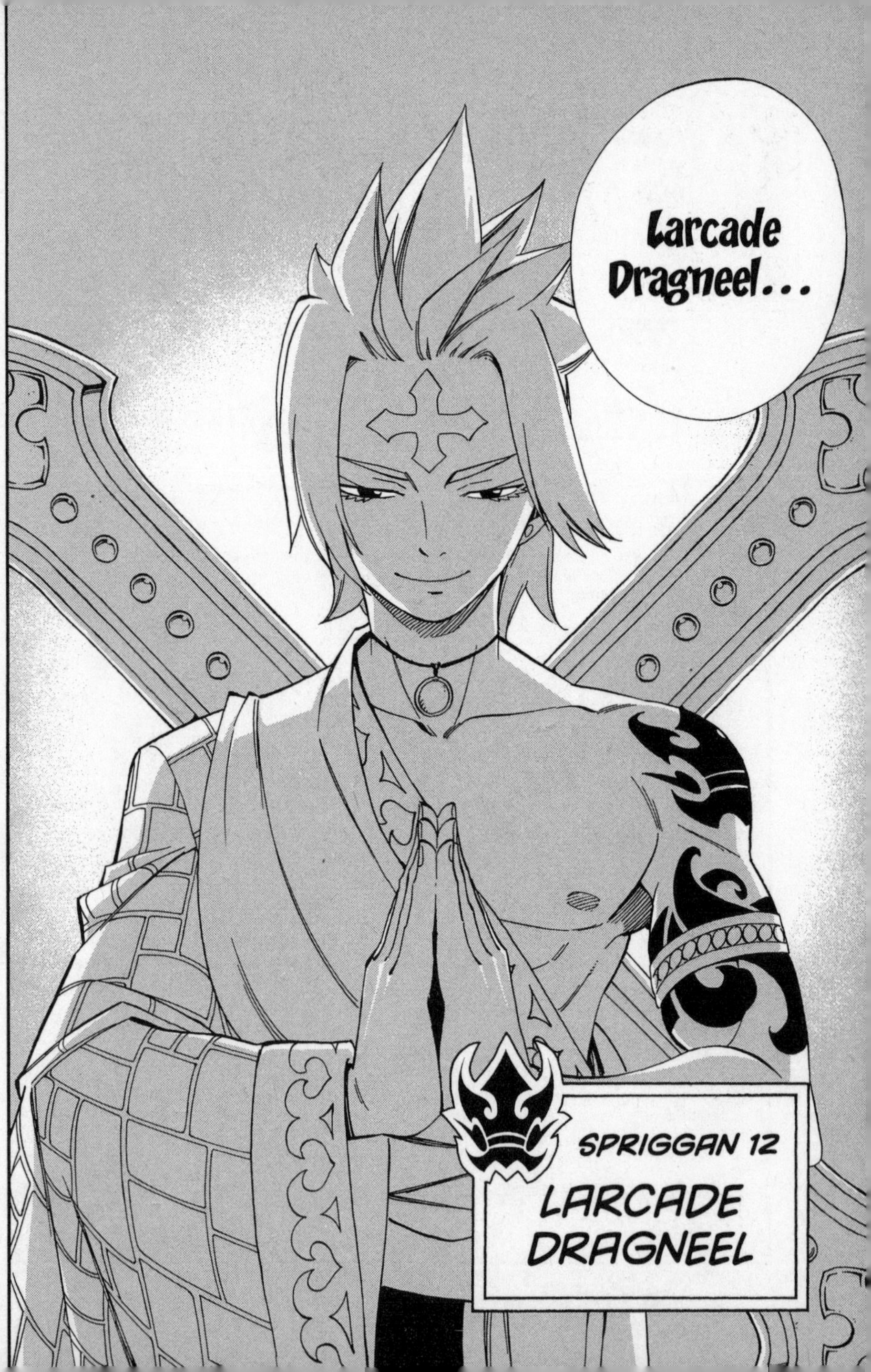
Larcade Dragneel...
SPRIGGAN 12
LARCADE DRAGNEEL

Chapter 494: The Hill That Leads to Tomorrow

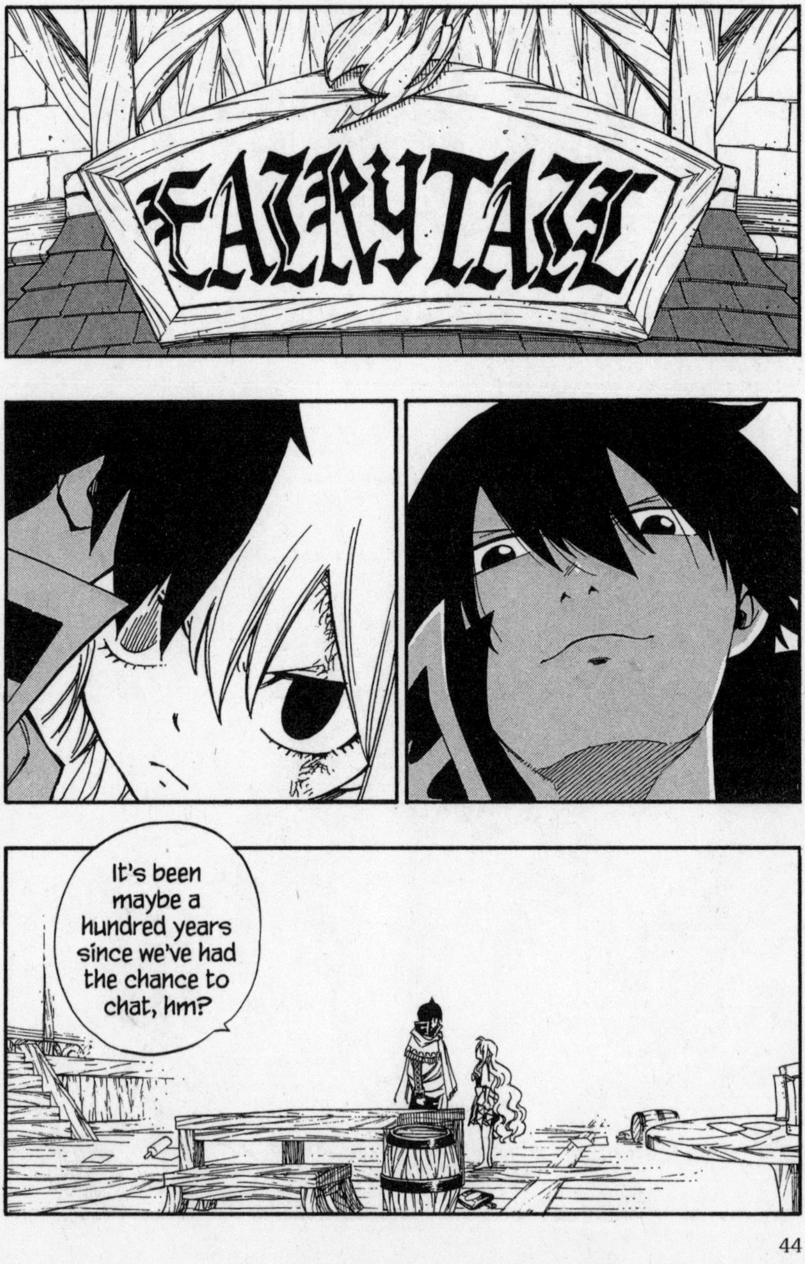
FAIRY TAIL
It's been maybe a hundred years since we've had the chance to chat, hm?

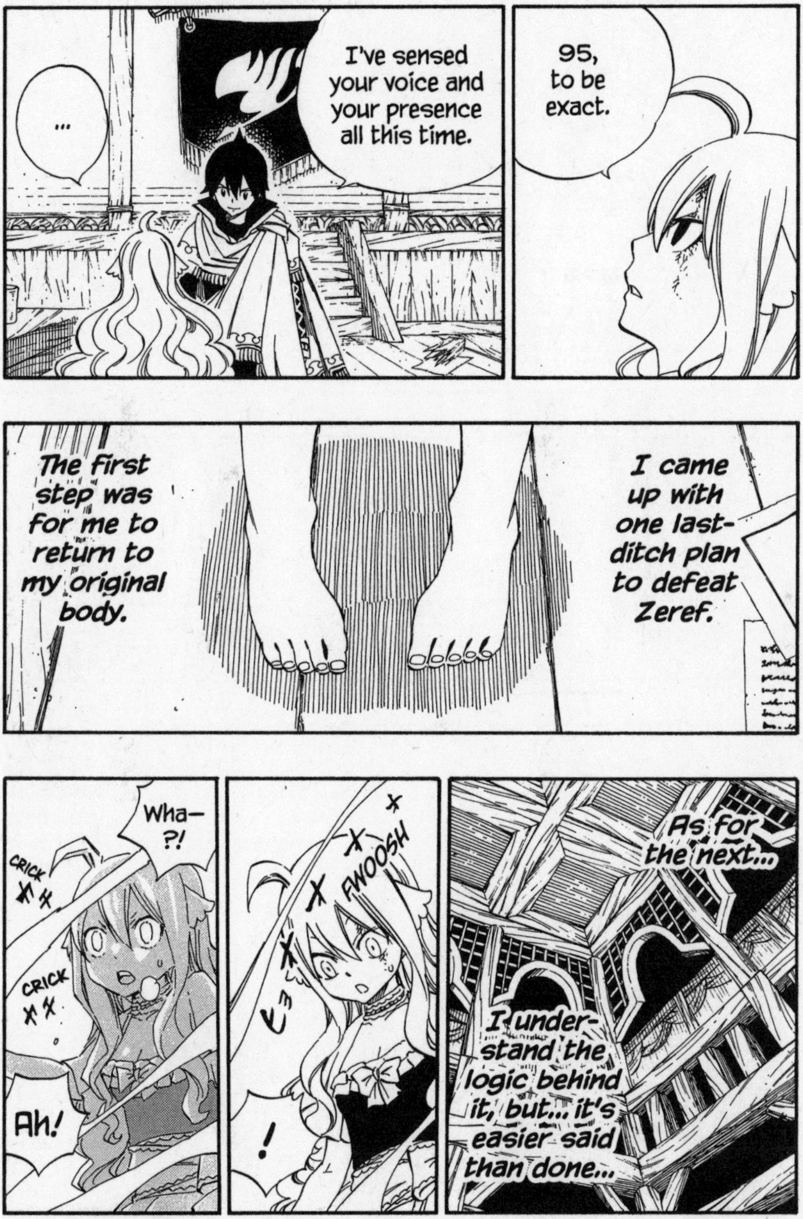
95, to be exact.
I've sensed your voice and your presence all this time.
...
I came up with one last-ditch plan to defeat Zeref.
The first step was for me to return to my original body.
As for the next...
I understand the logic behind it, but... it's easier said than done...
FWOOSH
!
Wha—?!
CRICK
CRICK
Ah!

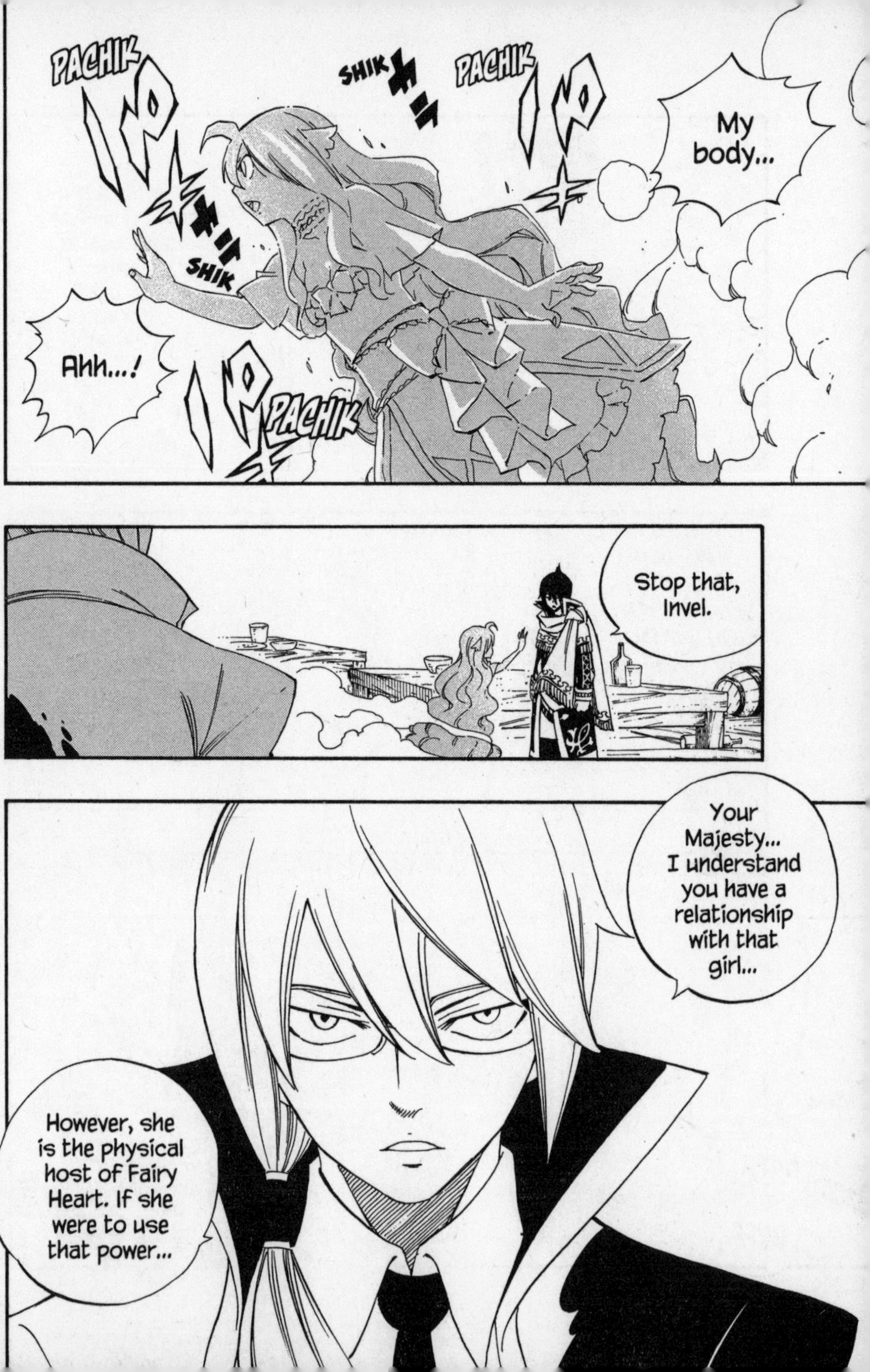
My body...
PACHIK
SHIK
PACHIK
SHIK
Ahh...!
PACHIK
Stop that, Invel.
Your Majesty... I understand you have a relationship with that girl...
However, she is the physical host of Fairy Heart. If she were to use that power...

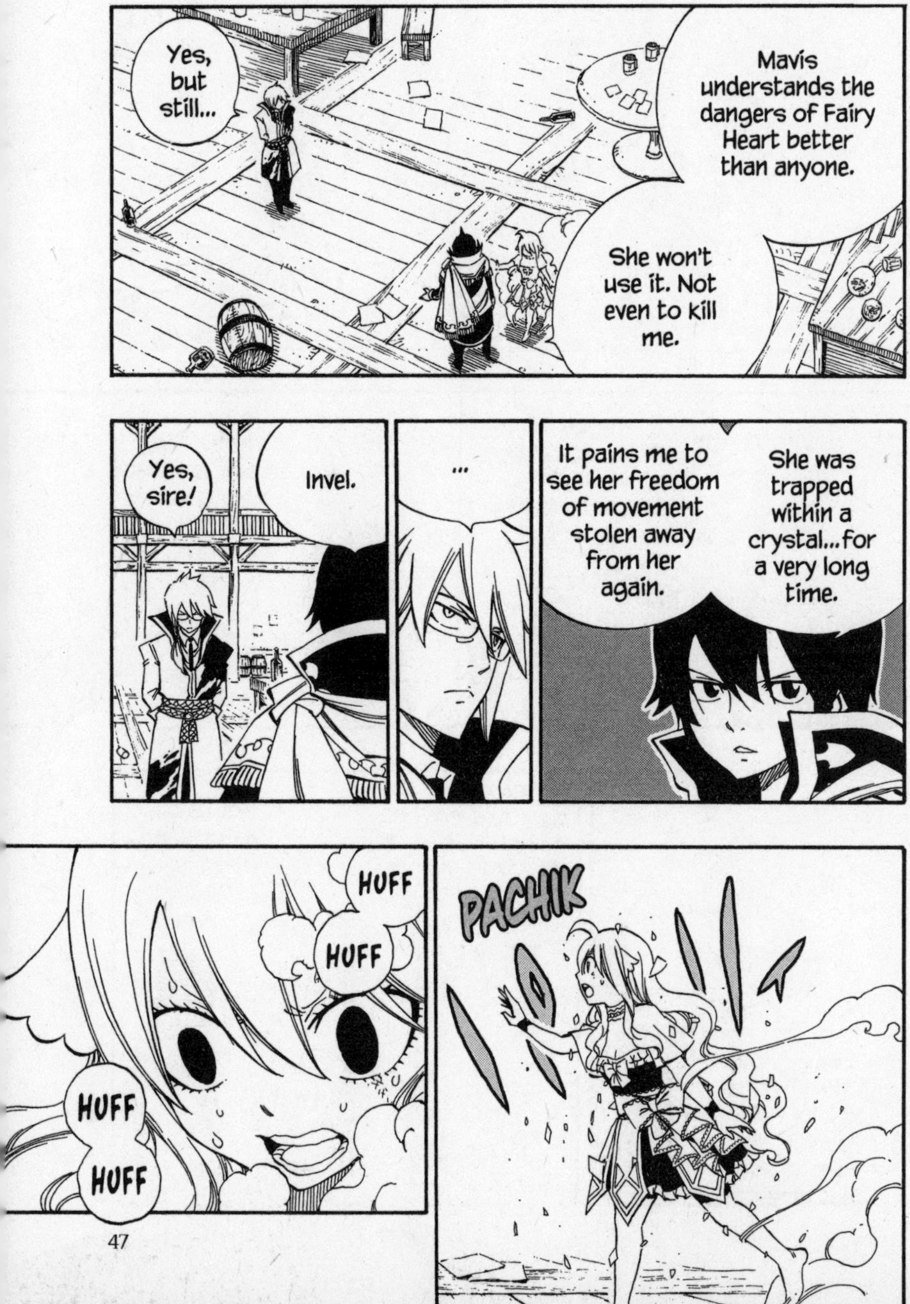

Mavis understands the dangers of Fairy Heart better than anyone.
She won't use it. Not even to kill me.
Yes, but still...
She was trapped within a crystal...for a very long time.
It pains me to see her freedom of movement stolen away from her again.
...
Invel.
Yes, sire!
PACHIK
HUFF
HUFF
HUFF
HUFF

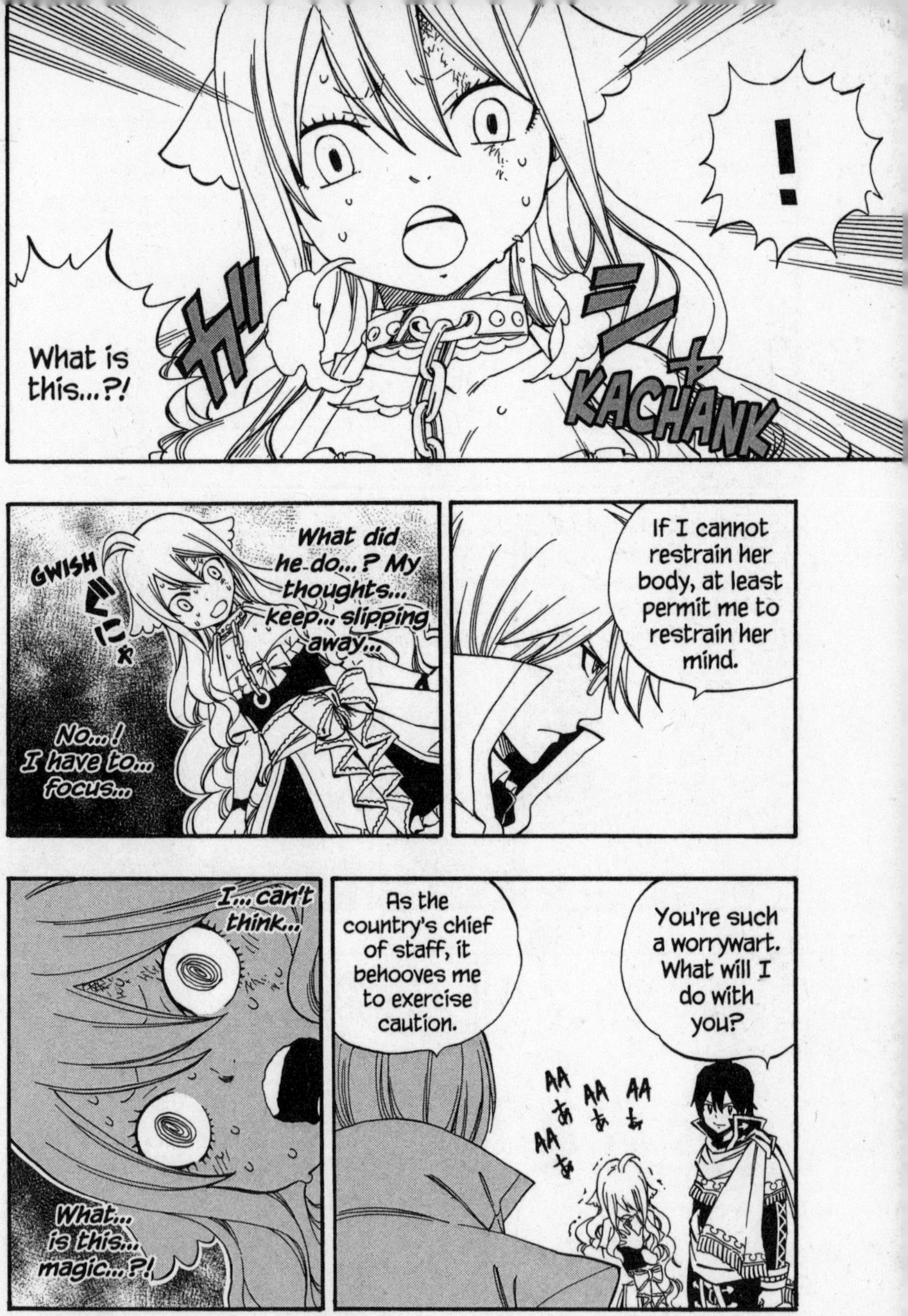
!
KACHANK
What is this...?!
If I cannot restrain her body, at least permit me to restrain her mind.
What did he do...? My thoughts... keep... slipping away...
GWISH
No...! I have to... focus...
You're such a worrywart. What will I do with you?
As the country's chief of staff, it behooves me to exercise caution.
AA
AA
AA
AA
I... can't think...
What... is this... magic...?!

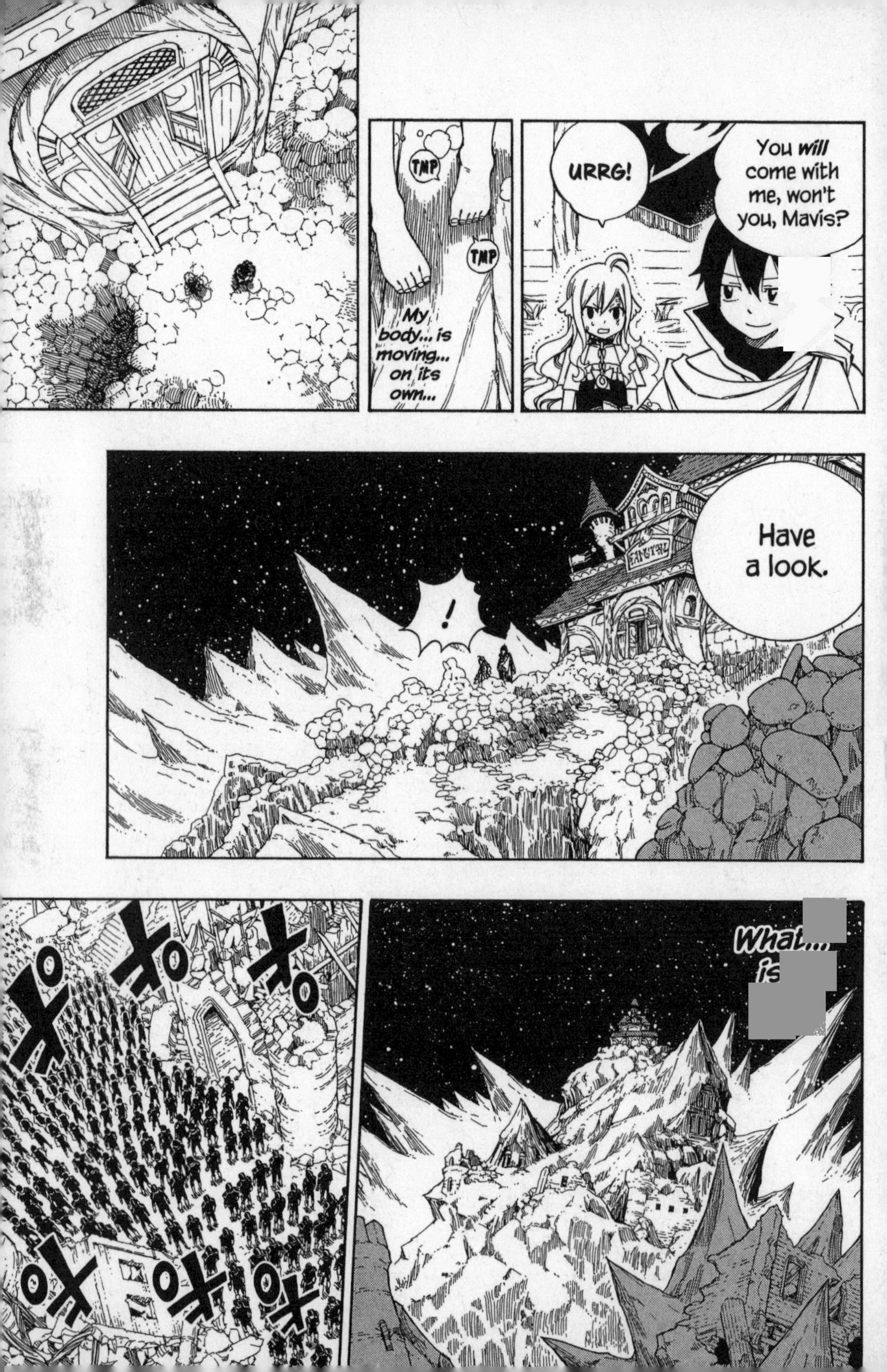
You will come with me, won't you, Mavis?
URRG!
TMP
TMP
My body... is moving... on its own...
Have a look.
!
What...
is

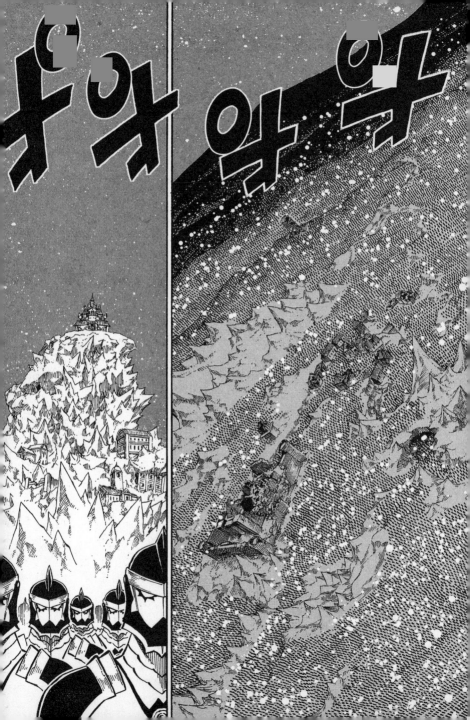

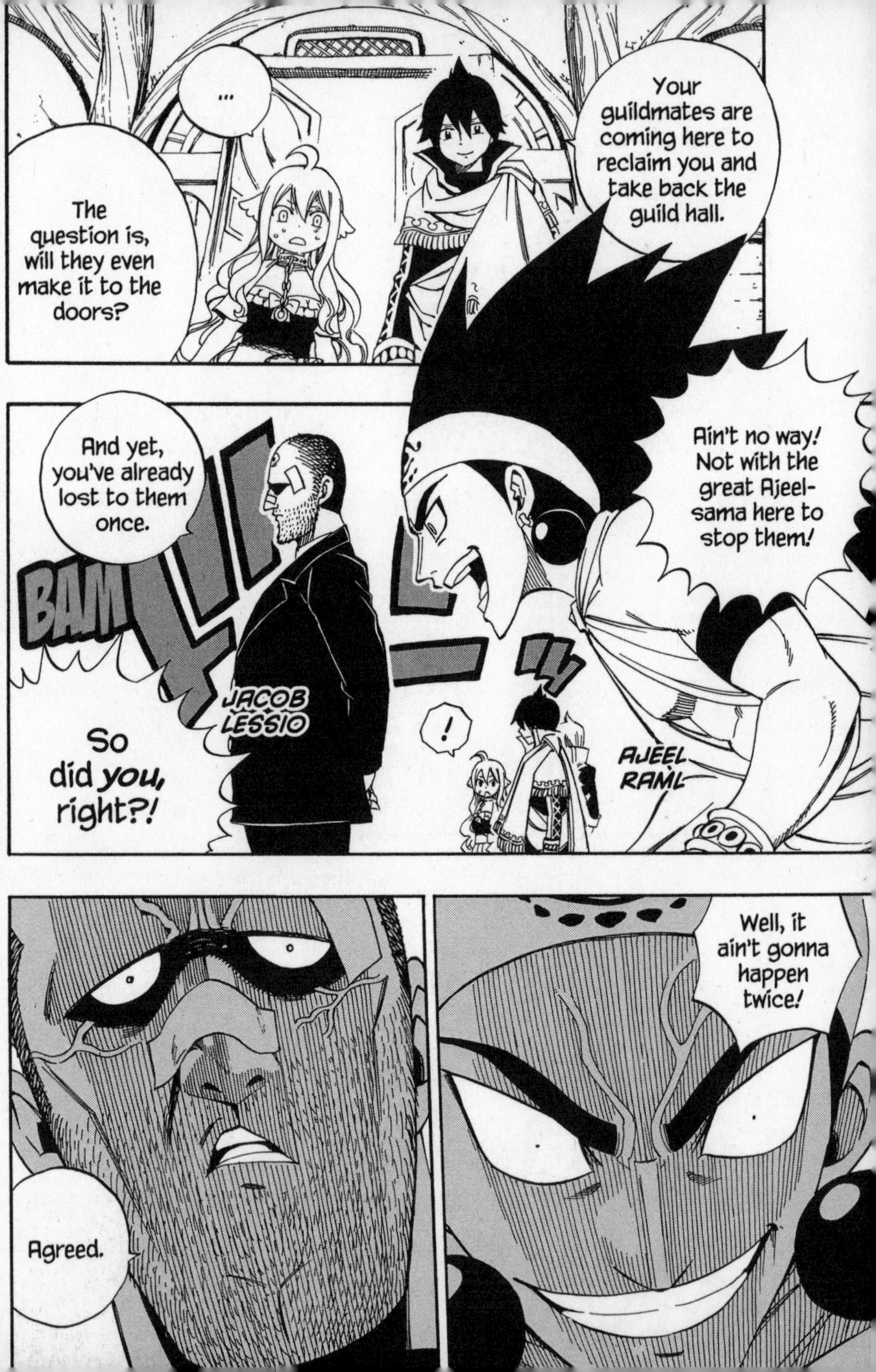
Your guildmates are coming here to reclaim you and take back the guild hall.
...
The question is, will they even make it to the doors?
Ain't no way! Not with the great Ajeel-sama here to stop them!
AJEEL RAML
!
And yet, you've already lost to them once.
BAM
JACOB LESSIO
So did *you*, right?!
Well, it ain't gonna happen twice!
Agreed.

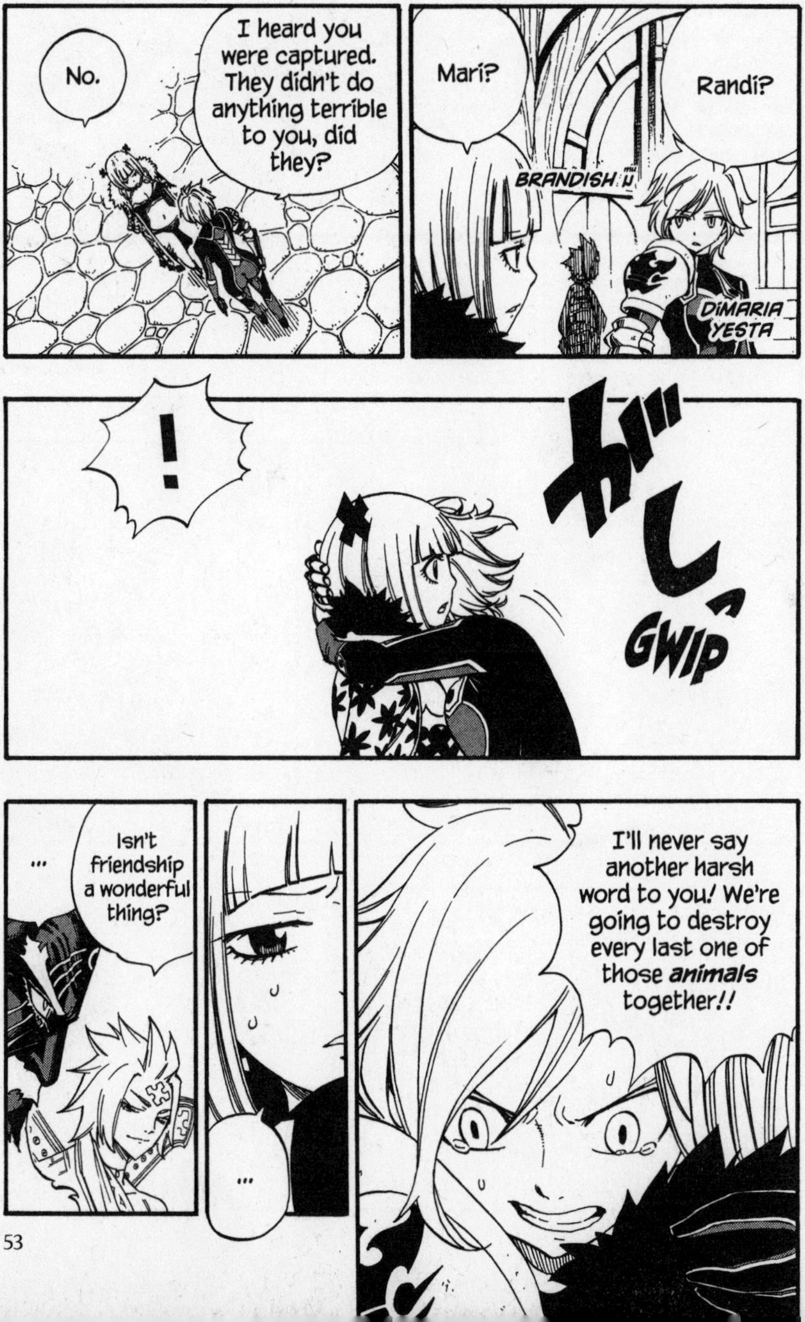
Randi?
Mari?
DIMARIA YESTA
BRANDISH μ
I heard you were captured. They didn't do anything terrible to you, did they?
No.
ガシッ
GWIP
!
I'll never say another harsh word to you! We're going to destroy every last one of those ***animals*** together!!
...
Isn't friendship a wonderful thing?
...

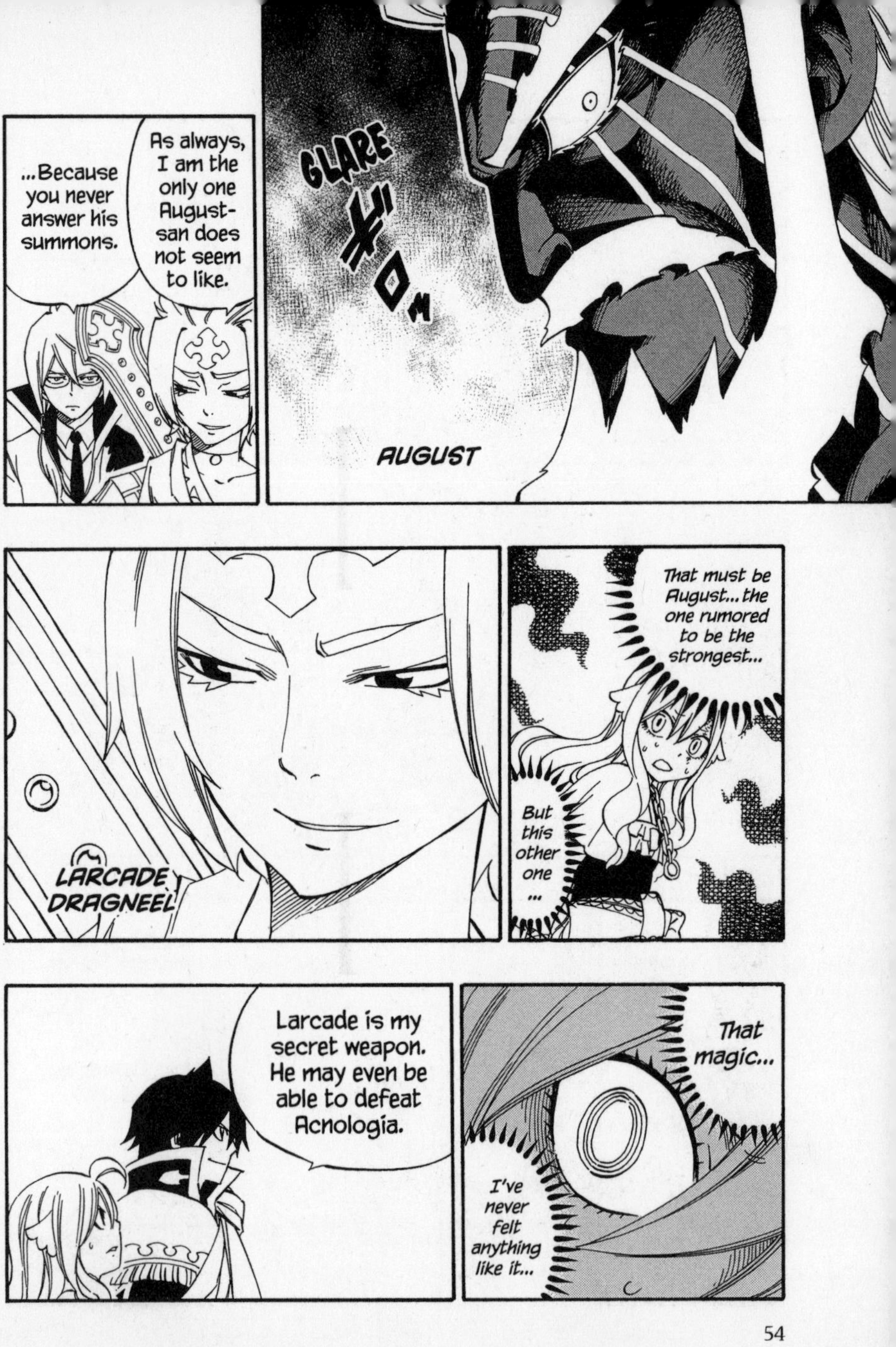
GLARE
AUGUST
As always, I am the only one August-san does not seem to like.
...Because you never answer his summons.
That must be August... the one rumored to be the strongest...
But this other one ...
LARCADE DRAGNEEL
That magic...
I've never felt anything like it...
Larcade is my secret weapon. He may even be able to defeat Acnologia.

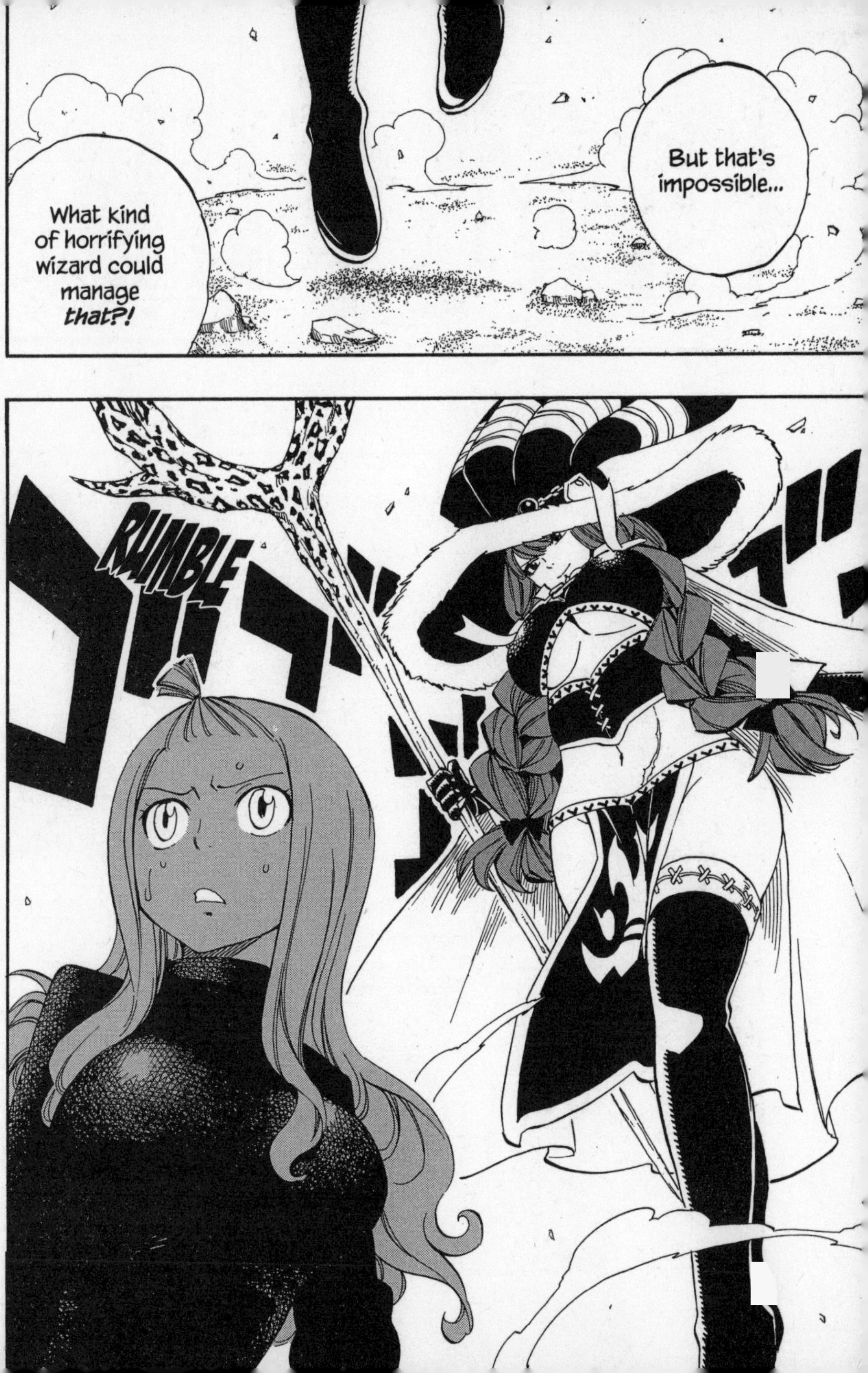
But that's impossible...
What kind of horrifying wizard could manage *that?!*
RUMBLE

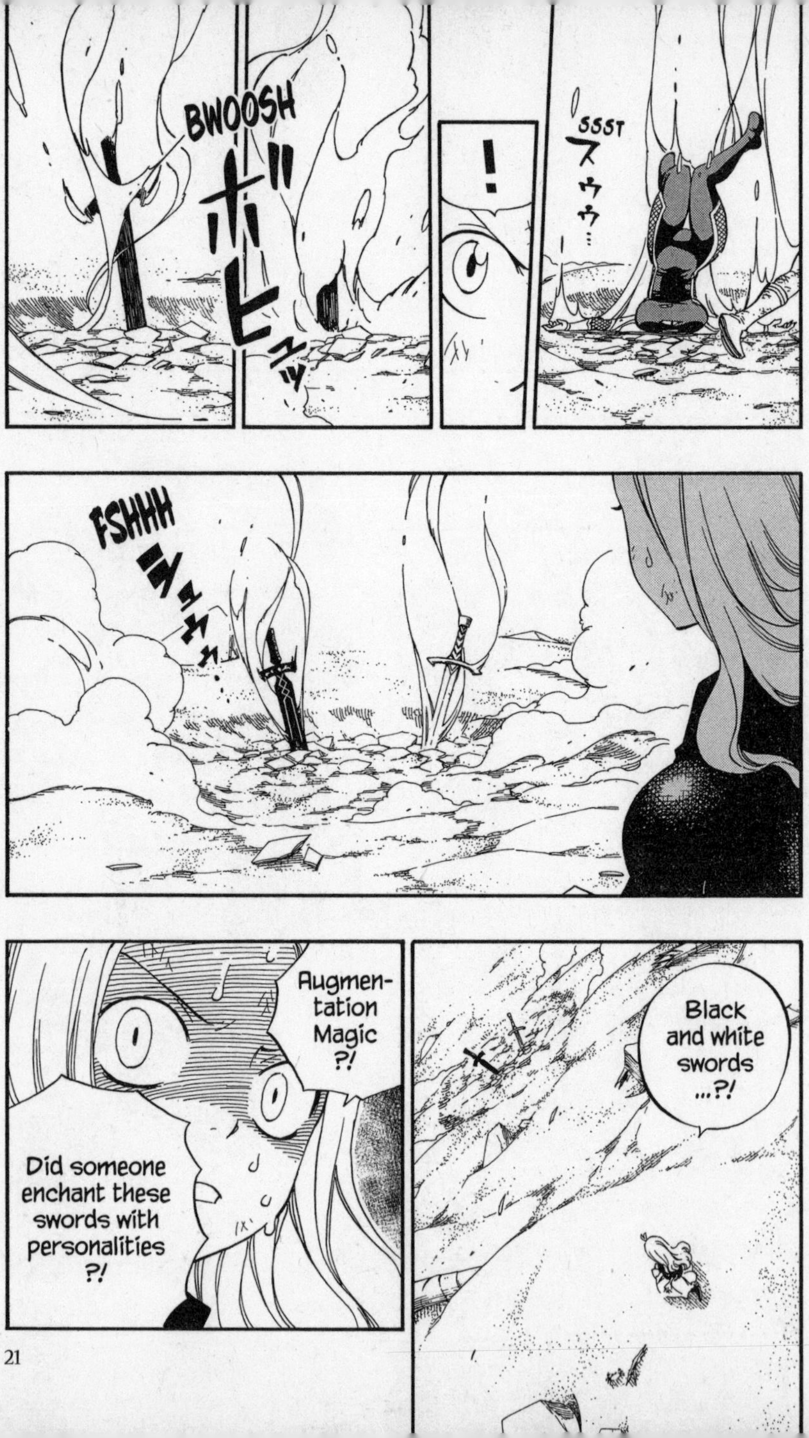
SSST
スゥゥ…
!
BWOOSH
ボヒュッ
FSHHH
Black and white swords ...?!
Augmentation Magic ?!
Did someone enchant these swords with personalities ?!

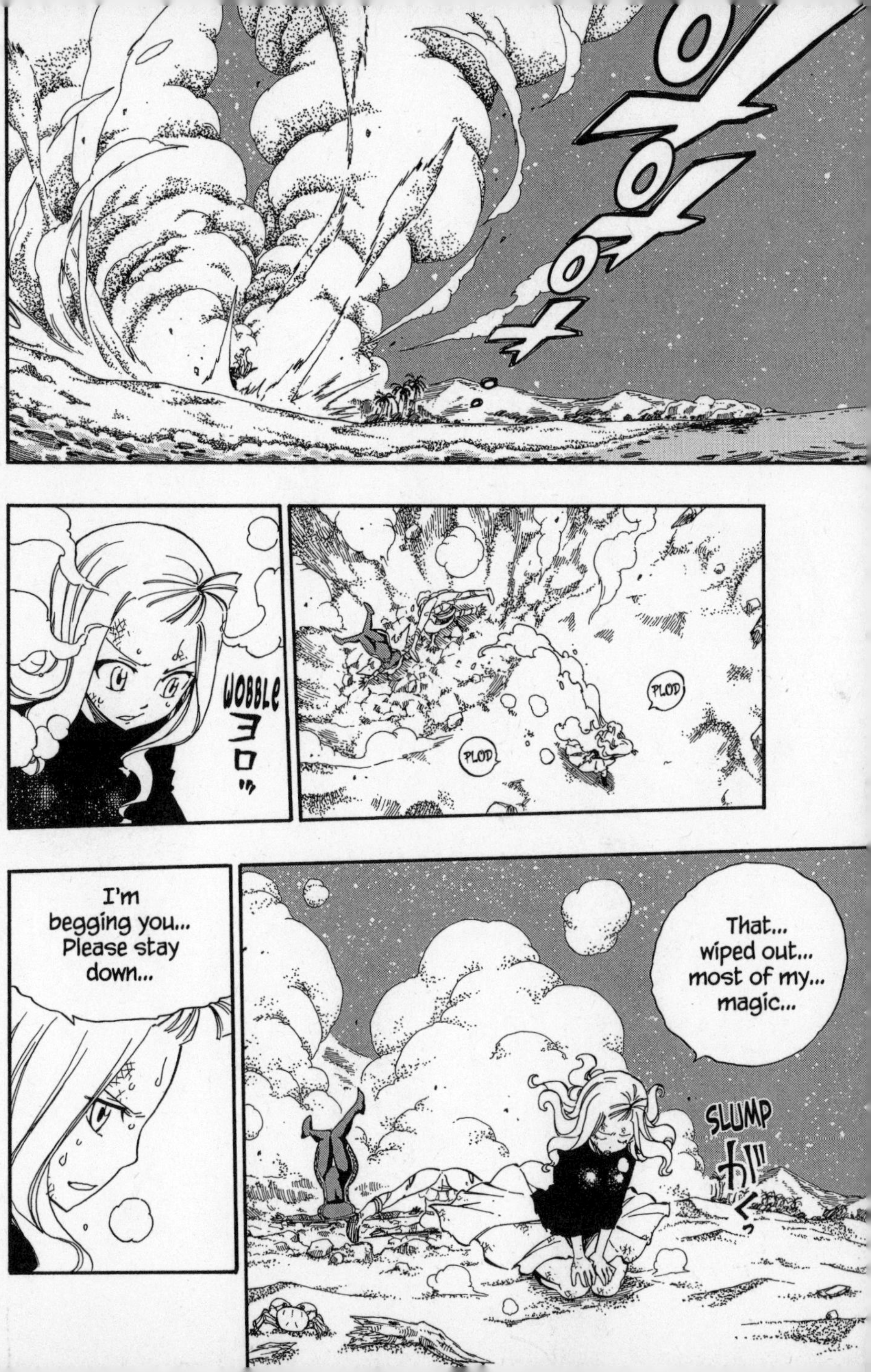
PLOD
PLOD
WOBBLE
ヨロッ
That... wiped out... most of my... magic...
SLUMP
かくっ
I'm begging you... Please stay down...

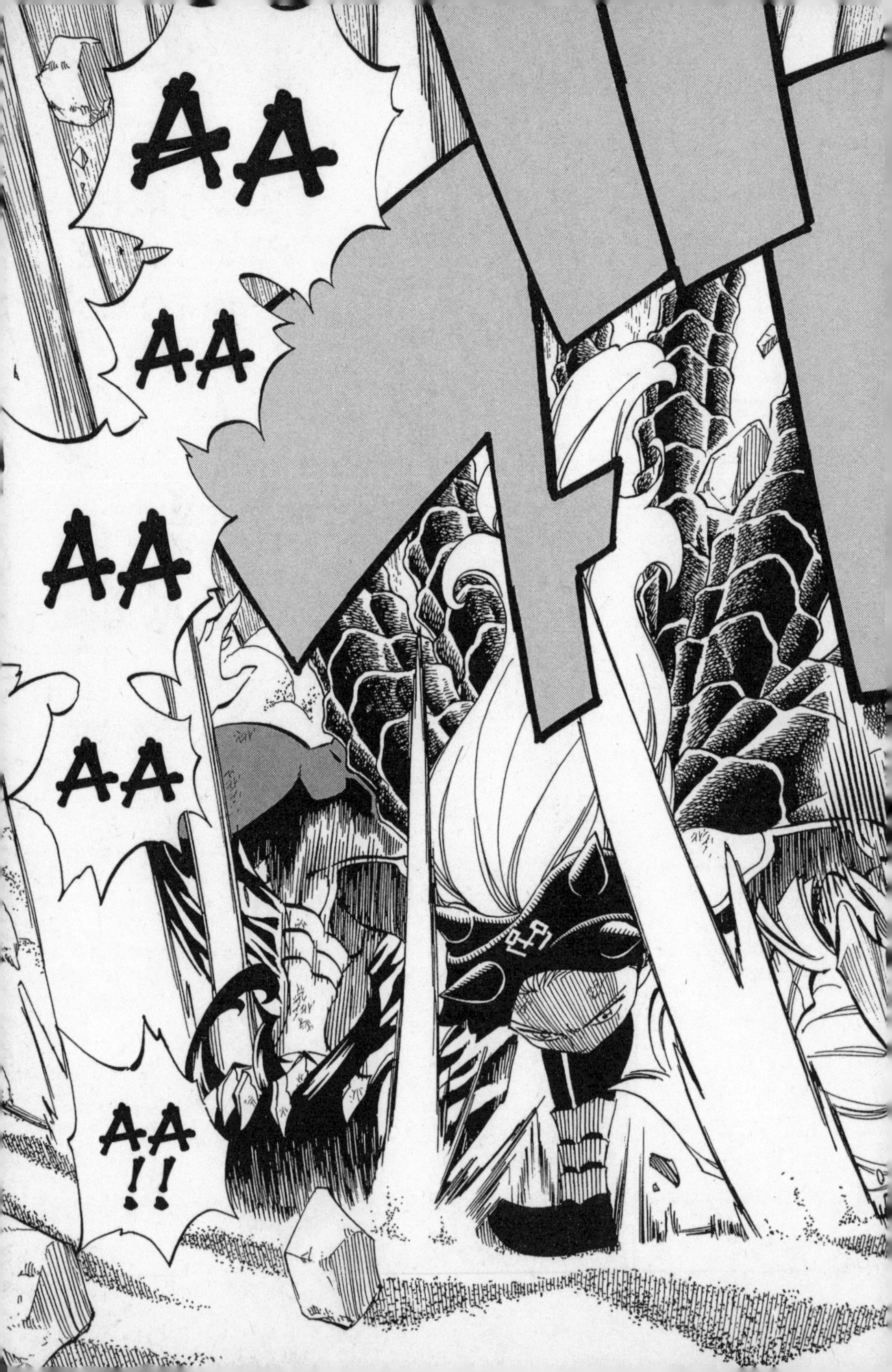
AA
AA
AA
AA
AA
!!

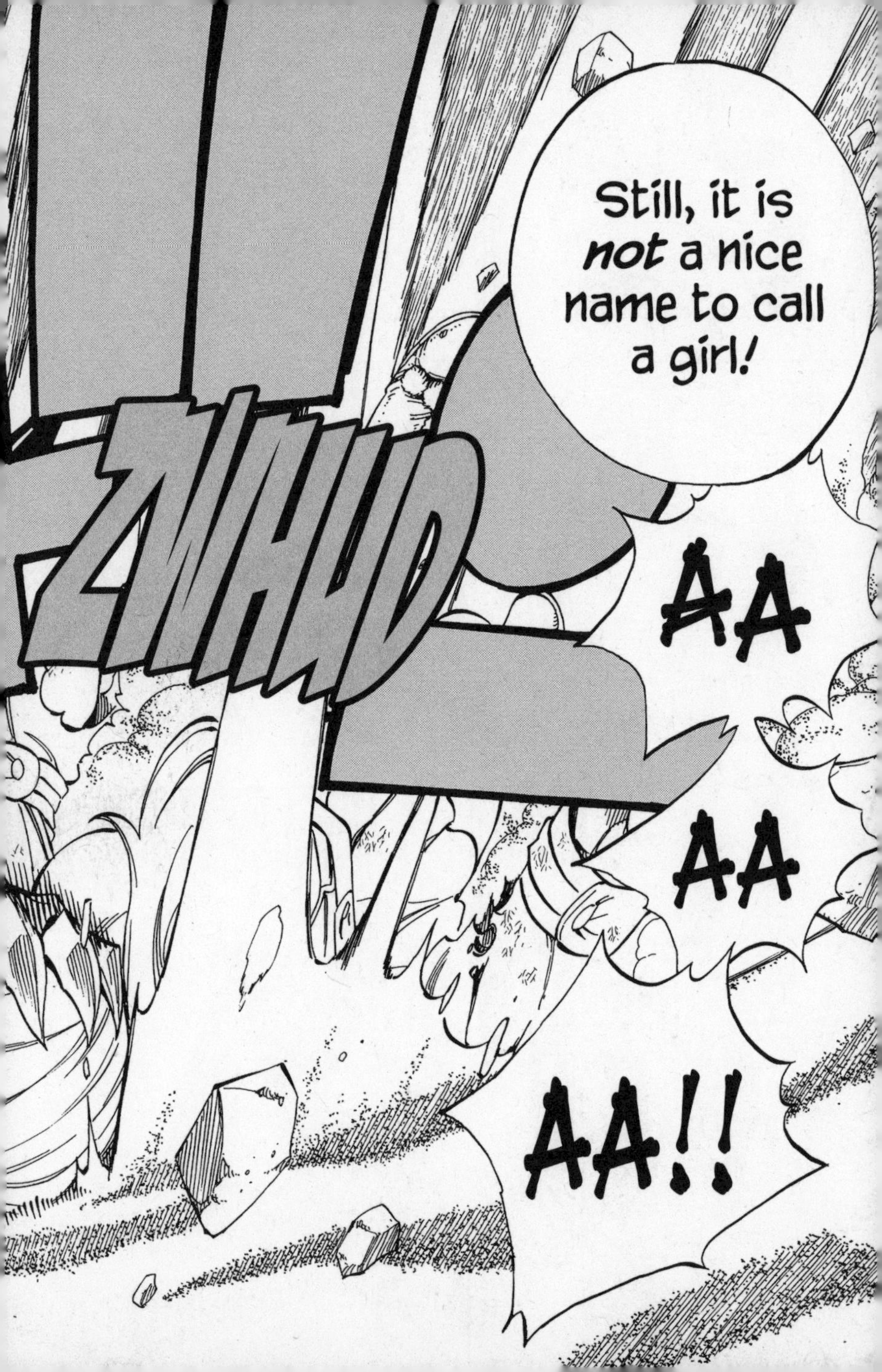
Still, it is *not* a nice name to call a girl!
ZWHUD
AA AA AA!!

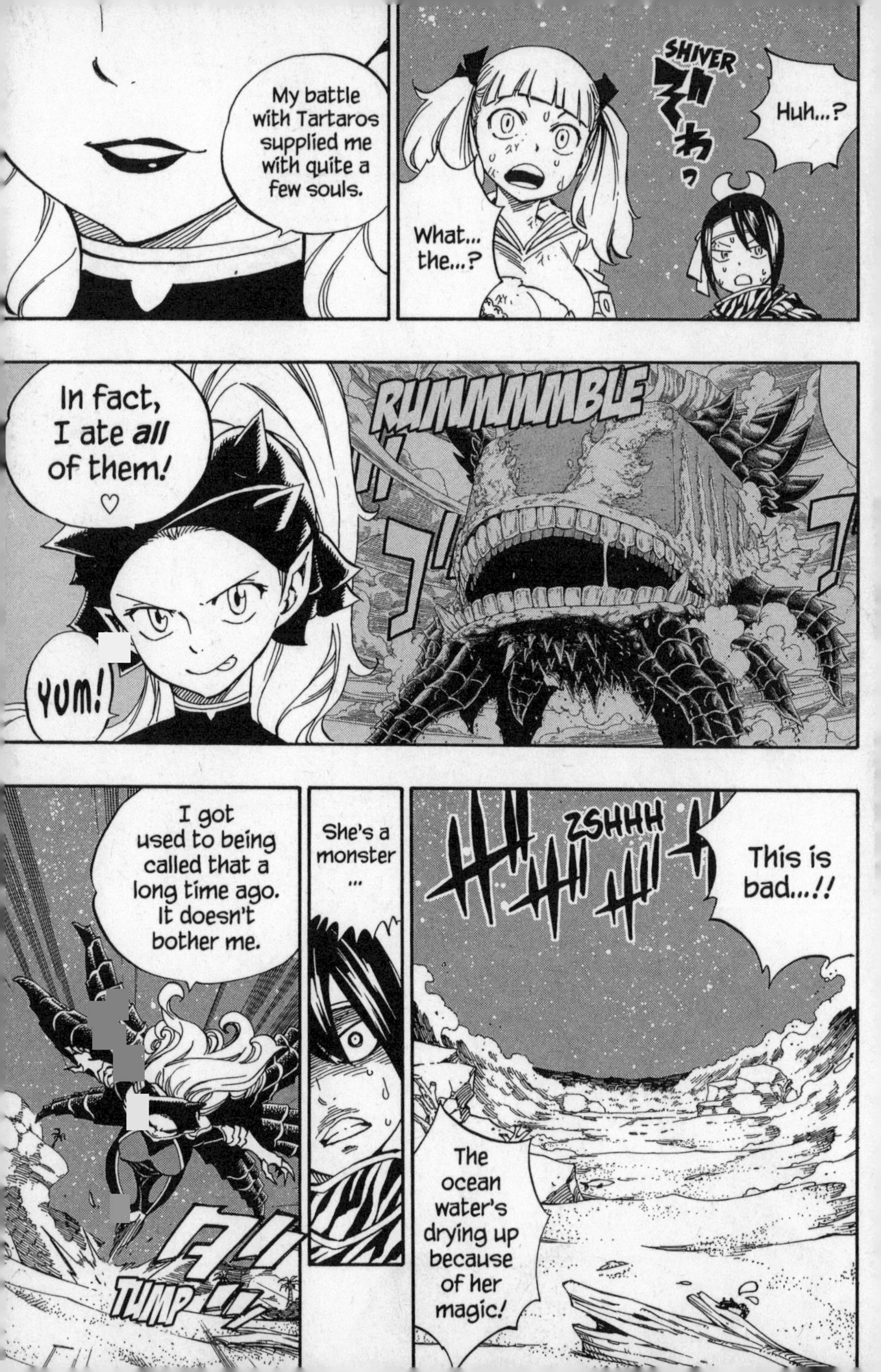
Huh...?
SHIVER
What... the...?
My battle with Tartaros supplied me with quite a few souls.
RUMMMMBLE
In fact, I ate *all* of them! ♡
YUM!
ZSHHH
This is bad...!!
The ocean water's drying up because of her magic!
She's a monster ...
I got used to being called that a long time ago. It doesn't bother me.
TUMP

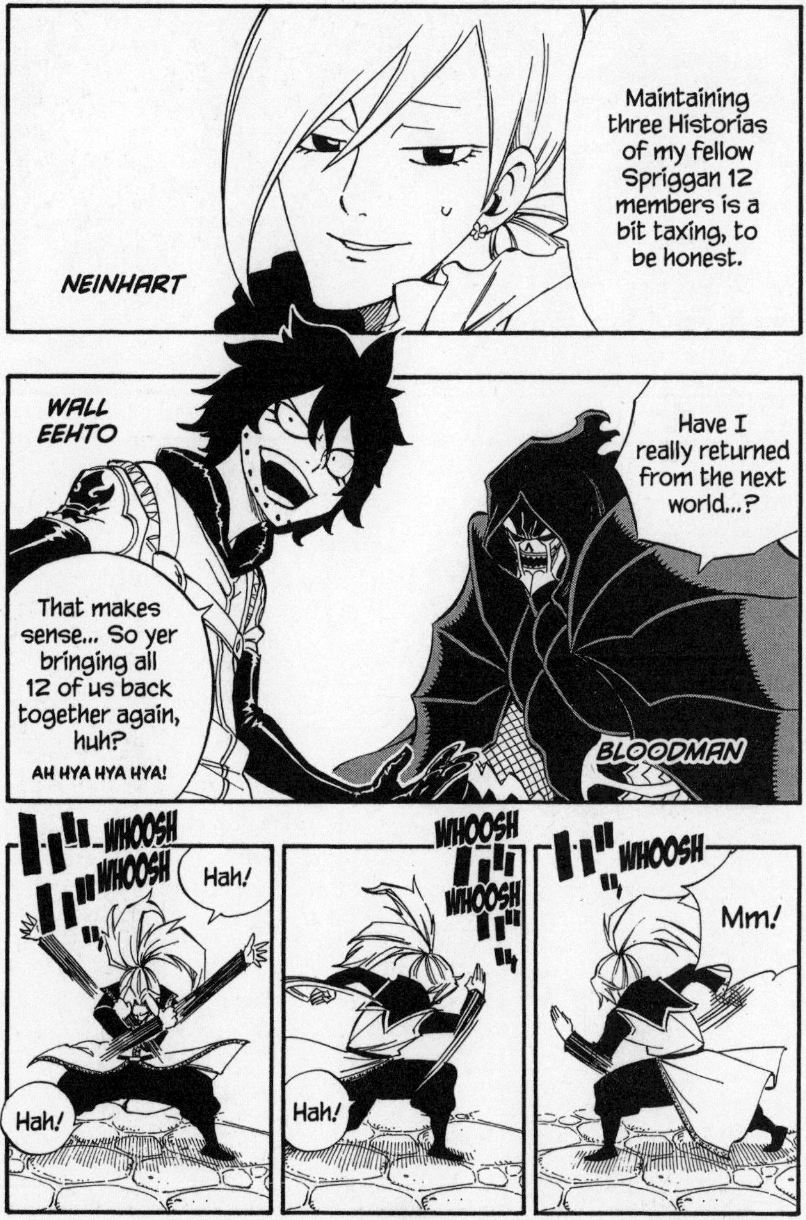
Maintaining three Historias of my fellow Spriggan 12 members is a bit taxing, to be honest.
NEINHART
Have I really returned from the next world...?
WALL EEHTO
That makes sense... So yer bringing all 12 of us back together again, huh?
AH HYA HYA HYA!
BLOODMAN
WHOOSH
Mm!
WHOOSH
WHOOSH
Hah!
WHOOSH
WHOOSH
Hah!
Hah!

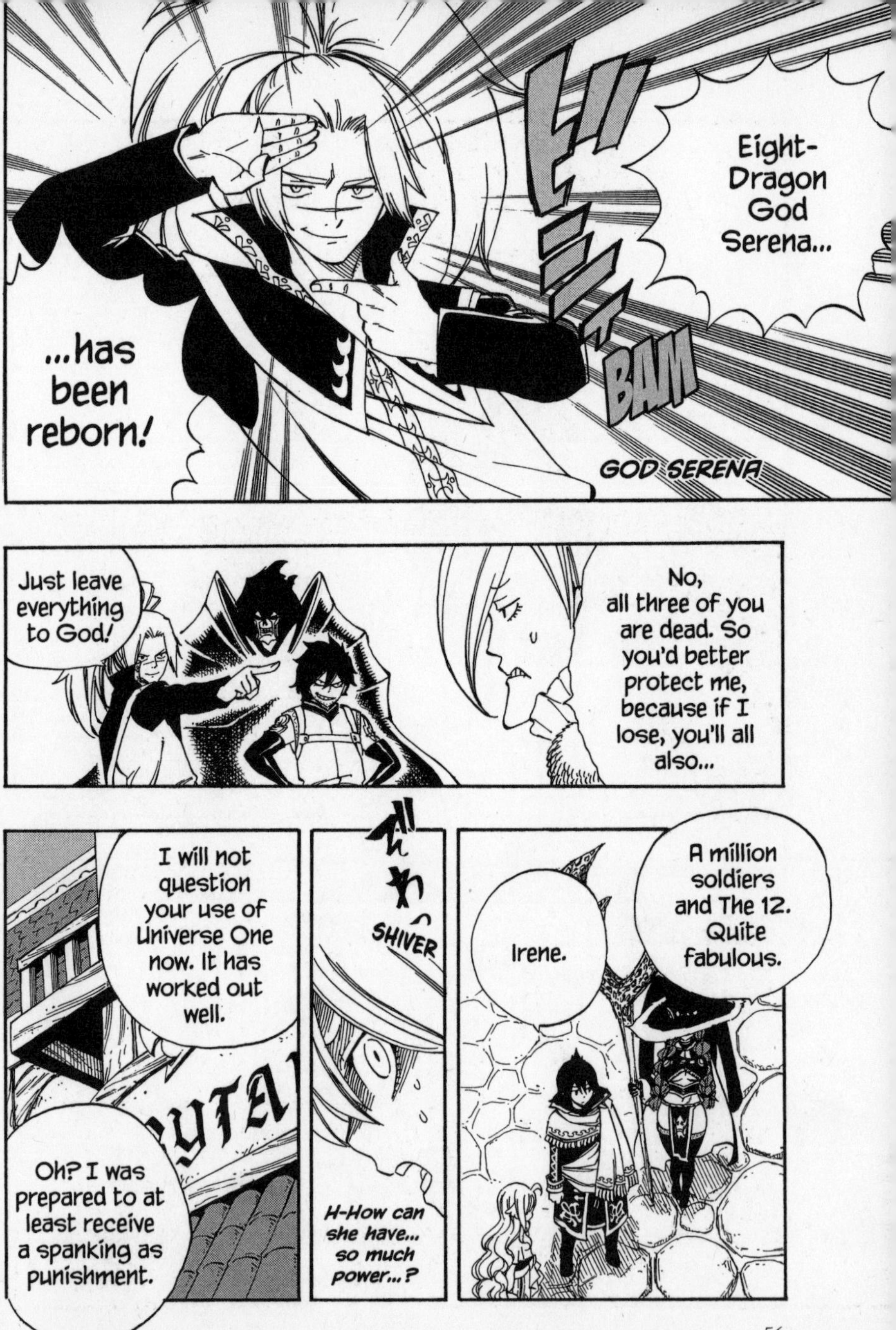
Eight-Dragon God Serena...
BAM
...has been reborn!
GOD SERENA
No, all three of you are dead. So you'd better protect me, because if I lose, you'll all also...
Just leave everything to God!
A million soldiers and The 12. Quite fabulous.
Irene.
ぞわ
SHIVER
H-How can she have... so much power...?
I will not question your use of Universe One now. It has worked out well.
Oh? I was prepared to at least receive a spanking as punishment.

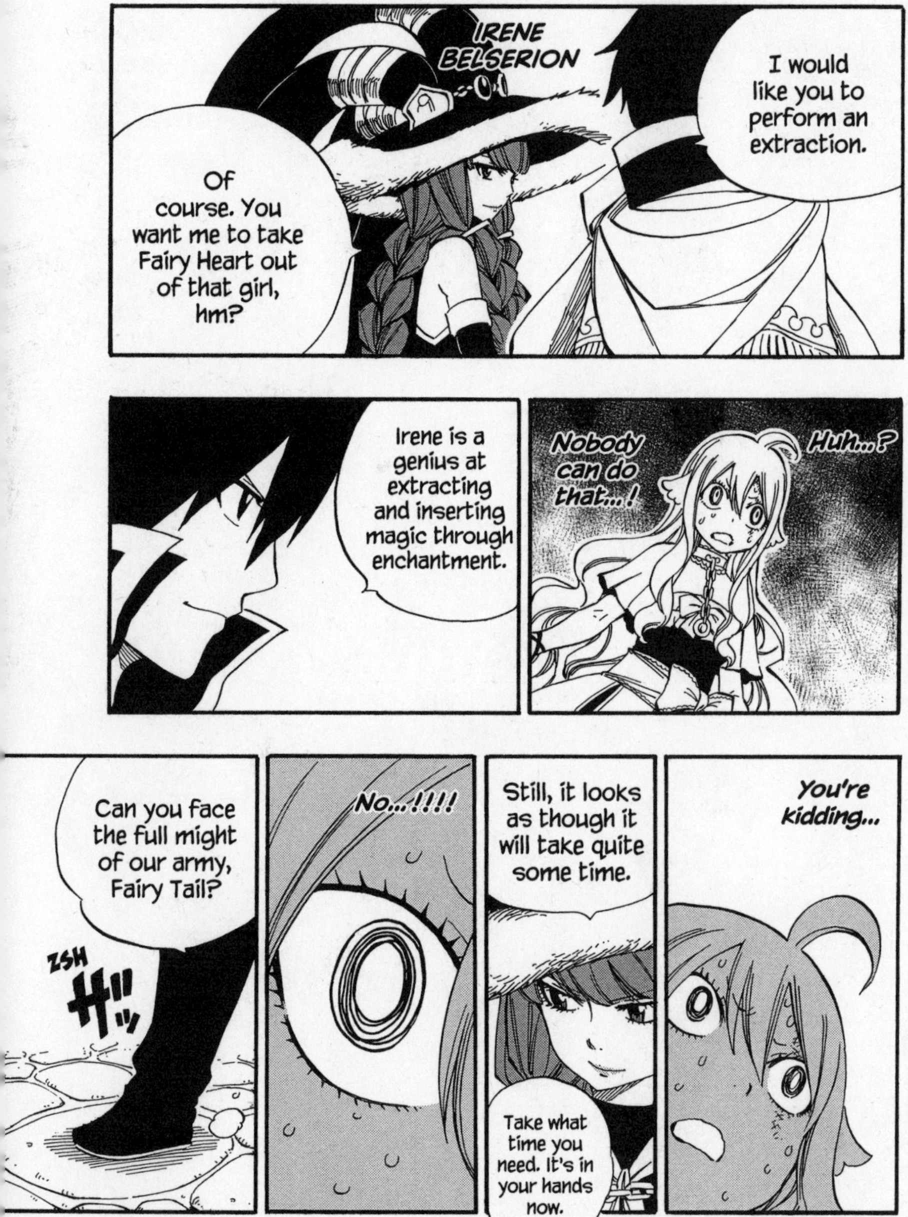

I would like you to perform an extraction.
IRENE BELSERION
Of course. You want me to take Fairy Heart out of that girl, hm?
Huh...?
Nobody can do that...!
Irene is a genius at extracting and inserting magic through enchantment.
You're kidding...
Still, it looks as though it will take quite some time.
Take what time you need. It's in your hands now.
No...!!!!
Can you face the full might of our army, Fairy Tail?
ZSH

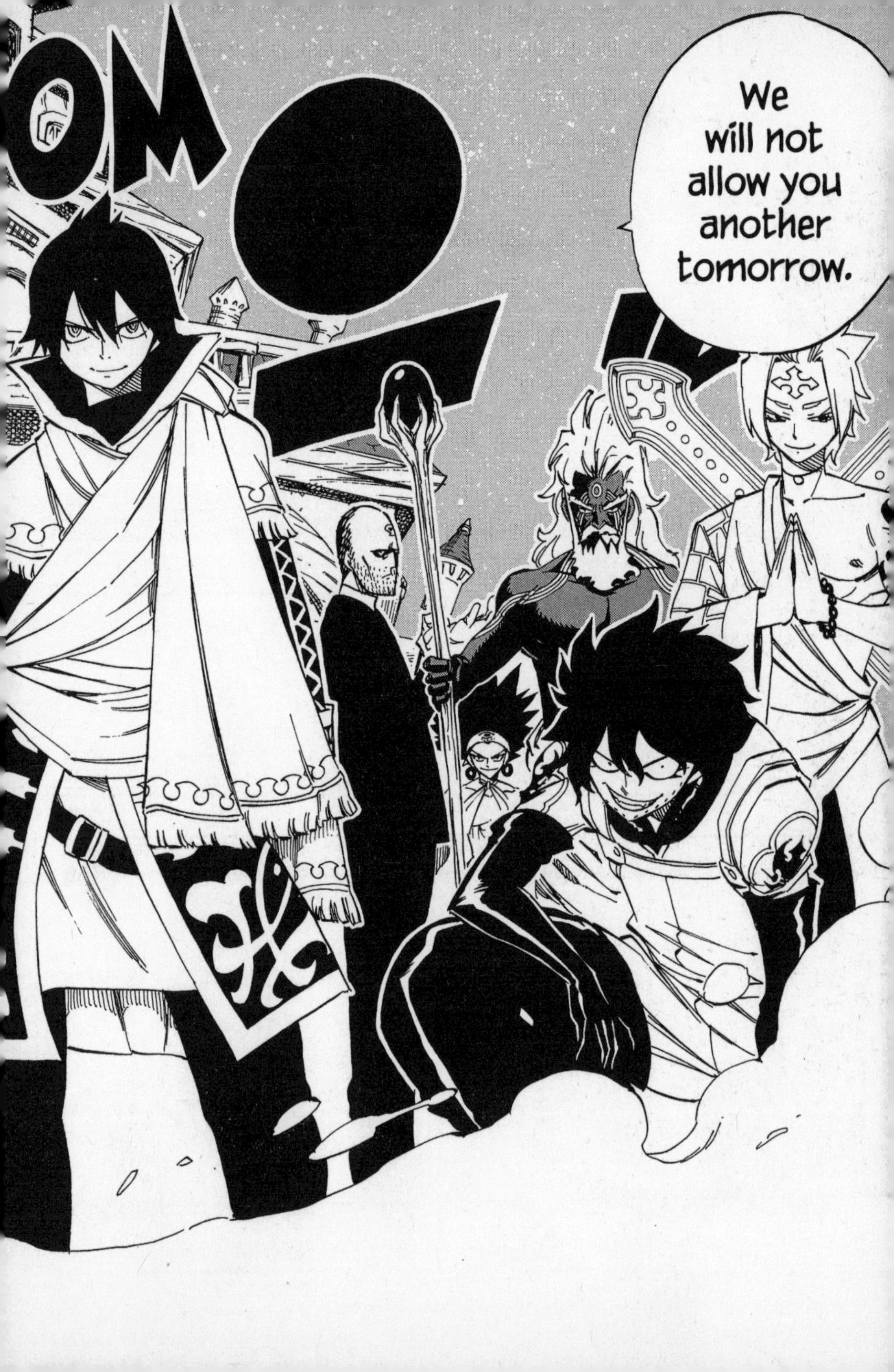
We will not allow you another tomorrow.

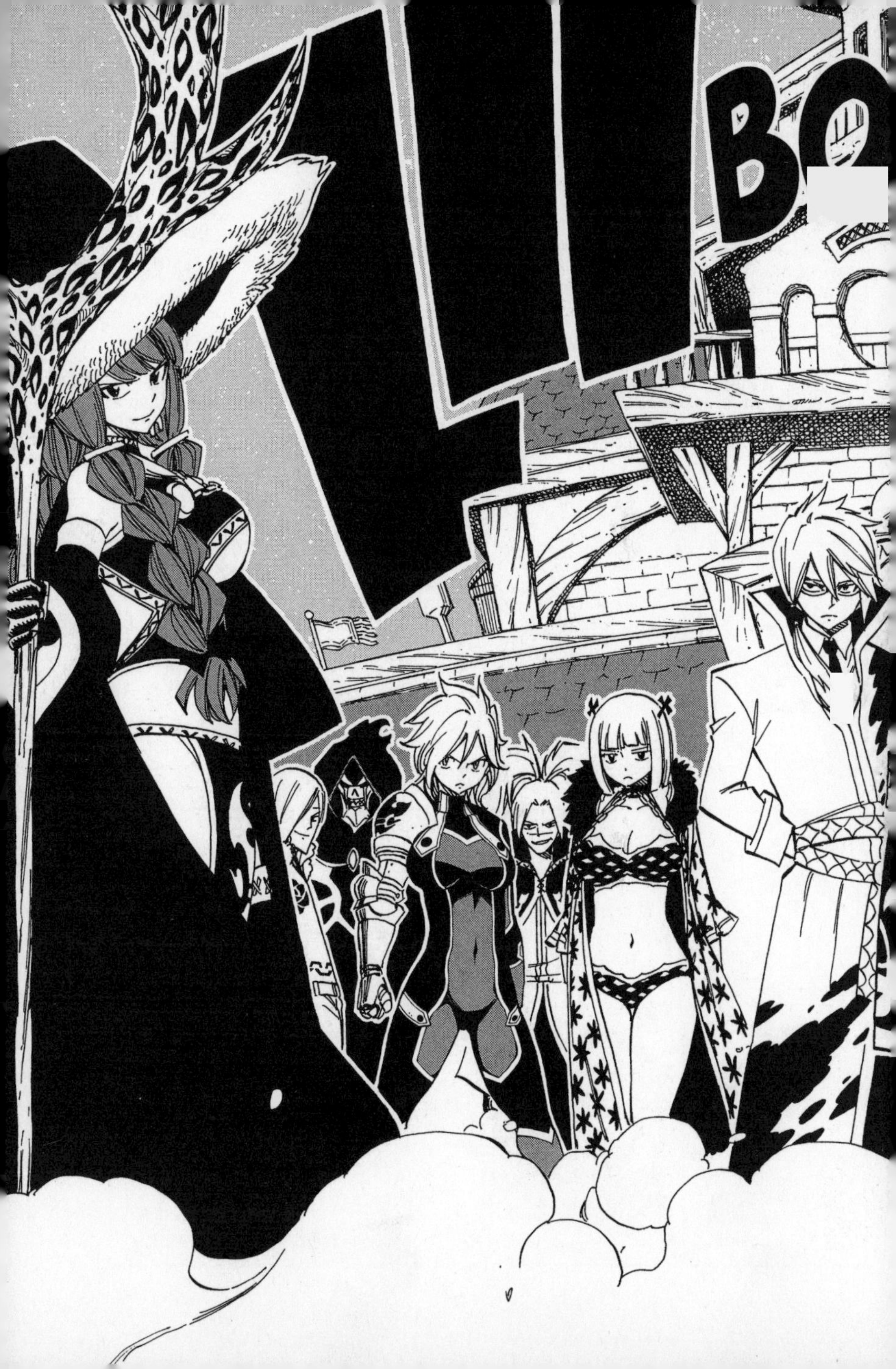
BO

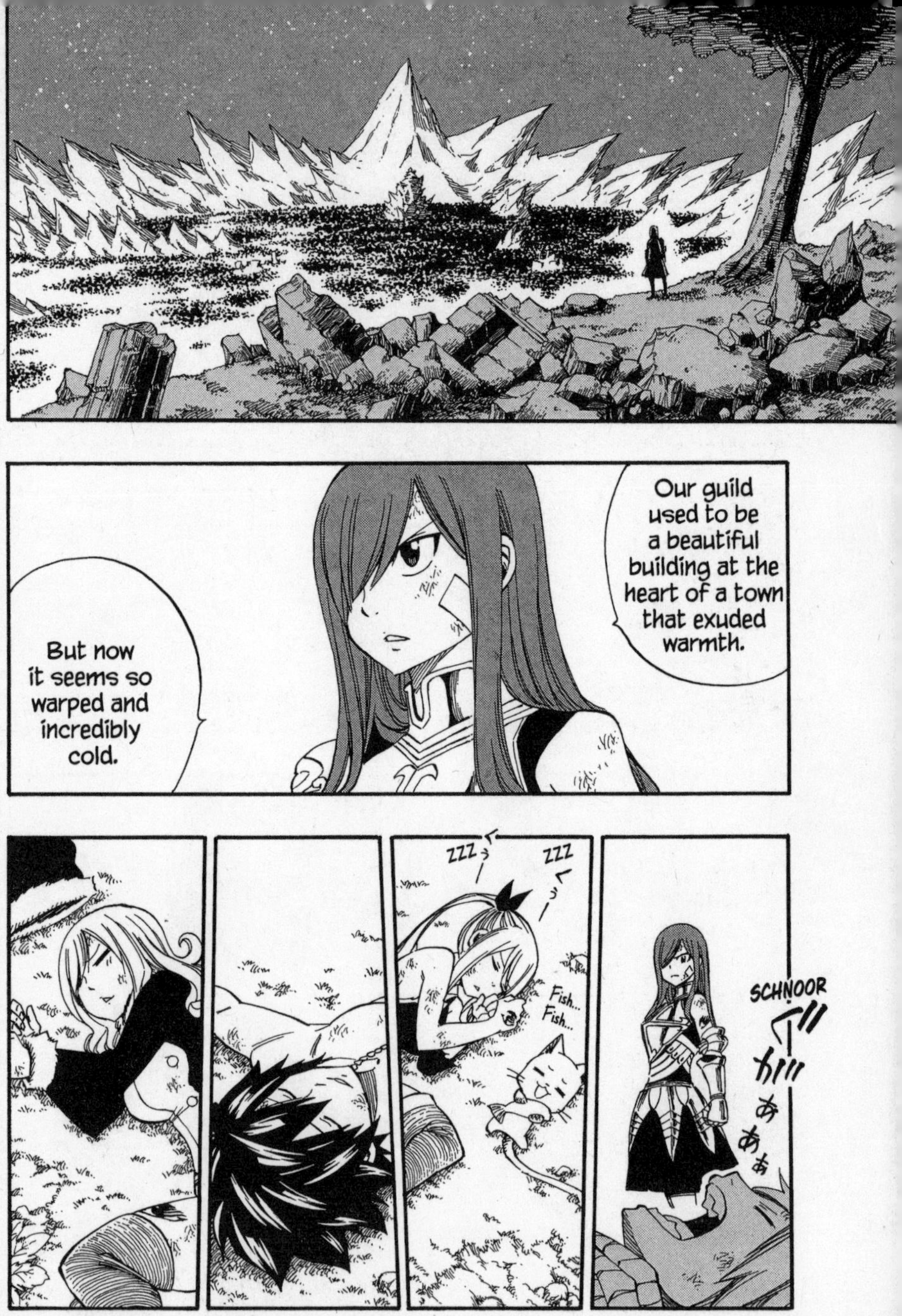
Our guild used to be a beautiful building at the heart of a town that exuded warmth.
But now it seems so warped and incredibly cold.
SCHNOOR
ZZZ
ZZZ
Fish... Fish...

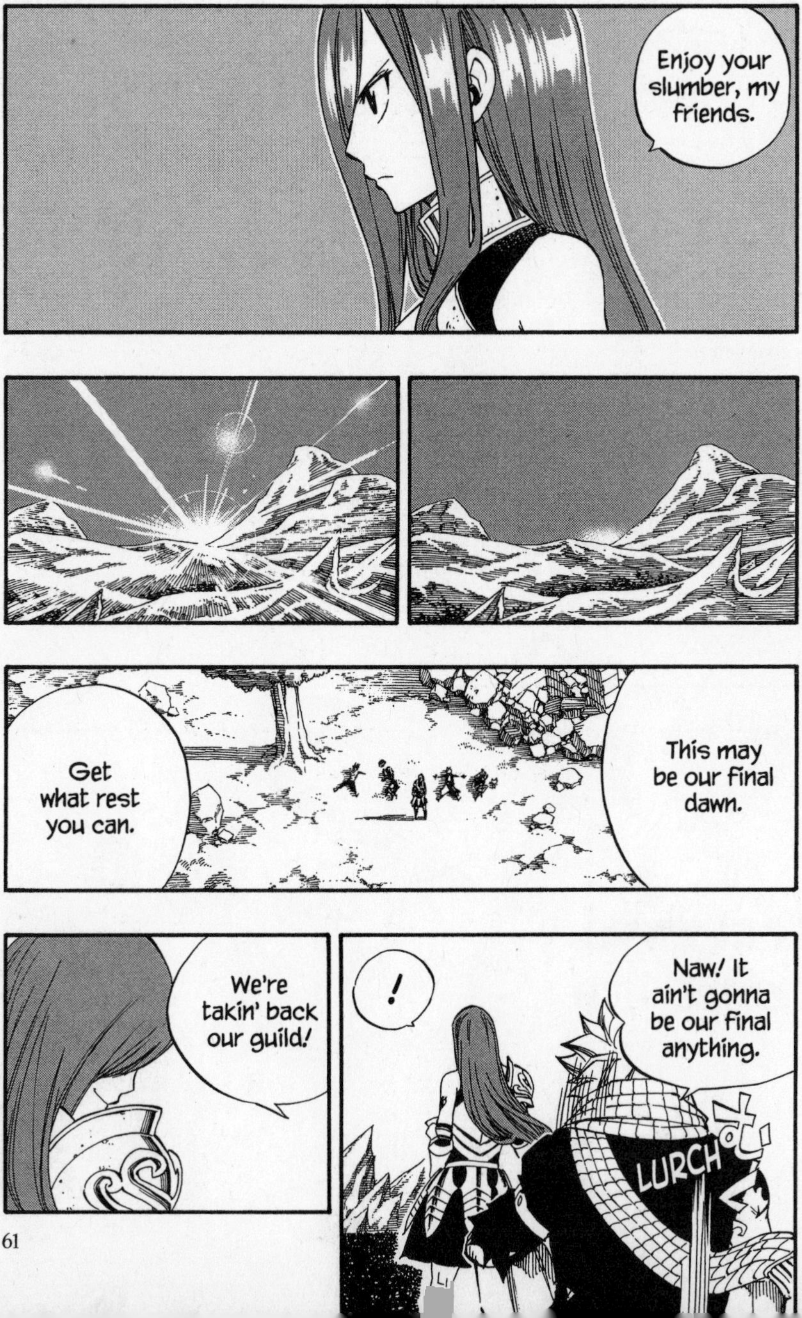
Enjoy your slumber, my friends.
This may be our final dawn.
Get what rest you can.
Naw! It ain't gonna be our final anything.
!
LURCH
We're takin' back our guild!

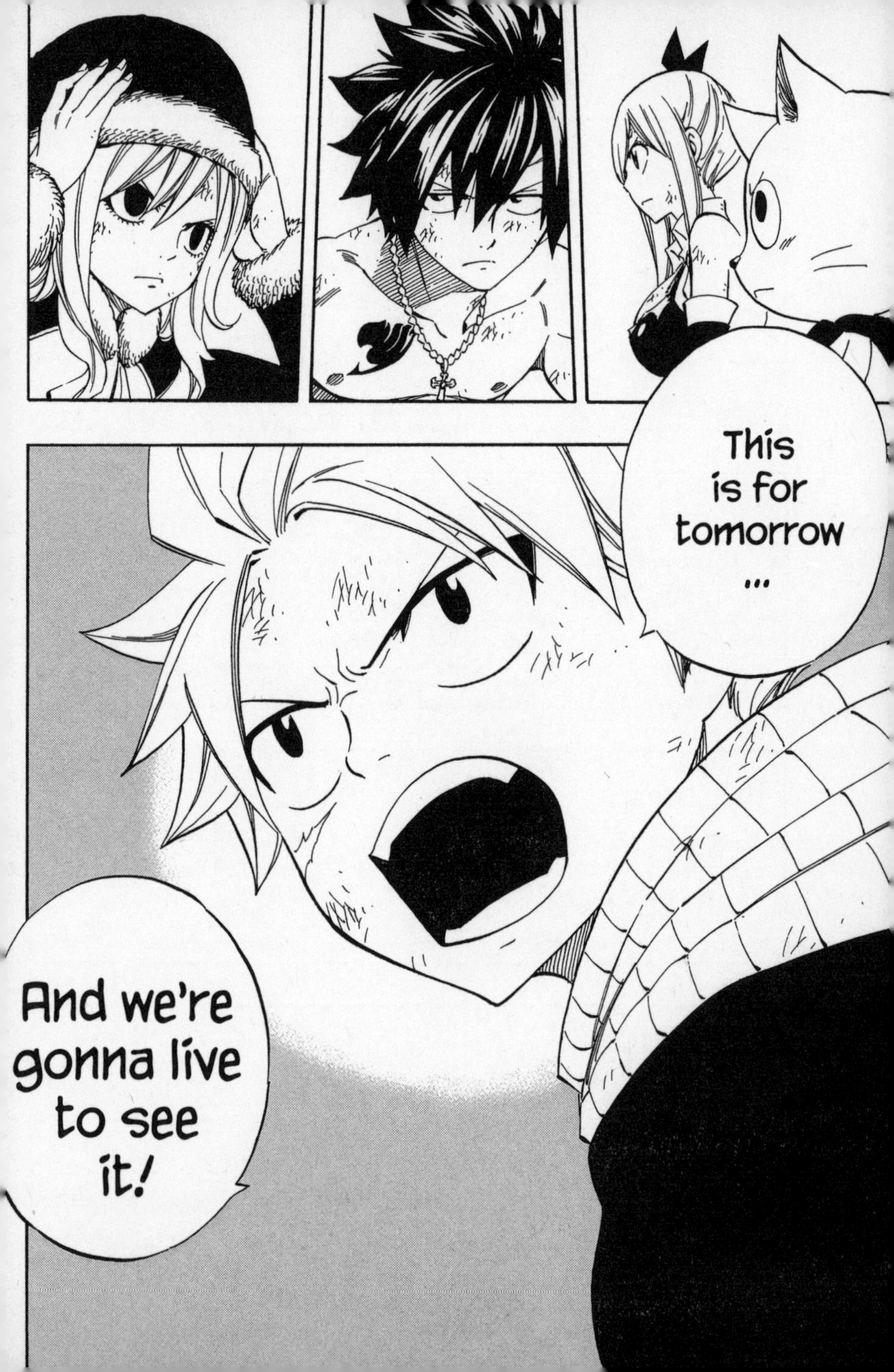
This is for tomorrow ...
And we're gonna live to see it!

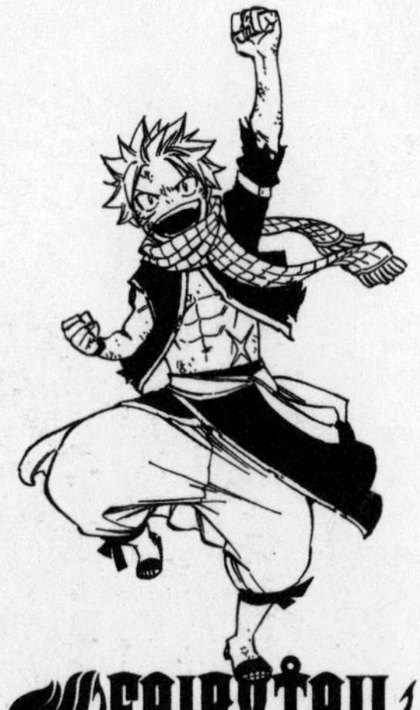
FAIRY TAIL

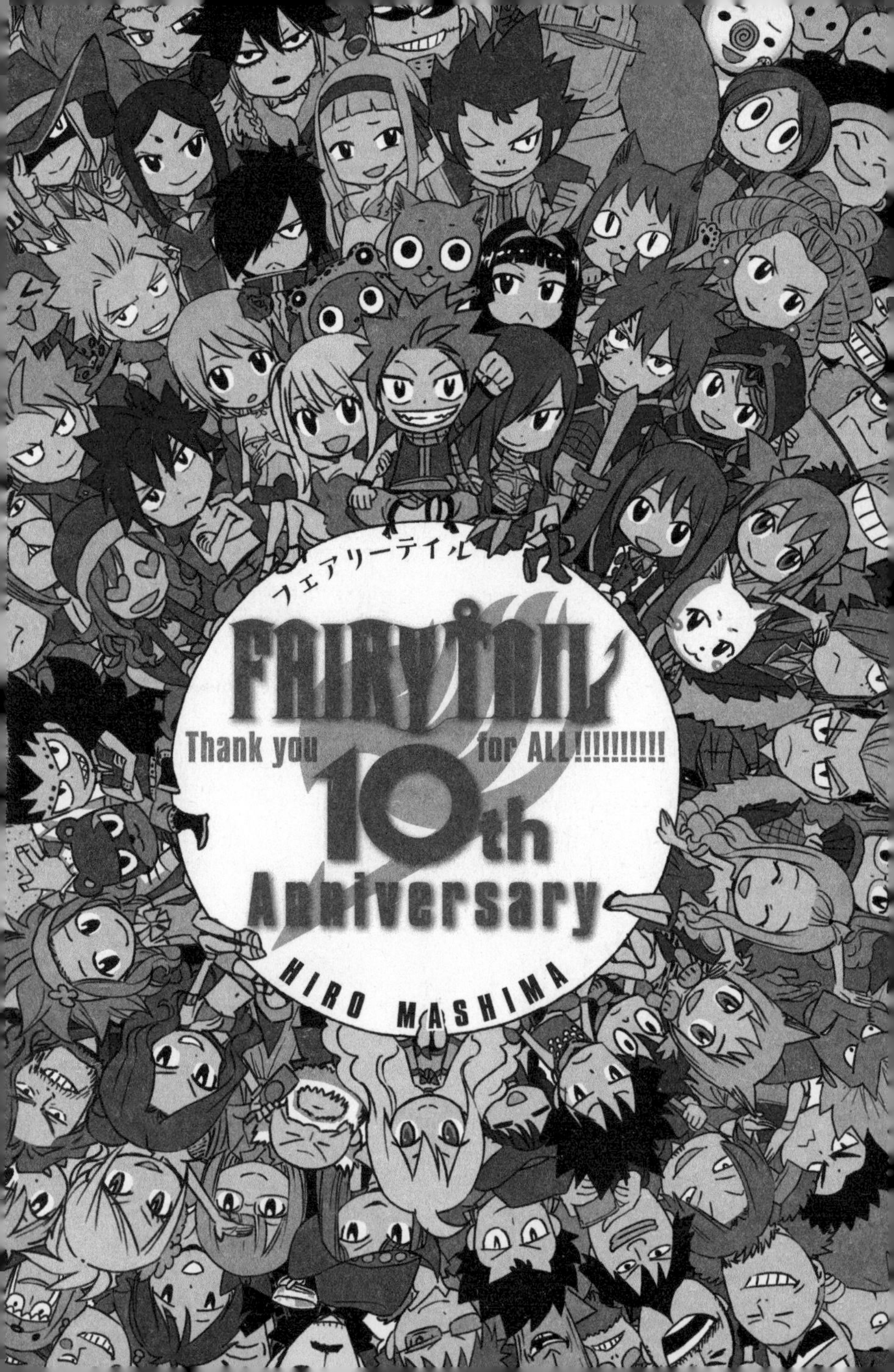
フェアリーテイル
FAIRY TAIL
Thank you for ALL!!!!!!!!!!
10th Anniversary
HIRO MASHIMA

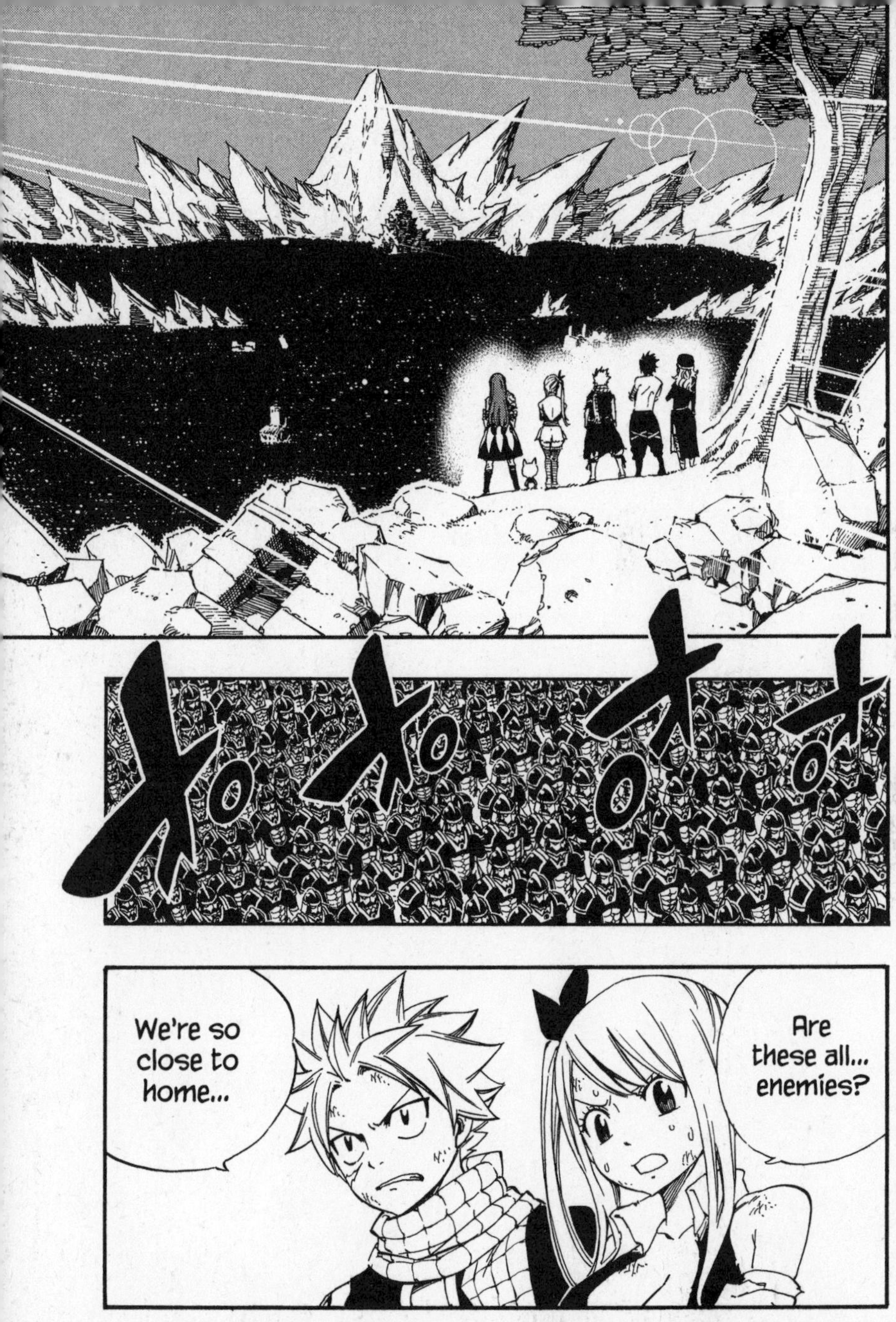
Are these all... enemies?
We're so close to home...

Chapter 495: I'm Hungry

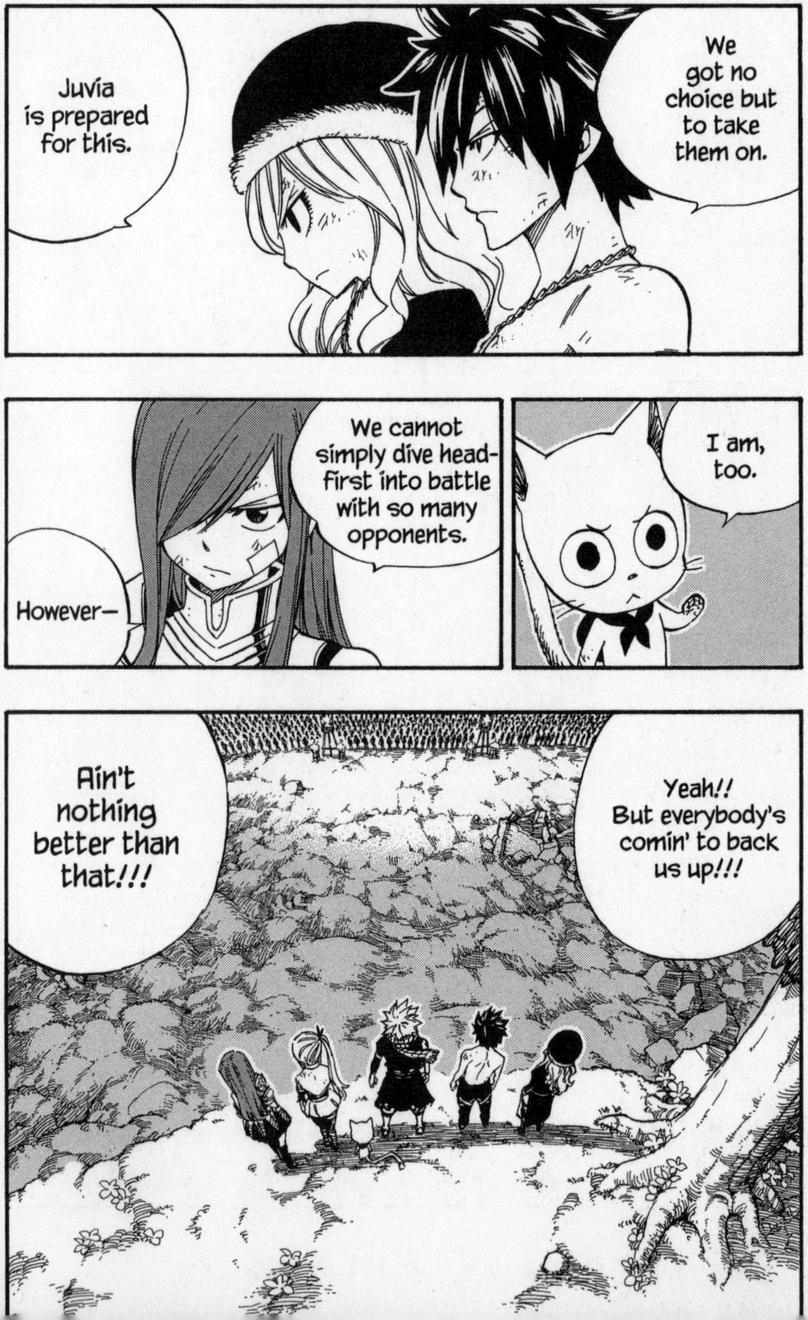
We got no choice but to take them on.
Juvia is prepared for this.
I am, too.
We cannot simply dive head-first into battle with so many opponents.
However—
Yeah!! But everybody's comin' to back us up!!!
Ain't nothing better than that!!!

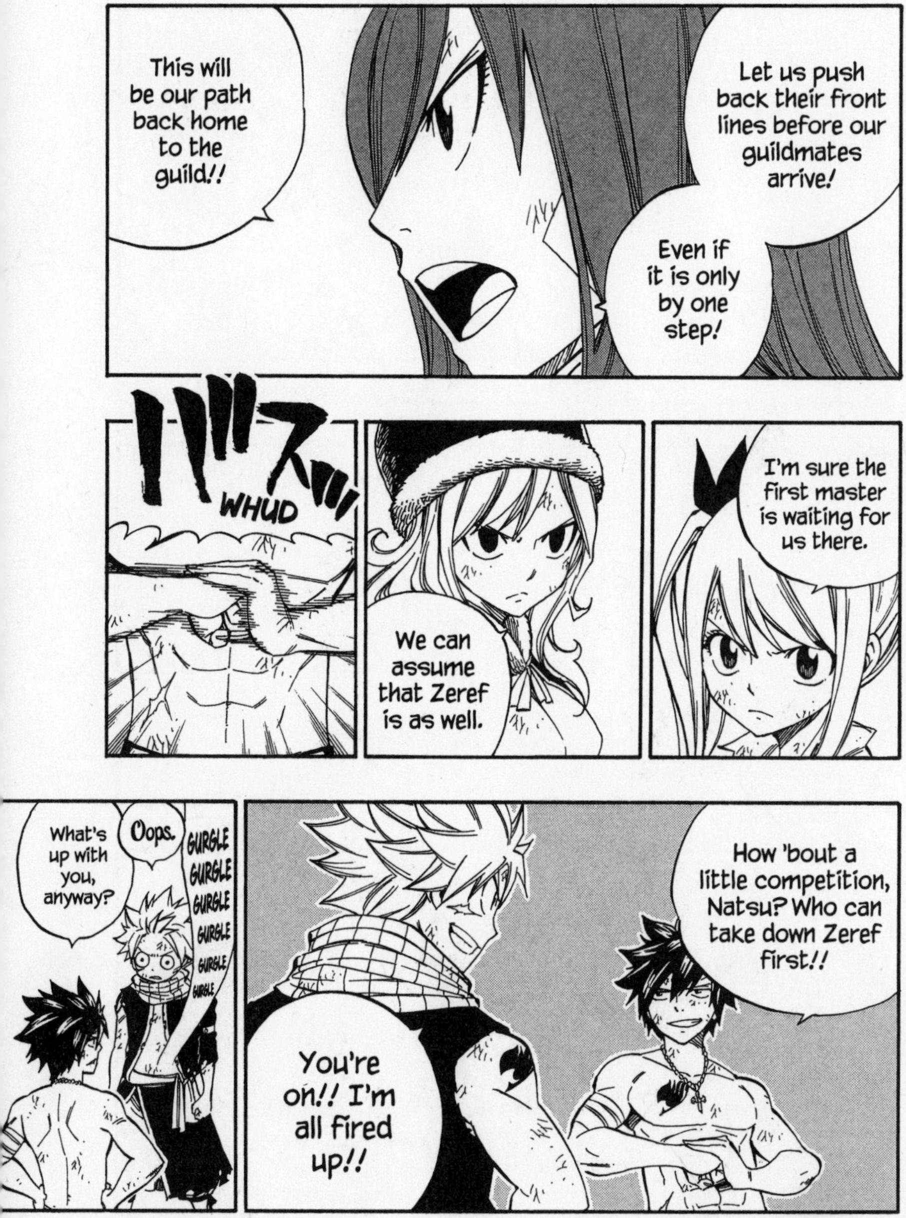
Let us push back their front lines before our guildmates arrive!
Even if it is only by one step!
This will be our path back home to the guild!!
I'm sure the first master is waiting for us there.
We can assume that Zeref is as well.
WHUD
How 'bout a little competition, Natsu? Who can take down Zeref first!!
You're on!! I'm all fired up!!
Oops.
GURGLE GURGLE GURGLE GURGLE GURGLE GURGLE
What's up with you, anyway?

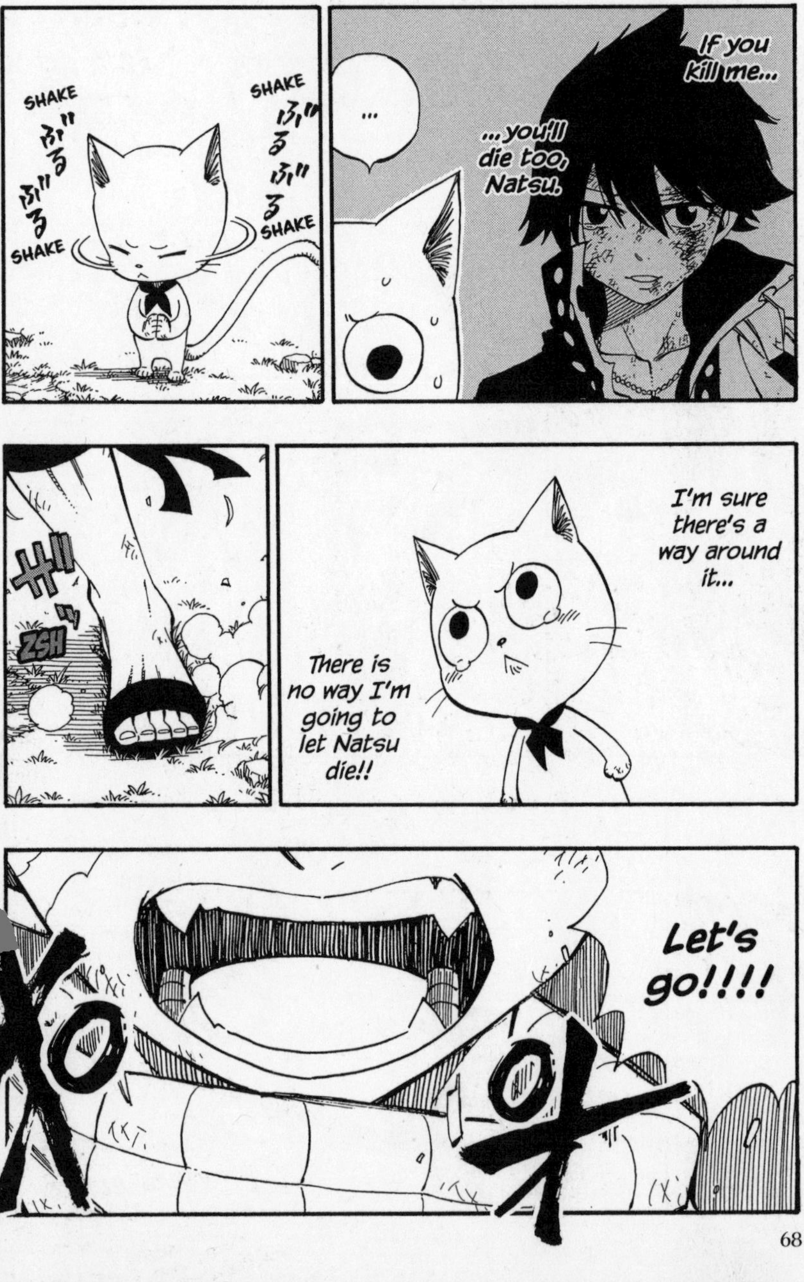

If you kill me...
...you'll die too, Natsu.
...
SHAKE
ぶるぶる
SHAKE
SHAKE
ぶるぶる
SHAKE
I'm sure there's a way around it...
There is no way I'm going to let Natsu die!!
ザッ
ZSH
Let's go!!!!

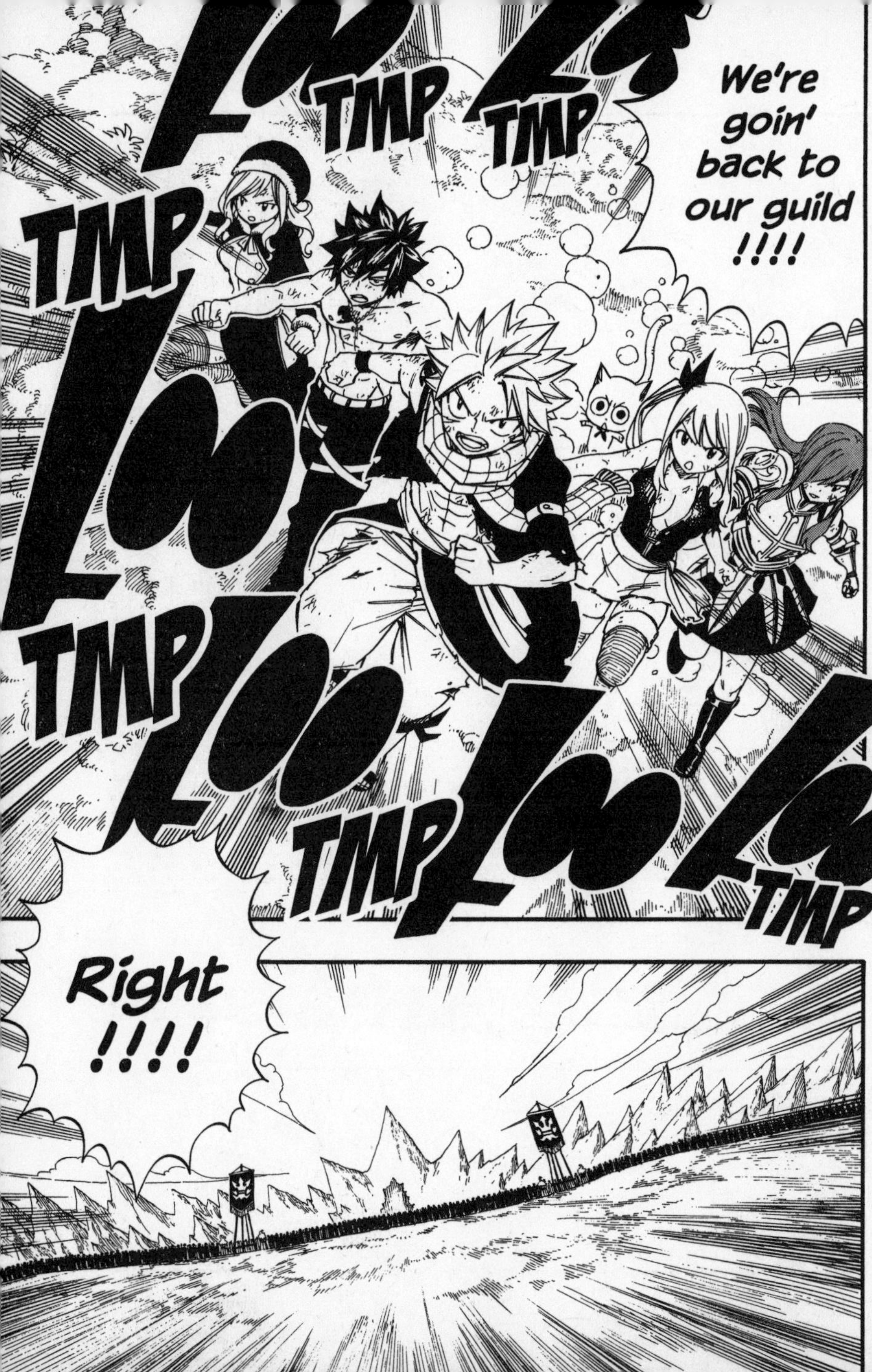
We're goin' back to our guild !!!!
TMP
TMP
TMP
TMP
TMP
TMP
TMP
Right !!!!

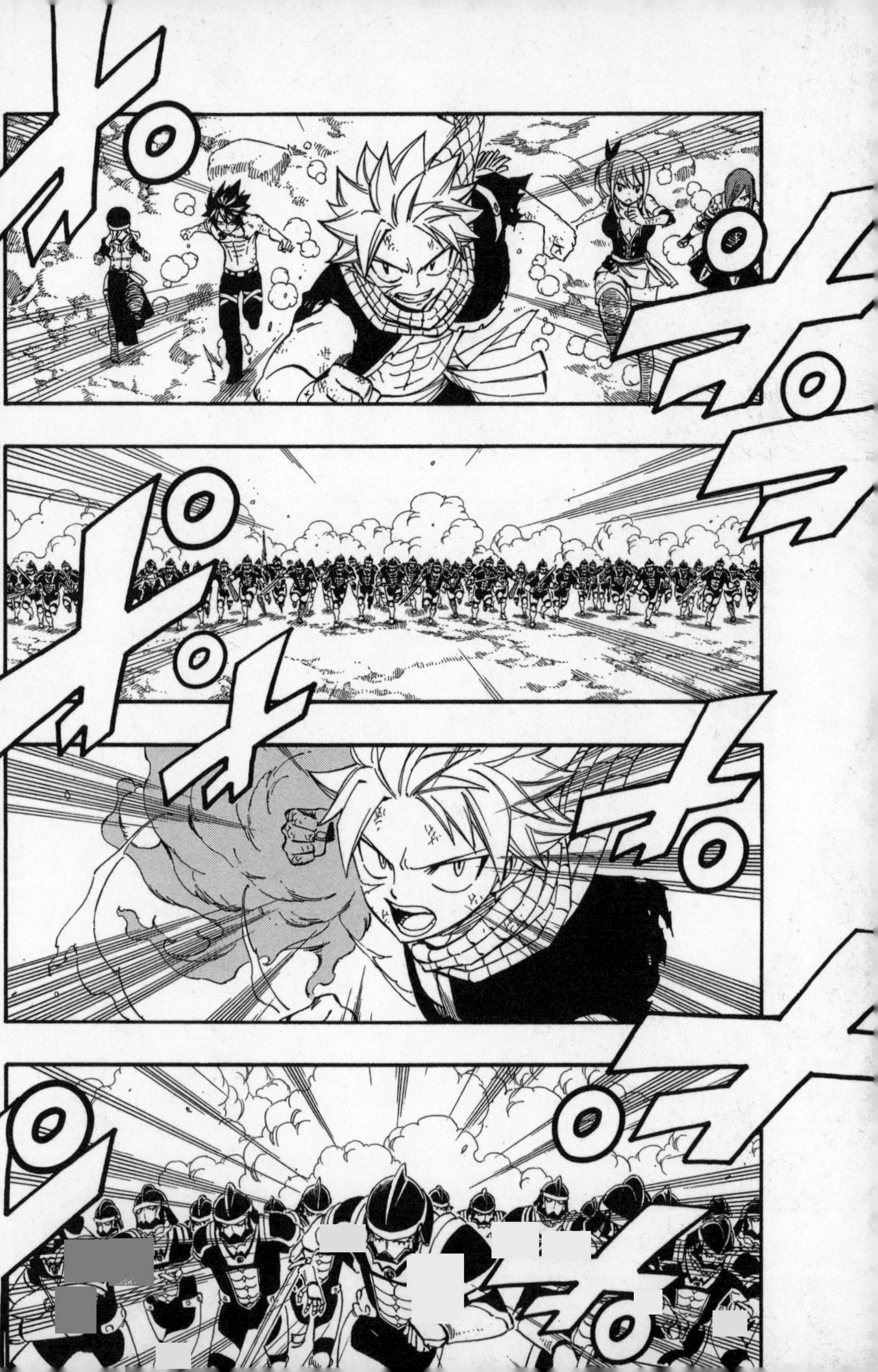

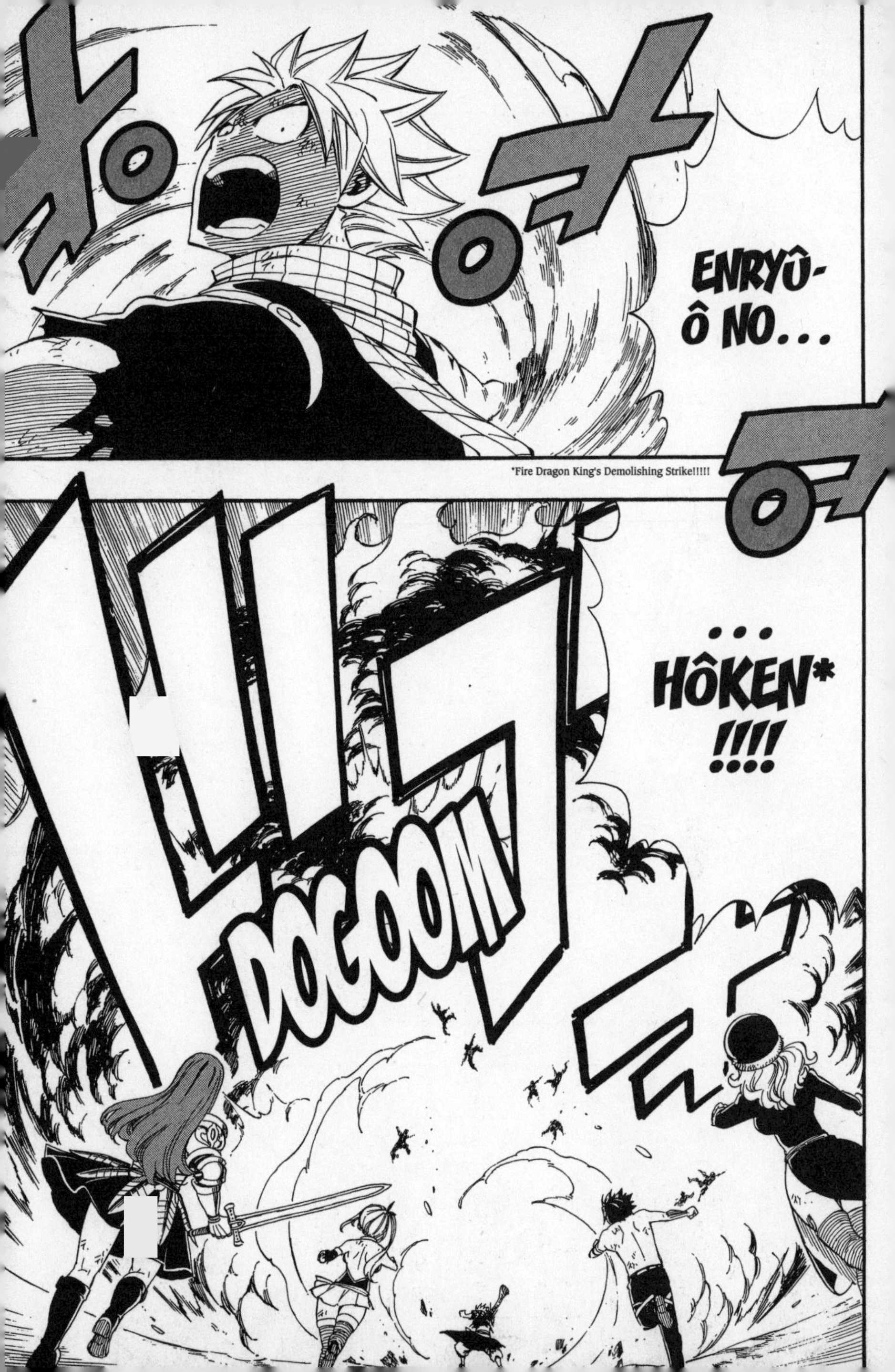
ENRYÛ-
Ô NO...
...
HÔKEN*
!!!!
DOGOOM
*Fire Dragon King's Demolishing Strike!!!!!

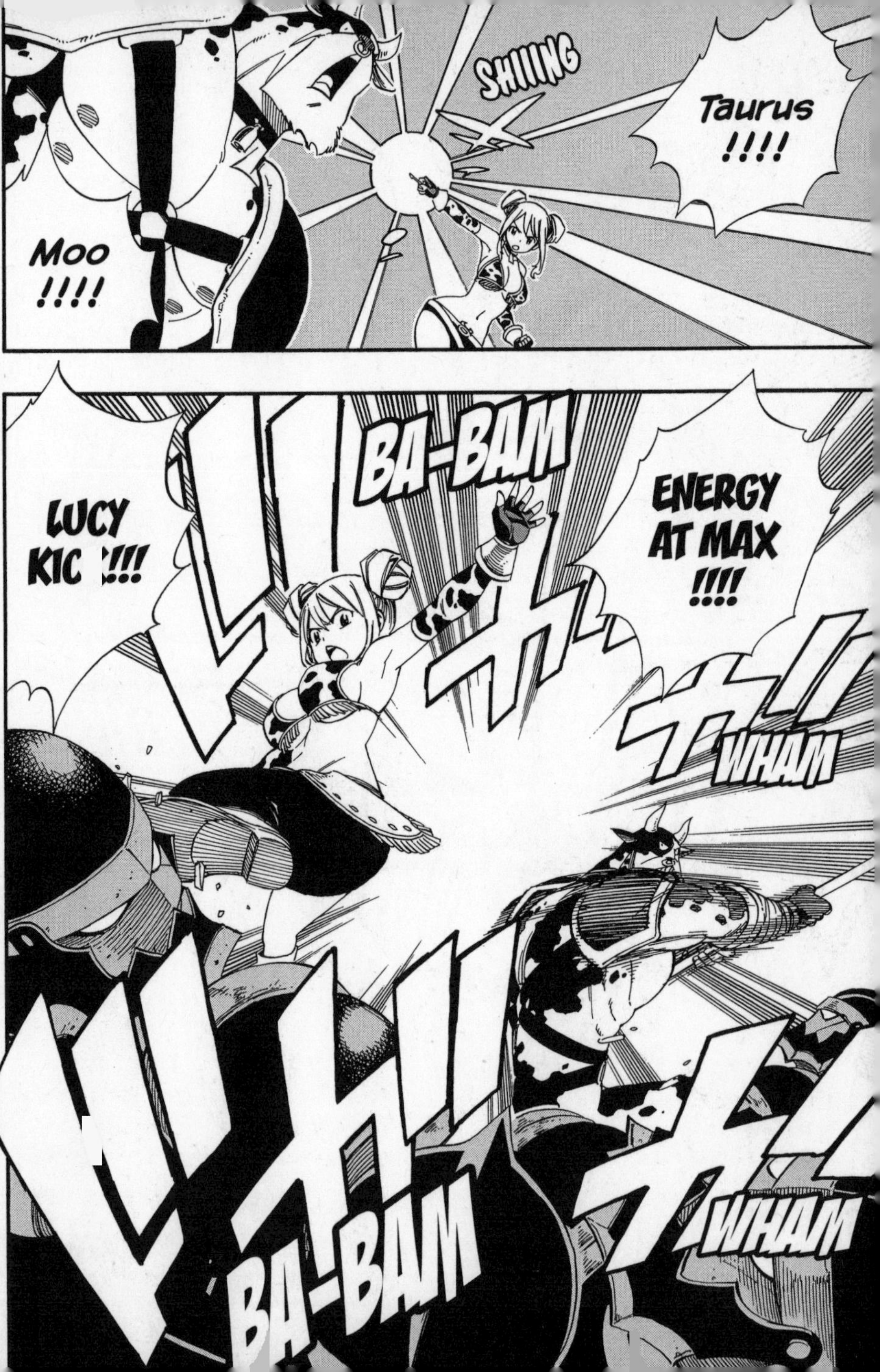
Taurus !!!!
SHIIING
Moo !!!!
ENERGY AT MAX !!!!
BA-BAM
LUCY KIC !!!
WHAM
WHAM
BA-BAM

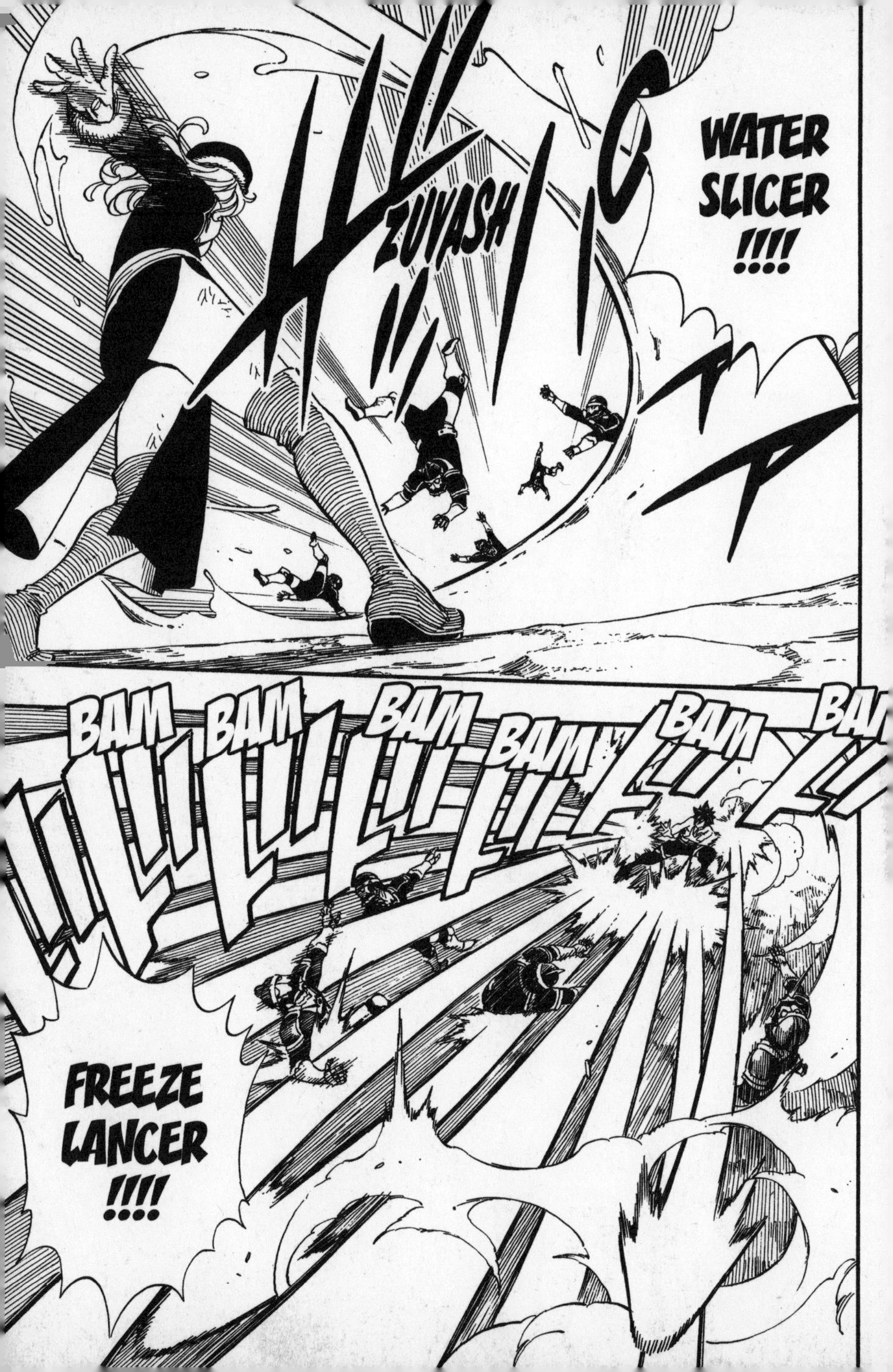
WATER SLICER !!!!
ZUVASH
BAM BAM BAM BAM BAM
FREEZE LANCER !!!!

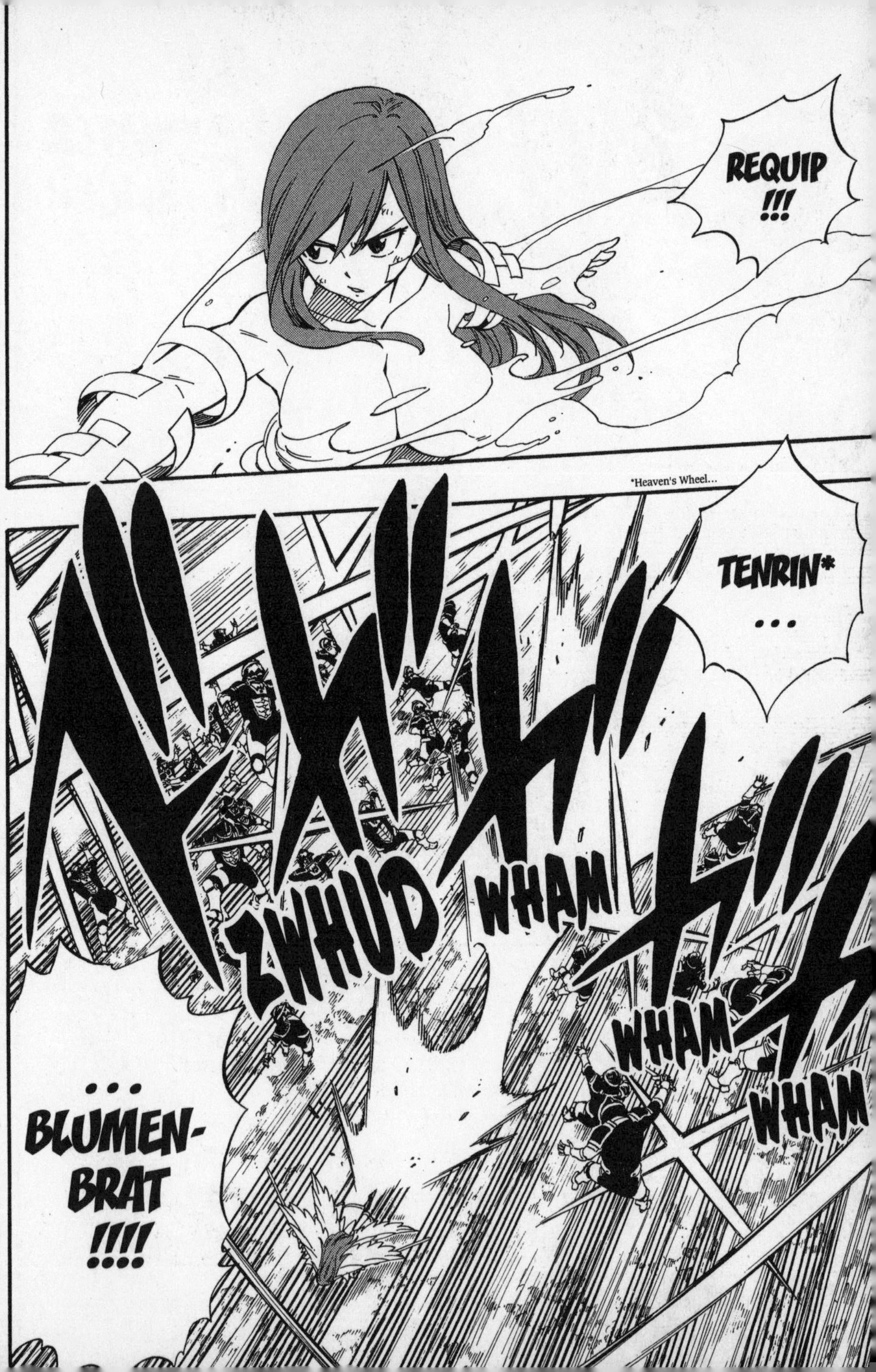
REQUIP !!!
TENRIN* ...
WHAM
WHAM
WHAM
ZWHUD
... BLUMEN-BRAT !!!!
*Heaven's Wheel...

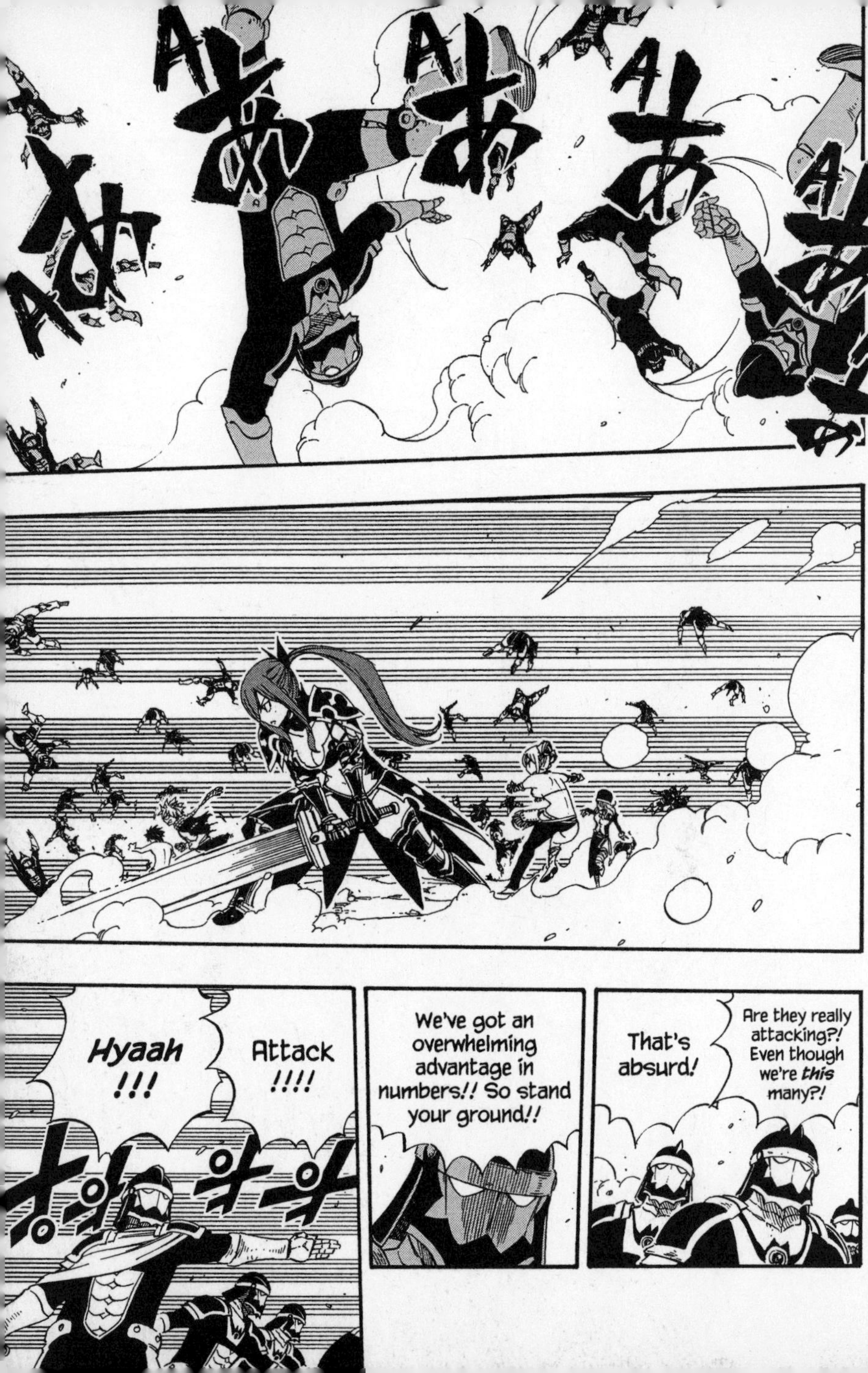
Are they really attacking?! Even though we're *this* many?!
That's absurd!
We've got an overwhelming advantage in numbers!! So stand your ground!!
Attack !!!!
Hyaah !!!

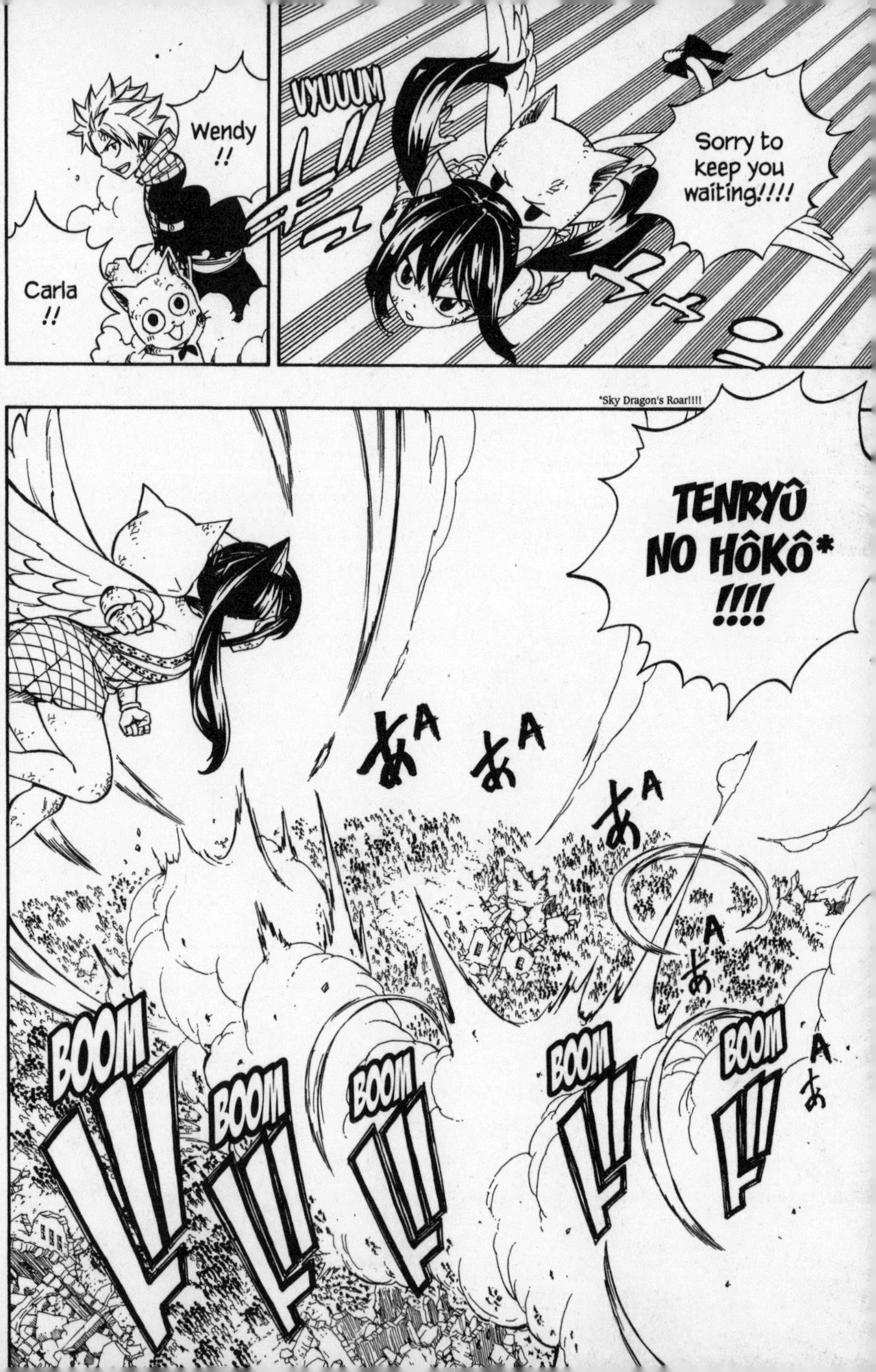
VYUUUM
Sorry to keep you waiting!!!!
Wendy!!
Carla!!
*Sky Dragon's Roar!!!!
TENRYÛ NO HÔKÔ*!!!!
あ A
あ A
あ A
あ A
あ A
BOOM
BOOM
BOOM
BOOM
BOOM

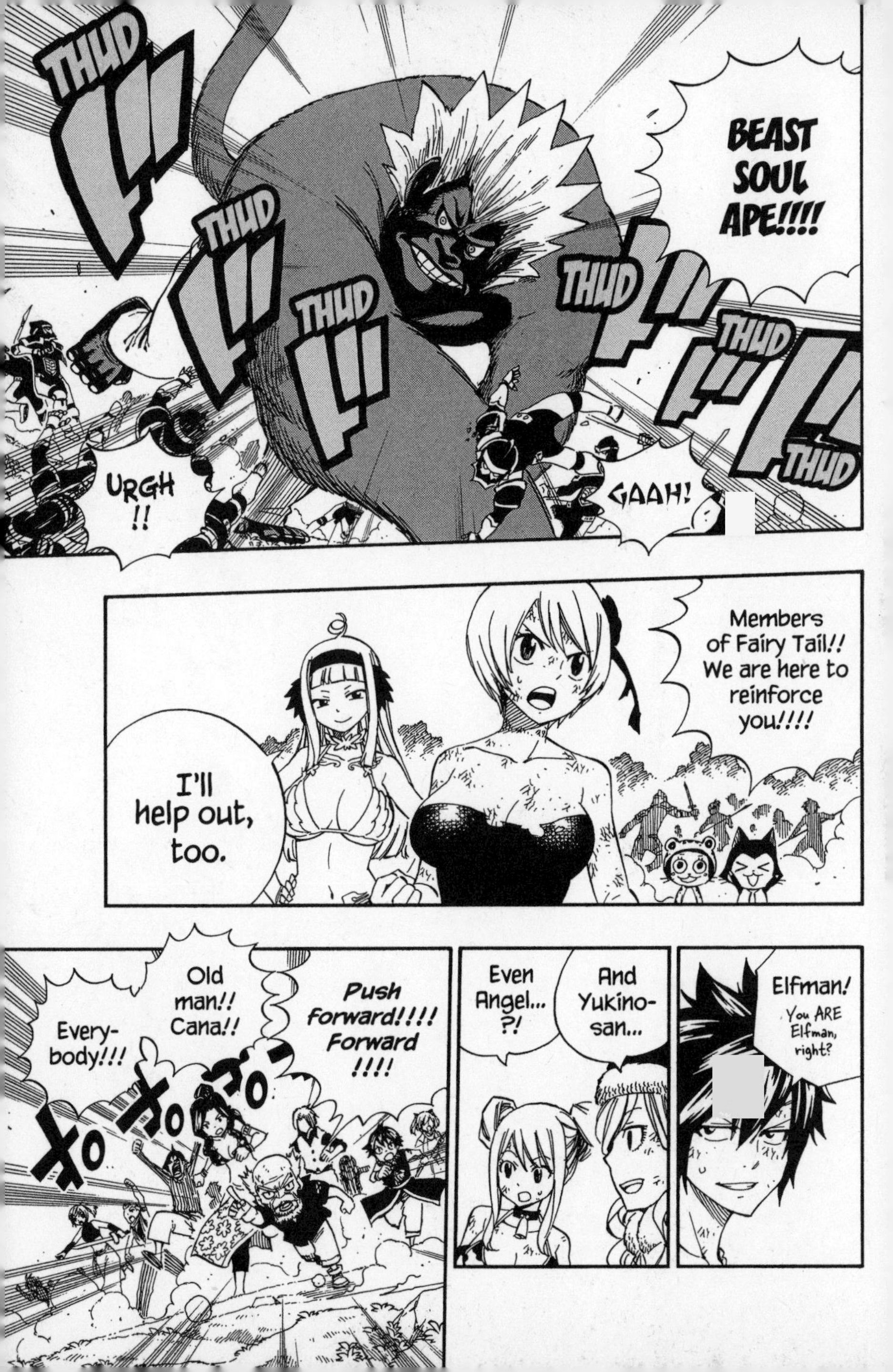
BEAST SOUL APE!!!!
THUD
THUD
THUD
GAAH!
THUD
THUD
THUD
THUD
URGH !!
Members of Fairy Tail!! We are here to reinforce you!!!!
I'll help out, too.
Elfman!
You ARE Elfman, right?
And Yukino-san...
Even Angel... ?!
Push forward!!!! Forward !!!!
Old man!! Cana!!
Every-body!!!

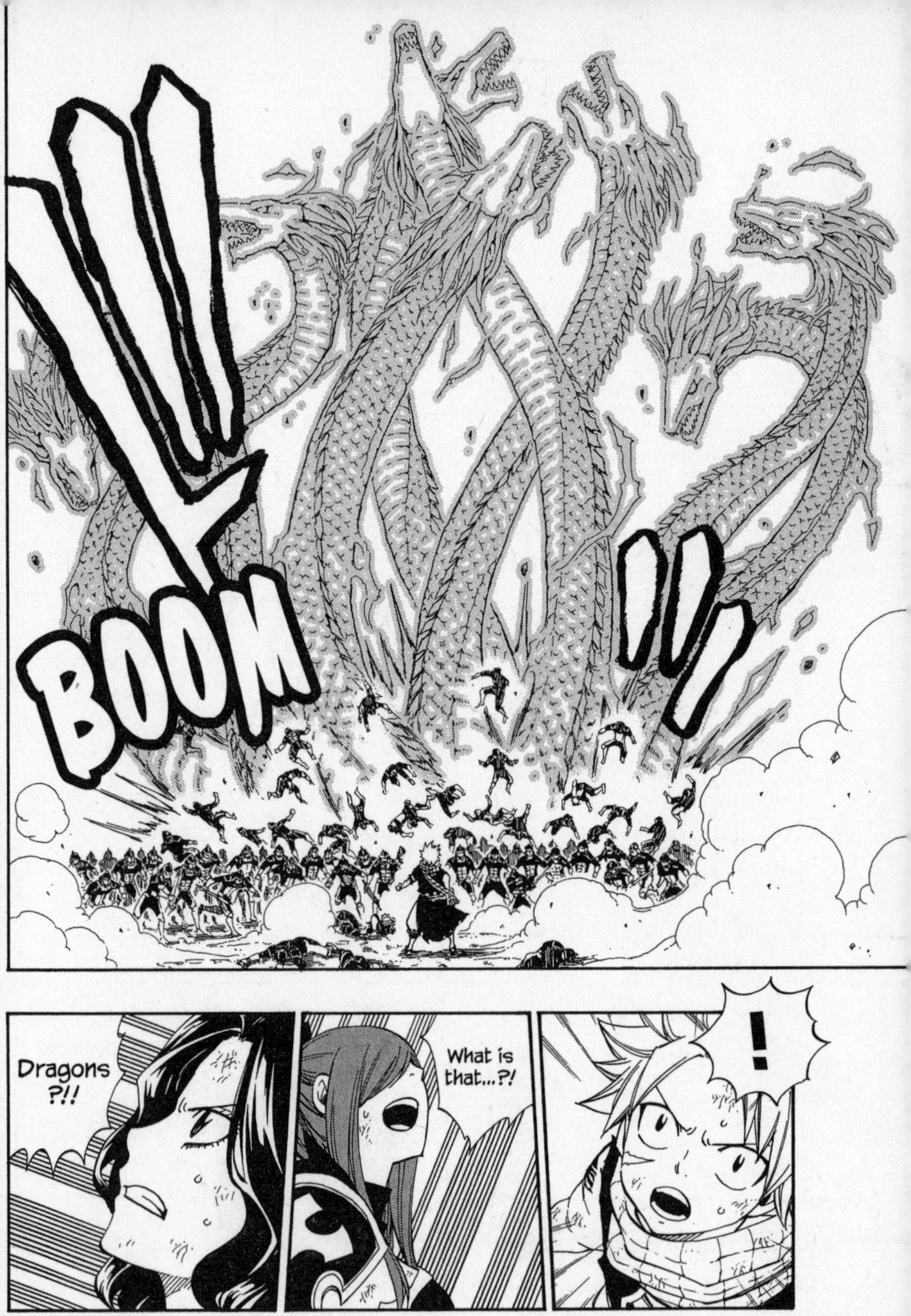
BOOM
!
What is that...?!
Dragons ?!!

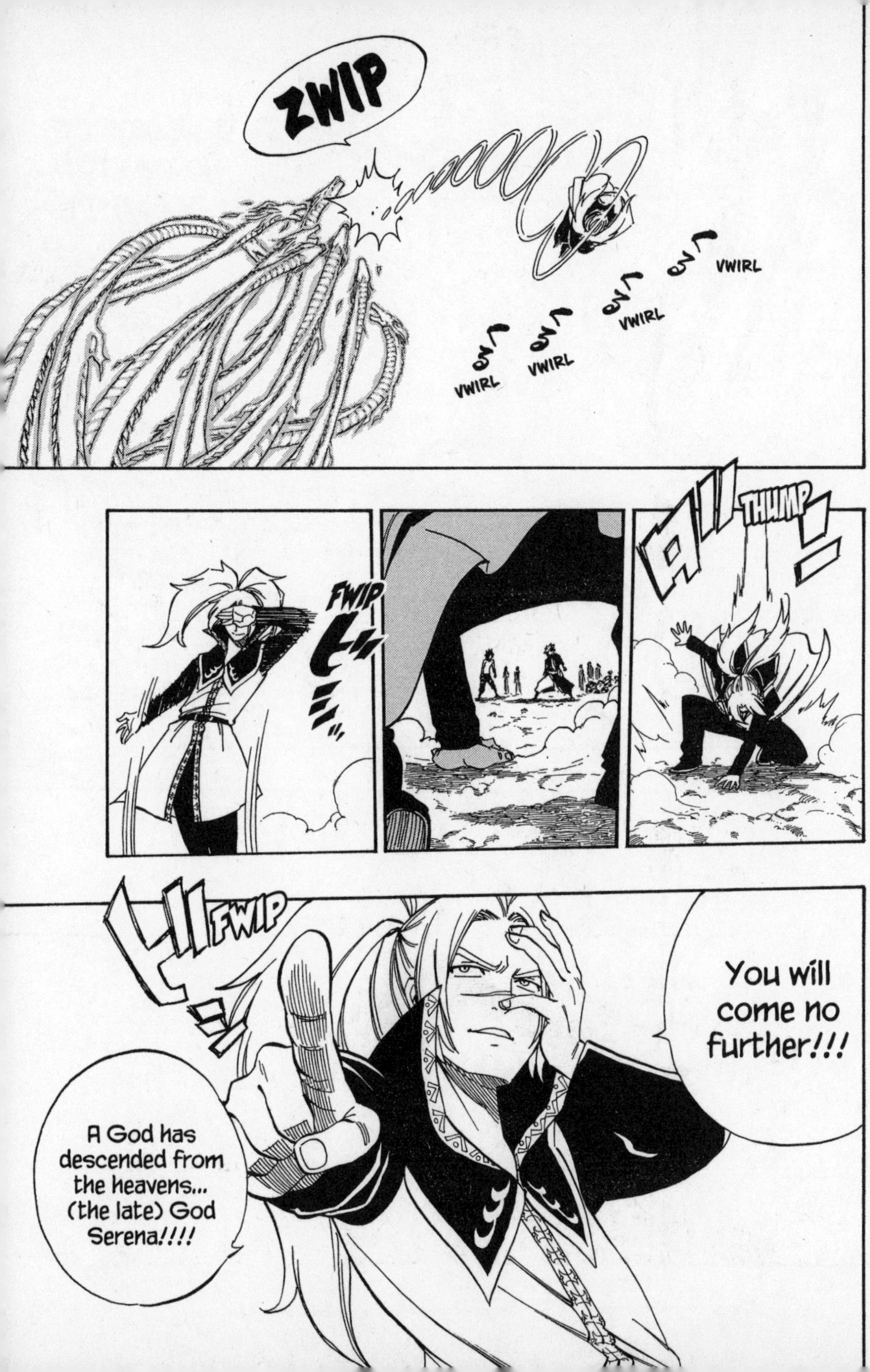
ZWIP
VWIRL
VWIRL
VWIRL
VWIRL
THUMP
FWIP
You will come no further!!!
FWIP
A God has descended from the heavens... (the late) God Serena!!!!

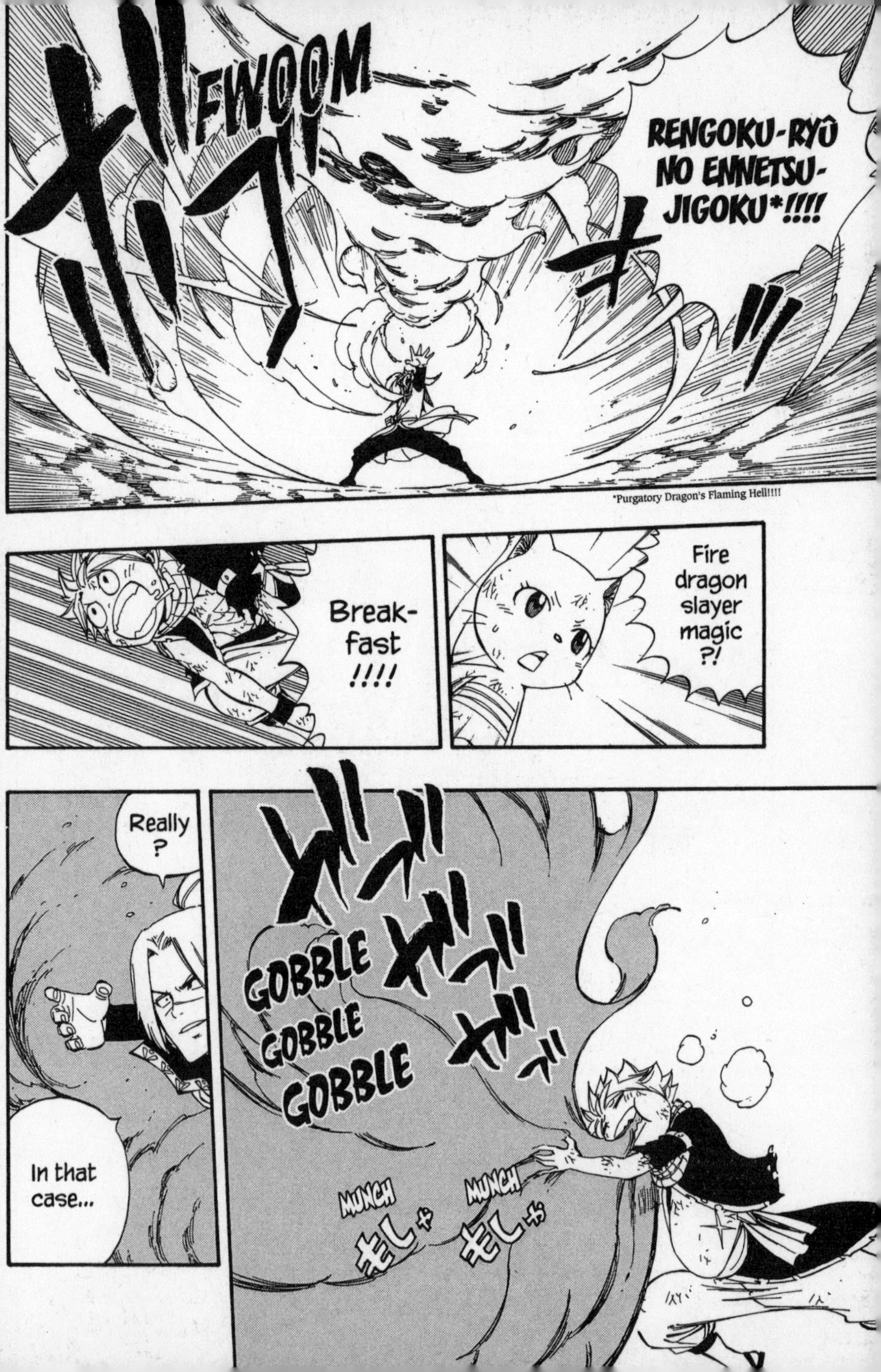
FWOOM
RENGOKU-RYÛ NO ENNETSU-JIGOKU*!!!!
Fire dragon slayer magic?!
Breakfast!!!!
GOBBLE GOBBLE GOBBLE
MUNCH
もしゃ
MUNCH
もしゃ
Really?
In that case...
*Purgatory Dragon's Flaming Hell!!!!

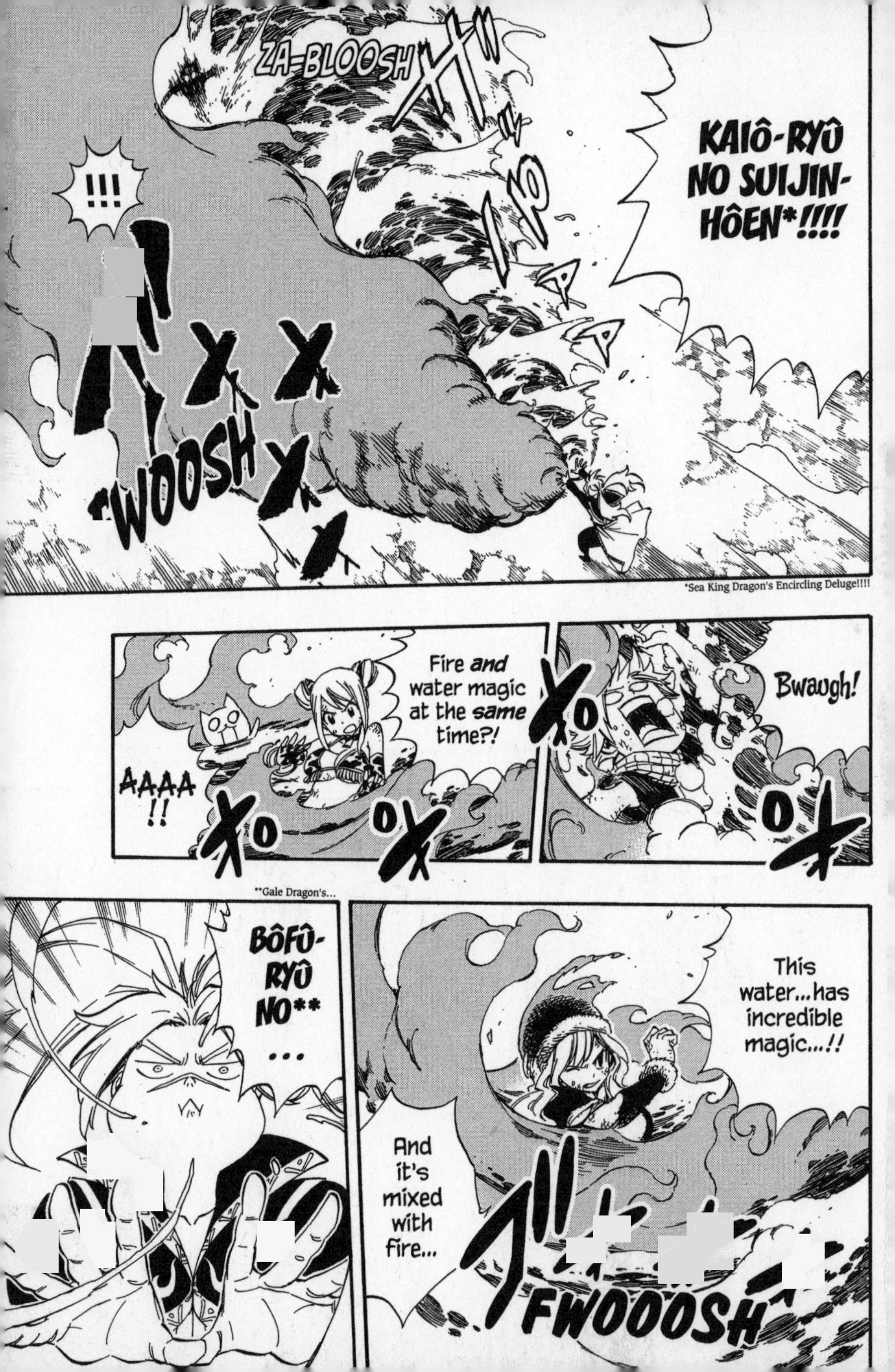
KAIÔ-RYÛ NO SUIJIN-HÔEN*!!!!
ZA-BLOOSH
!!!
FWOOSH
Bwaugh!
Fire and water magic at the same time?!
AAAA!!
This water...has incredible magic...!!
And it's mixed with fire...
FWOOOSH
BÔFÛ-RYÛ NO** ...

*Sea King Dragon's Encircling Deluge!!!!

**Gale Dragon's...

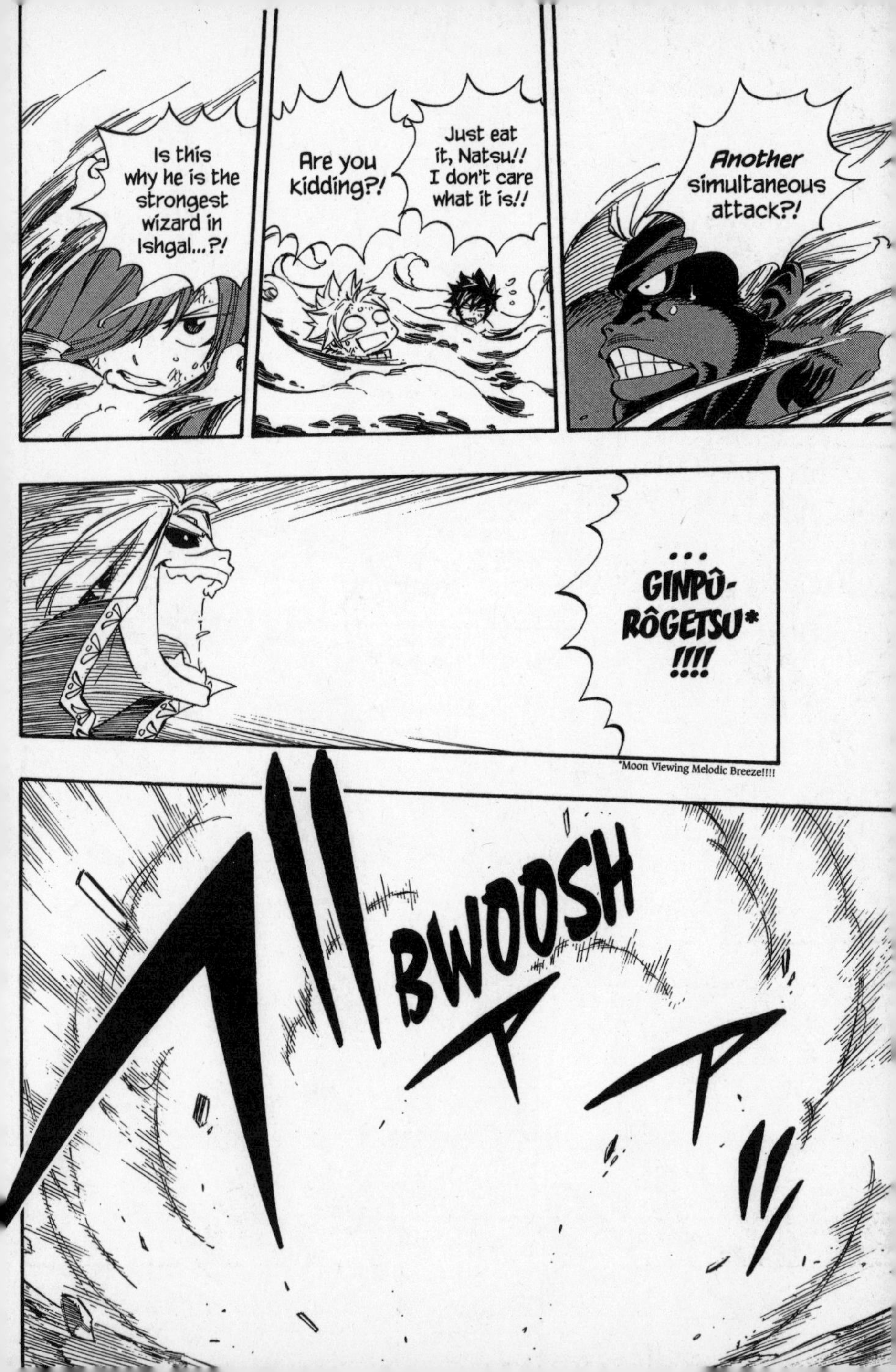
Another simultaneous attack?!
Just eat it, Natsu!! I don't care what it is!!
Are you kidding?!
Is this why he is the strongest wizard in Ishgal...?!
... GINPÛ-RÔGETSU* !!!!
*Moon Viewing Melodic Breeze!!!!
BWOOSH

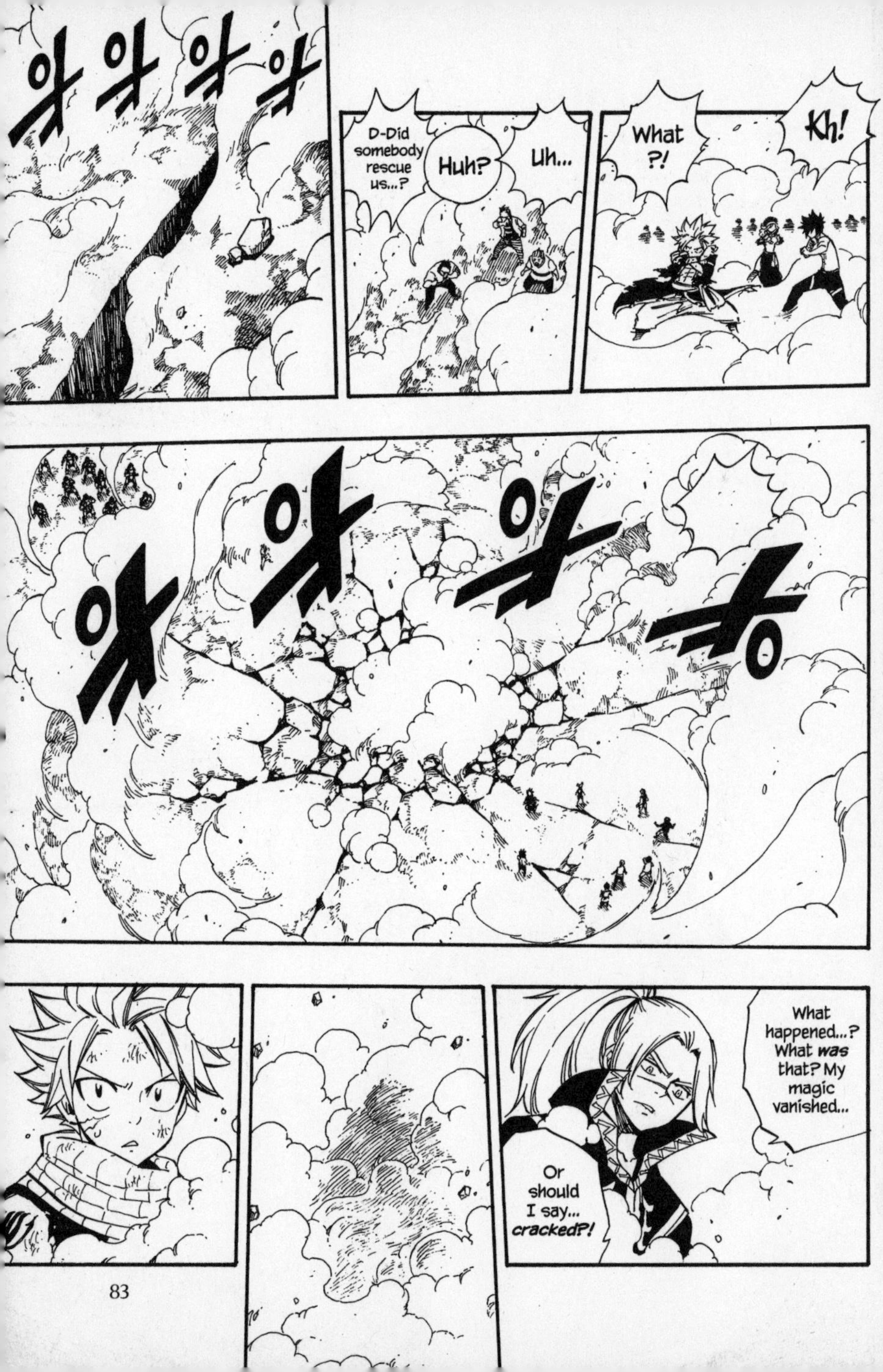

Kh!
What ?!
Uh...
Huh?
D-Did somebody rescue us...?
What happened...? What *was* that? My magic vanished...
Or should I say... *cracked*?!

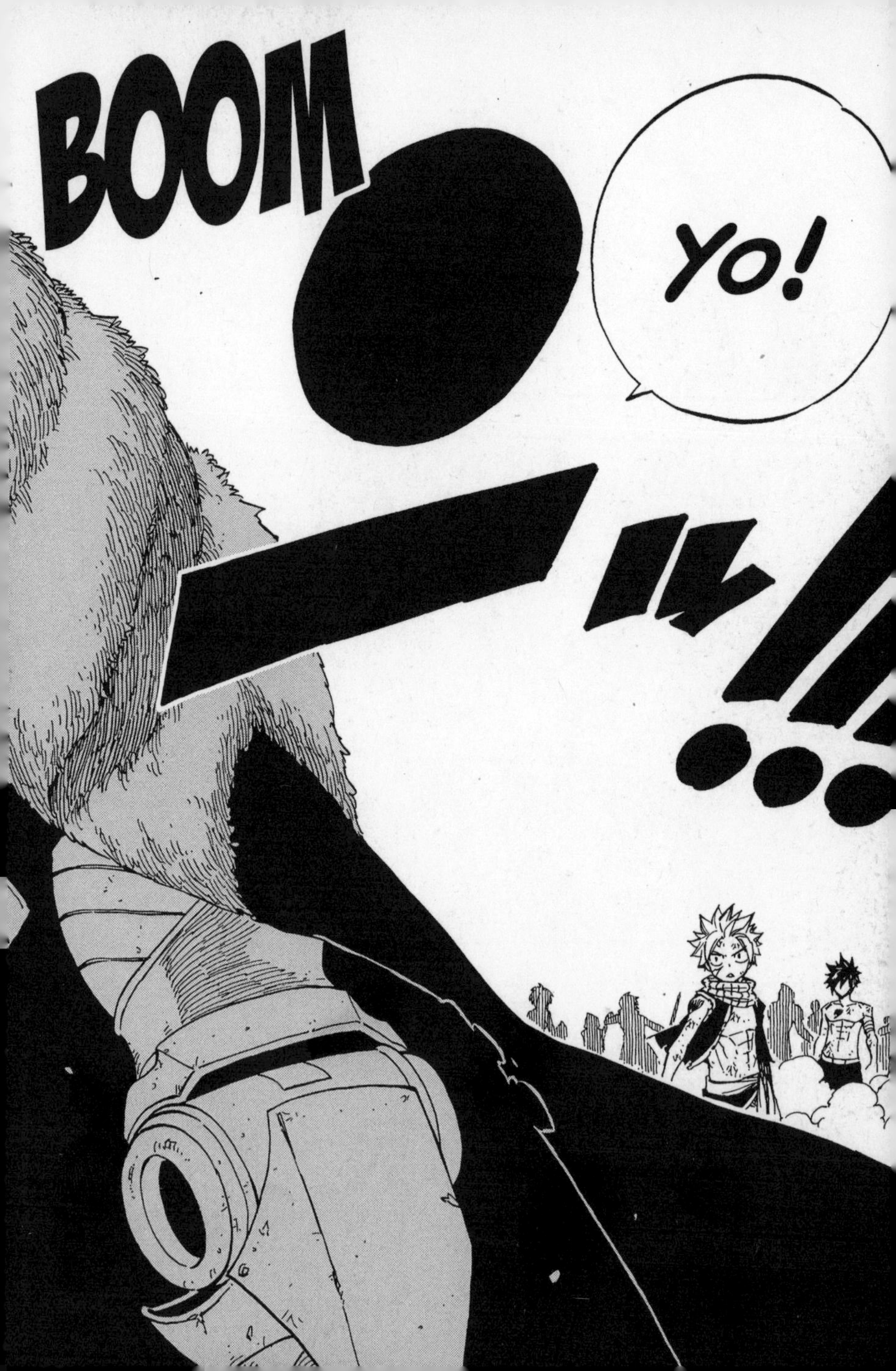
YO!
BOOM

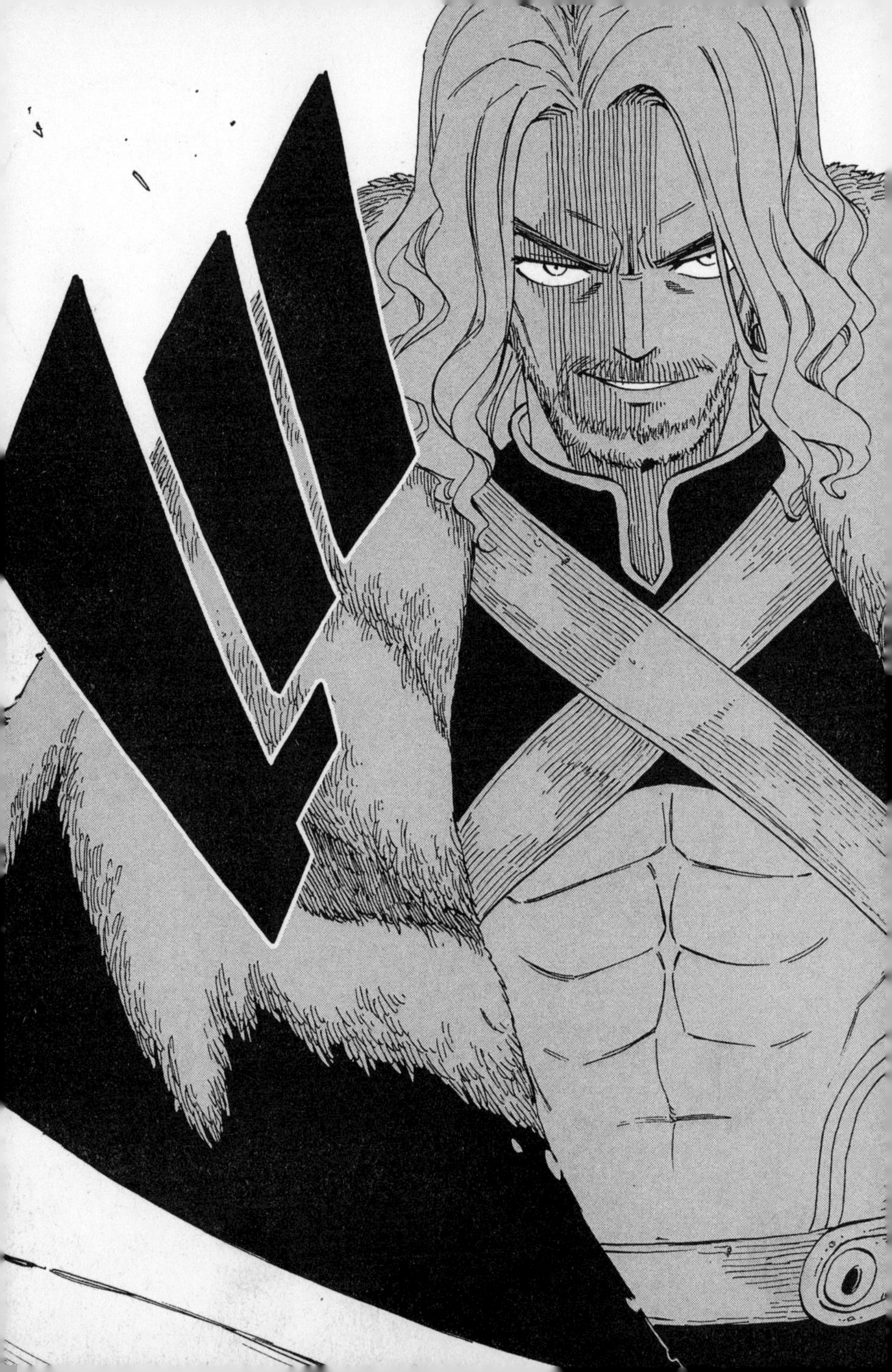

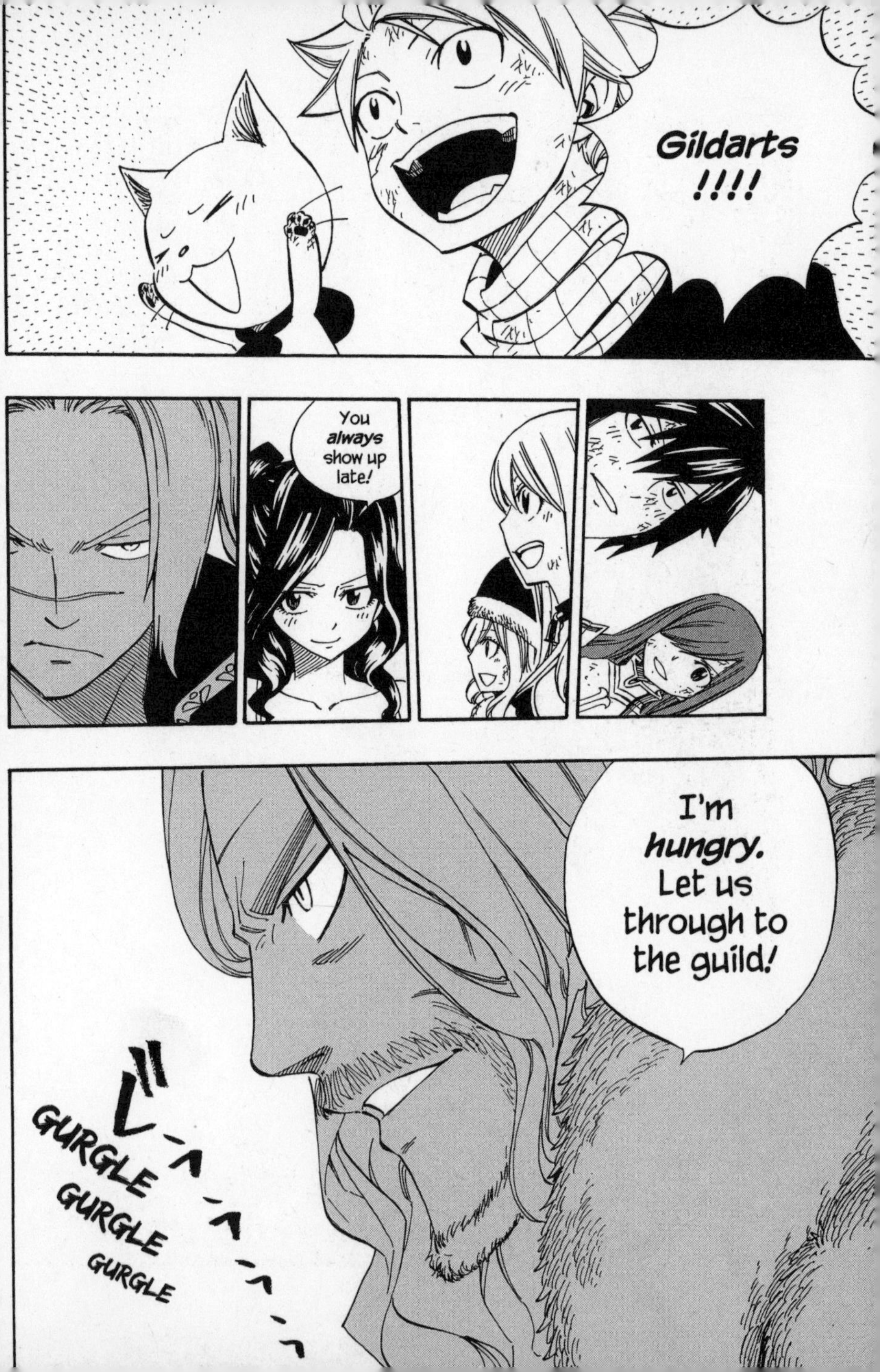
Gildarts !!!!
You *always* show up late!
I'm *hungry.* Let us through to the guild!
GURGLE GURGLE GURGLE

FAIRY TAIL

フェアリーテイル

Chapter 496: Forward!!!!

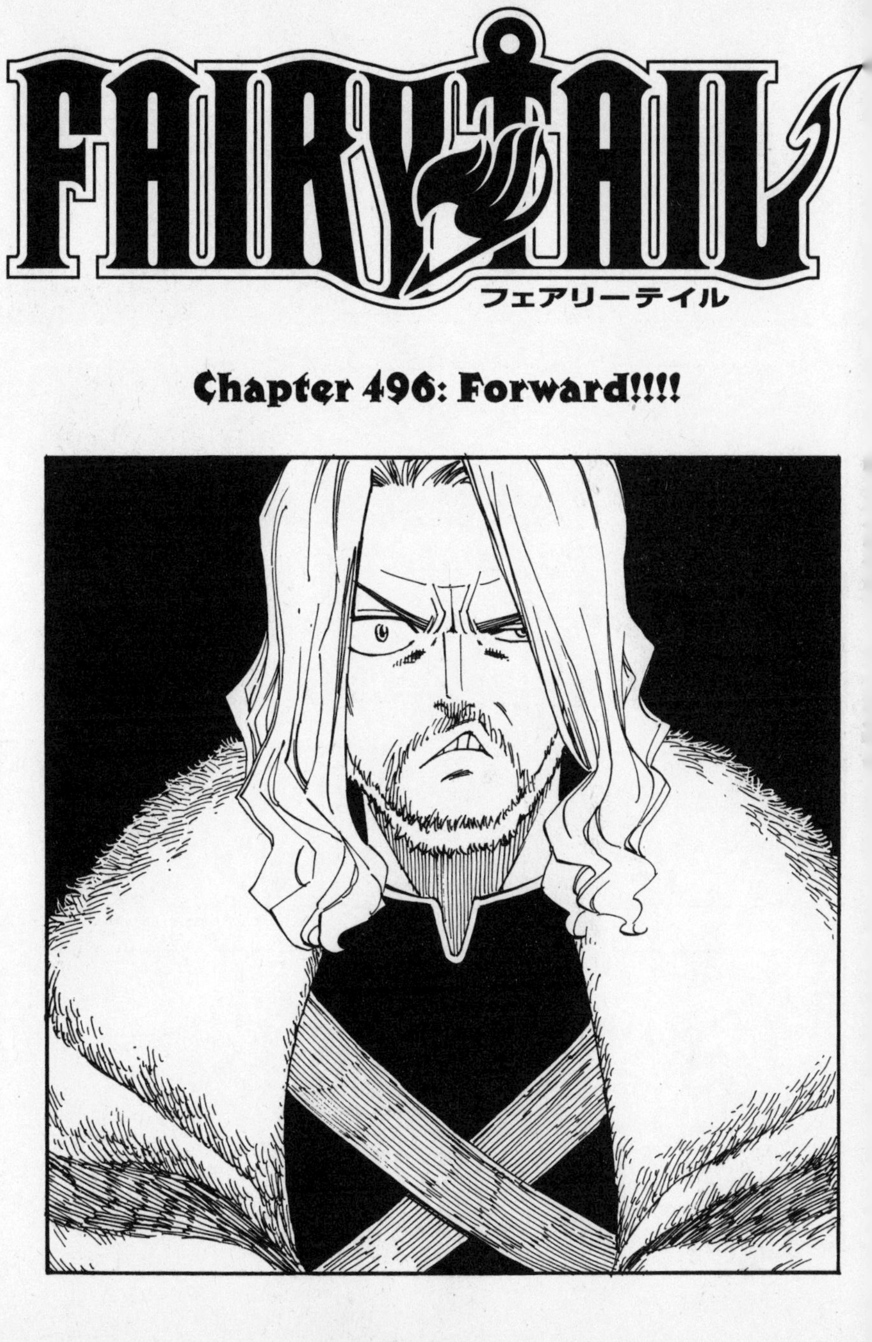

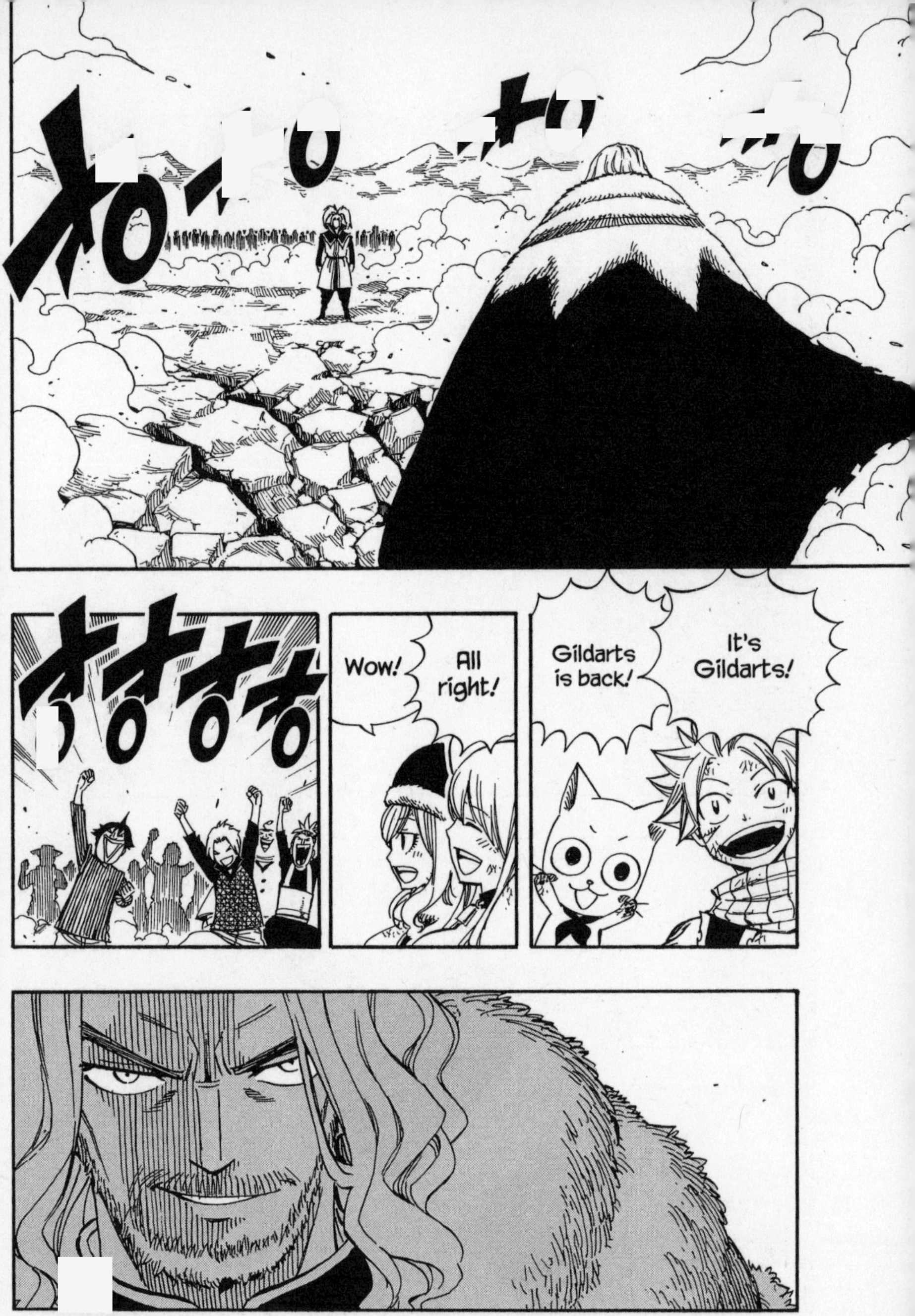
It's Gildarts!
Gildarts is back!
All right!
Wow!

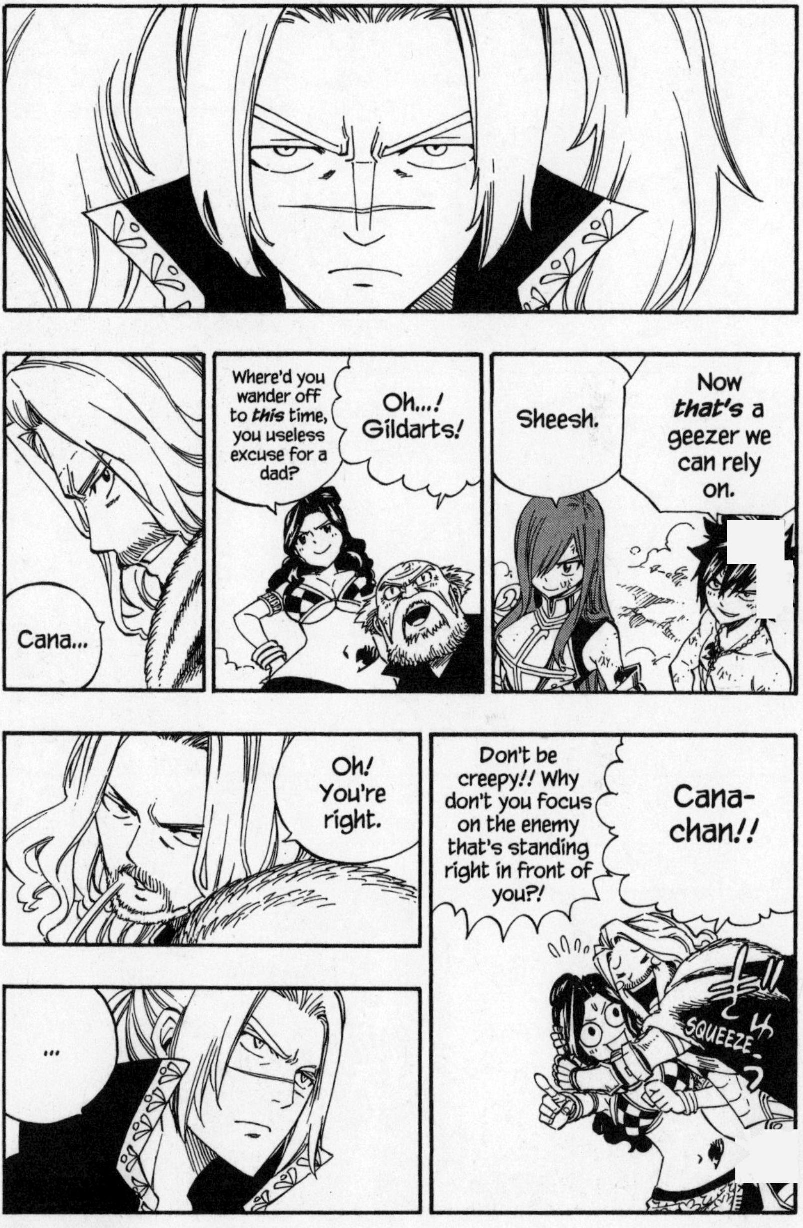
Now *that's* a geezer we can rely on.
Sheesh.
Oh...! Gildarts!
Where'd you wander off to *this* time, you useless excuse for a dad?
Cana...
Cana-chan!!
Don't be creepy!! Why don't you focus on the enemy that's standing right in front of you?!
SQUEEZE
Oh! You're right.
...

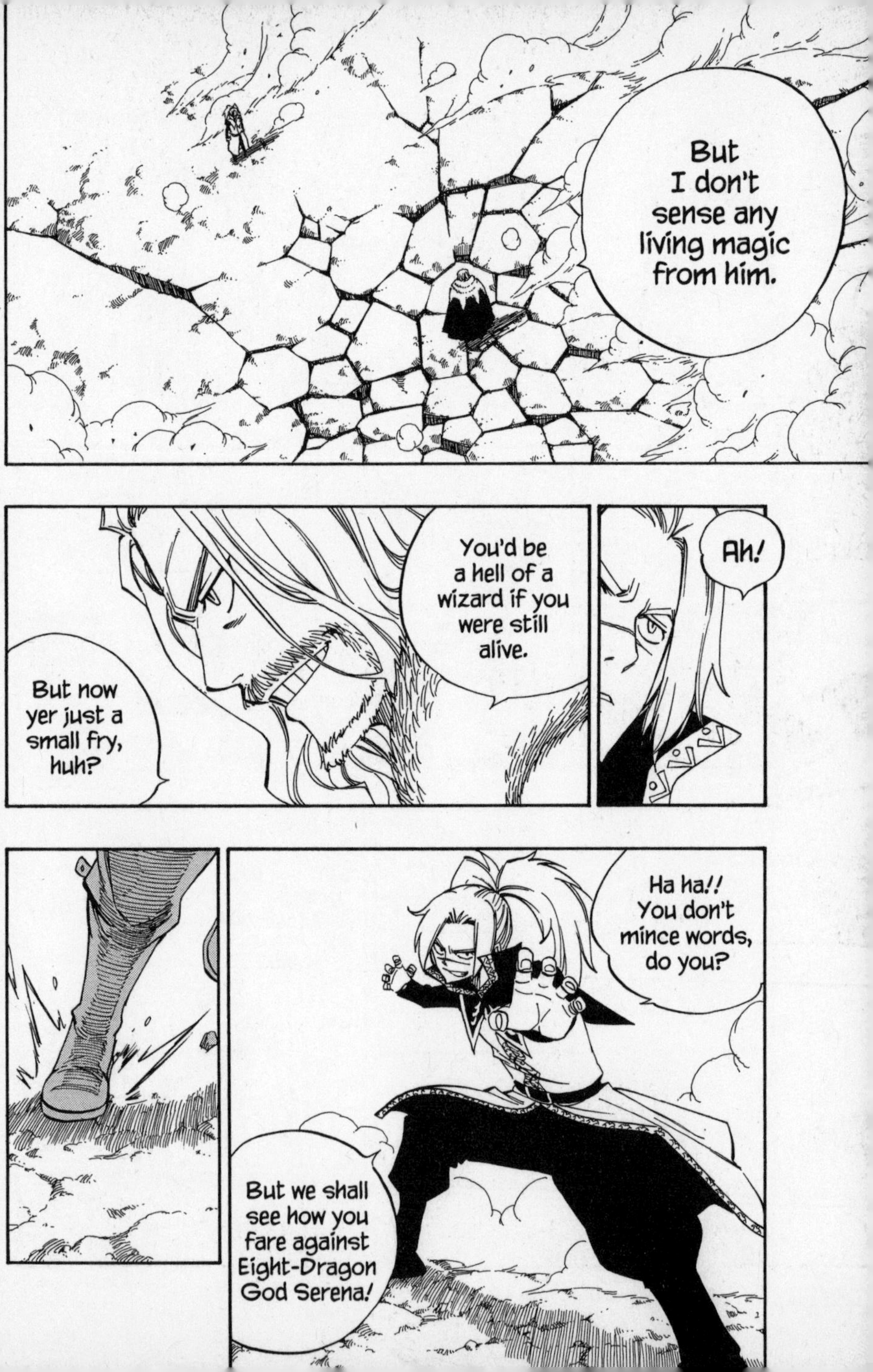

But I don't sense any living magic from him.
Ah!
You'd be a hell of a wizard if you were still alive.
But now yer just a small fry, huh?
Ha ha!! You don't mince words, do you?
But we shall see how you fare against Eight-Dragon God Serena!

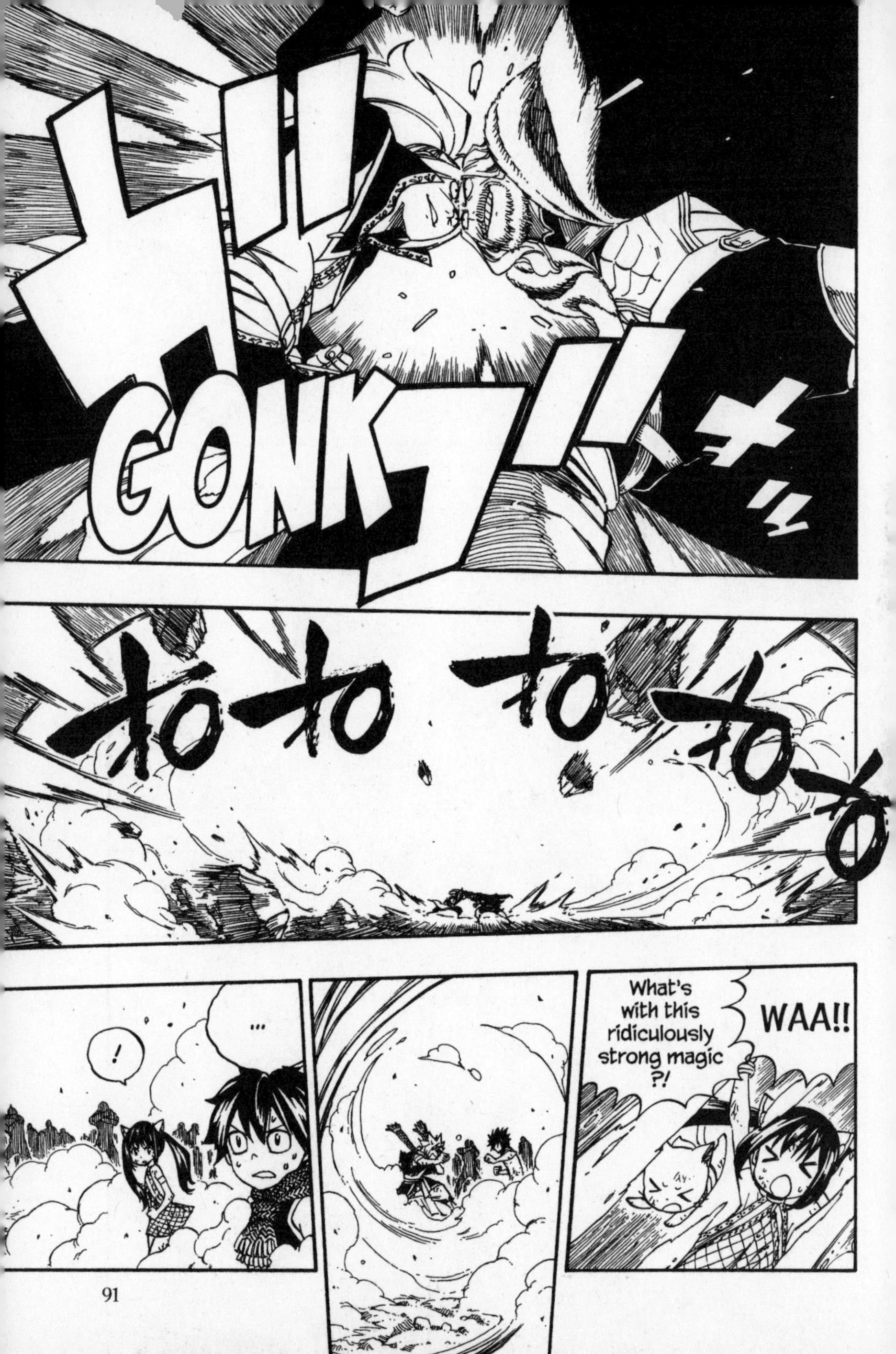
GONK!!
WAA!!
What's with this ridiculously strong magic?!
...
!

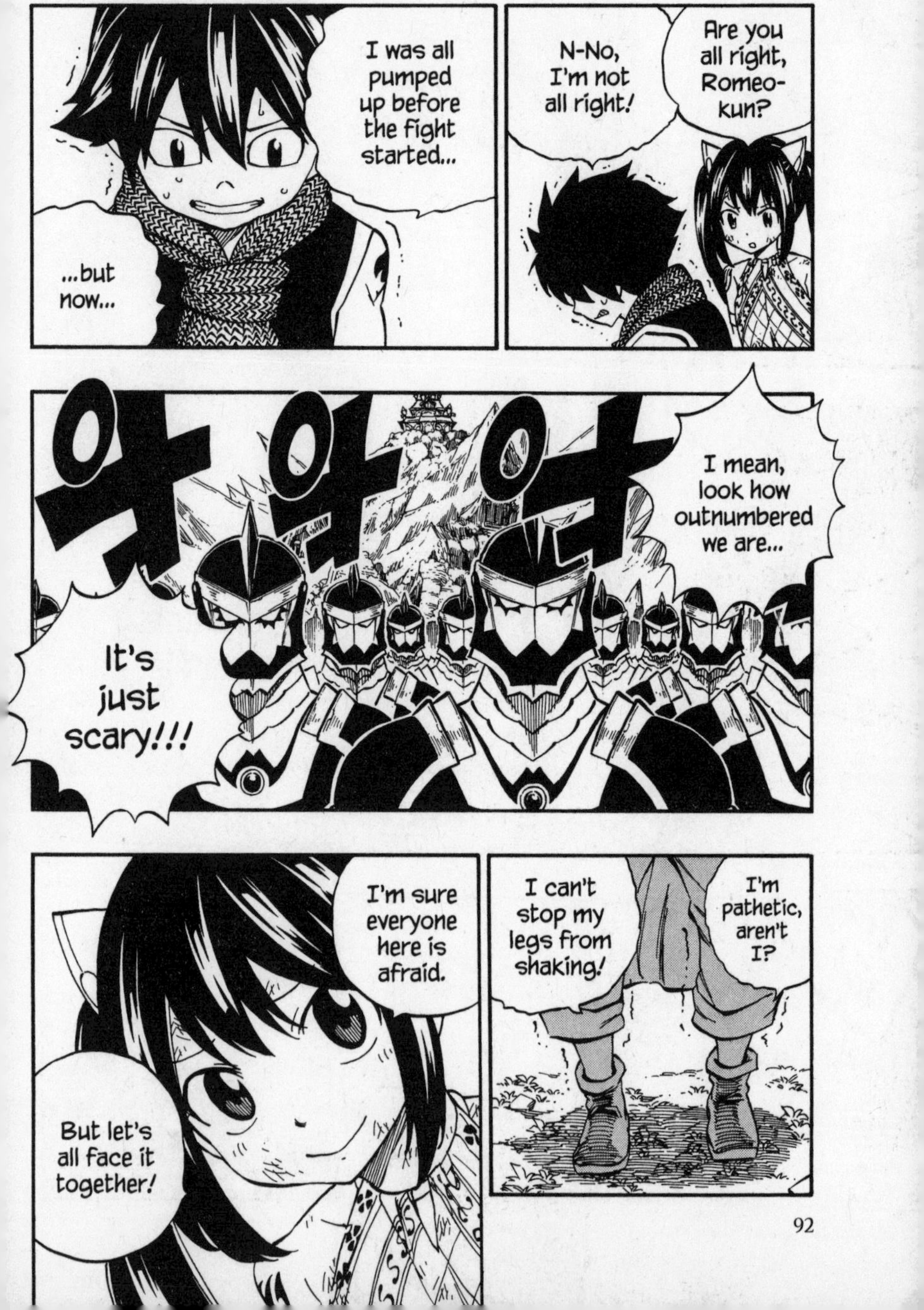
Are you all right, Romeo-kun?
N-No, I'm not all right!
I was all pumped up before the fight started...
...but now...
I mean, look how outnumbered we are...
It's just scary!!!
I'm pathetic, aren't I?
I can't stop my legs from shaking!
I'm sure everyone here is afraid.
But let's all face it together!

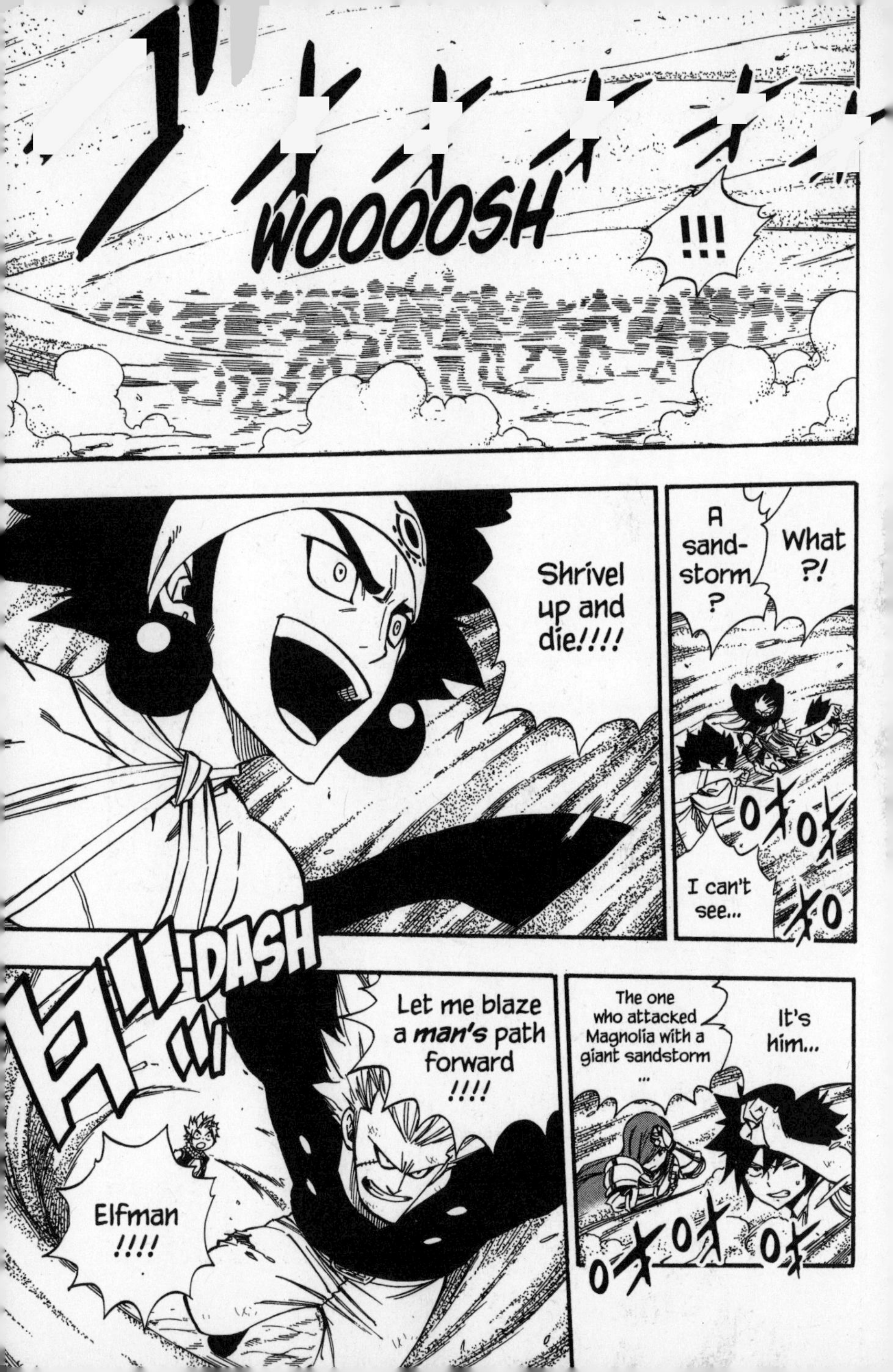
WOOOOSH
!!!
What ?!
A sandstorm ?
I can't see...
Shrivel up and die!!!!
It's him...
The one who attacked Magnolia with a giant sandstorm ...
DASH
Let me blaze a *man's* path forward !!!!
Elfman !!!!

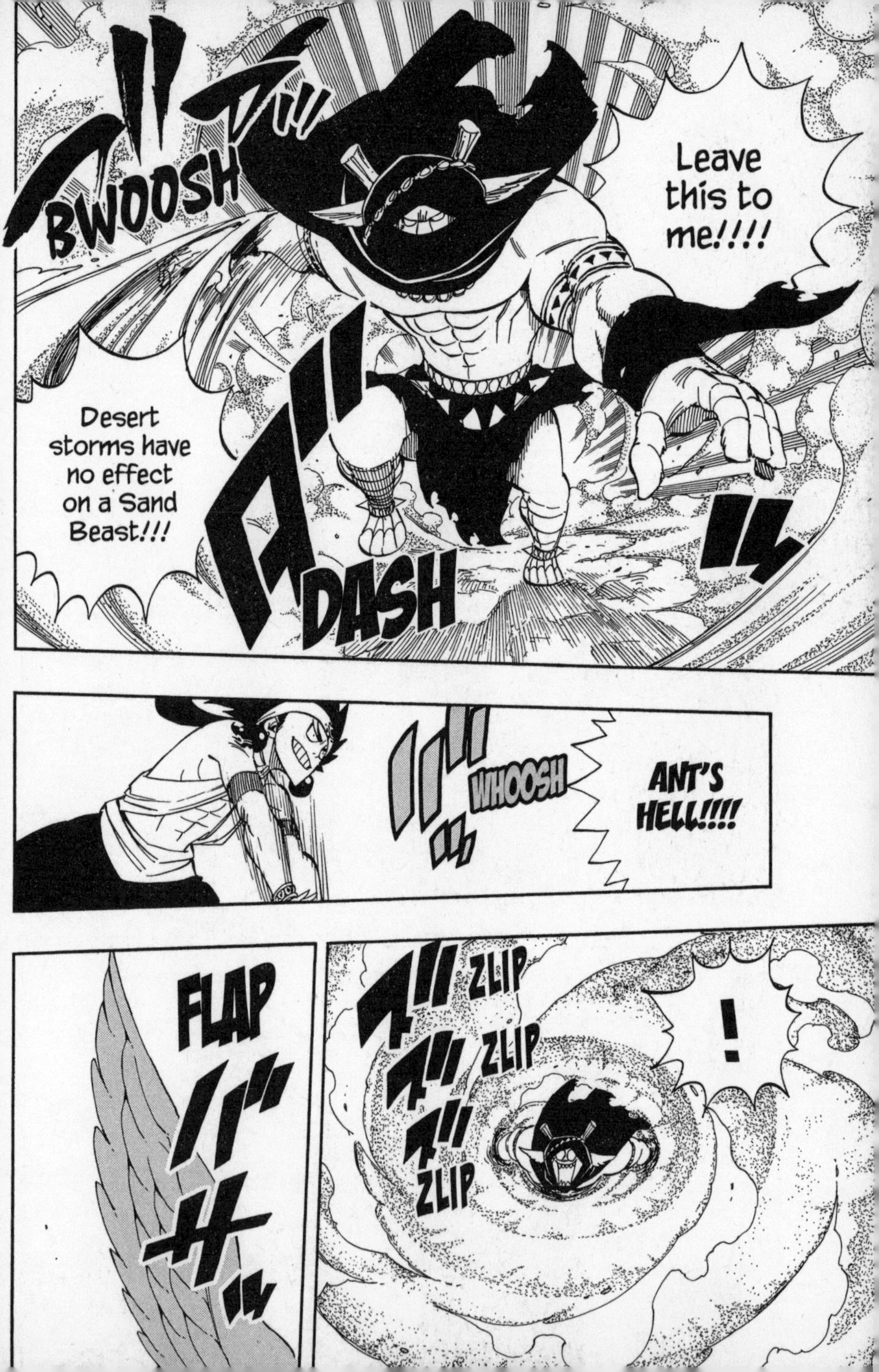

Leave this to me!!!!
BWOOSH
Desert storms have no effect on a Sand Beast!!!
DASH
ANT'S HELL!!!!
WHOOSH
!
ZLIP
ZLIP
ZLIP
FLAP

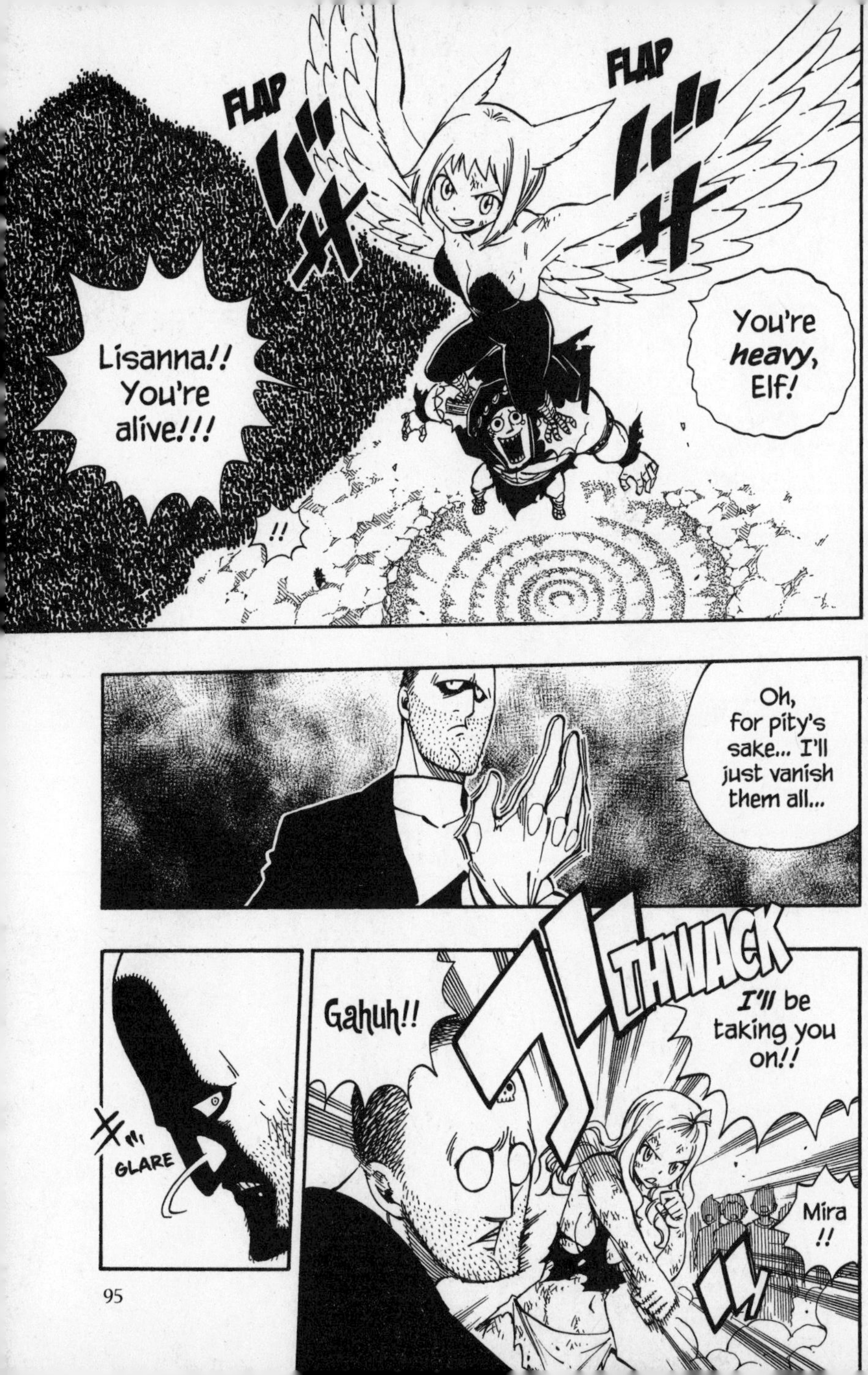
FLAP
FLAP
You're *heavy*, Elf!
Lisanna!! You're alive!!!
!!
Oh, for pity's sake... I'll just vanish them all...
THWACK
I'll be taking you on!!
Gahuh!!
Mira !!
GLARE

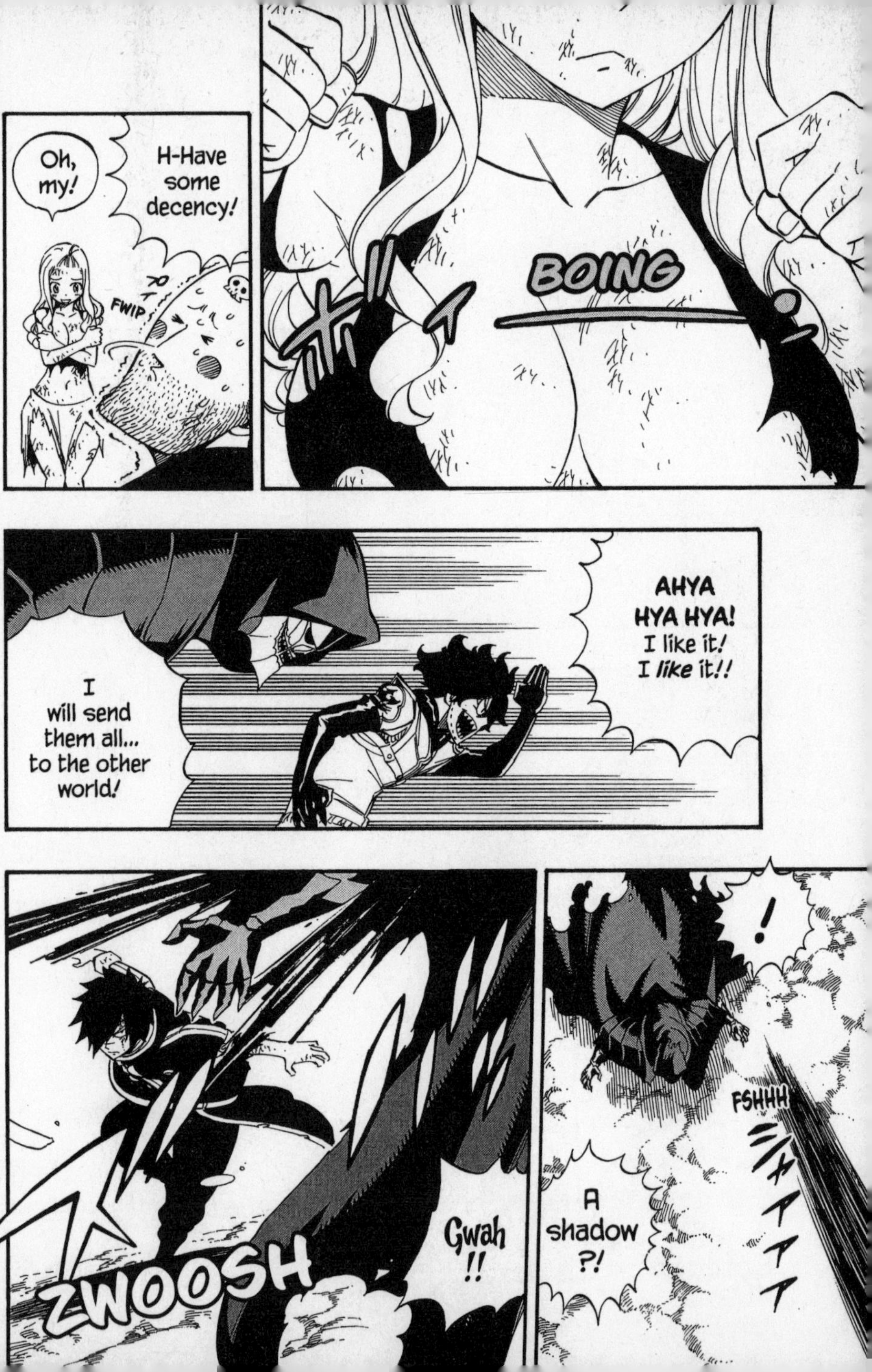
BOING
H-Have some decency!
Oh, my!
FWIP
AHYA HYA HYA! I like it! I like it!!
I will send them all... to the other world!
!
FSHHH
A shadow ?!
Gwah !!
ZWOOSH

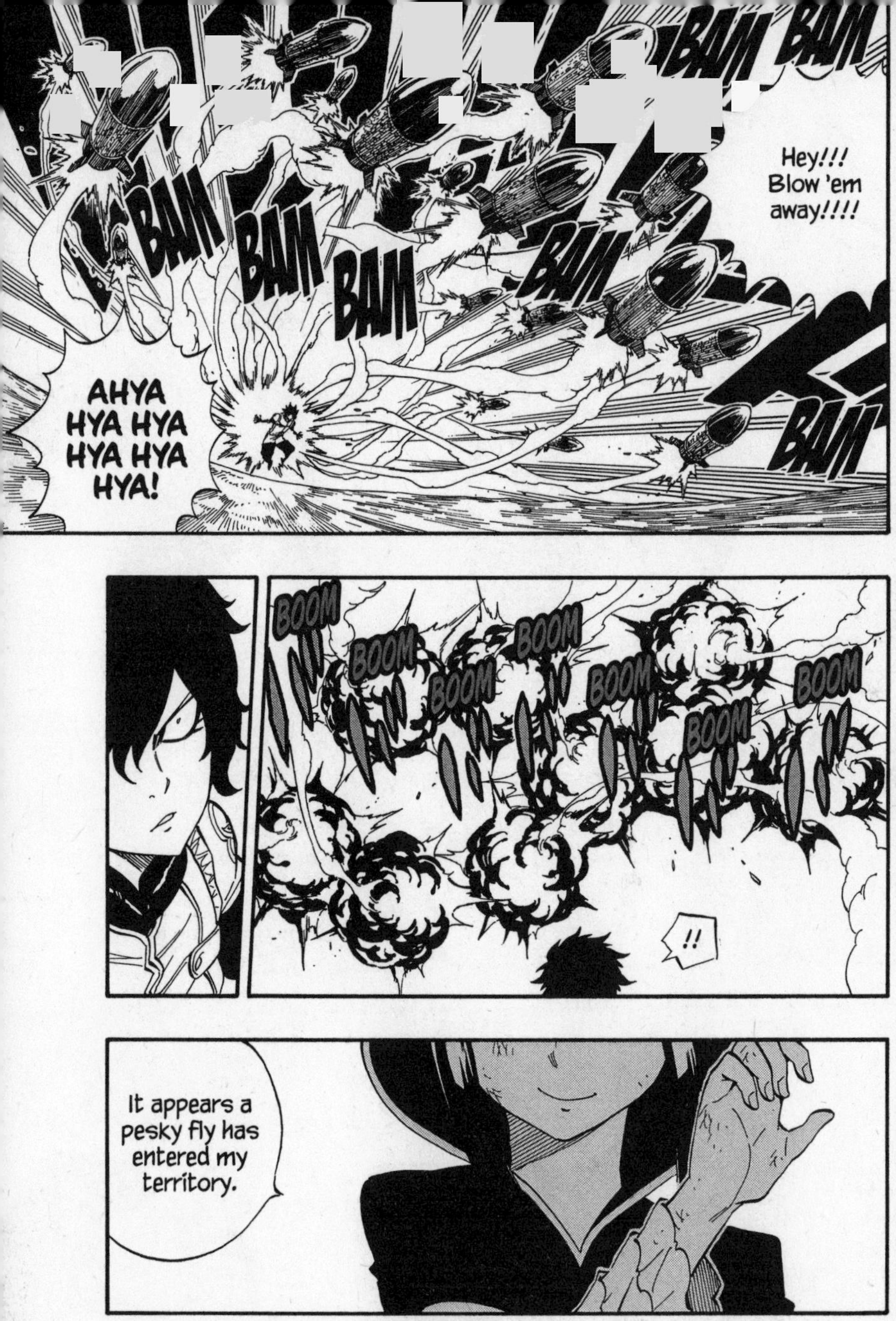
BAM BAM
Hey!!!
Blow 'em
away!!!!
BAM
BAM
BAM
BAM
BAM
AHYA
HYA HYA
HYA HYA
HYA!
BOOM
BOOM
BOOM
BOOM
BOOM
BOOM
BOOM
!!
It appears a
pesky fly has
entered my
territory.

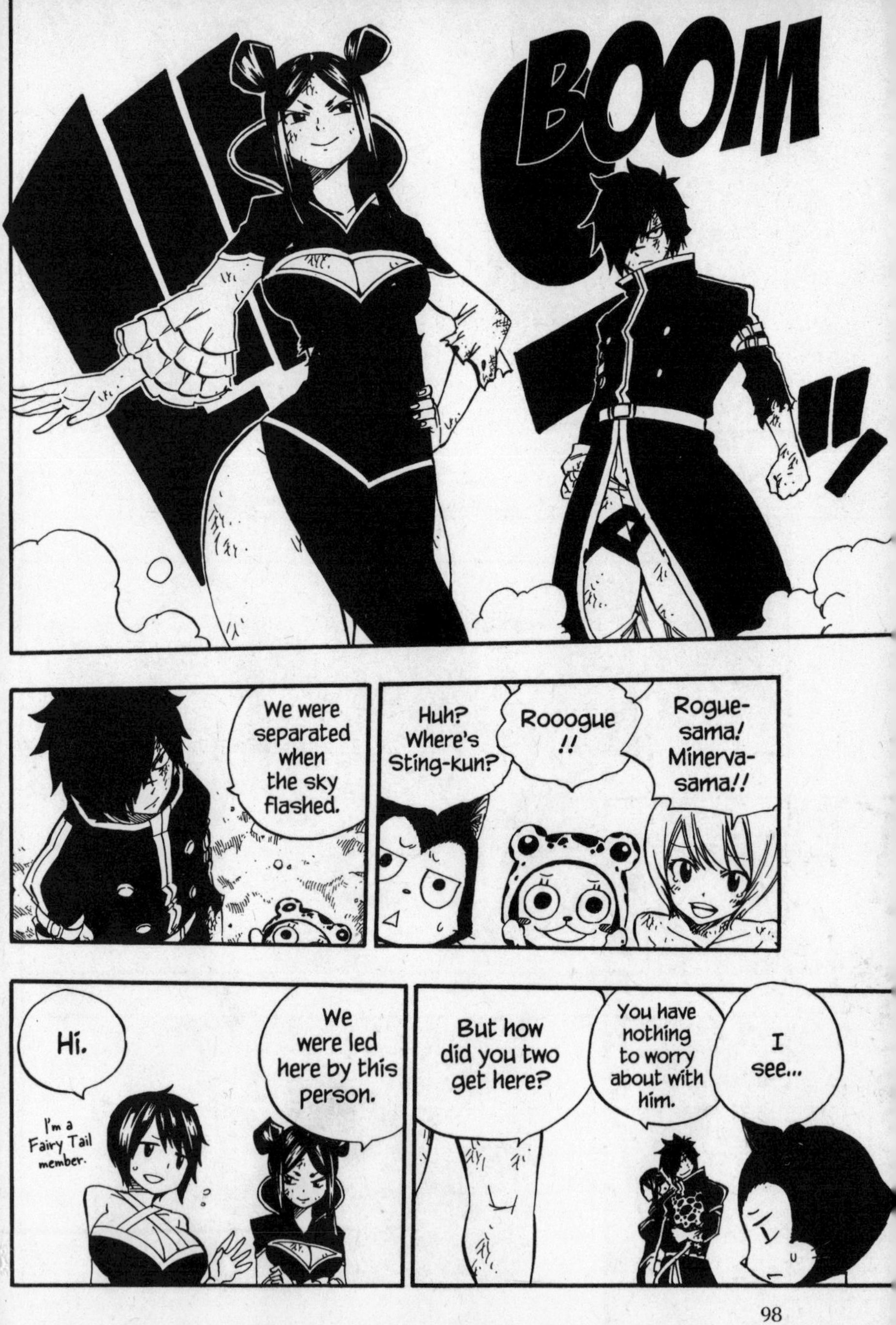
BOOM
Rogue-sama! Minerva-sama!!
Rooogue !!
Huh? Where's Sting-kun?
We were separated when the sky flashed.
I see...
You have nothing to worry about with him.
But how did you two get here?
We were led here by this person.
Hi.
I'm a Fairy Tail member.

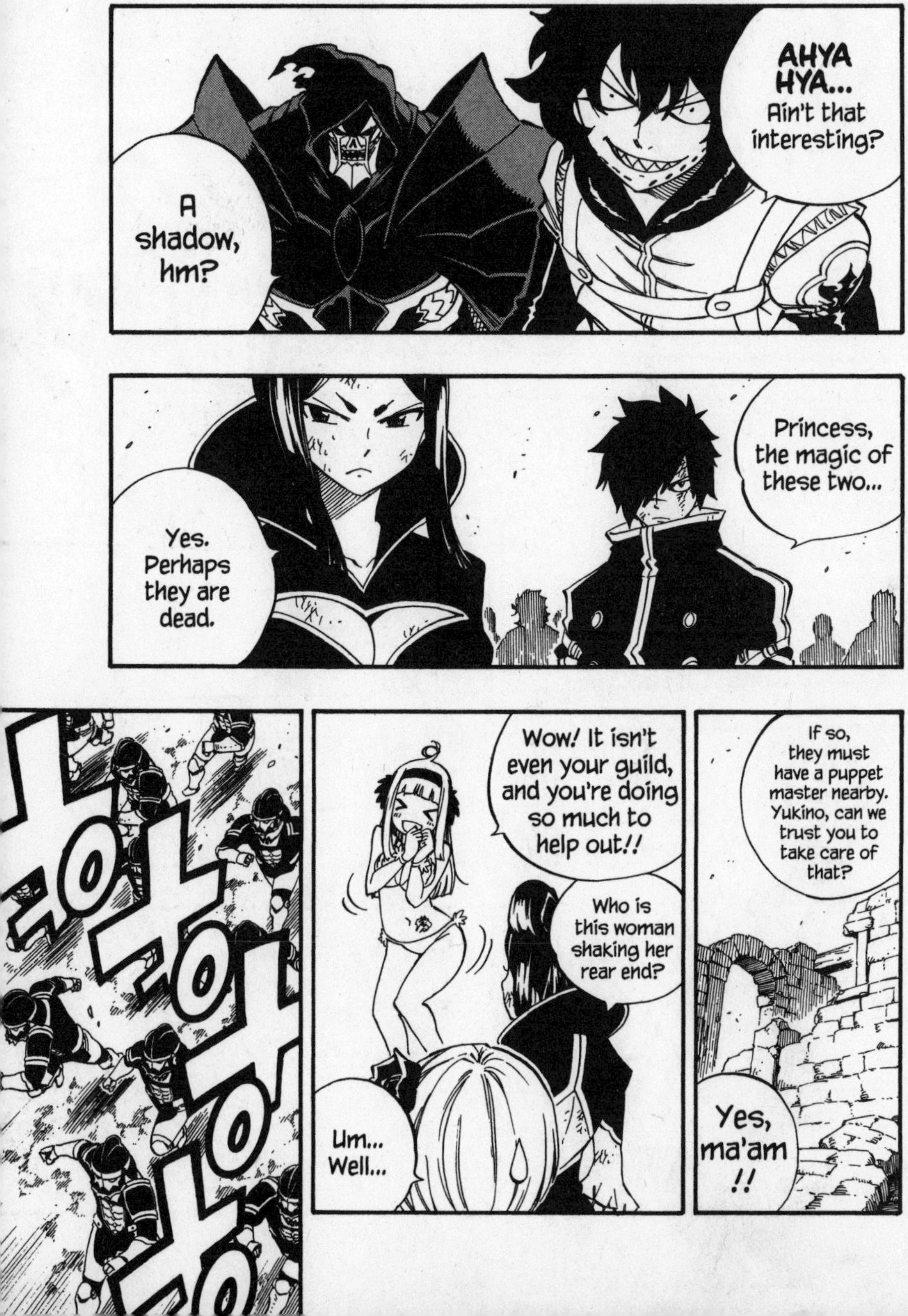
AHYA HYA... Ain't that interesting?
A shadow, hm?
Princess, the magic of these two...
Yes. Perhaps they are dead.
If so, they must have a puppet master nearby. Yukino, can we trust you to take care of that?
Yes, ma'am!!
Wow! It isn't even your guild, and you're doing so much to help out!!
Who is this woman shaking her rear end?
Um... Well...

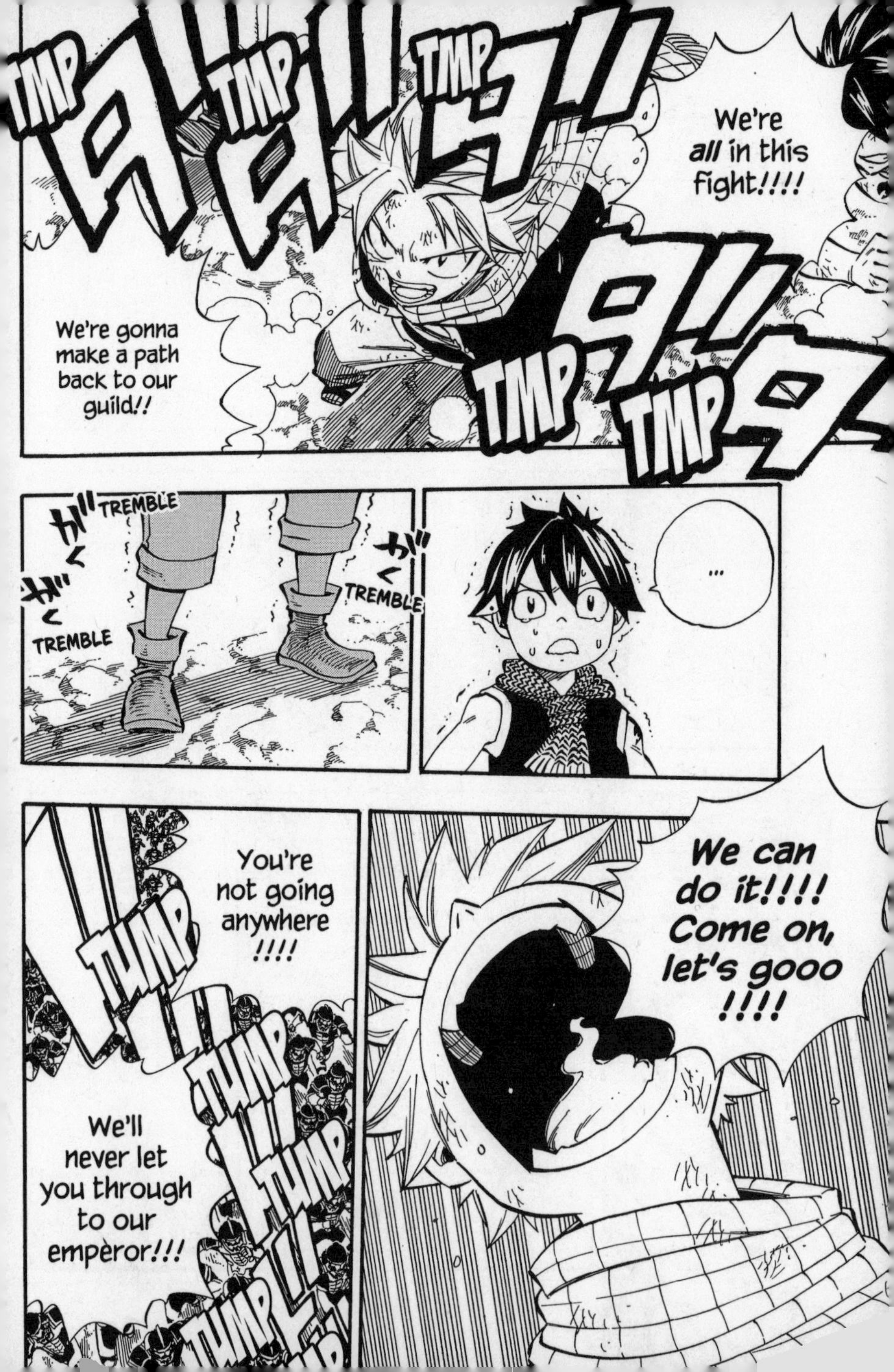
We're all in this fight!!!!
TMP TMP TMP
We're gonna make a path back to our guild!!
TMP TMP
...
TREMBLE
TREMBLE
TREMBLE
We can do it!!!! Come on, let's gooo!!!!
You're not going anywhere!!!!
We'll never let you through to our emperor!!!
THUMP THUMP THUMP THUMP

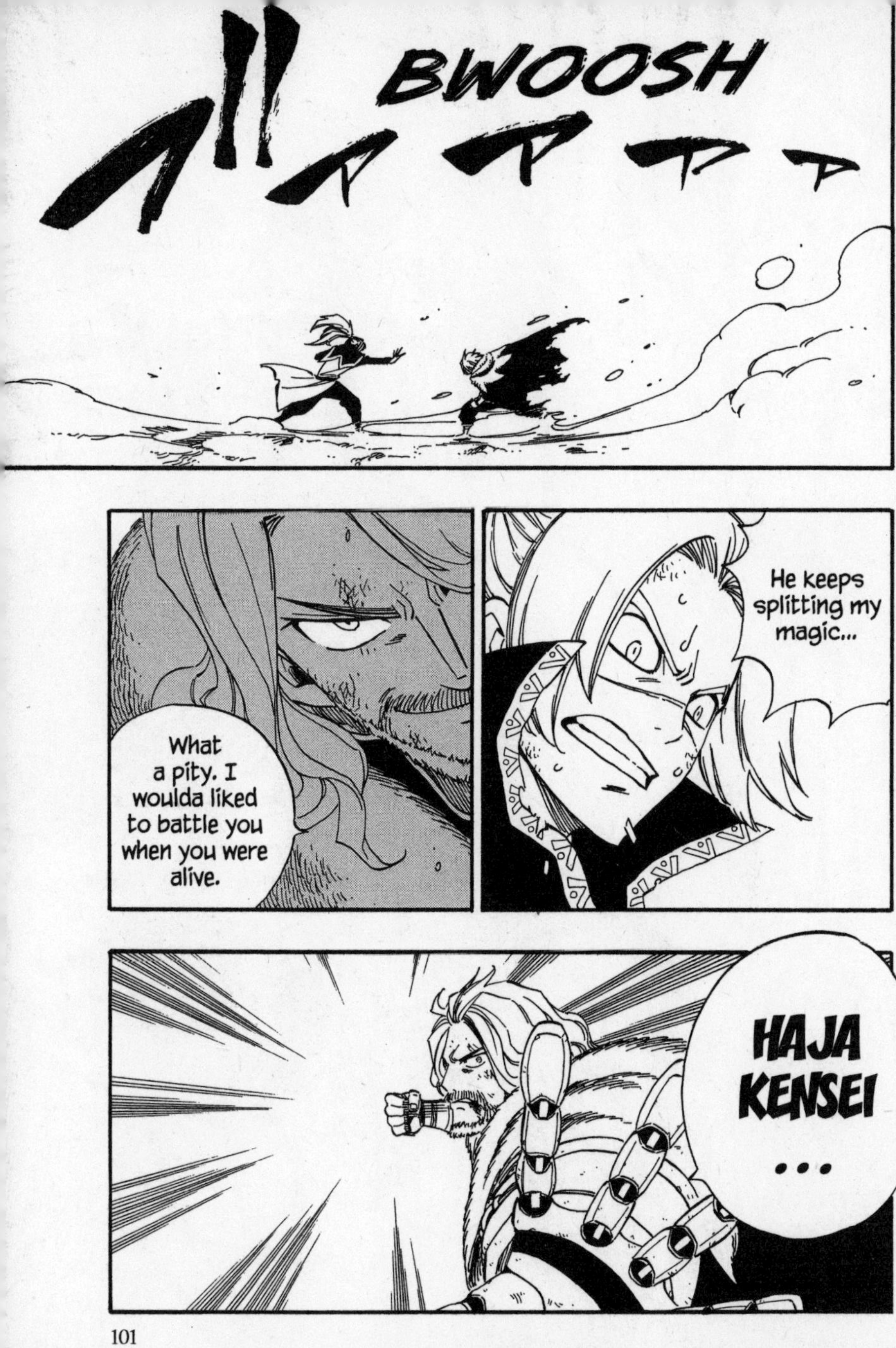
BWOOSH
He keeps splitting my magic...
What a pity. I woulda liked to battle you when you were alive.
HAJA KENSEI ...

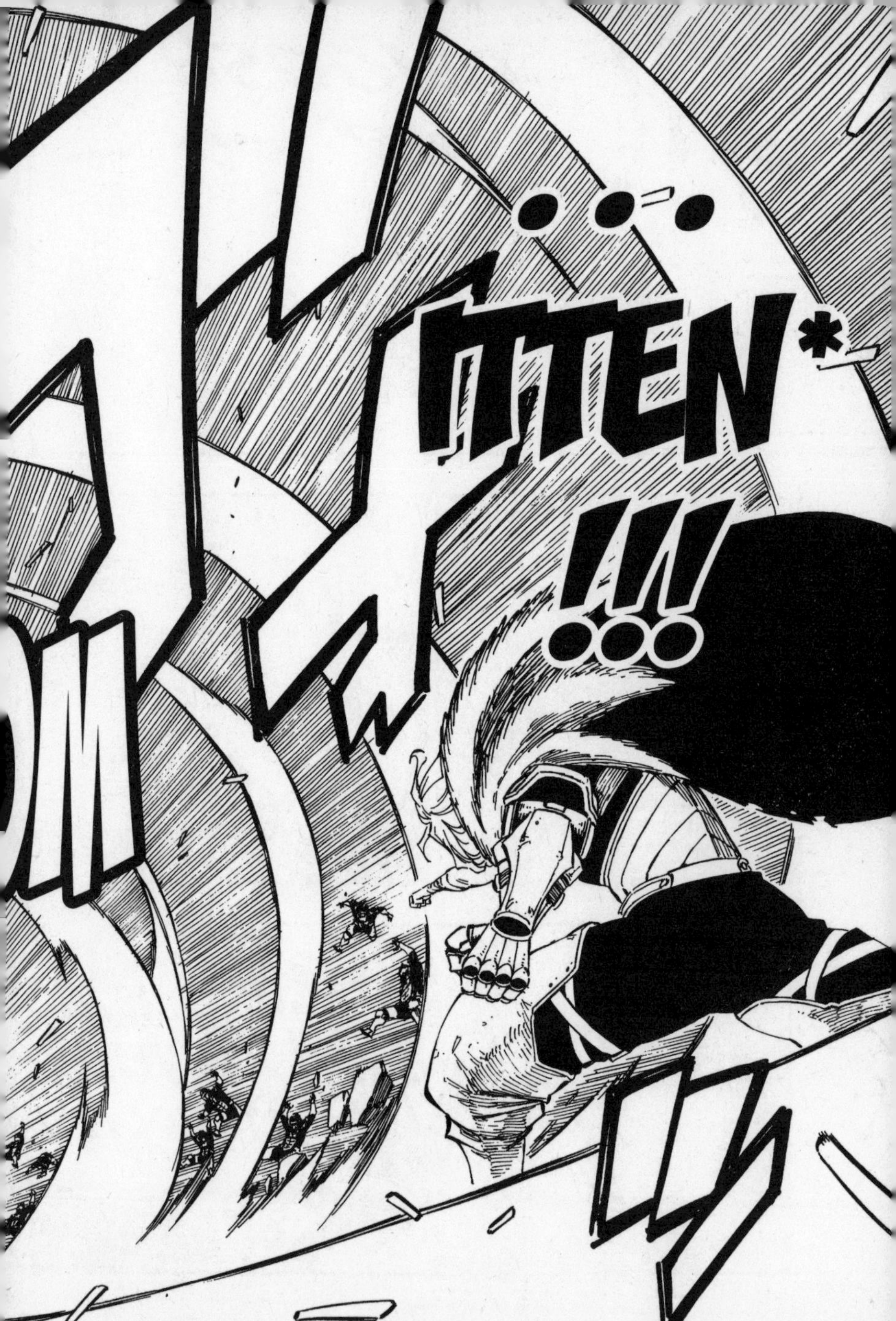
...TTEN*!!

*Firmament!!!

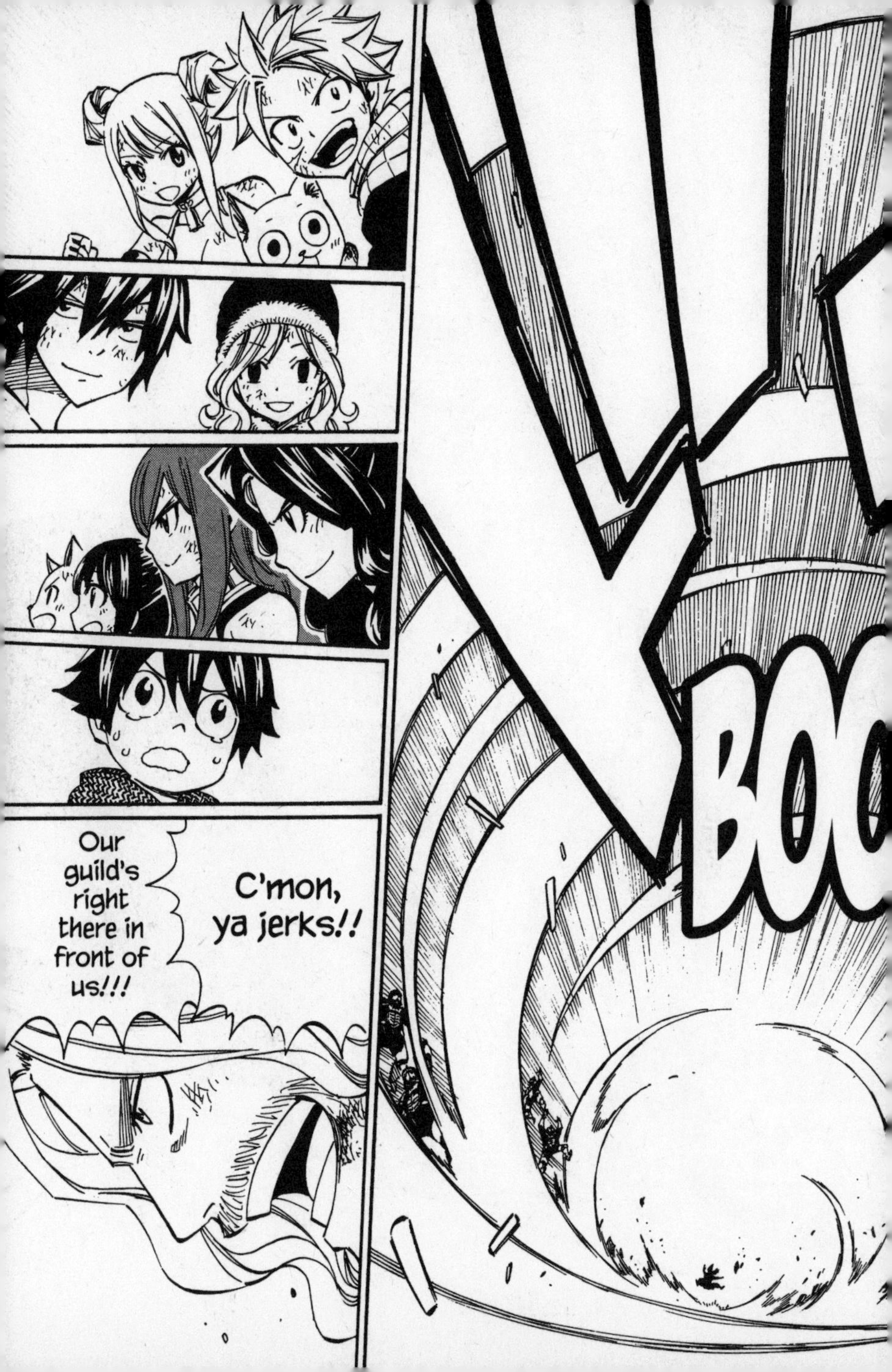
BOO
C'mon, ya jerks!!
Our guild's right there in front of us!!!

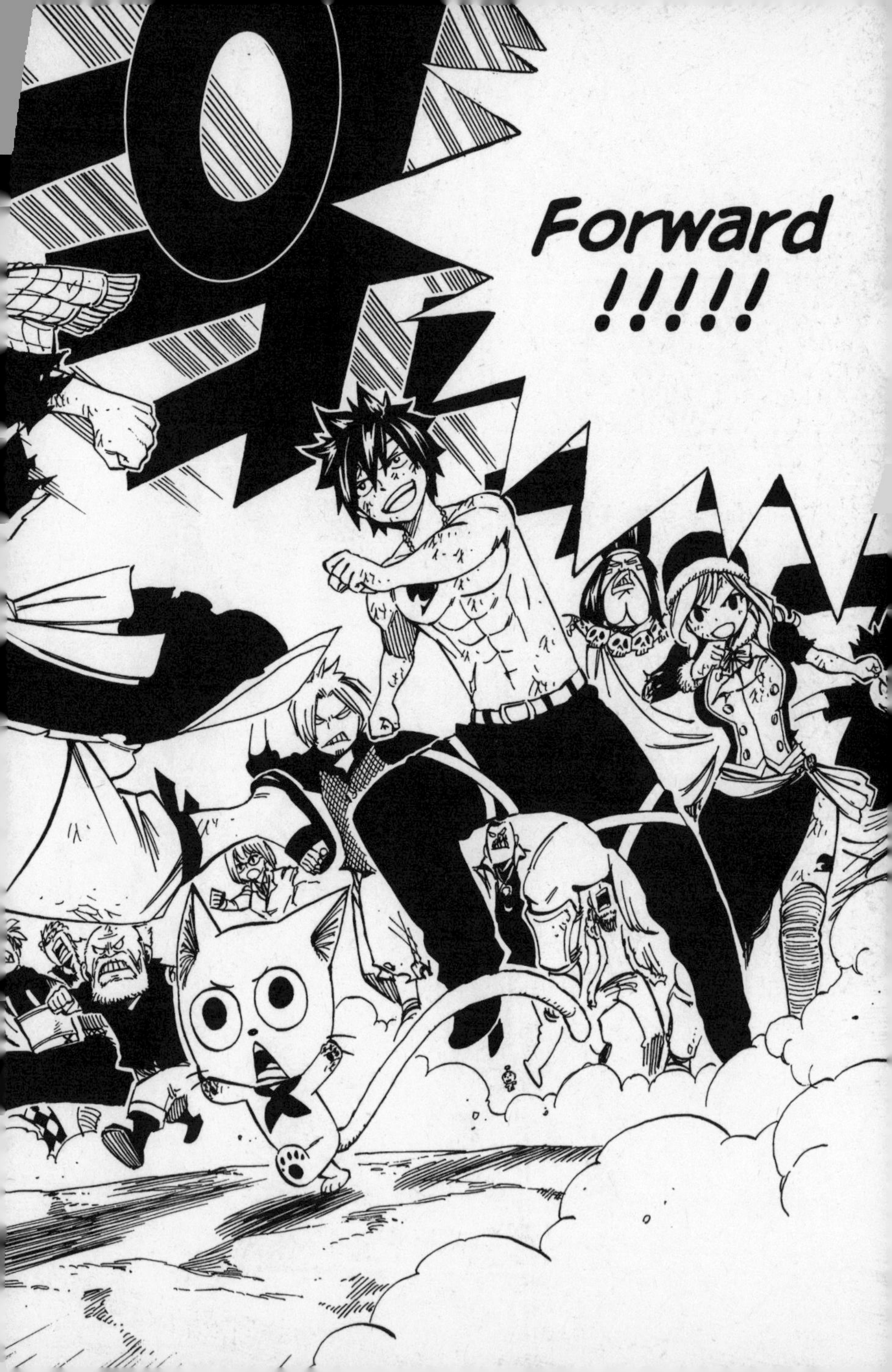
Forward !!!!!

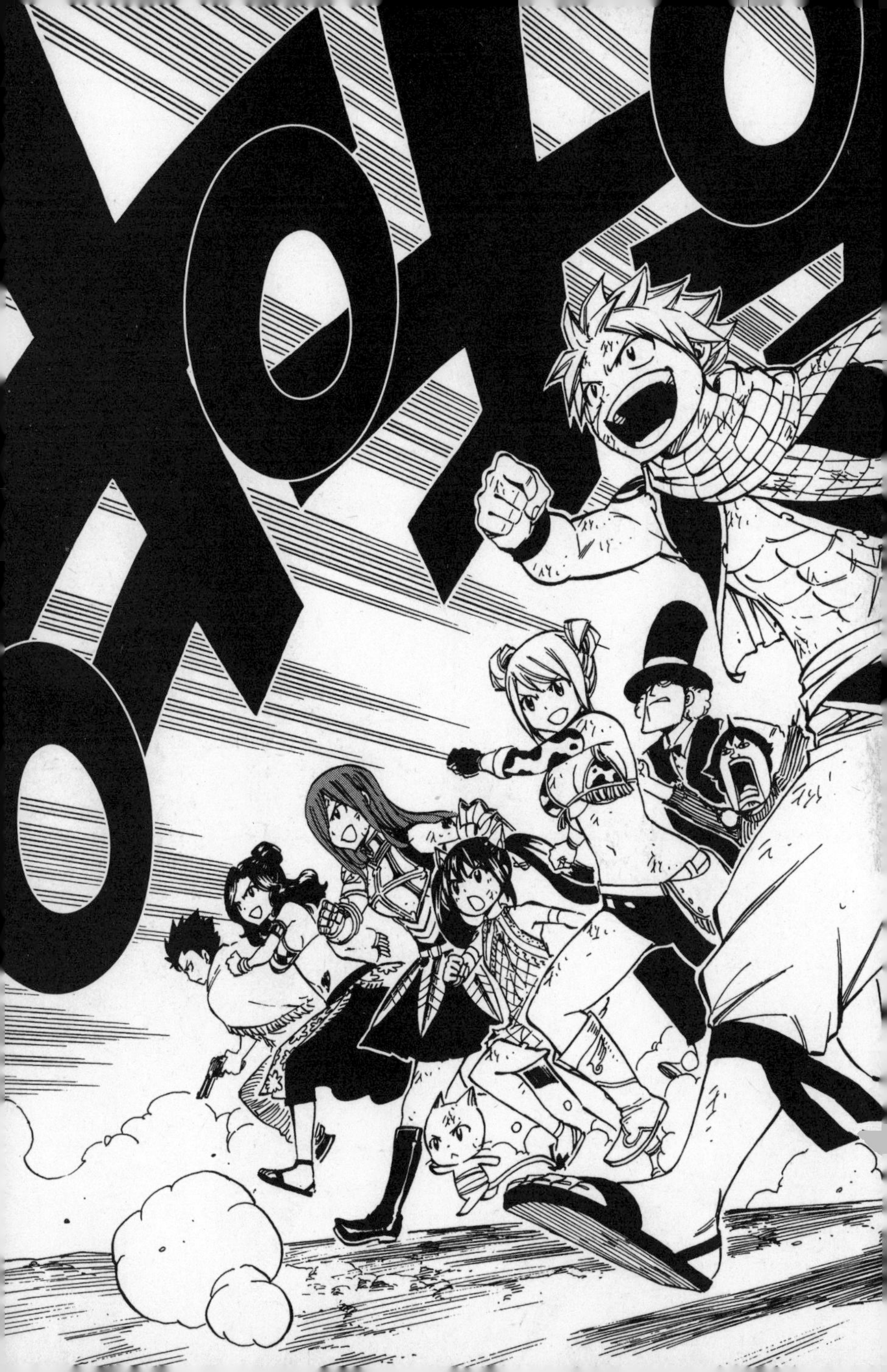

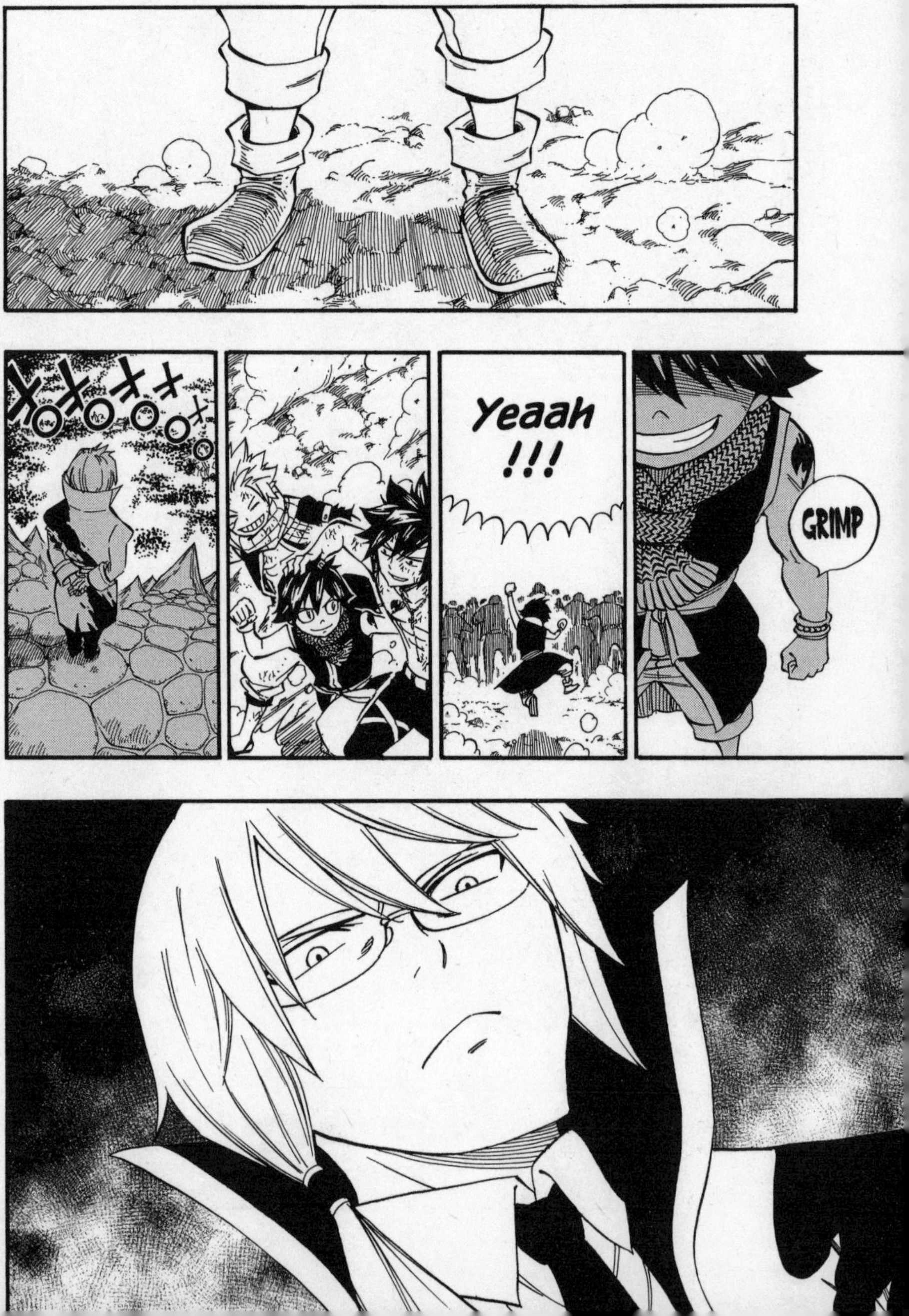
GRIMP
Yeaah !!!

Chapter 497: The Winter Wizard

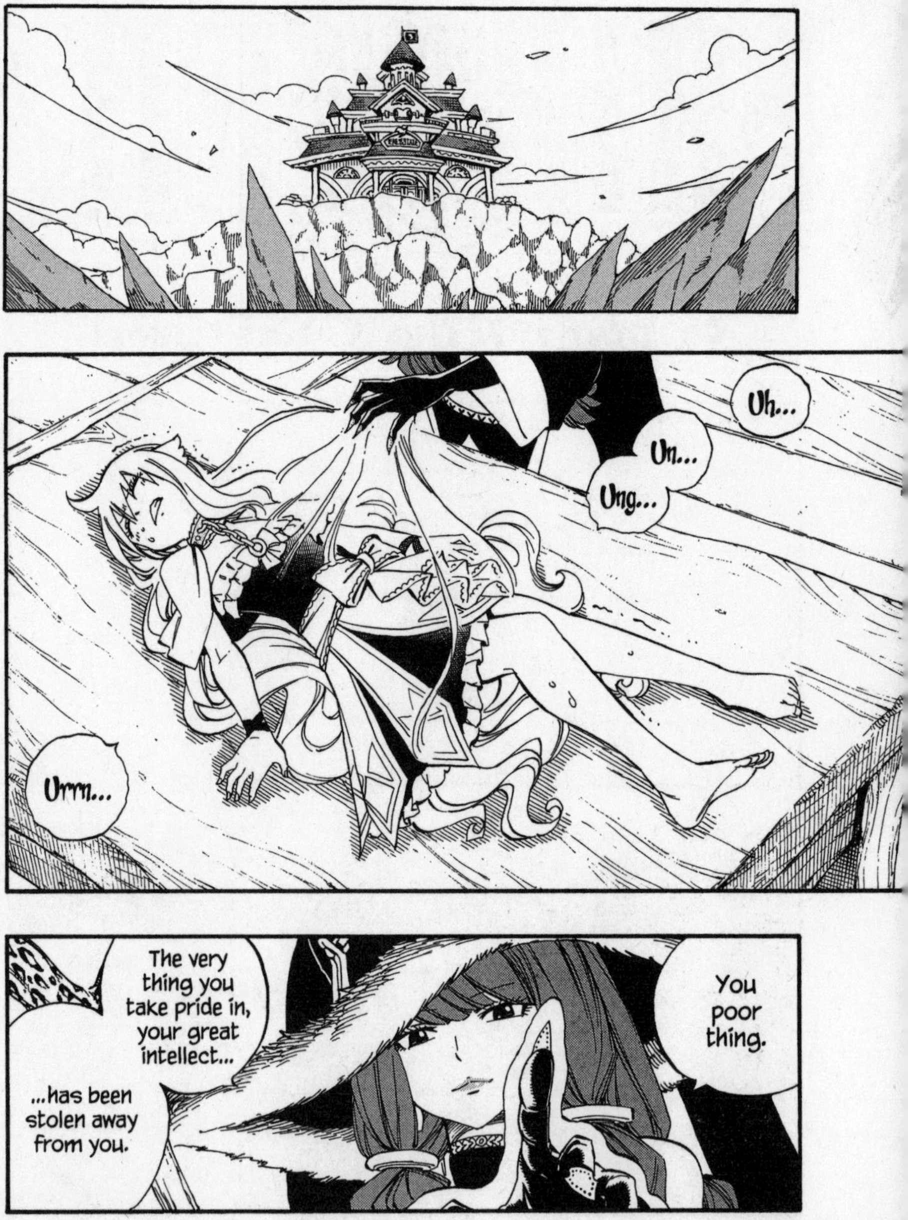
Uh...
Un...
Ung...
Urrn...
You poor thing.
The very thing you take pride in, your great intellect...
...has been stolen away from you.

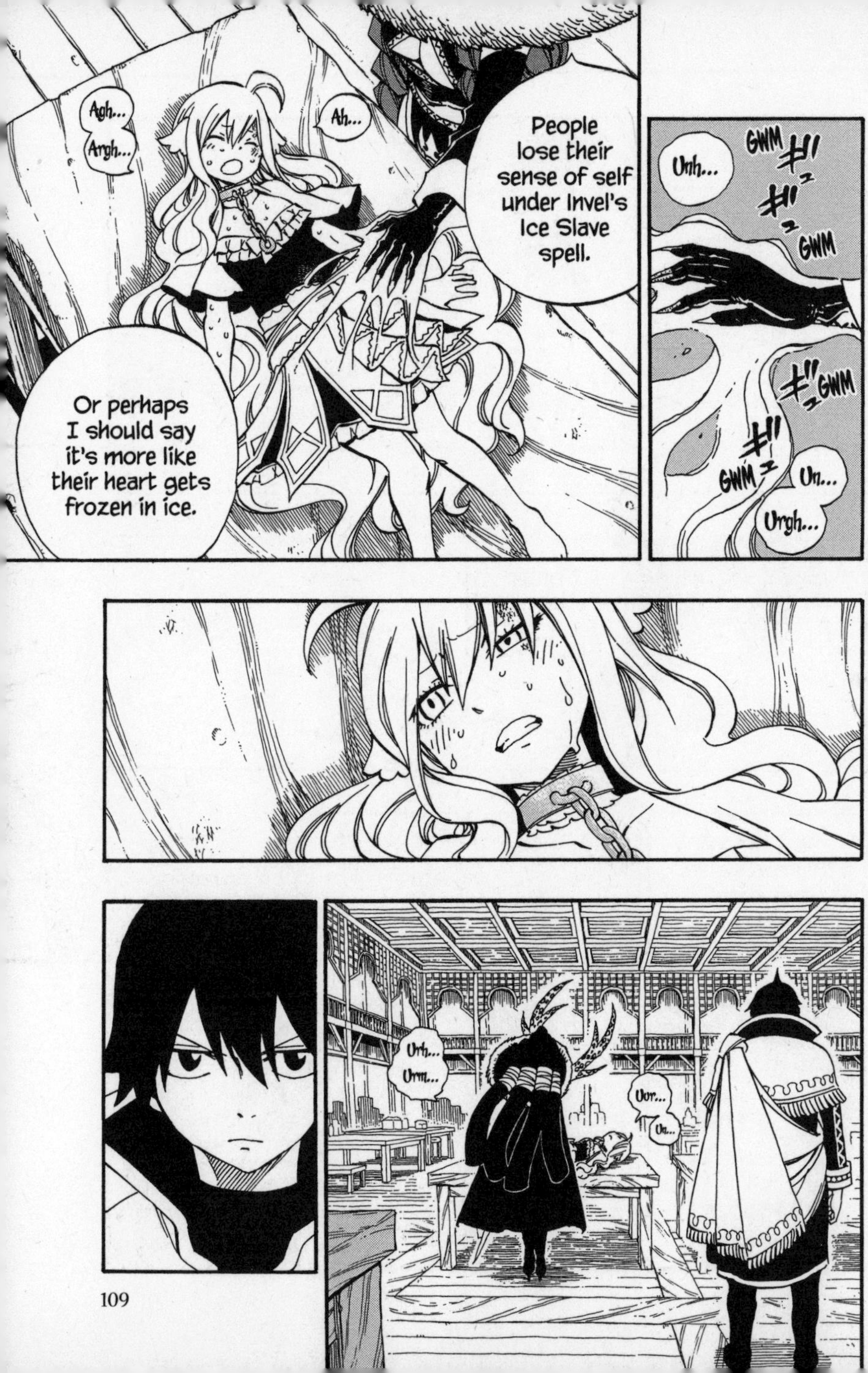
Unh...
GWM
GWM
GWM
GWM
Un...
Urgh...
People lose their sense of self under Invel's Ice Slave spell.
Ah...
Agh...
Argh...
Or perhaps I should say it's more like their heart gets frozen in ice.
Uor...
Un...
Urh...
Urm...

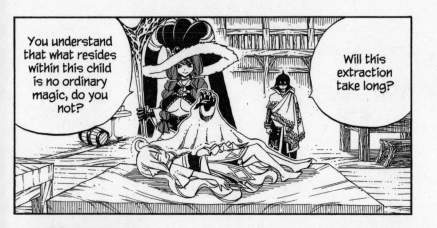

Will this extraction take long?
You understand that what resides within this child is no ordinary magic, do you not?
Urrg!
Unh!
Oww!
I would rather not see her suffer.
Oh, my. I wouldn't have imagined that even *you* feel such emotions, Your Majesty.
...
And though this may sound insolent, I must say it nevertheless.

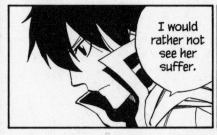

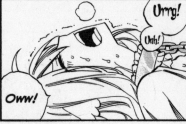

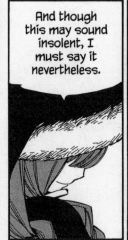

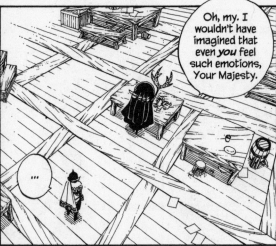

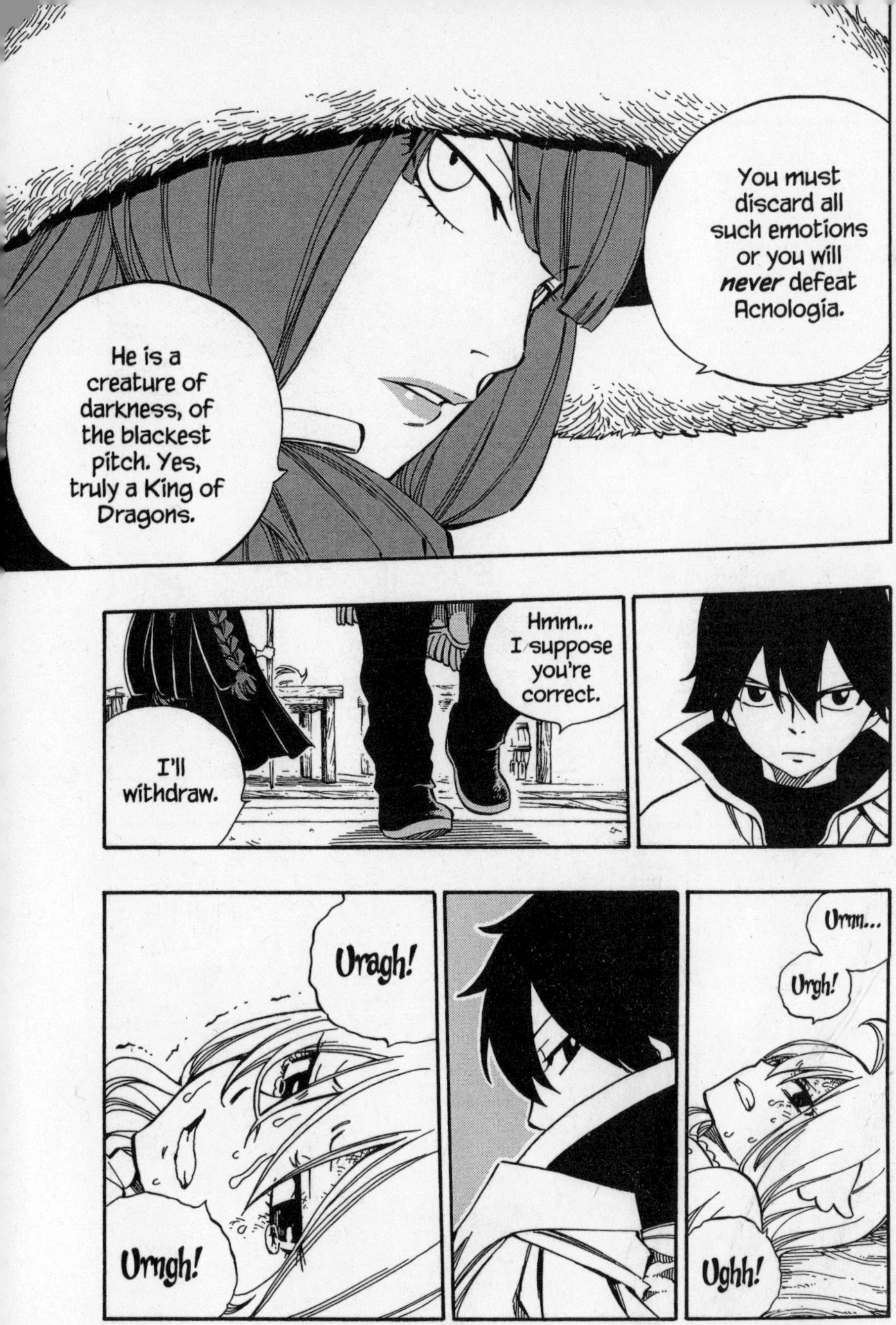
You must discard all such emotions or you will *never* defeat Acnologia.
He is a creature of darkness, of the blackest pitch. Yes, truly a King of Dragons.
Hmm... I suppose you're correct.
I'll withdraw.
Urrn...
Urgh!
Ughh!
Uragh!
Urngh!

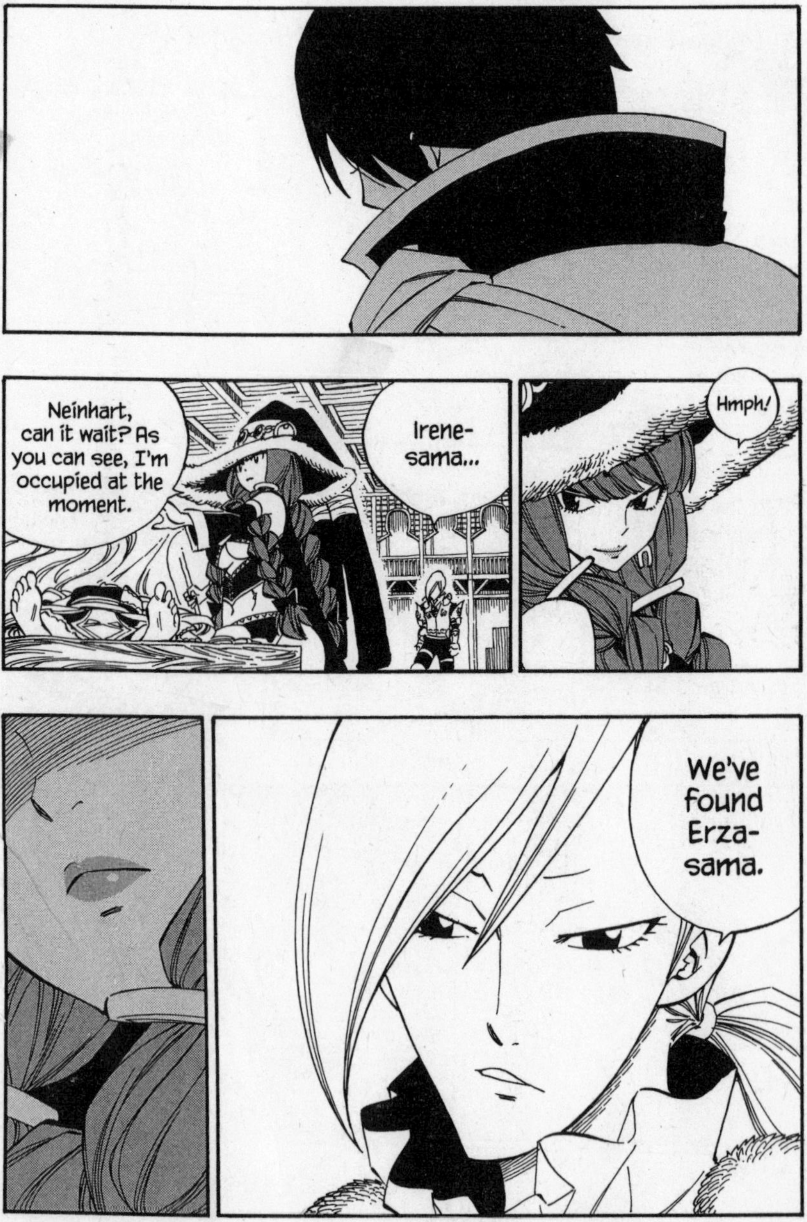

Hmph!
Irene-sama...
Neinhart, can it wait? As you can see, I'm occupied at the moment.
We've found Erza-sama.

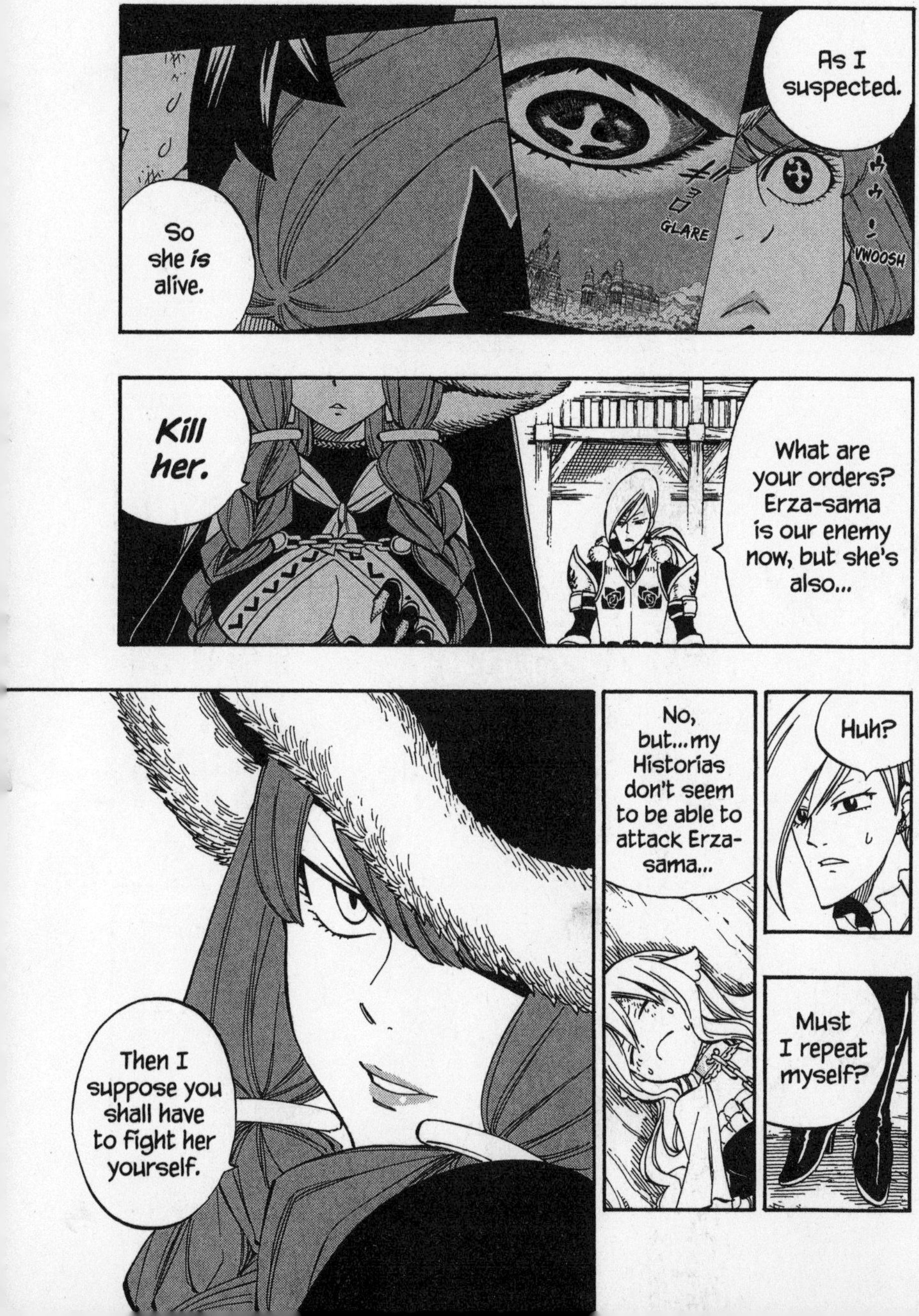
As I suspected.
VWOOSH
GLARE
So she *is* alive.
What are your orders? Erza-sama is our enemy now, but she's also...
Kill her.
Huh?
Must I repeat myself?
No, but...my Historias don't seem to be able to attack Erza-sama...
Then I suppose you shall have to fight her yourself.

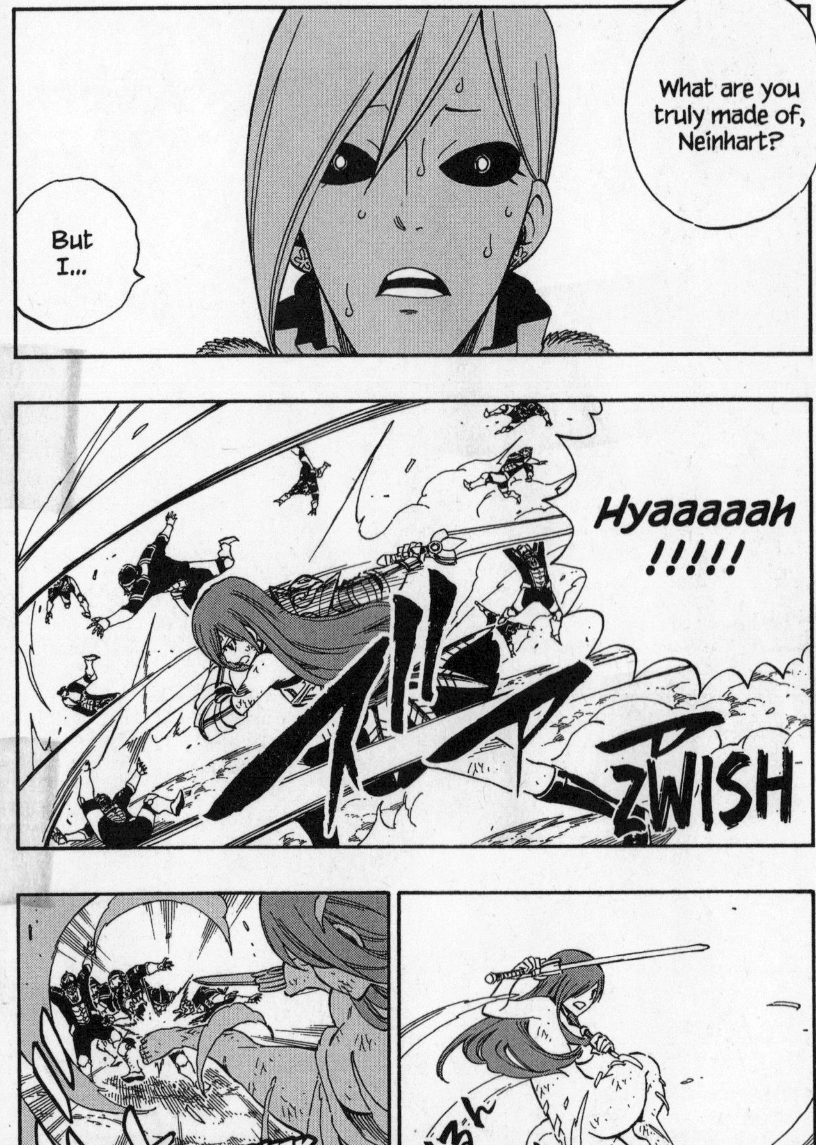
What are you truly made of, Neinhart?
But I...
Hyaaaaah!!!!!
ZWISH
VWIRL
THWAK

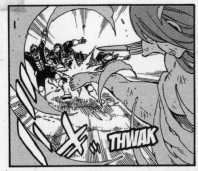

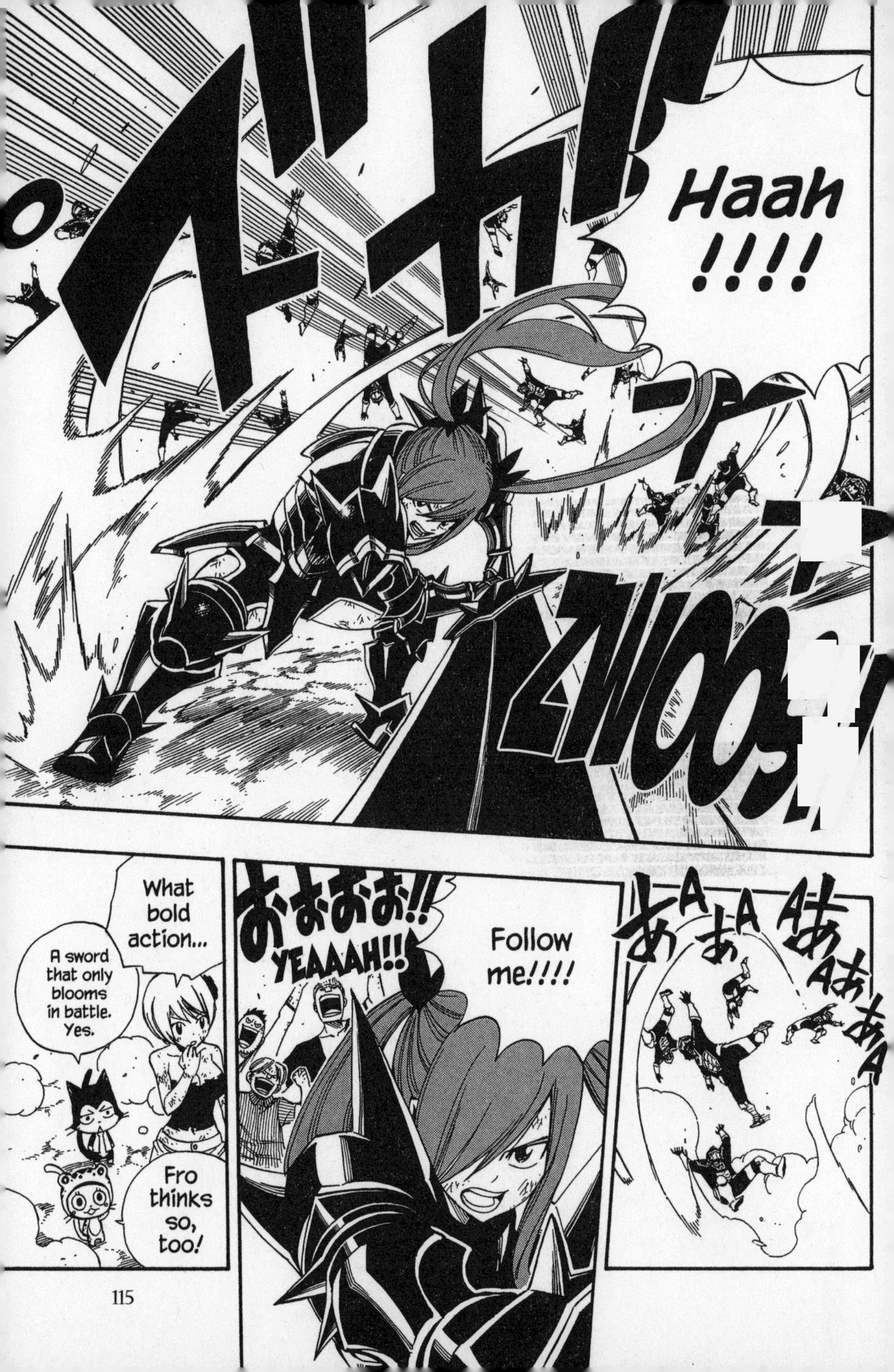
Haah
!!!!
YEAAAH!!
Follow me!!!!
What bold action...
A sword that only blooms in battle. Yes.
Fro thinks so, too!

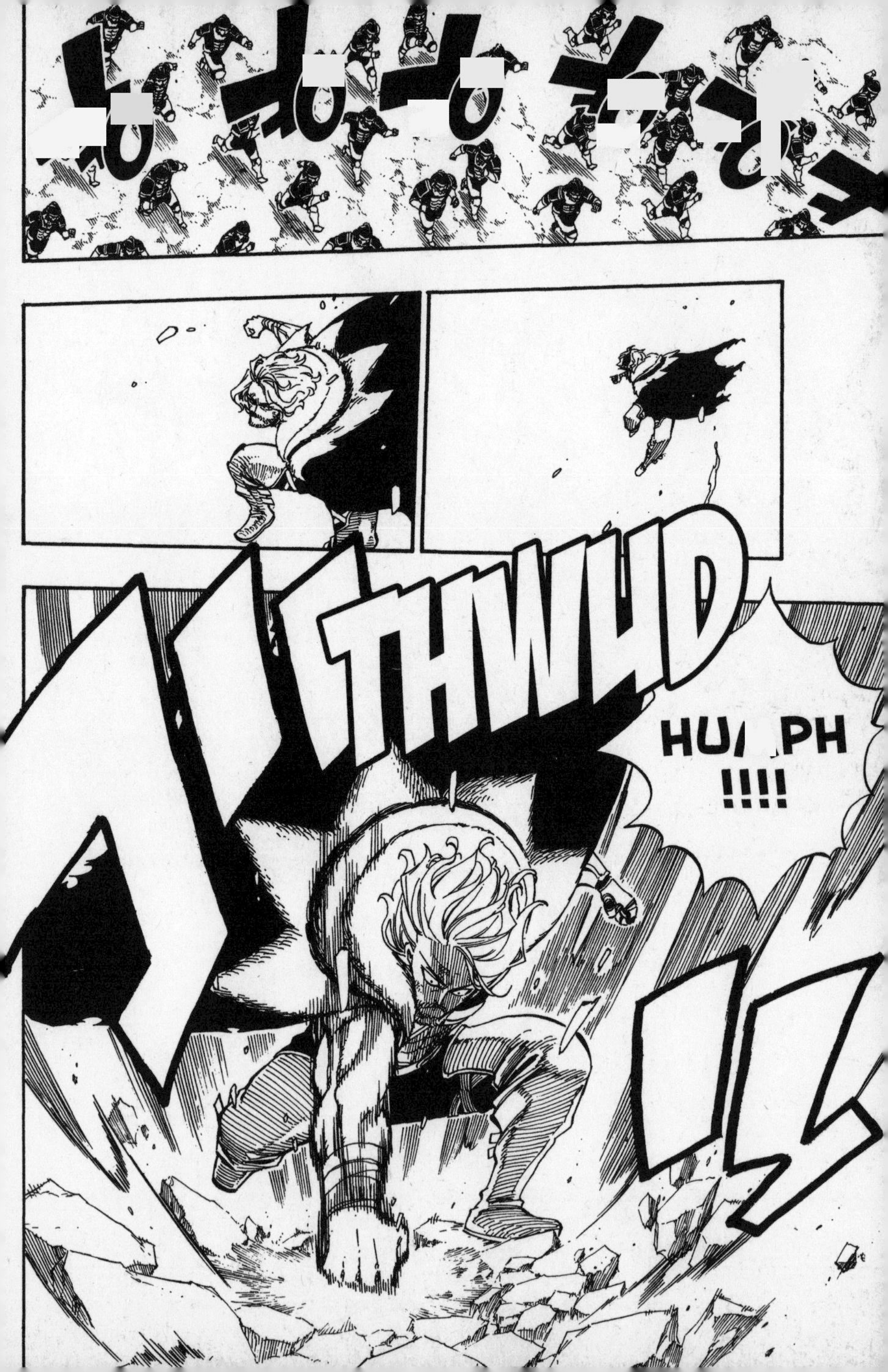
THWUD
HU[redacted]PH
!!!!

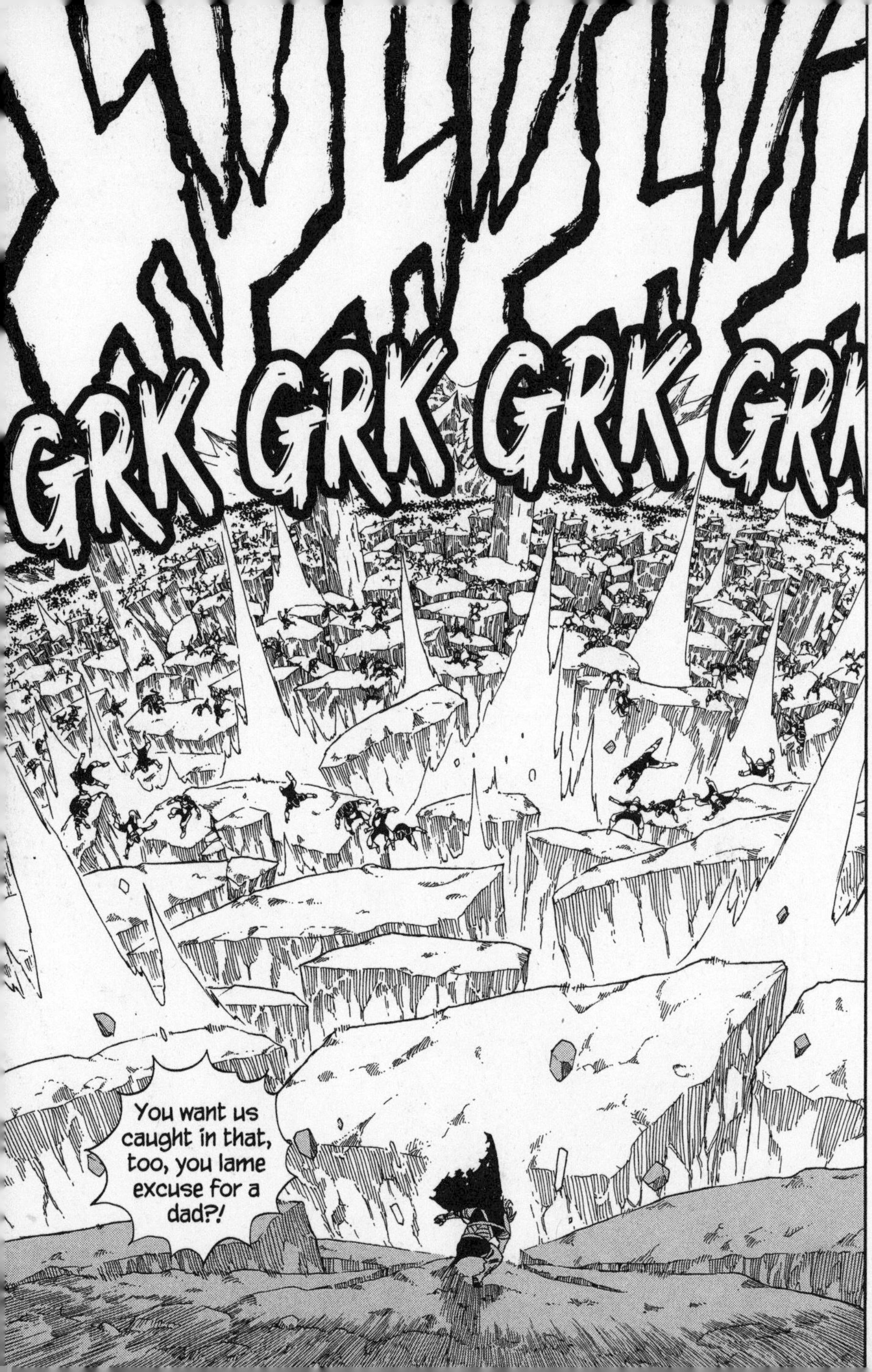
GRK GRK GRK
You want us caught in that, too, you lame excuse for a dad?!

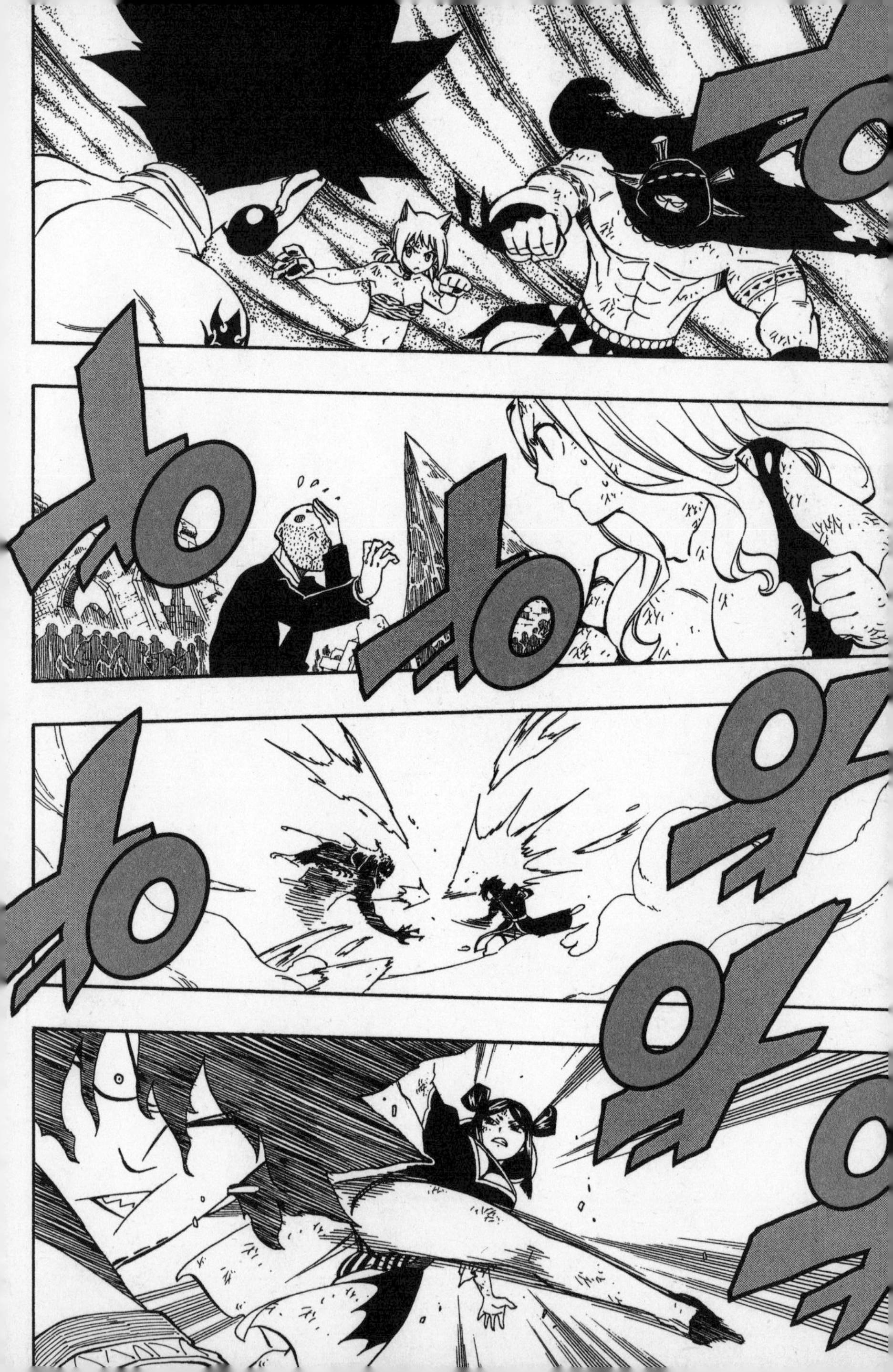

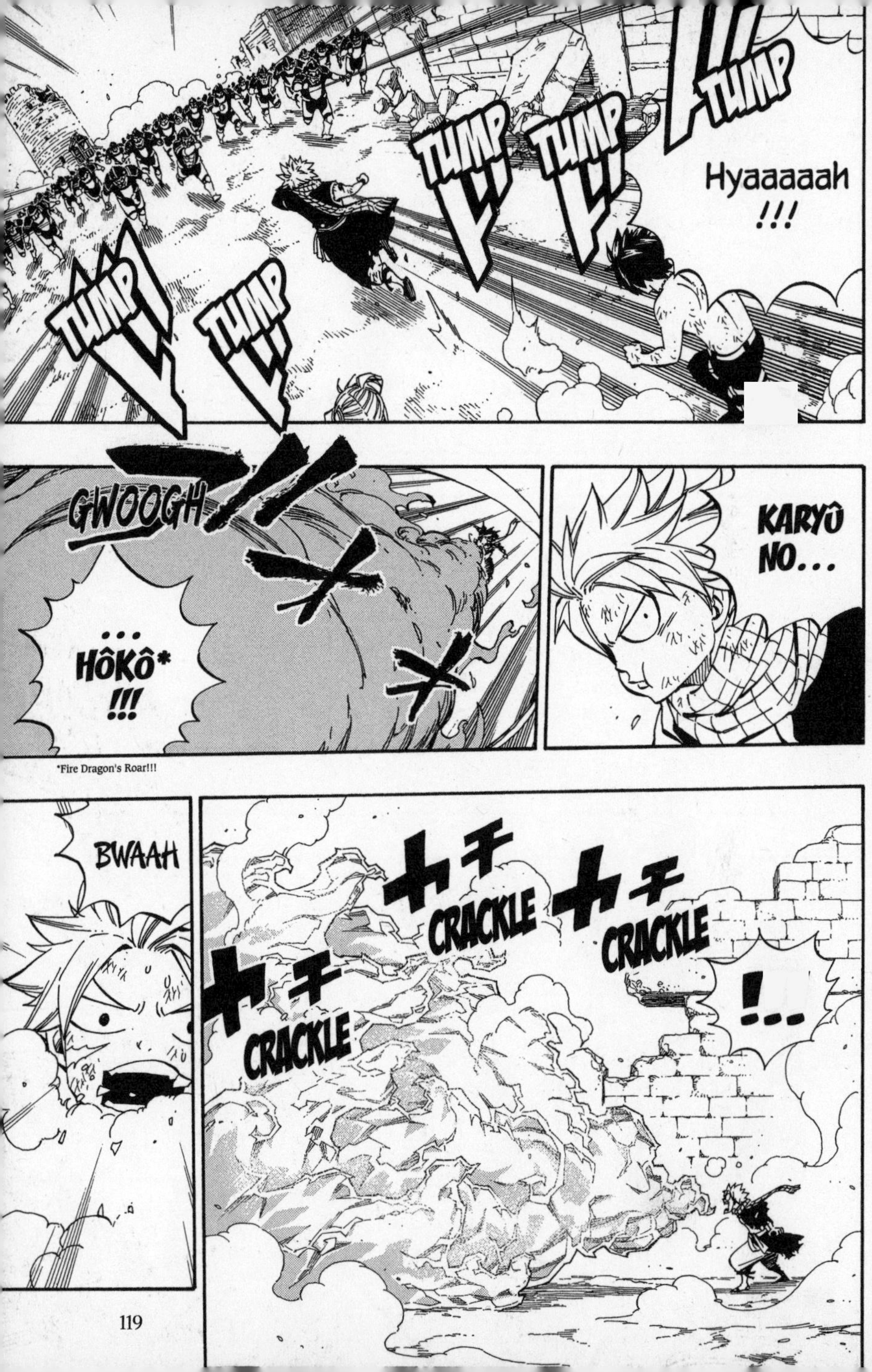
TUMP
Hyaaaaah !!!
TUMP
TUMP
TUMP
TUMP
KARYÛ NO...
GWOOGH
... HÔKÔ* !!!
CRACKLE
CRACKLE
CRACKLE
!..
BWAAH

*Fire Dragon's Roar!!!

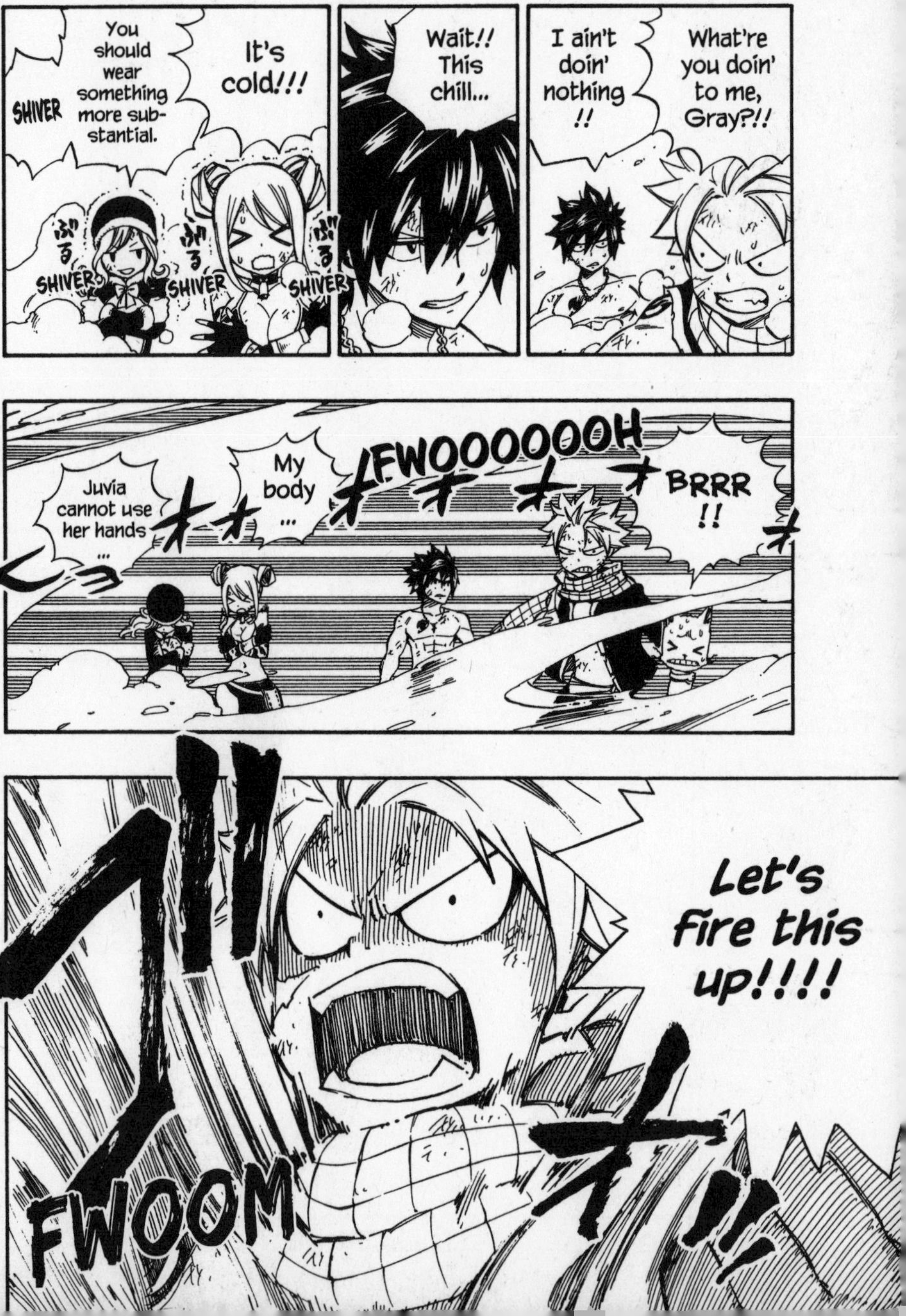
What're you doin' to me, Gray?!!
I ain't doin' nothing!!
Wait!! This chill...
It's cold!!!
You should wear something more substantial.
SHIVER
ぶる
SHIVER
ぶる
SHIVER
ぶる
SHIVER
BRRR!!
FWOOOOOOH
My body...
Juvia cannot use her hands...
Let's fire this up!!!!
FWOOM

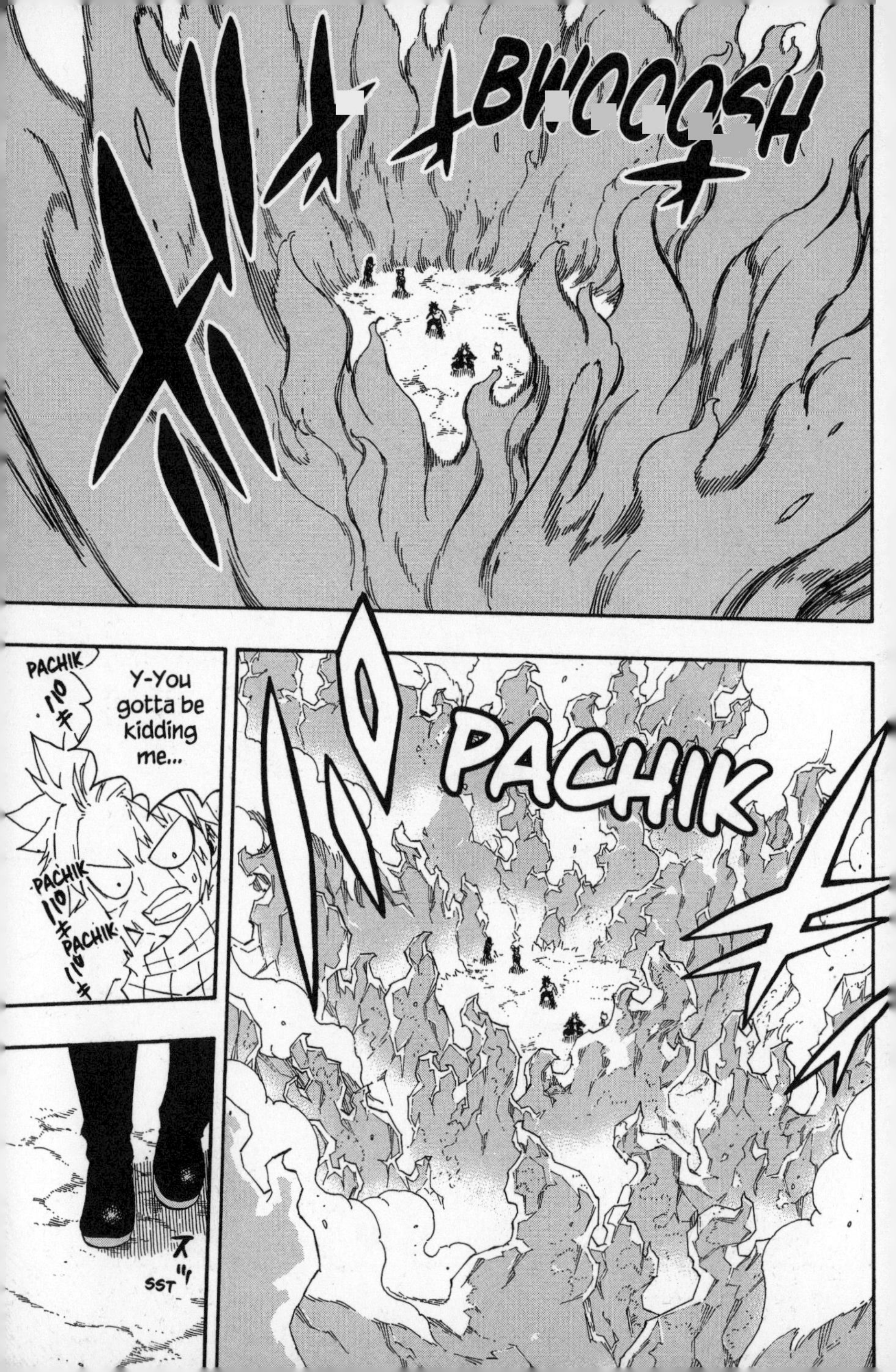
BWOOOSH
PACHIK
Y-You gotta be kidding me...
PACHIK
PACHIK
PACHIK
SST

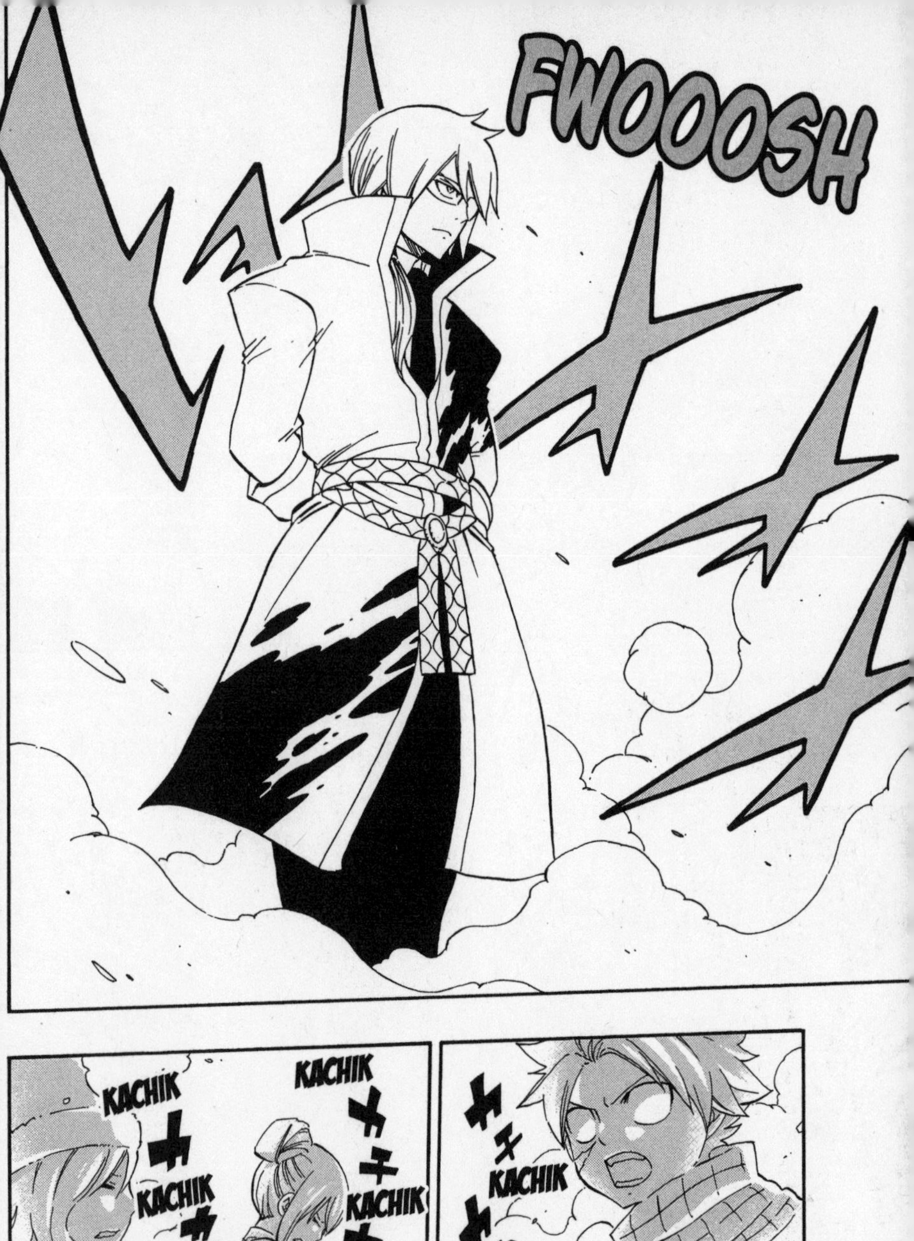
FWOOOSH
KACHIK
KACHIK
KACHIK
KACHIK
KACHIK
KACHIK

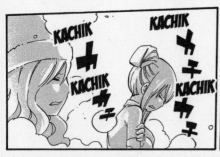

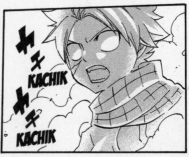

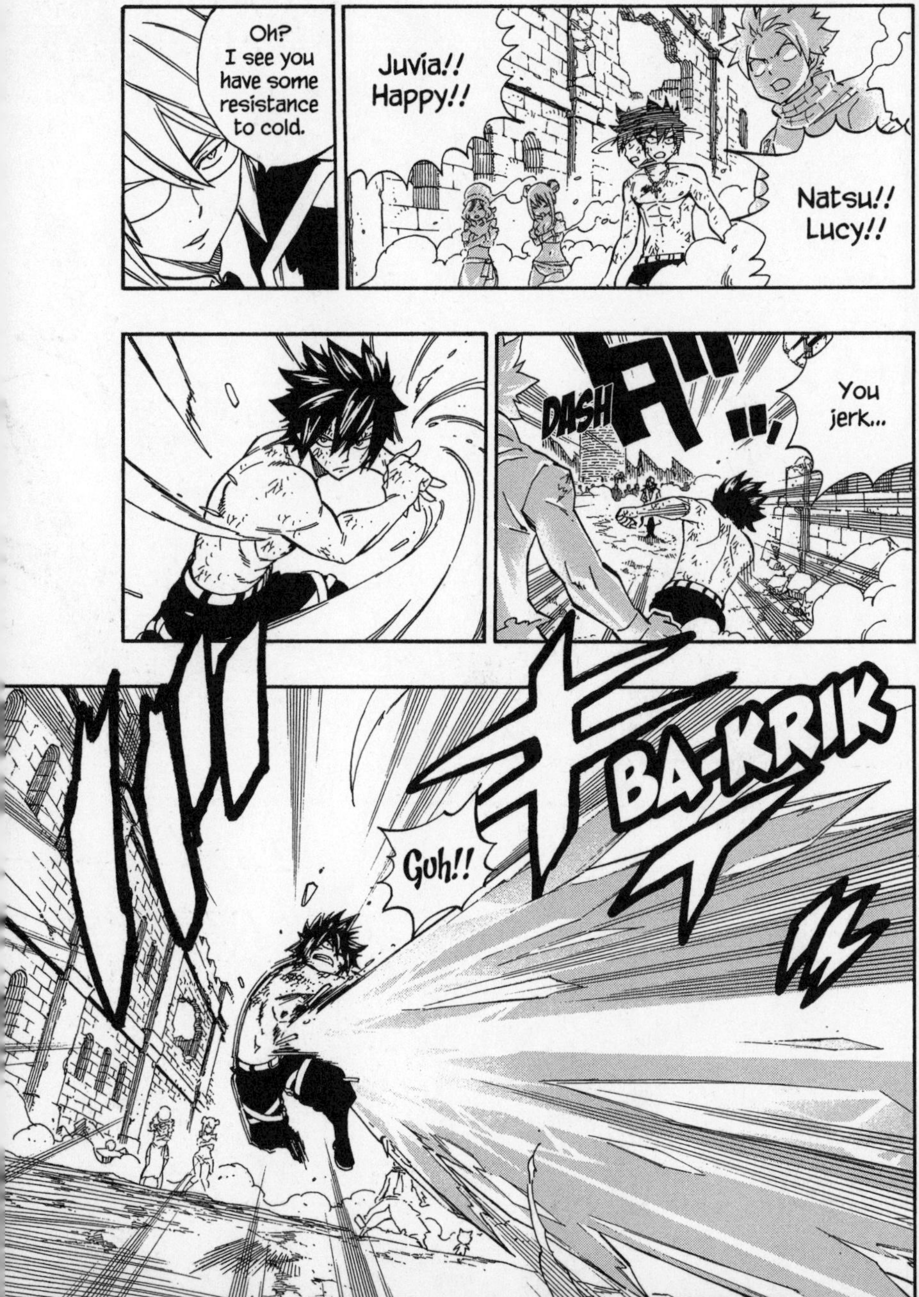

Juvia!! Happy!!
Natsu!! Lucy!!
Oh? I see you have some resistance to cold.
You jerk...
DASH
BA-KRIK
Guh!!

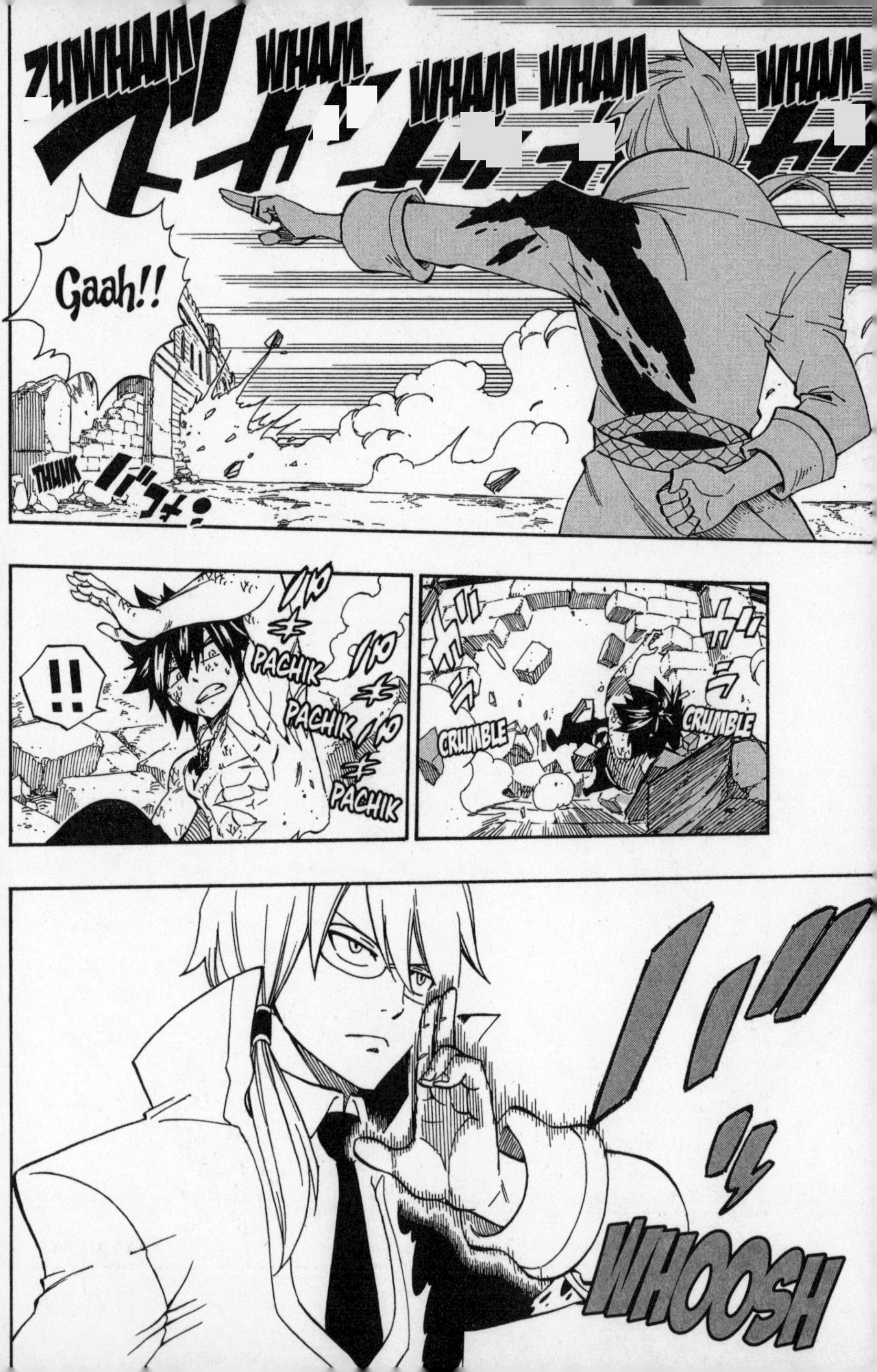
ZUWHAM!! WHAM WHAM WHAM WHAM
Gaah!!
THUNK
CRUMBLE
CRUMBLE
!!
PACHIK
PACHIK
PACHIK
WHOOSH

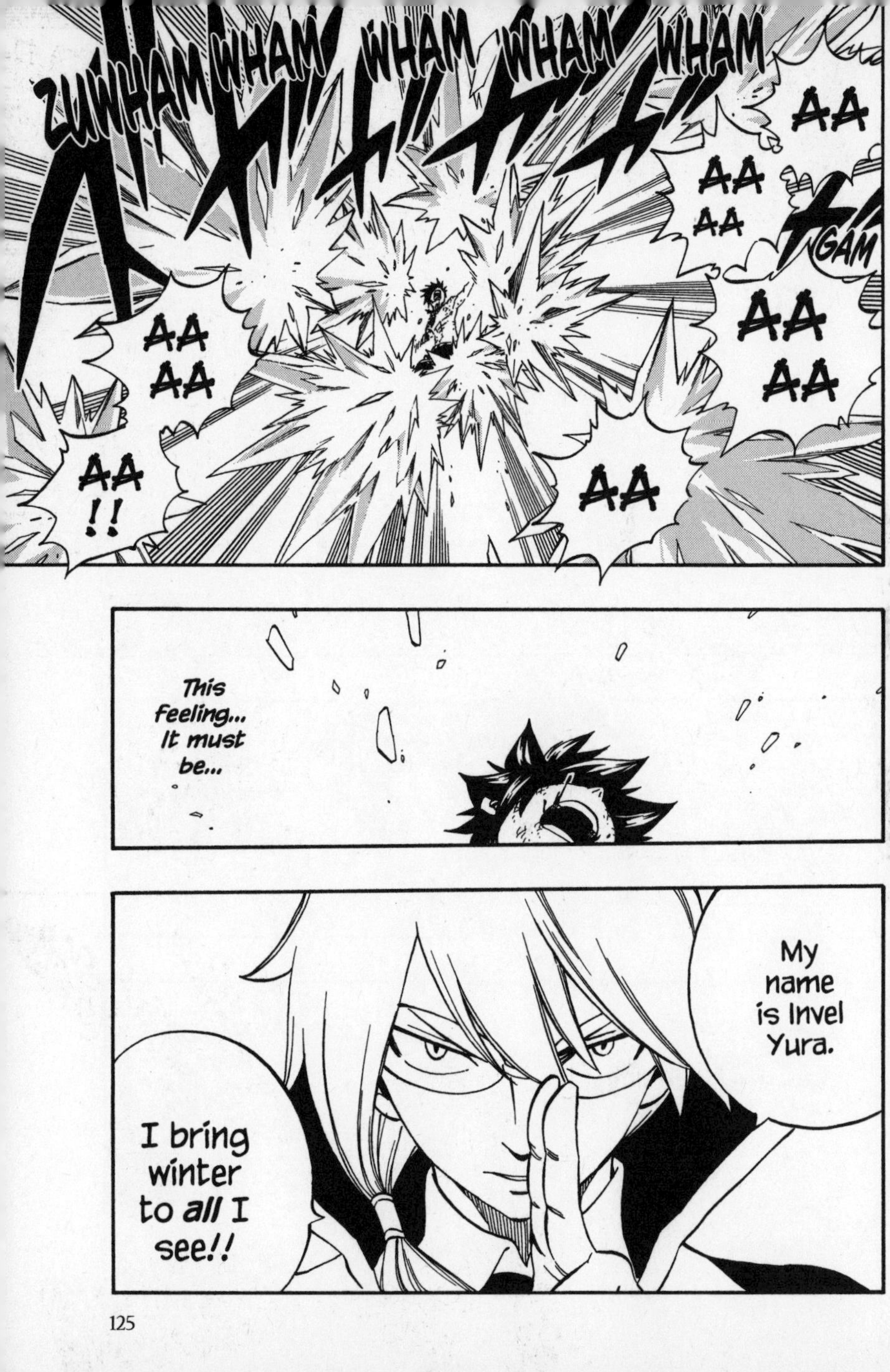
ZUWHAM WHAM WHAM WHAM WHAM
AA
AA
AA
GAM
AA
AA
AA
AA
AA
AA
!!
This feeling... It must be...
My name is Invel Yura.
I bring winter to *all* I see!!

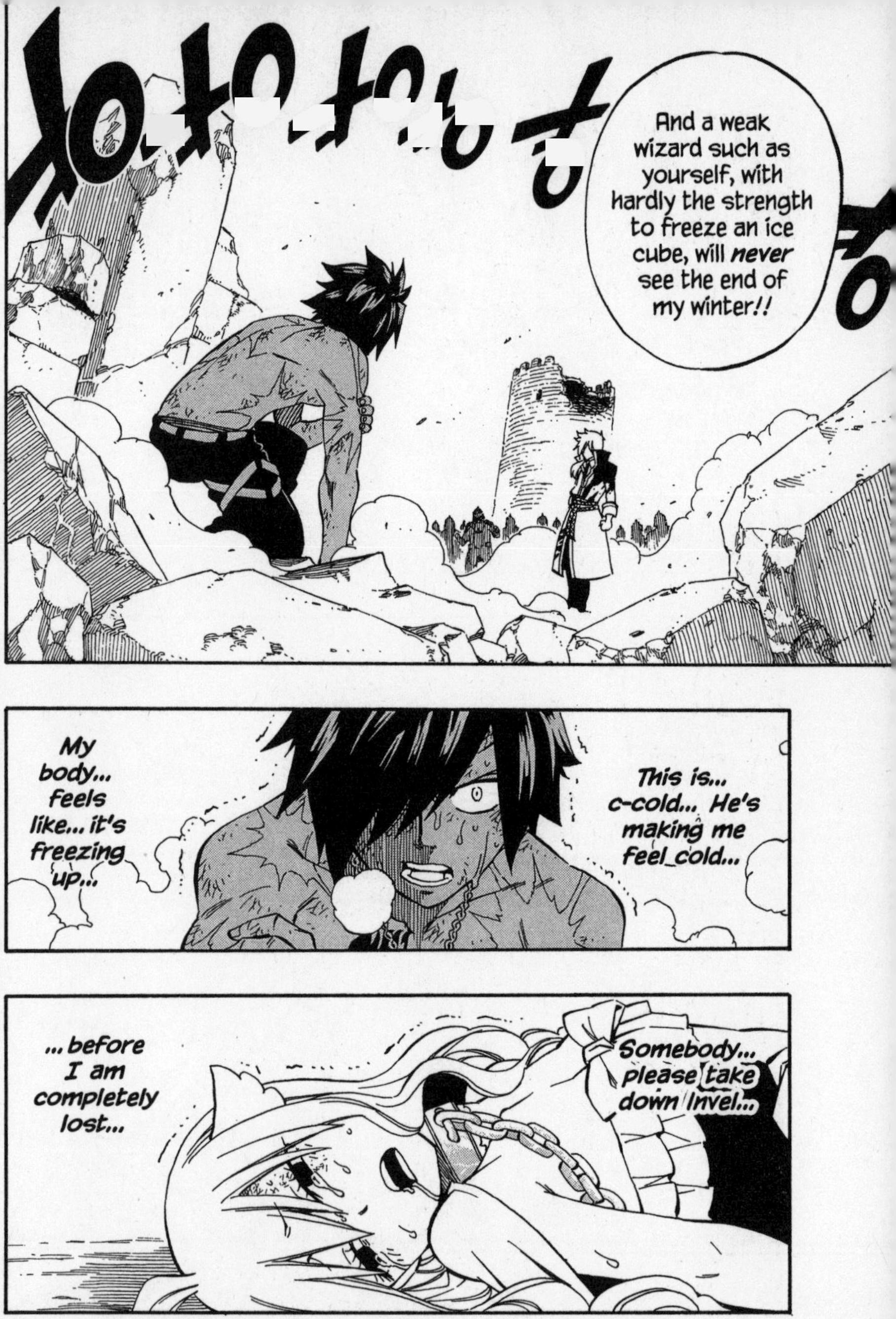
And a weak wizard such as yourself, with hardly the strength to freeze an ice cube, will *never* see the end of my winter!!
This is... c-cold... He's making me feel_cold...
My body... feels like... it's freezing up...
Somebody... please take down Invel...
...before I am completely lost...

FAIRY TAIL
フェアリーテイル

Chapter 498: Gray vs. Invel

Love me Tender

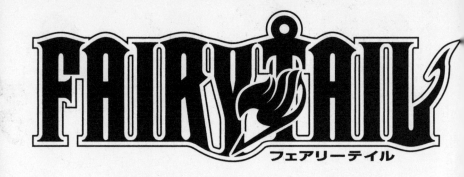

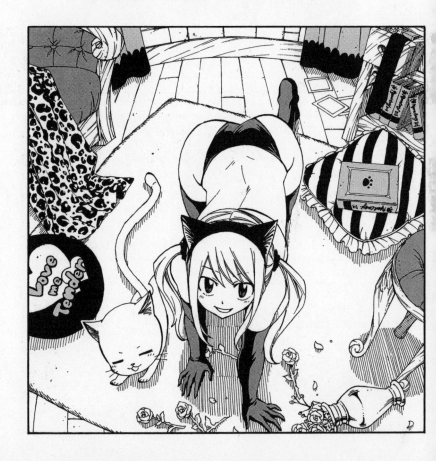

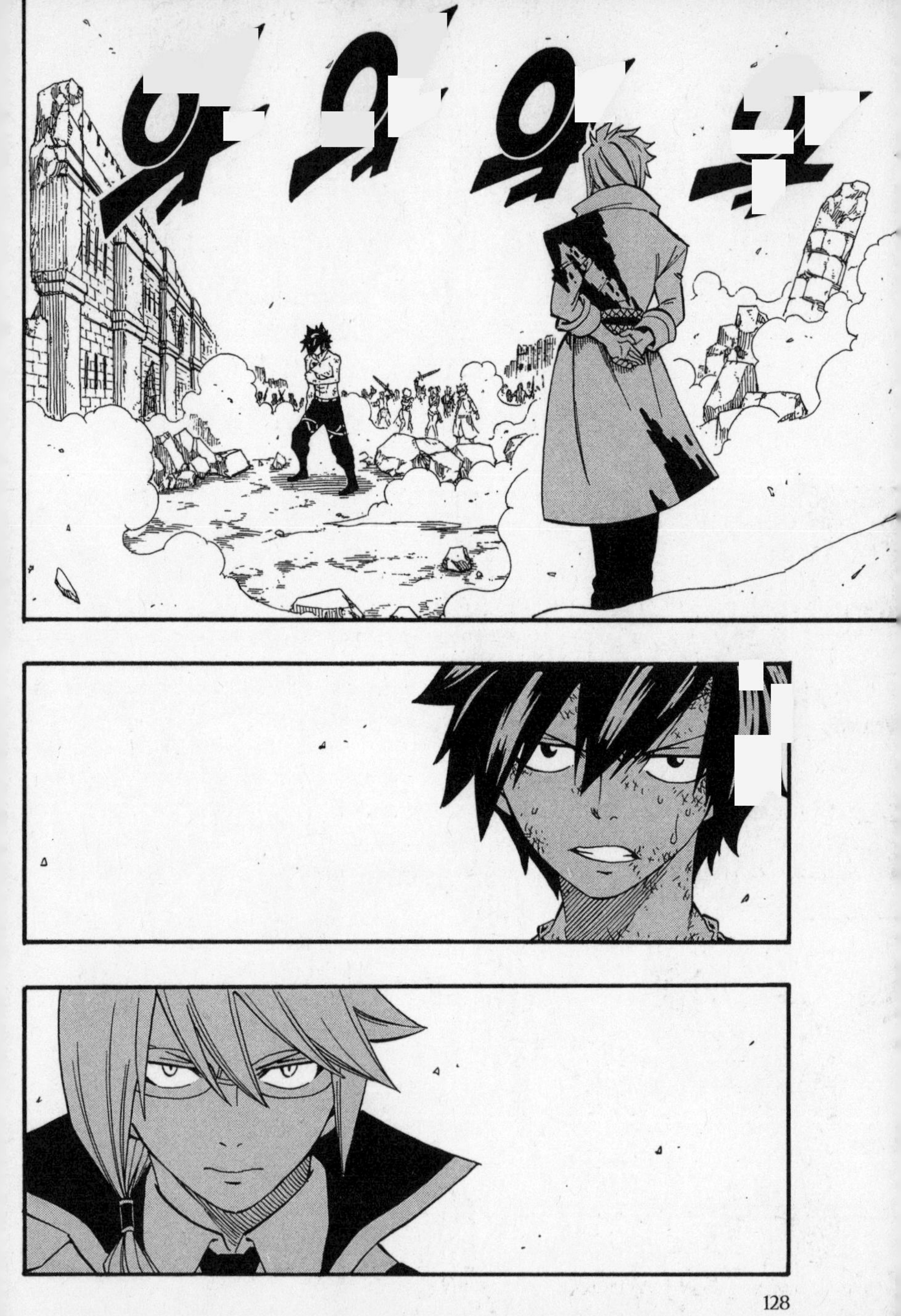

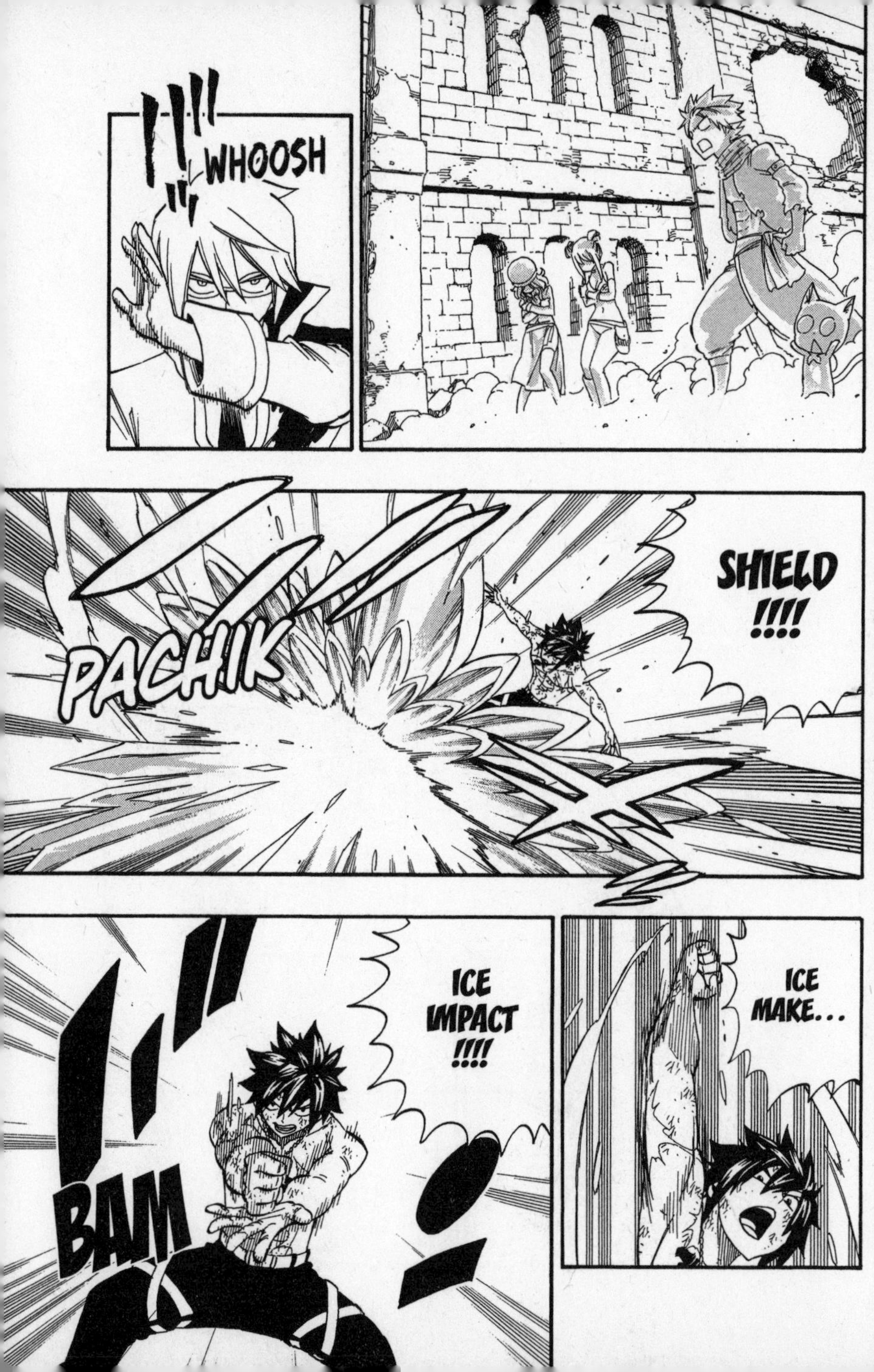
WHOOSH
SHIELD
!!!!
PACHIK
ICE
MAKE...
ICE
IMPACT
!!!!
BAM

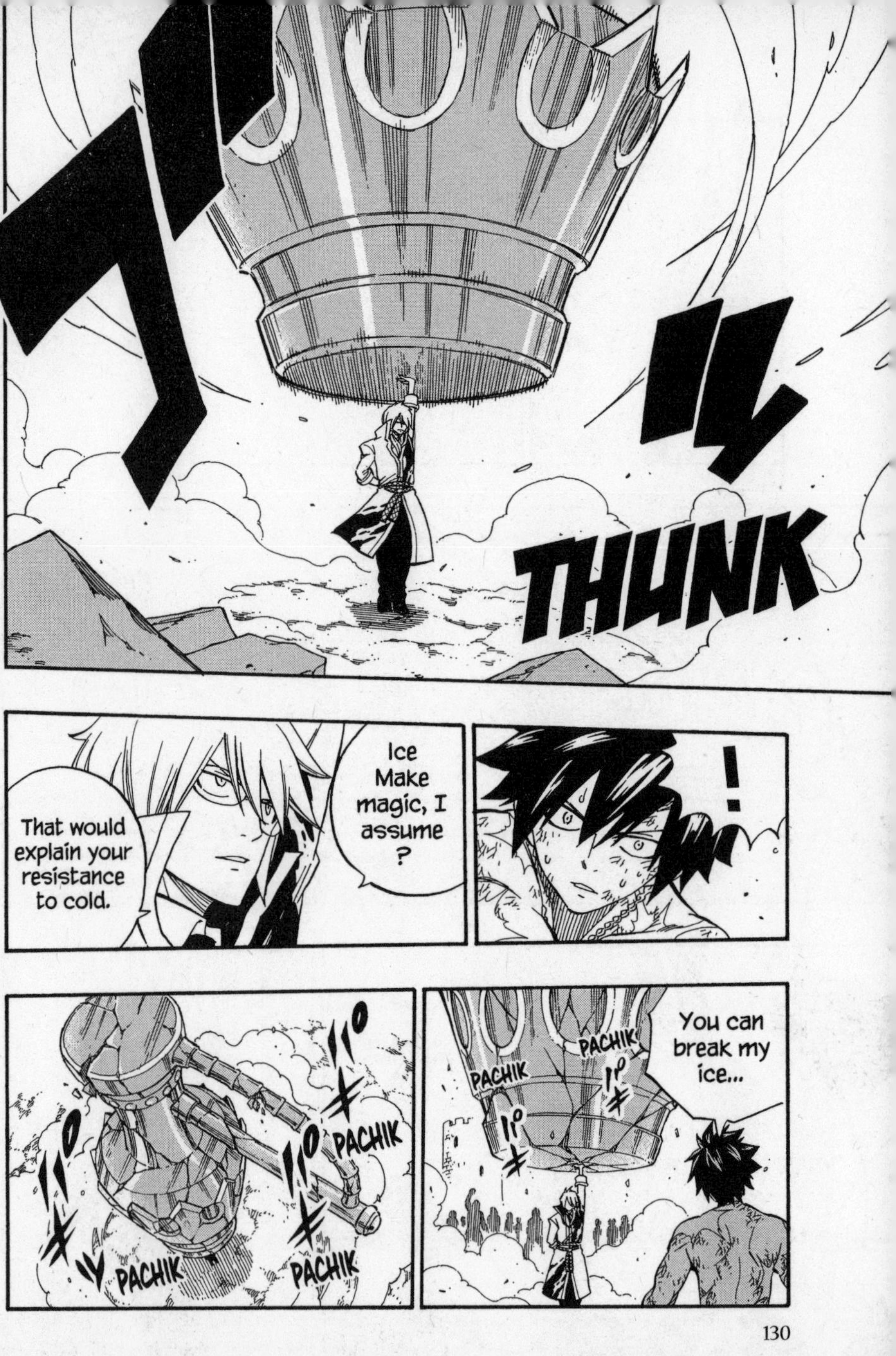
THUNK
!
Ice Make magic, I assume?
That would explain your resistance to cold.
PACHIK
PACHIK
You can break my ice...
PACHIK
PACHIK
PACHIK

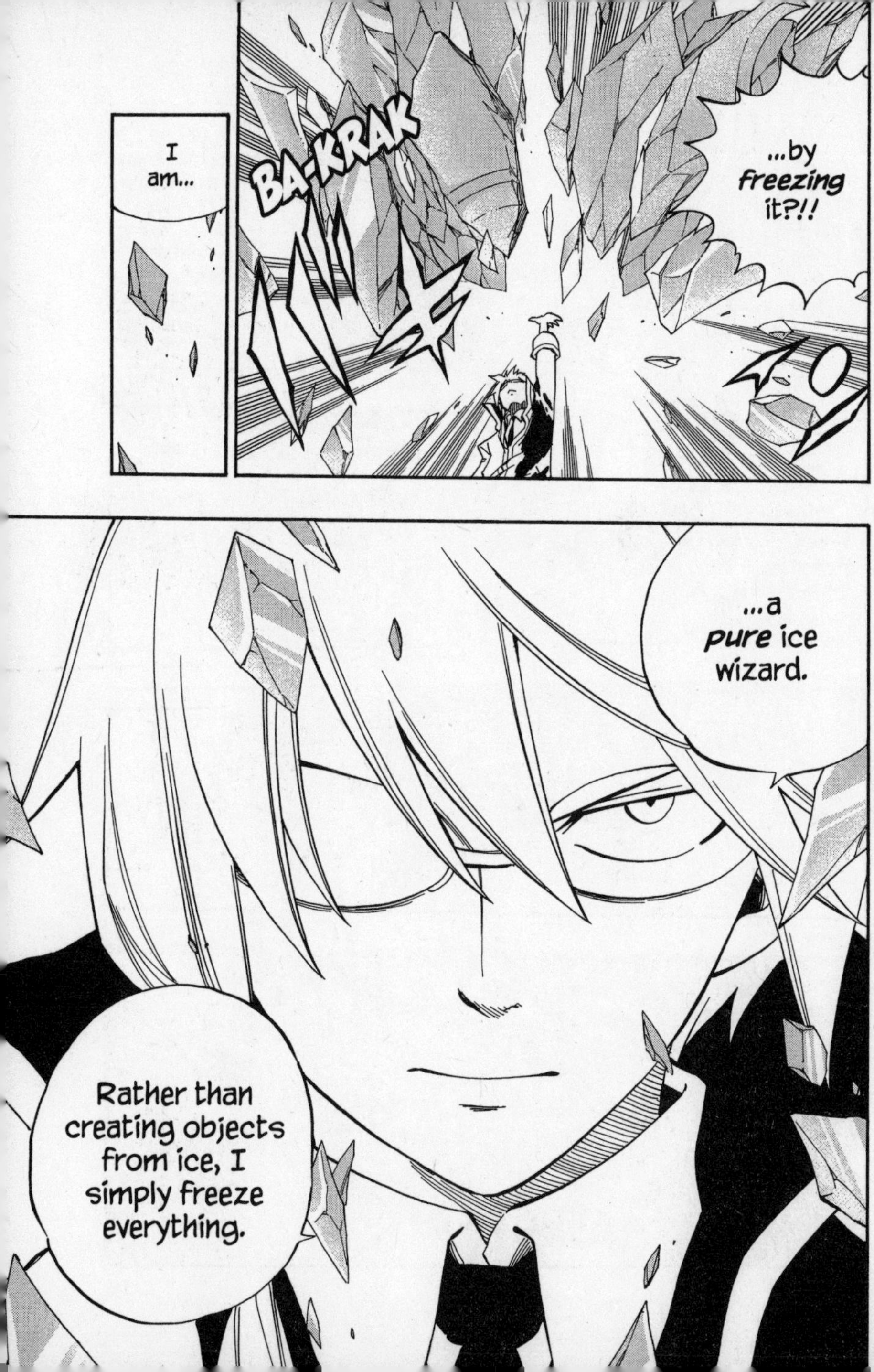
...by freezing it?!!
BA-KRAK
I am...
...a *pure* ice wizard.
Rather than creating objects from ice, I simply freeze everything.

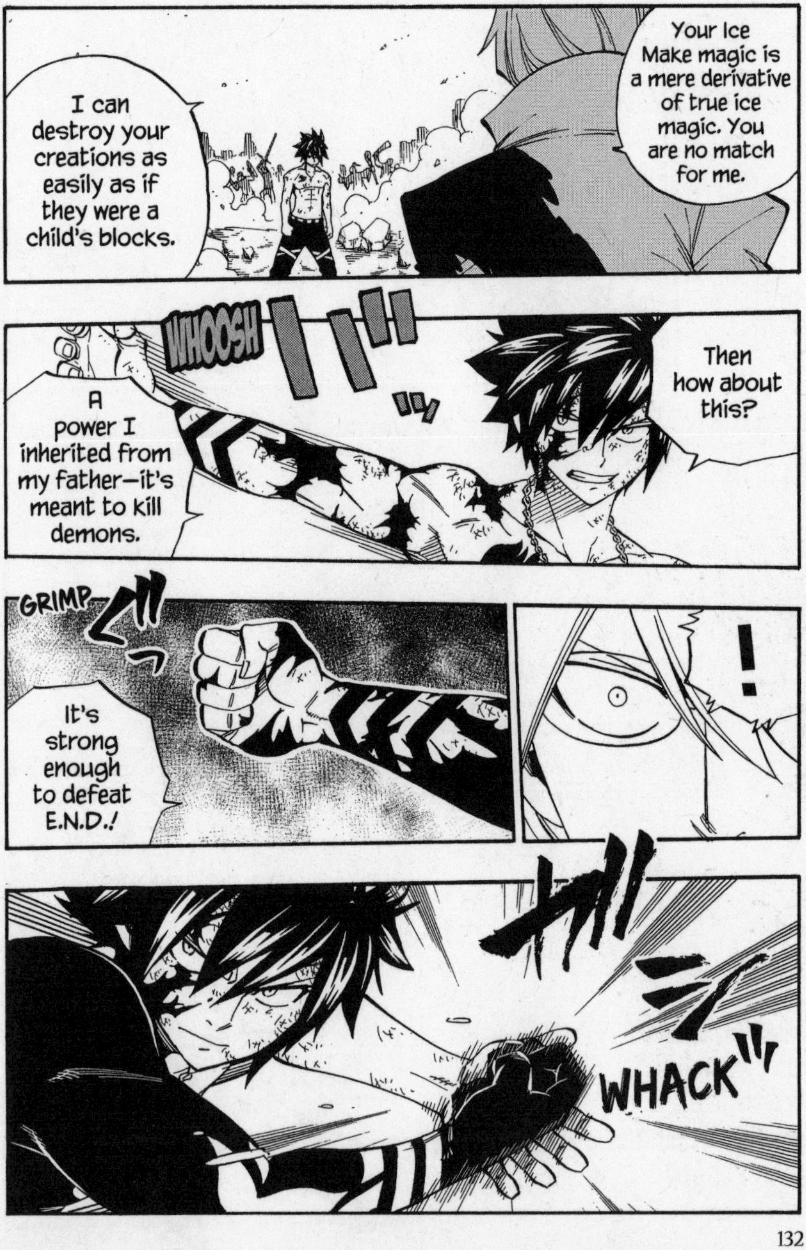
Your Ice Make magic is a mere derivative of true ice magic. You are no match for me.
I can destroy your creations as easily as if they were a child's blocks.
Then how about this?
WHOOSH
A power I inherited from my father—it's meant to kill demons.
!
GRIMP
It's strong enough to defeat E.N.D.!
WHACK

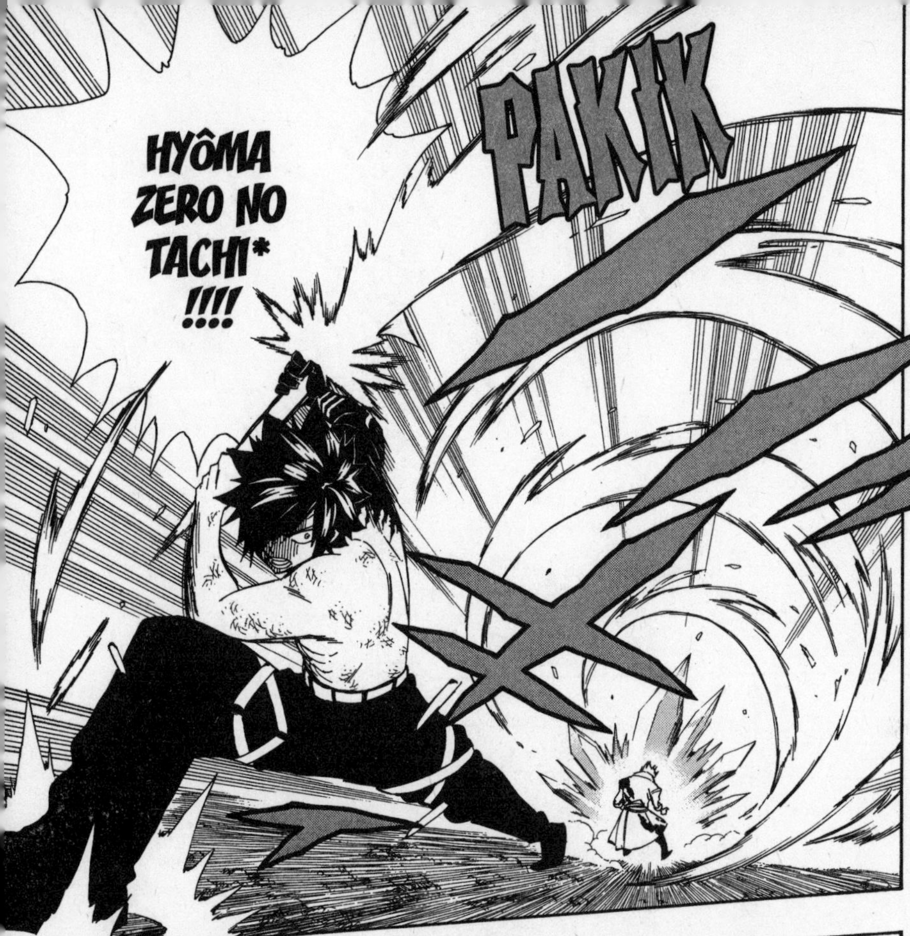
PAKIK
HYÔMA ZERO NO TACHI* !!!!

*Ice Demon Zero's Long Sword!!!!

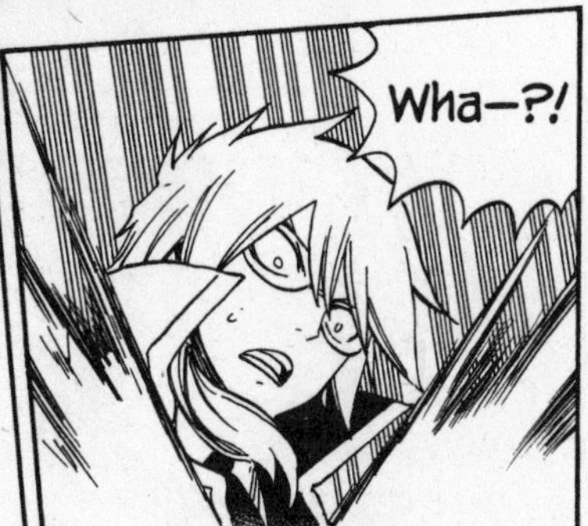
Wha-?!

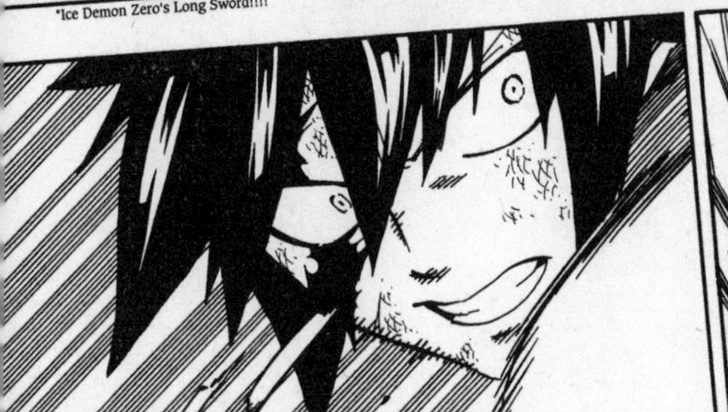

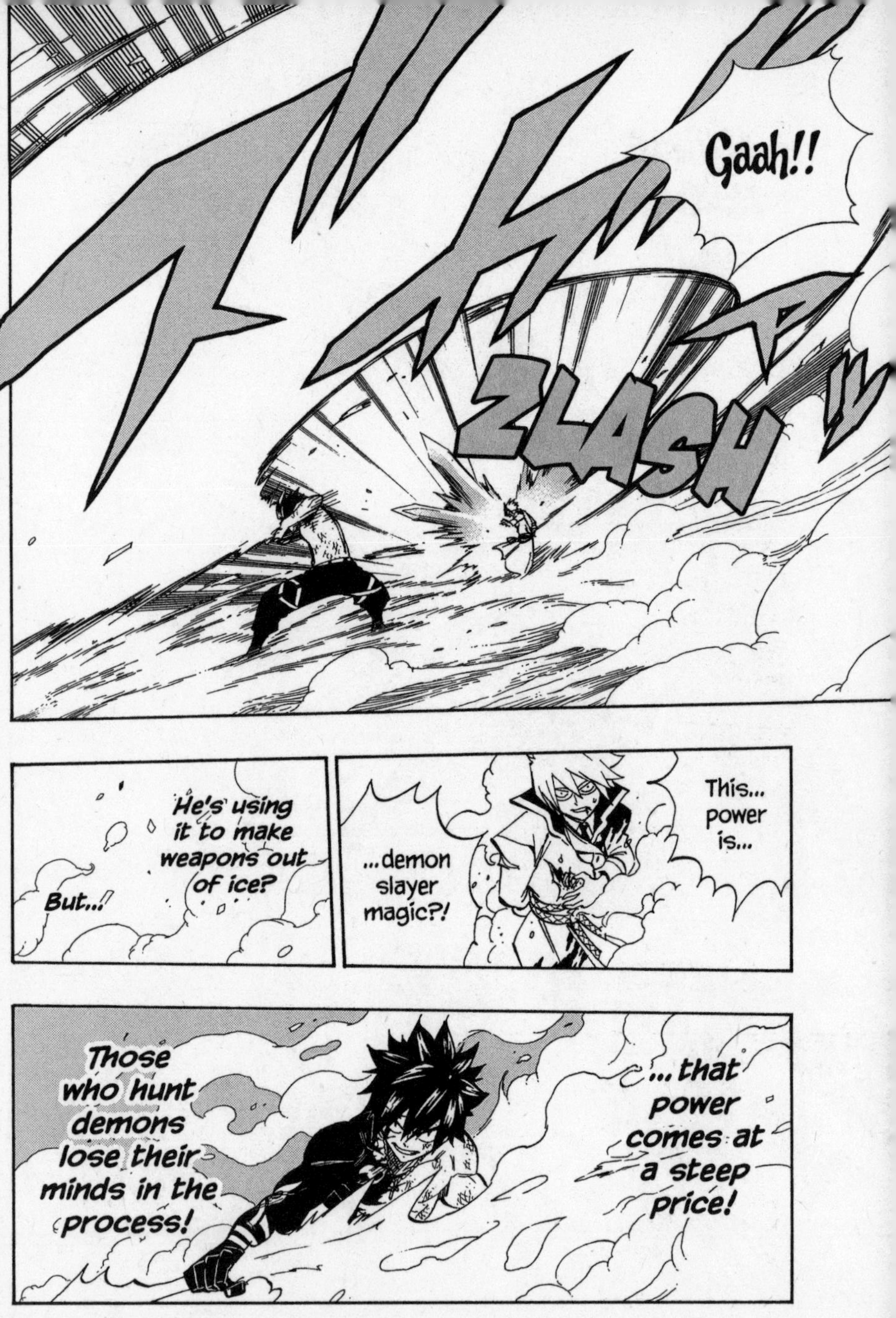
Gaah!!
ZLASH
This... power is...
...demon slayer magic?!
He's using it to make weapons out of ice?
But...!
...that power comes at a steep price!
Those who hunt demons lose their minds in the process!

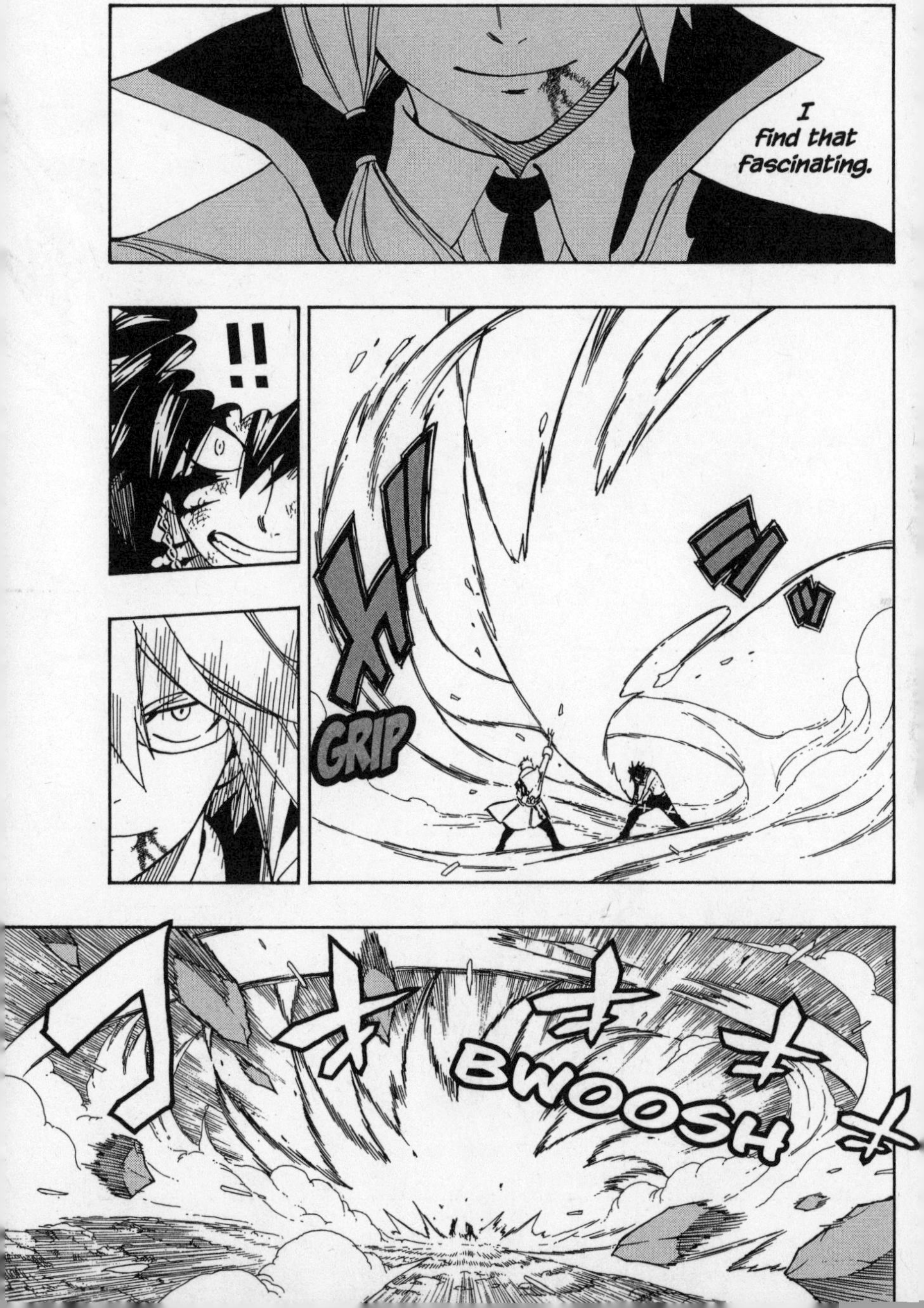
I find that fascinating.
GRIP
!!
BWOOSH

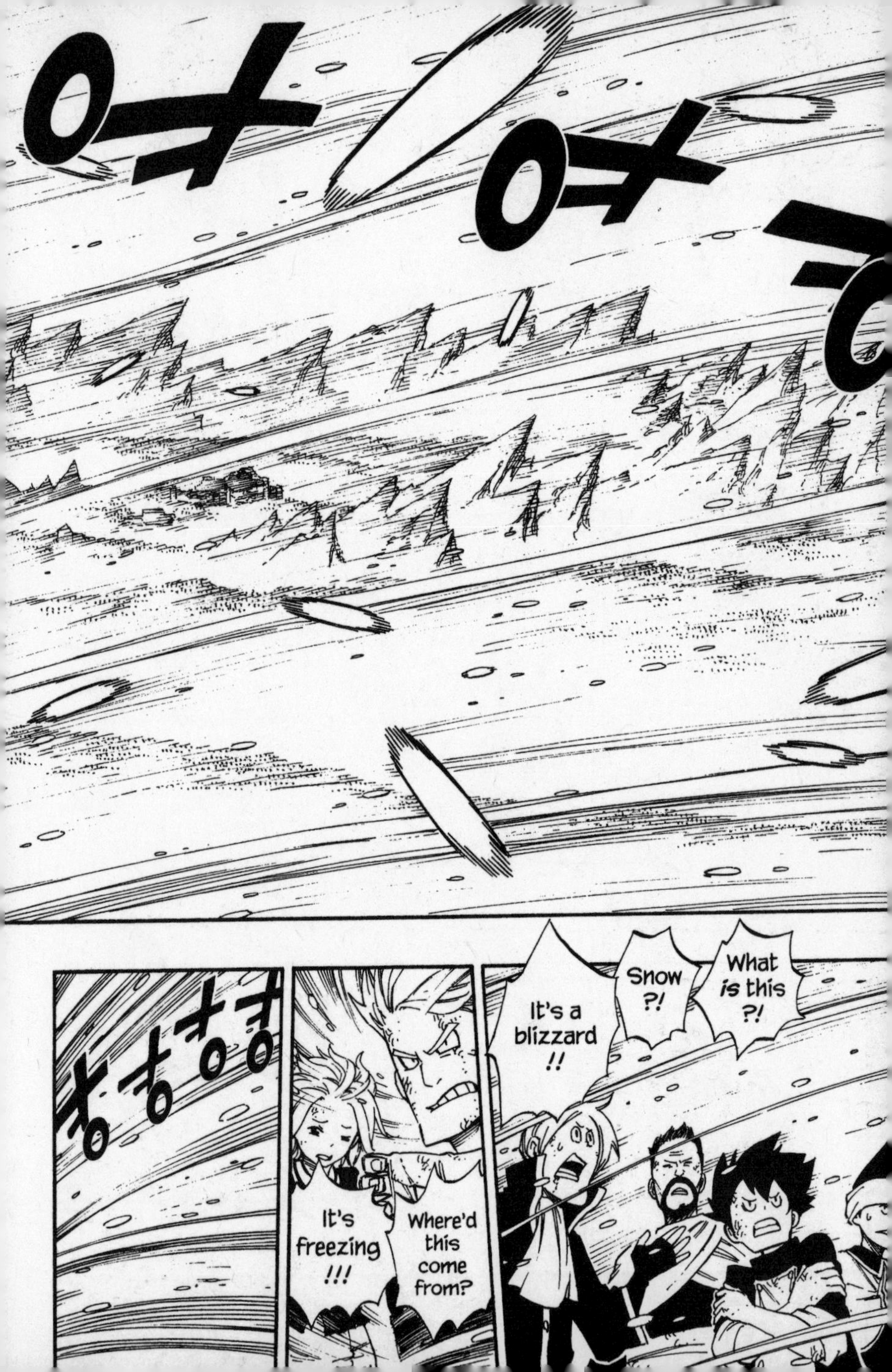
What is this ?!
Snow ?!
It's a blizzard !!
Where'd this come from?
It's freezing !!!

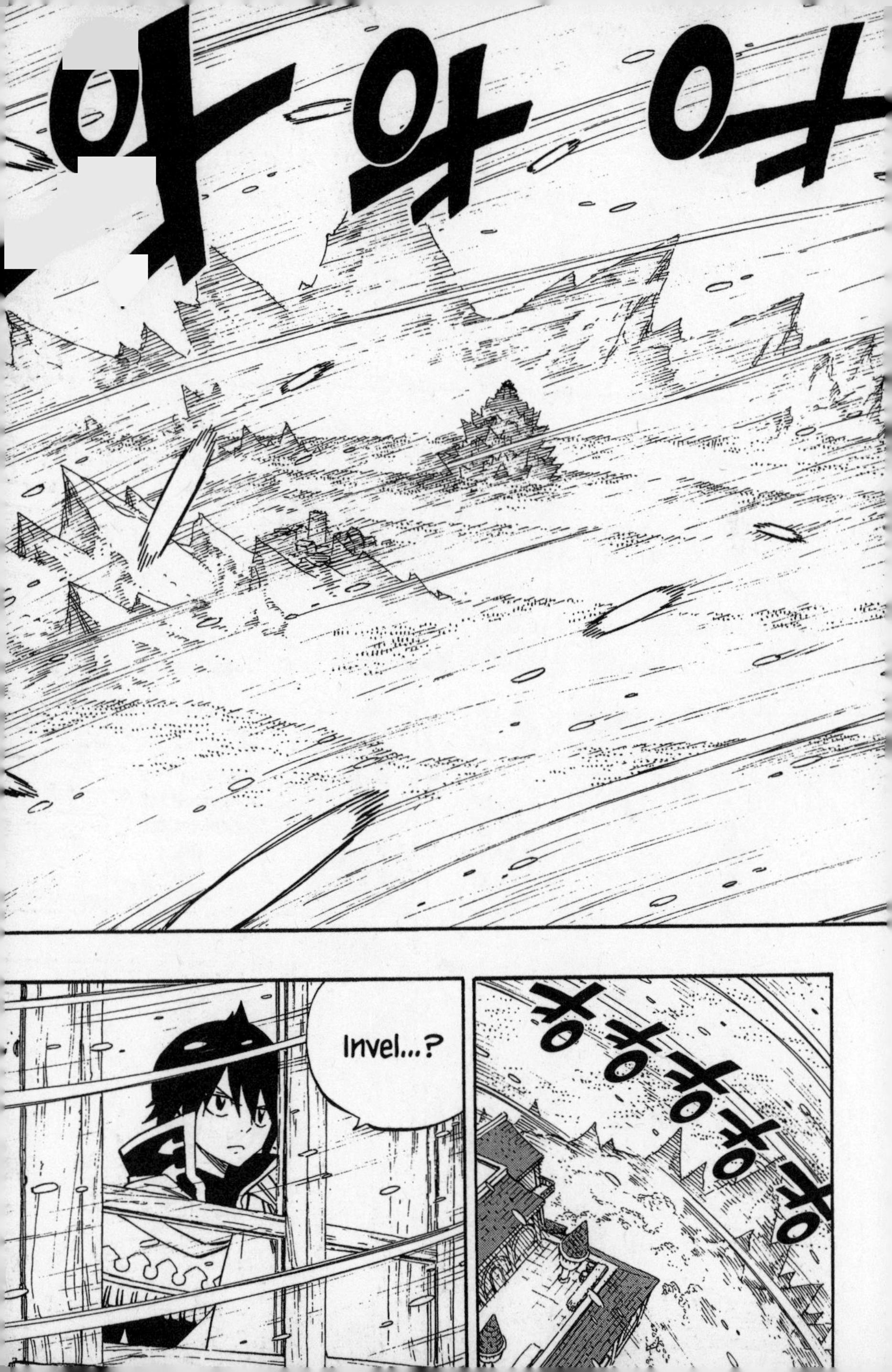
Invel...?

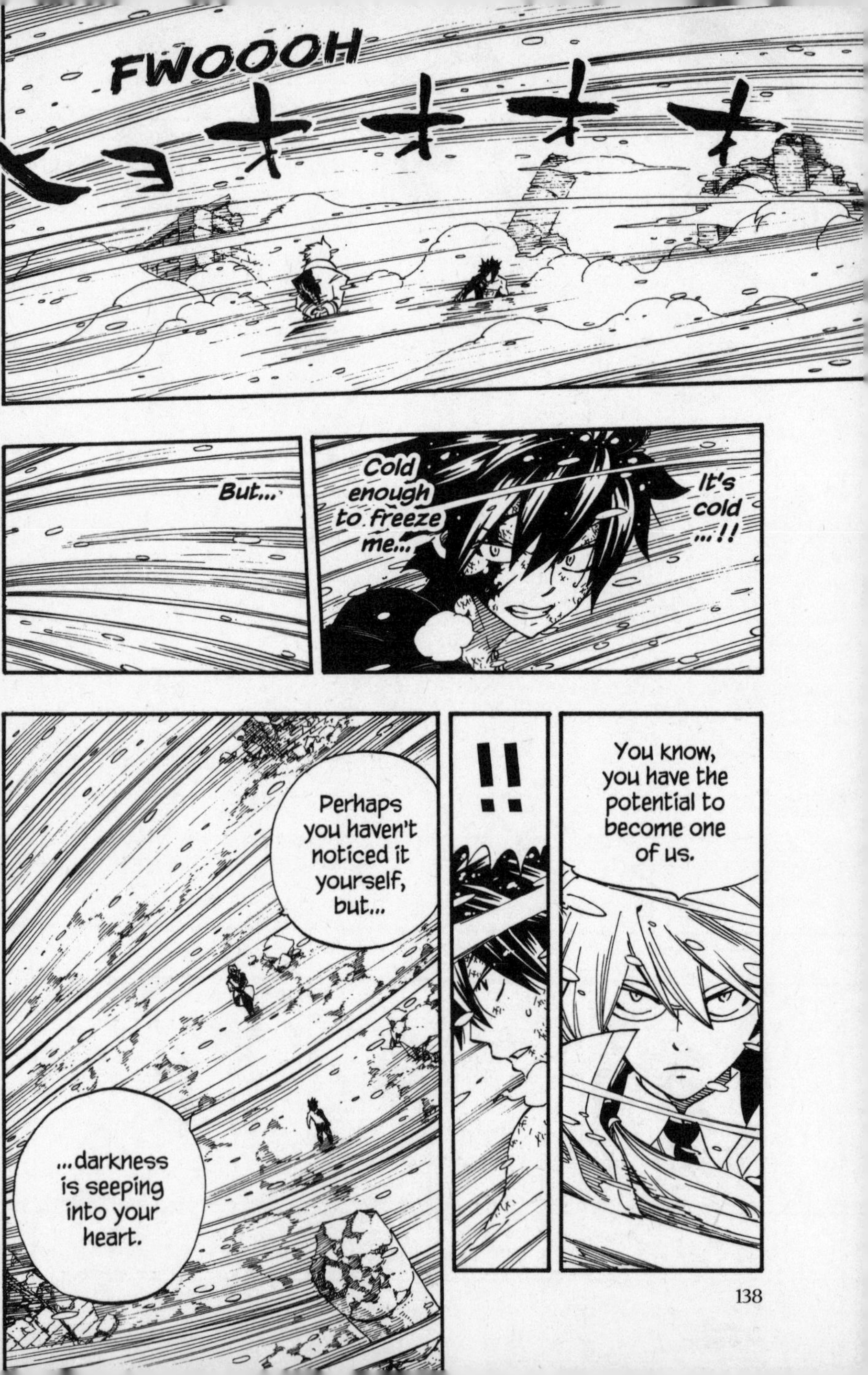
FWOOOH
It's cold ...!!
Cold enough to freeze me...
But...
You know, you have the potential to become one of us.
!!
Perhaps you haven't noticed it yourself, but...
...darkness is seeping into your heart.

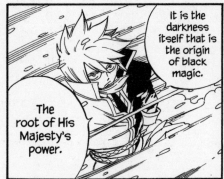

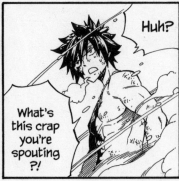

Huh?
What's this crap you're spouting?!
It is the darkness itself that is the origin of black magic.
The root of His Majesty's power.
Wait, you *know* you're the villains here?
It is a tremendous source of power, one that any human being can possess.
Darkness is unrelated to the concepts of good and evil.
And the darkness within *you* is on the verge of release.
Quit it with that nonsense.
I ain't never been the squeaky-clean hero type anyway!
CLENCH

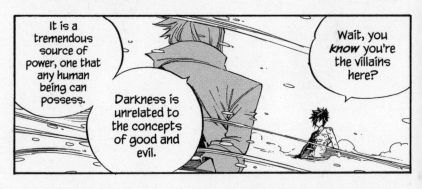

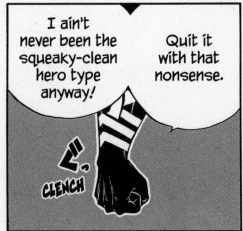

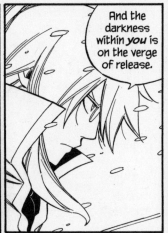

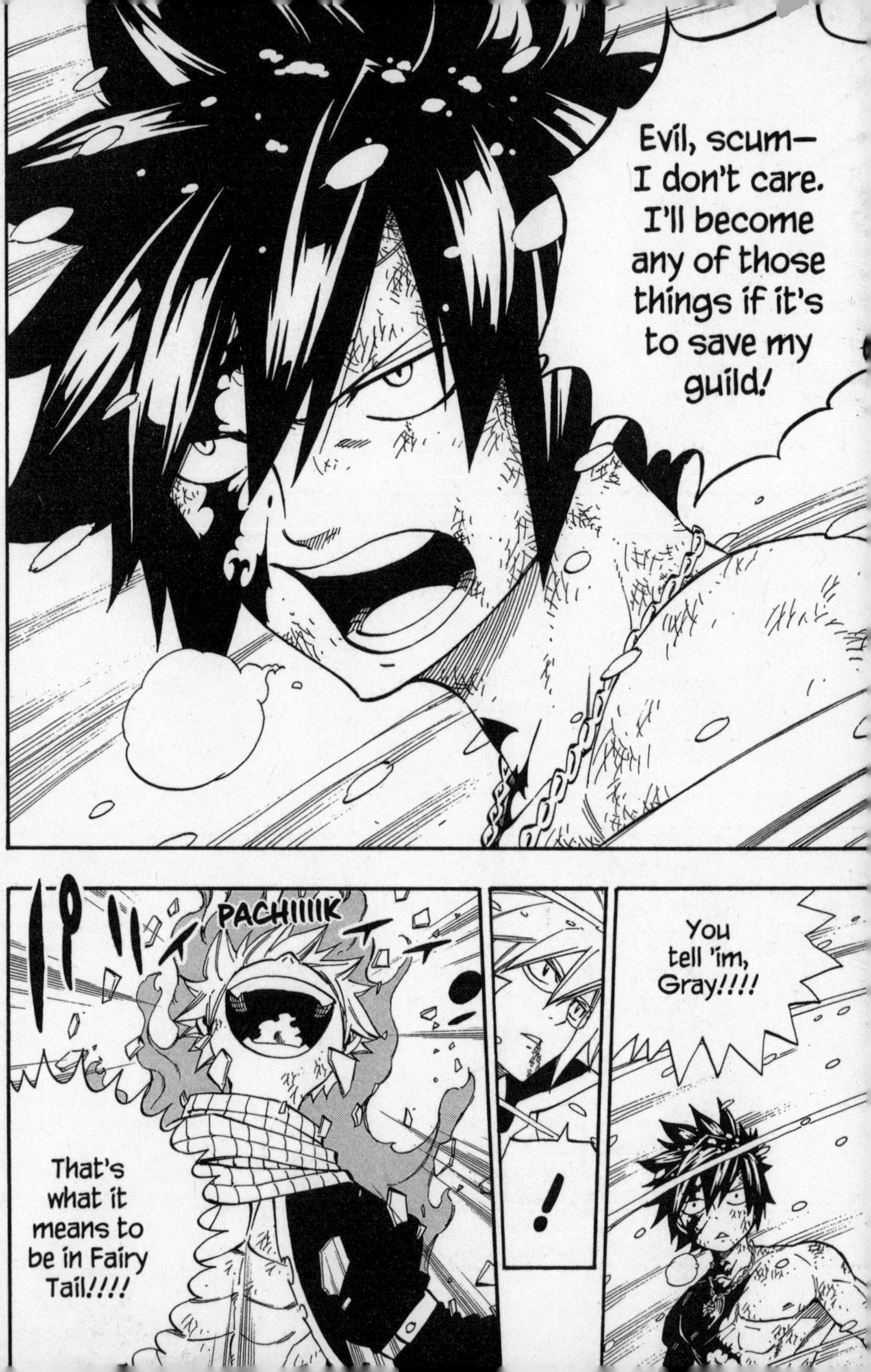
Evil, scum— I don't care. I'll become any of those things if it's to save my guild!
You tell 'im, Gray!!!!
!
PACHIIIIK
That's what it means to be in Fairy Tail!!!!

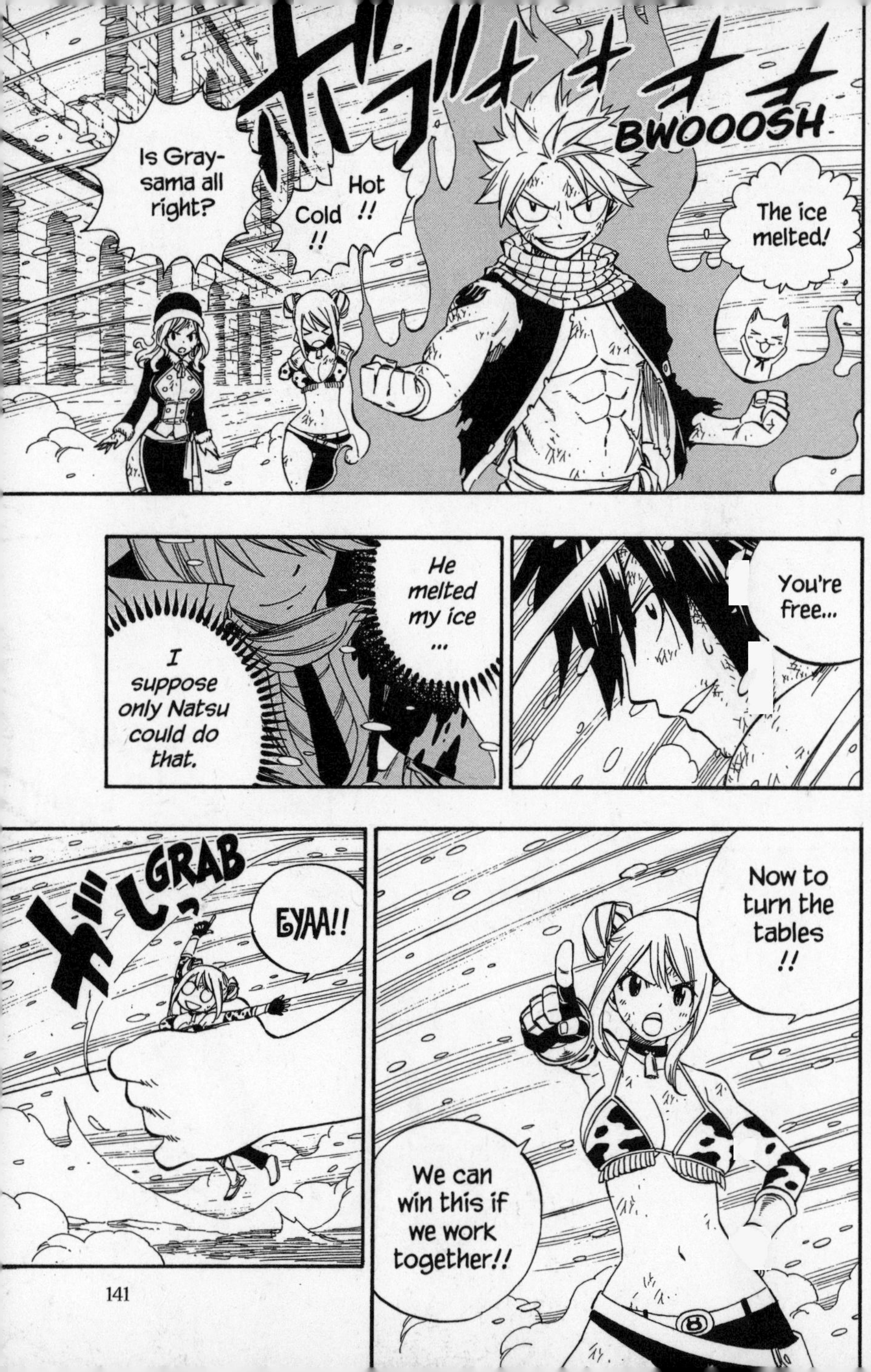
BWOOOSH
The ice melted!
Hot!!
Cold!!
Is Gray-sama all right?
You're free...
He melted my ice...
I suppose only Natsu could do that.
Now to turn the tables!!
We can win this if we work together!!
GRAB
EYAA!!

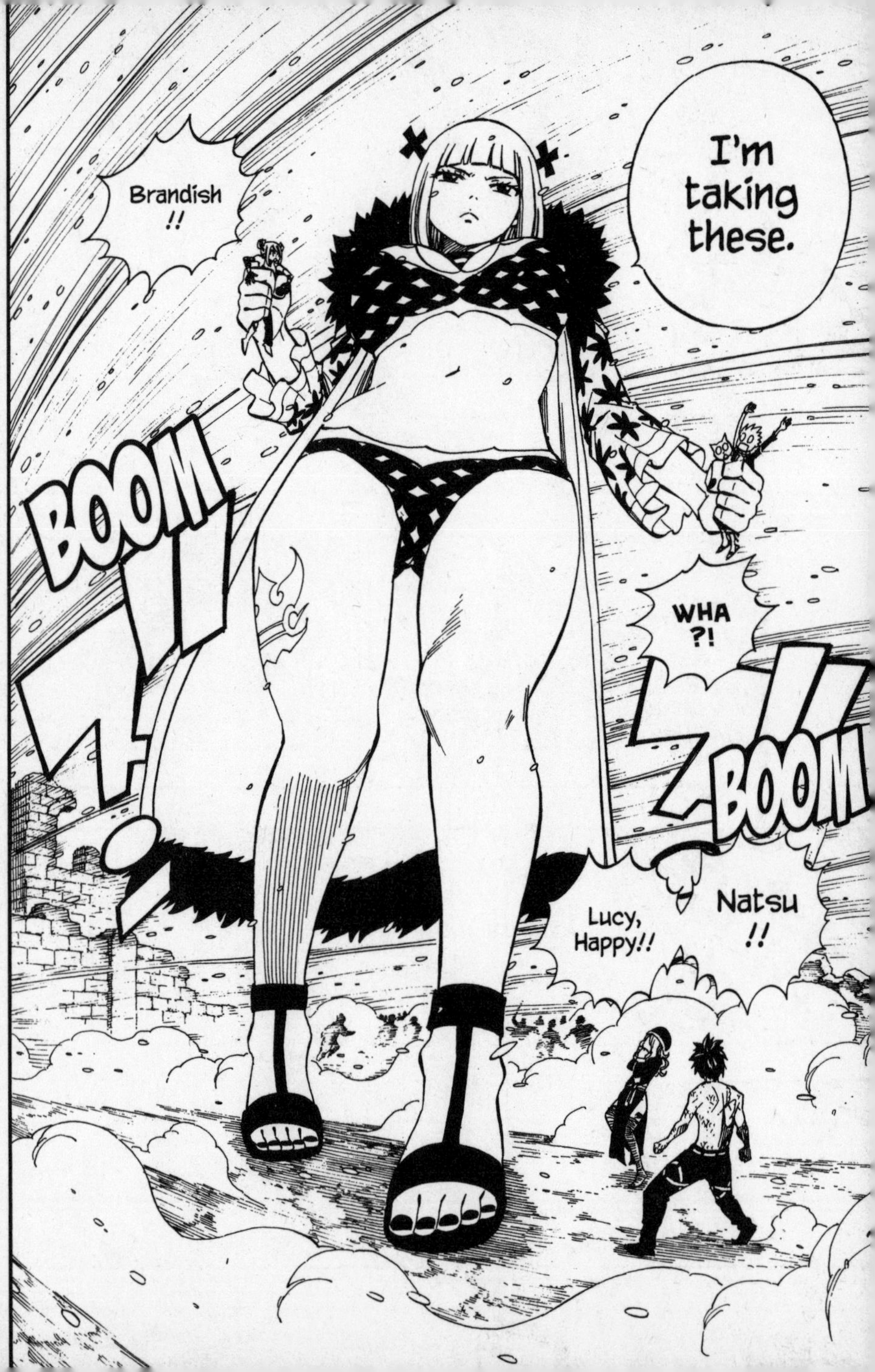
I'm taking these.
Brandish!!
WHA?!
BOOM
BOOM
Natsu!!
Lucy, Happy!!

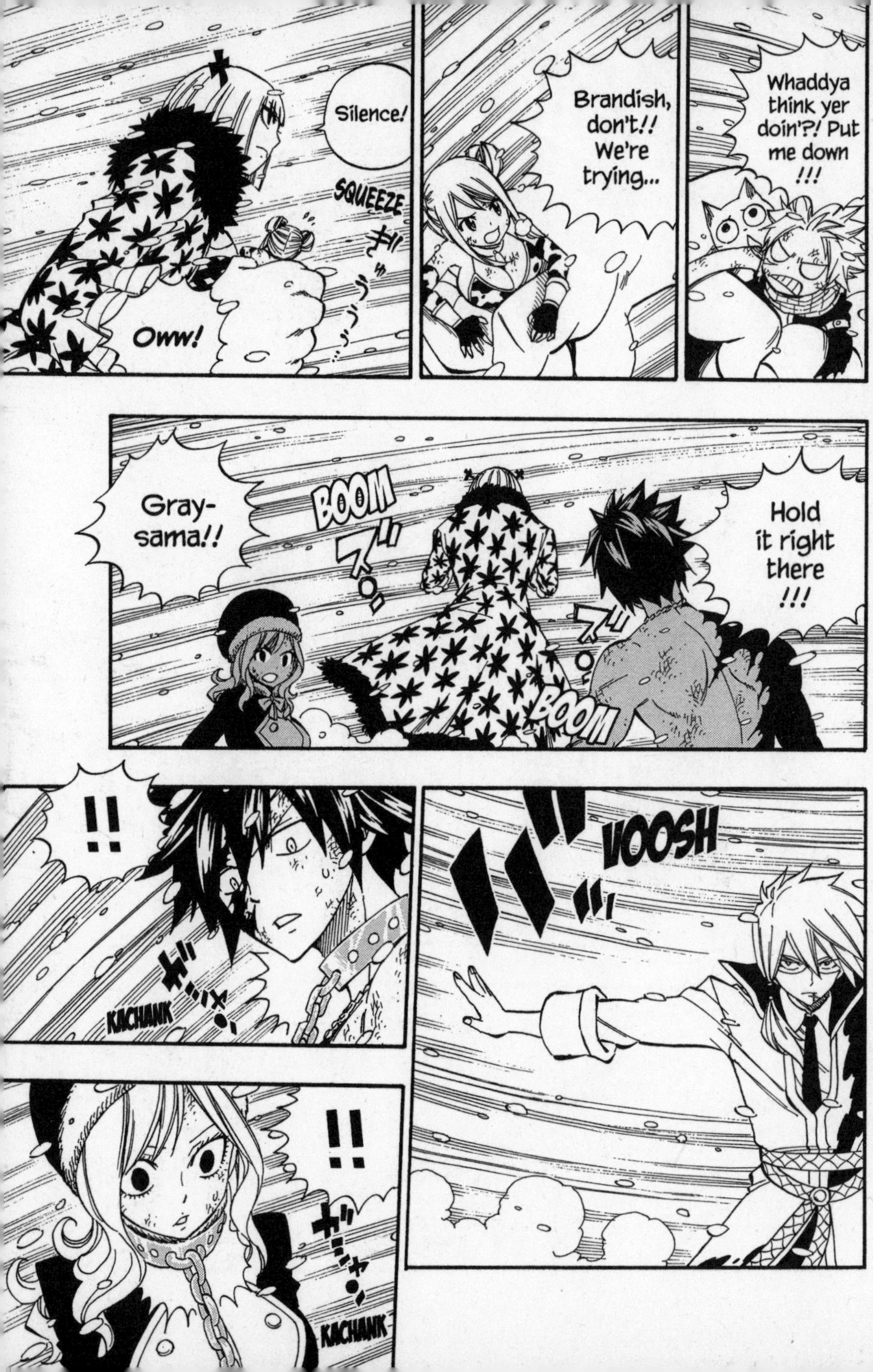

Whaddya think yer doin'?! Put me down !!!
Brandish, don't!! We're trying...
Silence!
SQUEEZE
Oww!
Hold it right there !!!
BOOM
Gray-sama!!
BOOM
VOOSH
!!
KACHANK
!!
KACHANK

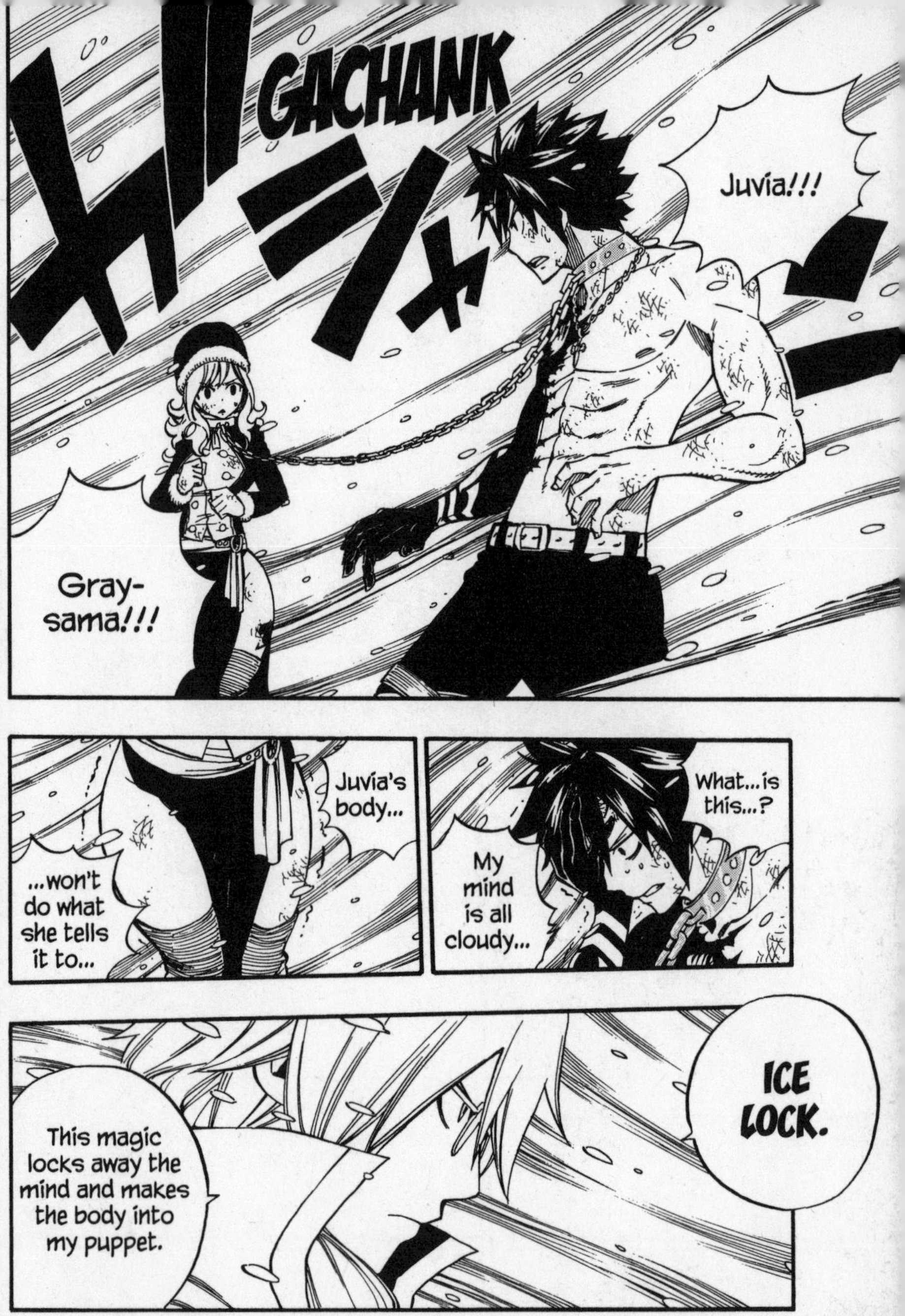
GACHANK
Juvia!!!
Gray-sama!!!
Juvia's body...
...won't do what she tells it to...
What...is this...?
My mind is all cloudy...
ICE LOCK.
This magic locks away the mind and makes the body into my puppet.

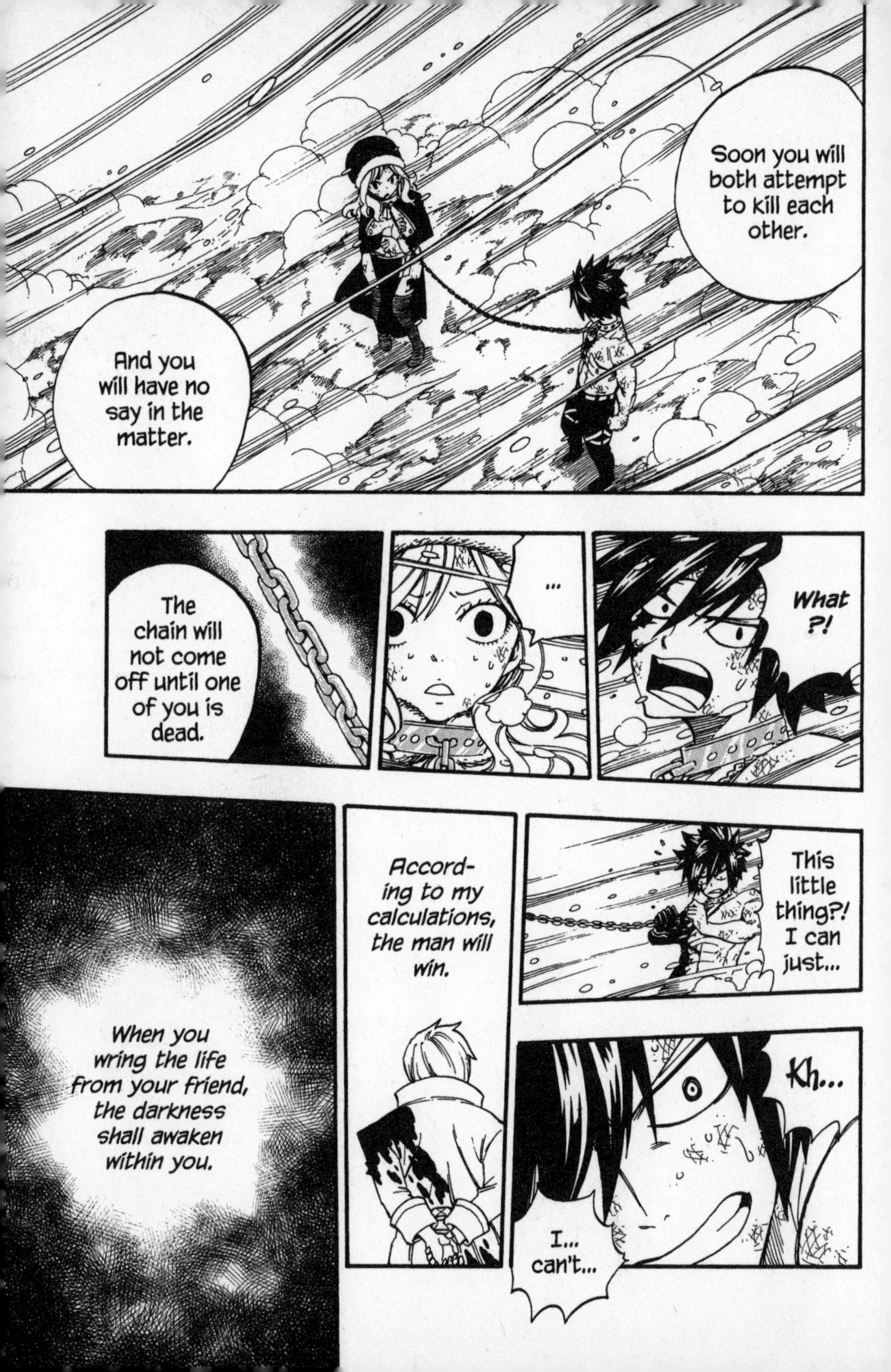

Soon you will both attempt to kill each other.
And you will have no say in the matter.
What?!
...
The chain will not come off until one of you is dead.
This little thing?! I can just...
Kh...
I... can't...
According to my calculations, the man will win.
When you wring the life from your friend, the darkness shall awaken within you.

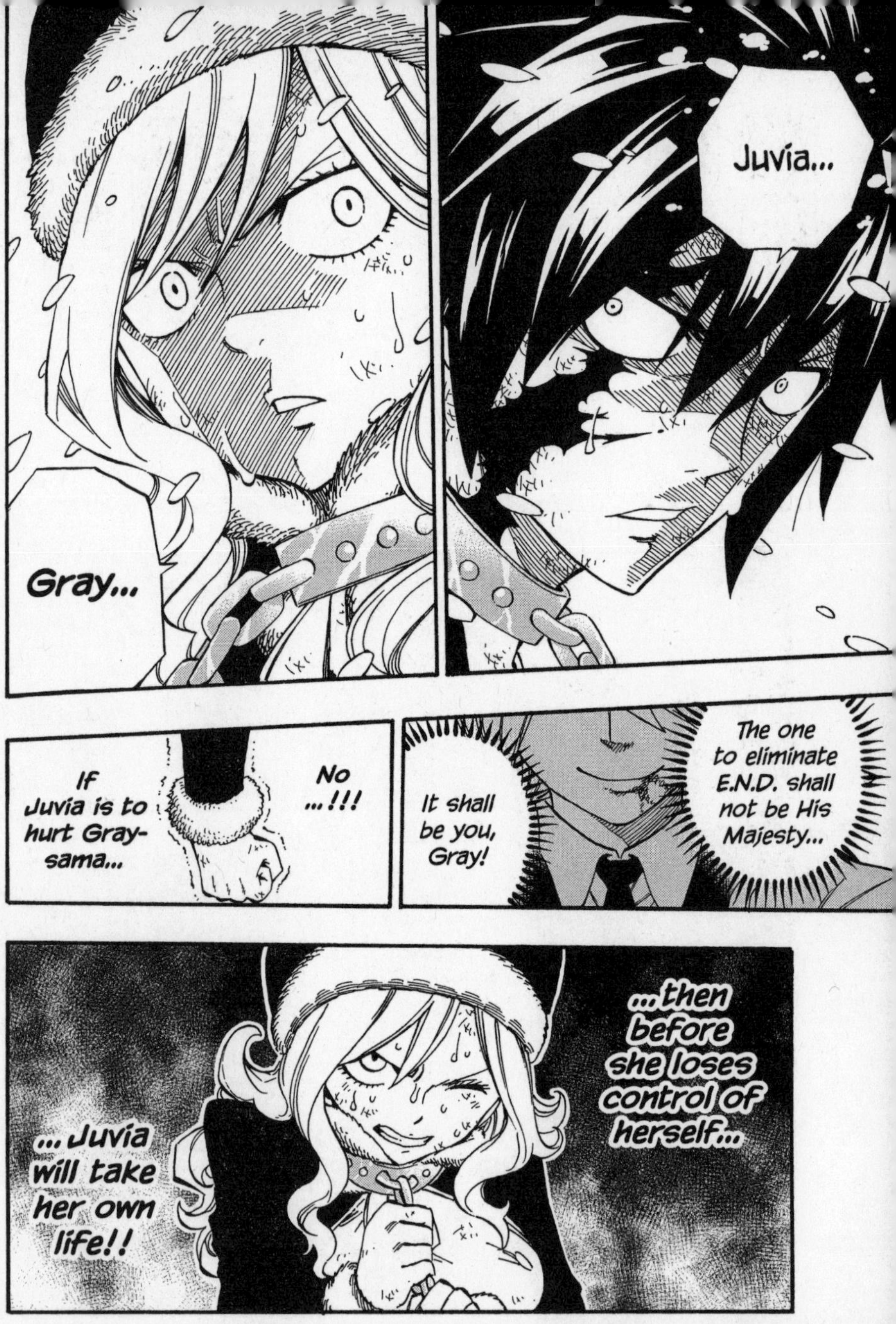
Juvia...
Gray...
The one to eliminate E.N.D. shall not be His Majesty...
It shall be you, Gray!
No ...!!!
If Juvia is to hurt Gray-sama...
...then before she loses control of herself...
...Juvia will take her own life!!

FAIRY TAIL

フェアリーテイル

Chapter 499: Gray and Juvia

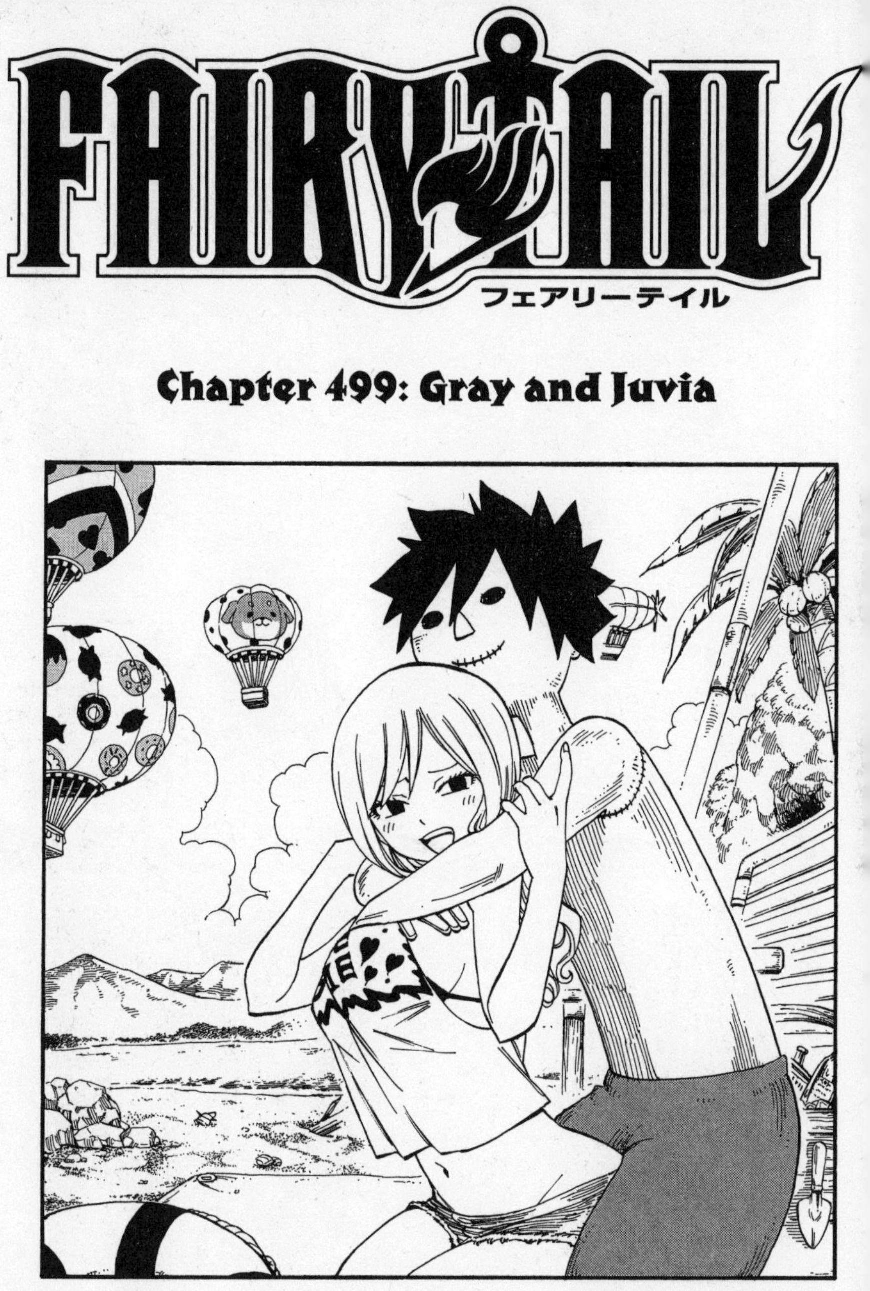

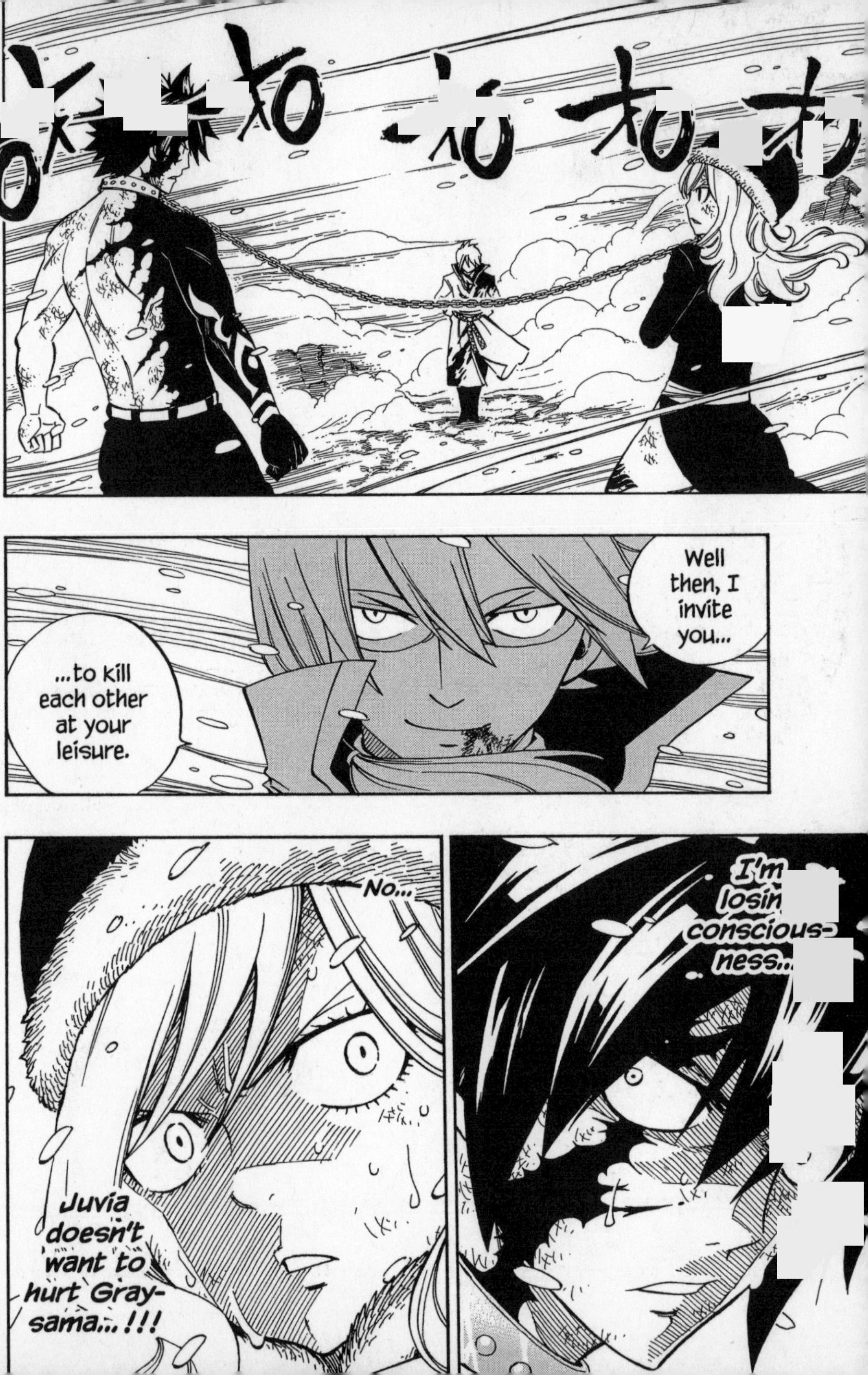
Well then, I invite you...
...to kill each other at your leisure.
I'm losin conscious-ness...
No...
Juvia doesn't want to hurt Gray-sama...!!!

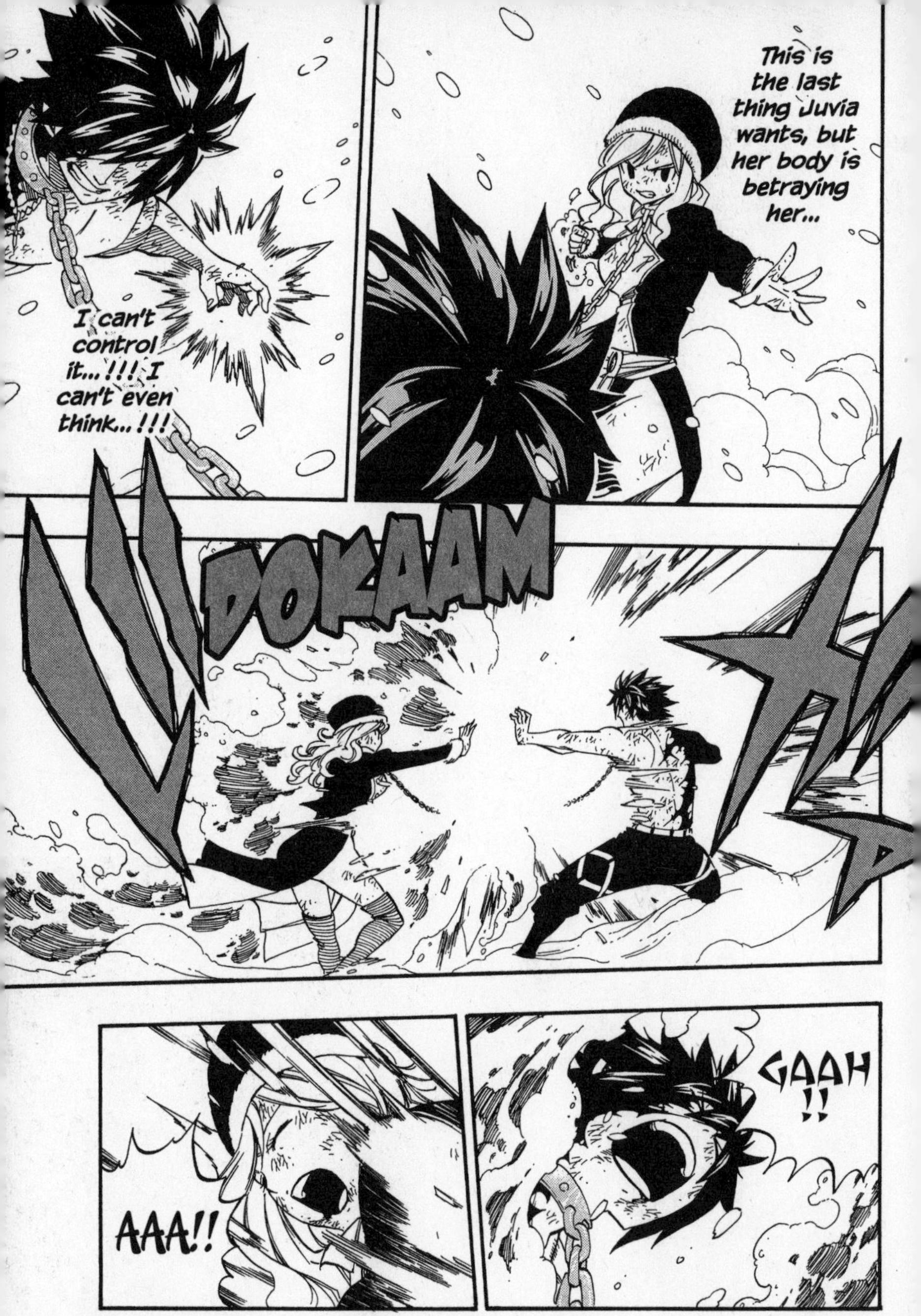
This is the last thing Juvia wants, but her body is betraying her...
I can't control it...!!! I can't even think...!!!
DOKAAM
GAAH!!
AAA!!

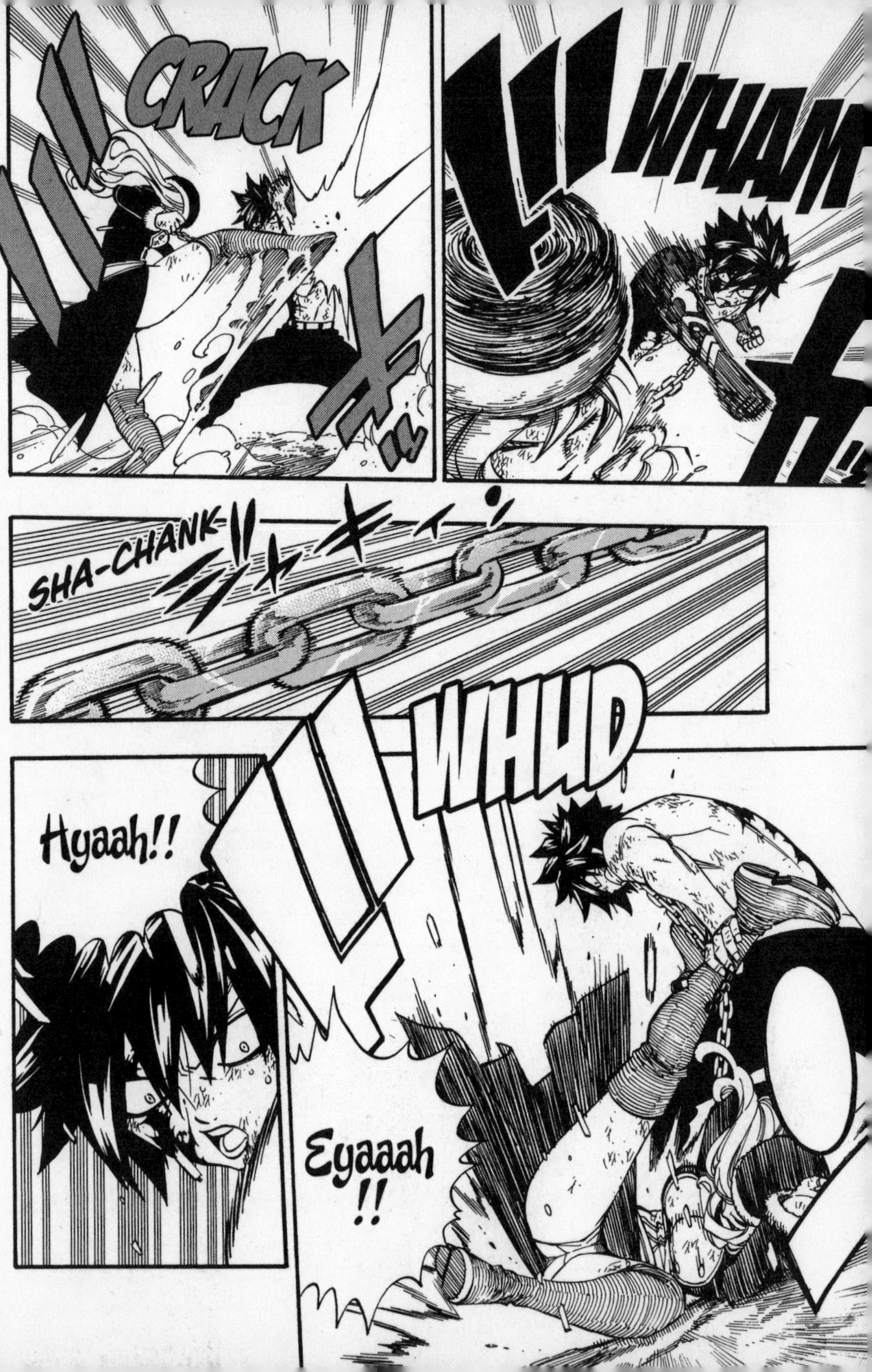
WHAM
CRACK
SHA-CHANK!!
WHUD
Eyaaah!!
Hyaah!!

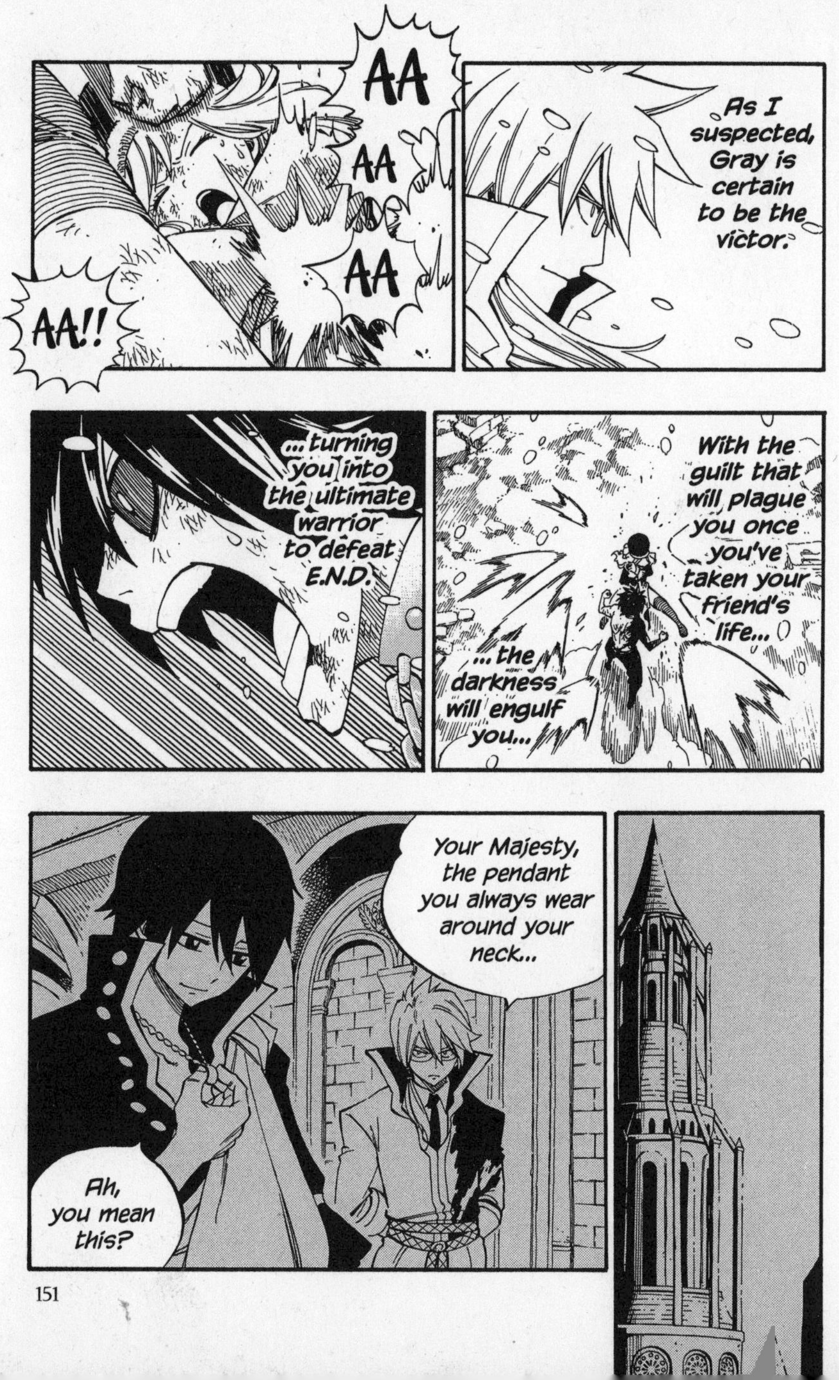

As I suspected, Gray is certain to be the victor.
AA
AA
AA
AA!!
With the guilt that will plague you once you've taken your friend's life...
...the darkness will engulf you...
...turning you into the ultimate warrior to defeat E.N.D.
Your Majesty, the pendant you always wear around your neck...
Ah, you mean this?

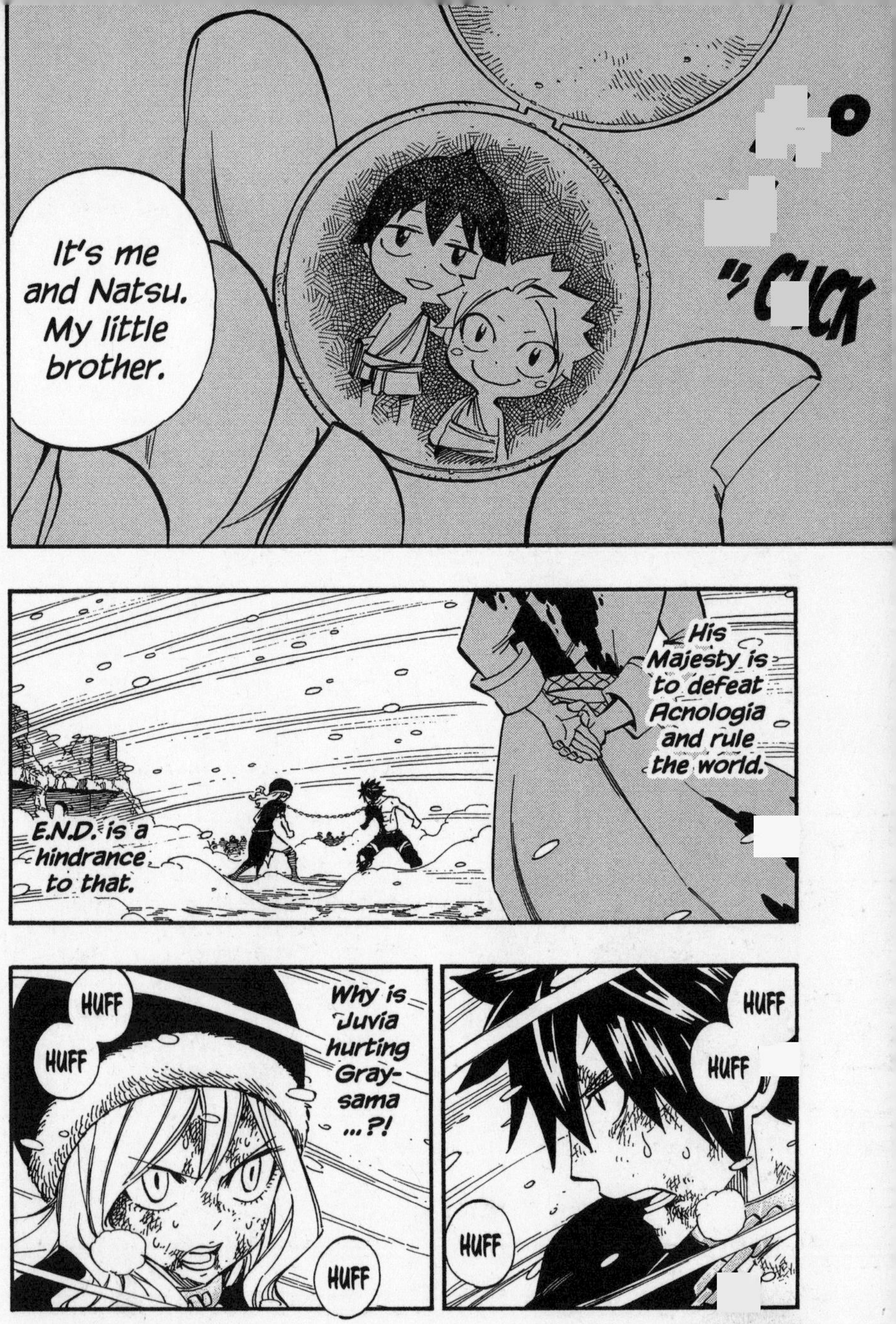
It's me and Natsu. My little brother.
His Majesty is to defeat Acnologia and rule the world.
E.N.D. is a hindrance to that.
HUFF
HUFF
HUFF
HUFF
HUFF
Why is Juvia hurting Gray-sama ...?!
HUFF

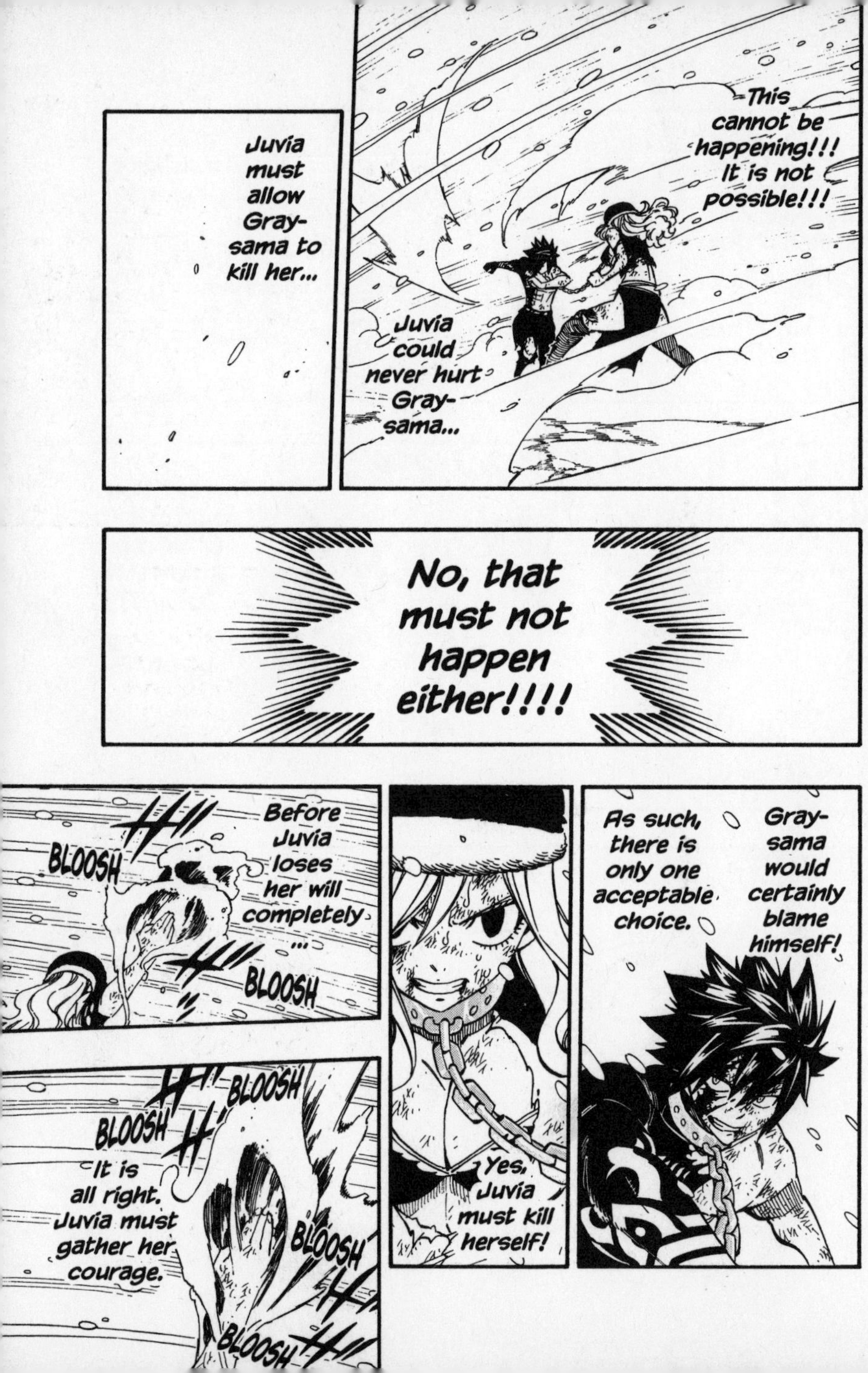
This cannot be happening!!! It is not possible!!!
Juvia could never hurt Gray-sama...
Juvia must allow Gray-sama to kill her...
No, that must not happen either!!!!
Gray-sama would certainly blame himself!
As such, there is only one acceptable choice.
Yes, Juvia must kill herself!
Before Juvia loses her will completely...
BLOOSH
BLOOSH
BLOOSH
BLOOSH
It is all right. Juvia must gather her courage.
BLOOSH
BLOOSH

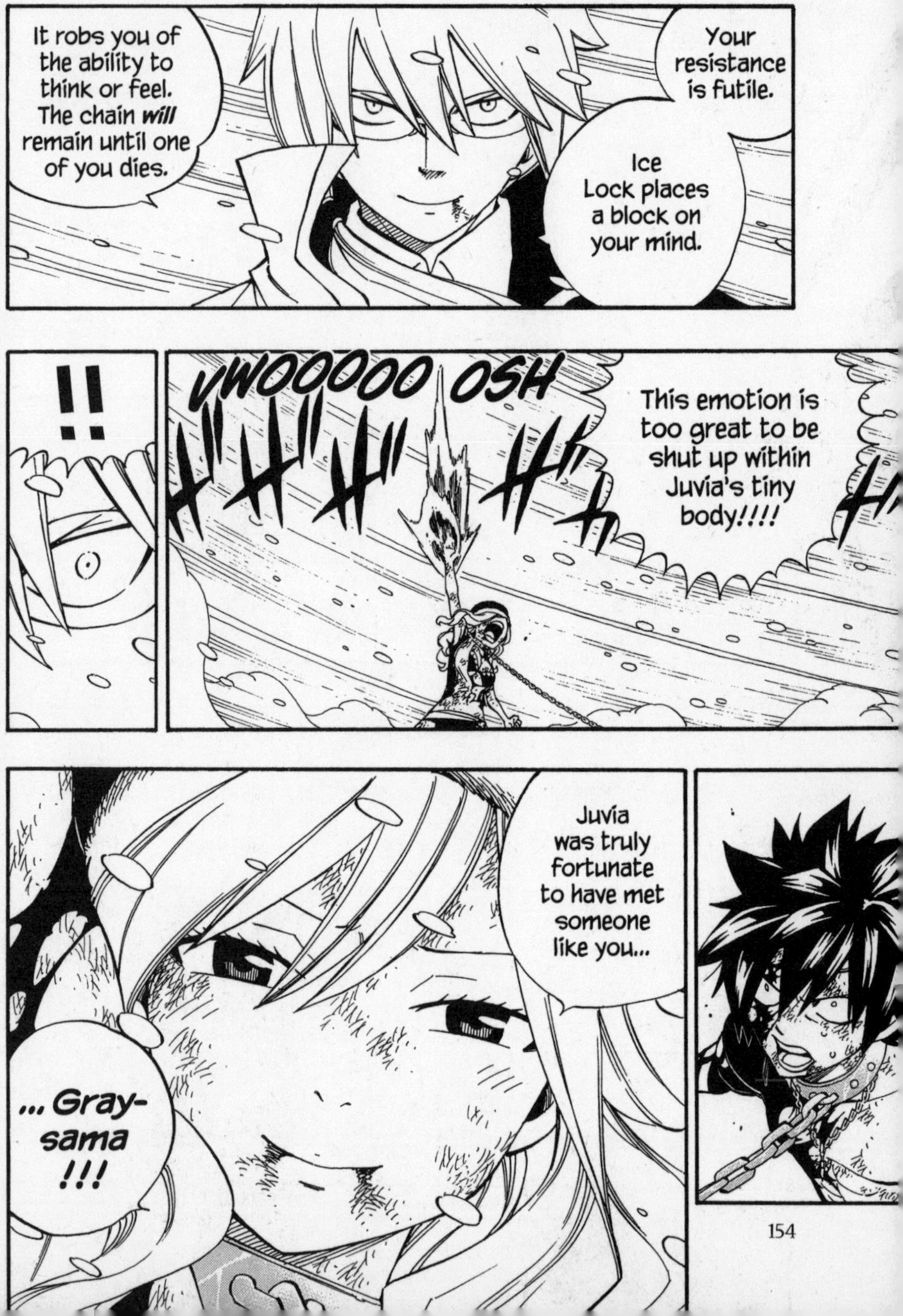
Your resistance is futile.
Ice Lock places a block on your mind.
It robs you of the ability to think or feel. The chain *will* remain until one of you dies.
VWOOOOO OSH
This emotion is too great to be shut up within Juvia's tiny body!!!!
!!
Juvia was truly fortunate to have met someone like you...
... Gray-sama !!!

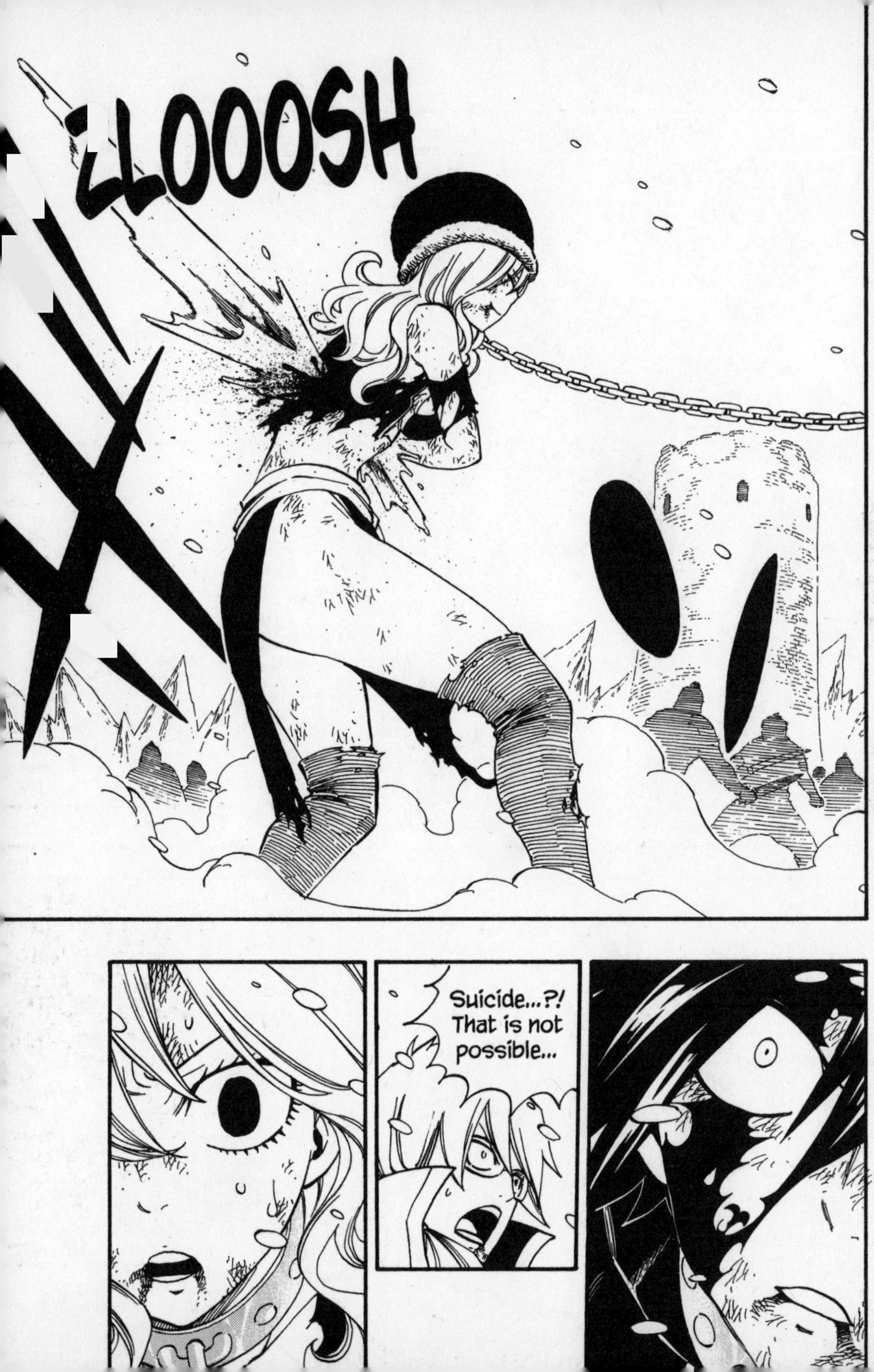
ZLOOOSH
Suicide...?! That is not possible...

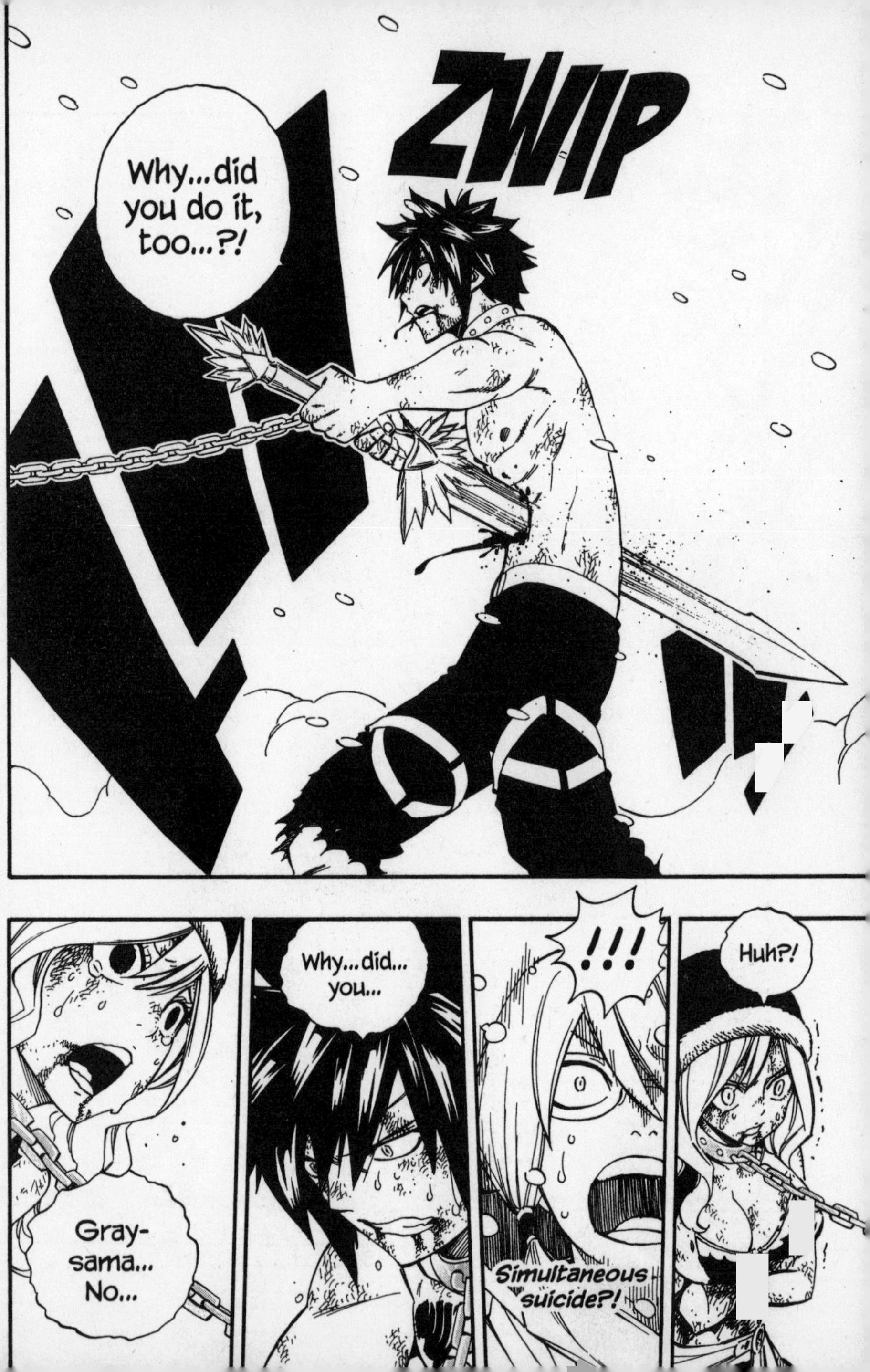
ZWIP
Why...did you do it, too...?!
Huh?!
!!!
Simultaneous suicide?!
Why...did... you...
Gray-sama... No...

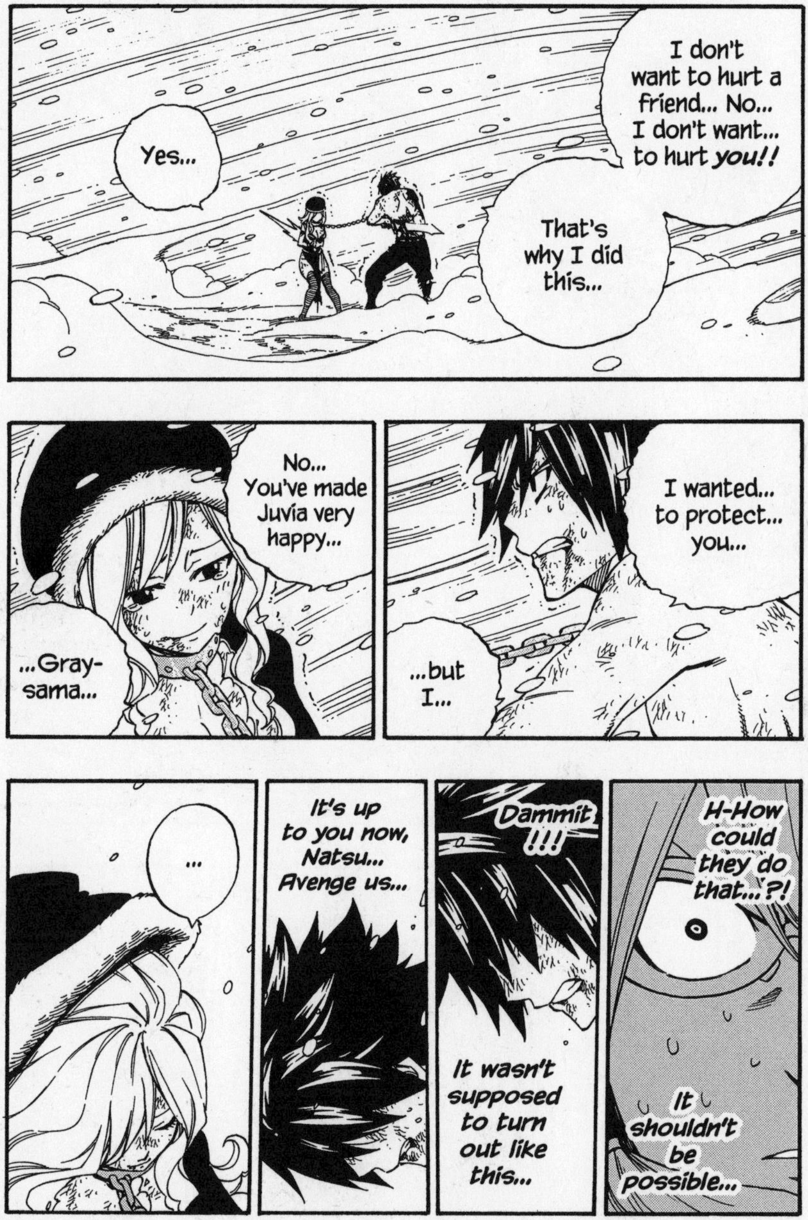
I don't want to hurt a friend... No... I don't want... to hurt *you!!*
That's why I did this...
Yes...
I wanted... to protect... you...
...but I...
No... You've made Juvia very happy...
...Gray-sama...
H-How could they do that...?!
It shouldn't be possible...
Dammit!!!
It wasn't supposed to turn out like this...
It's up to you now, Natsu... Avenge us...
...

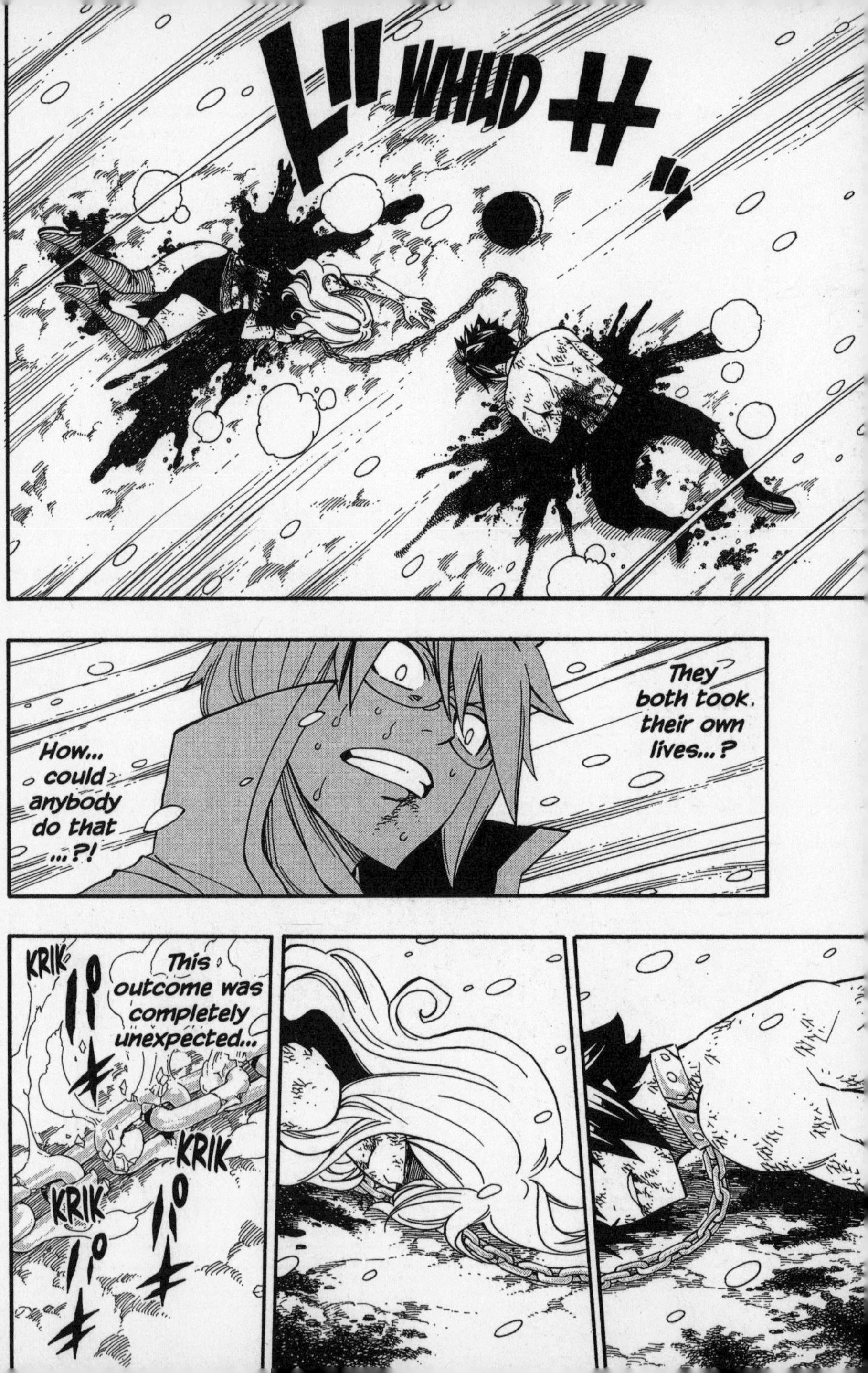
WHUD
They both took their own lives...?
How... could anybody do that ...?!
This outcome was completely unexpected...
KRIK
KRIK
KRIK

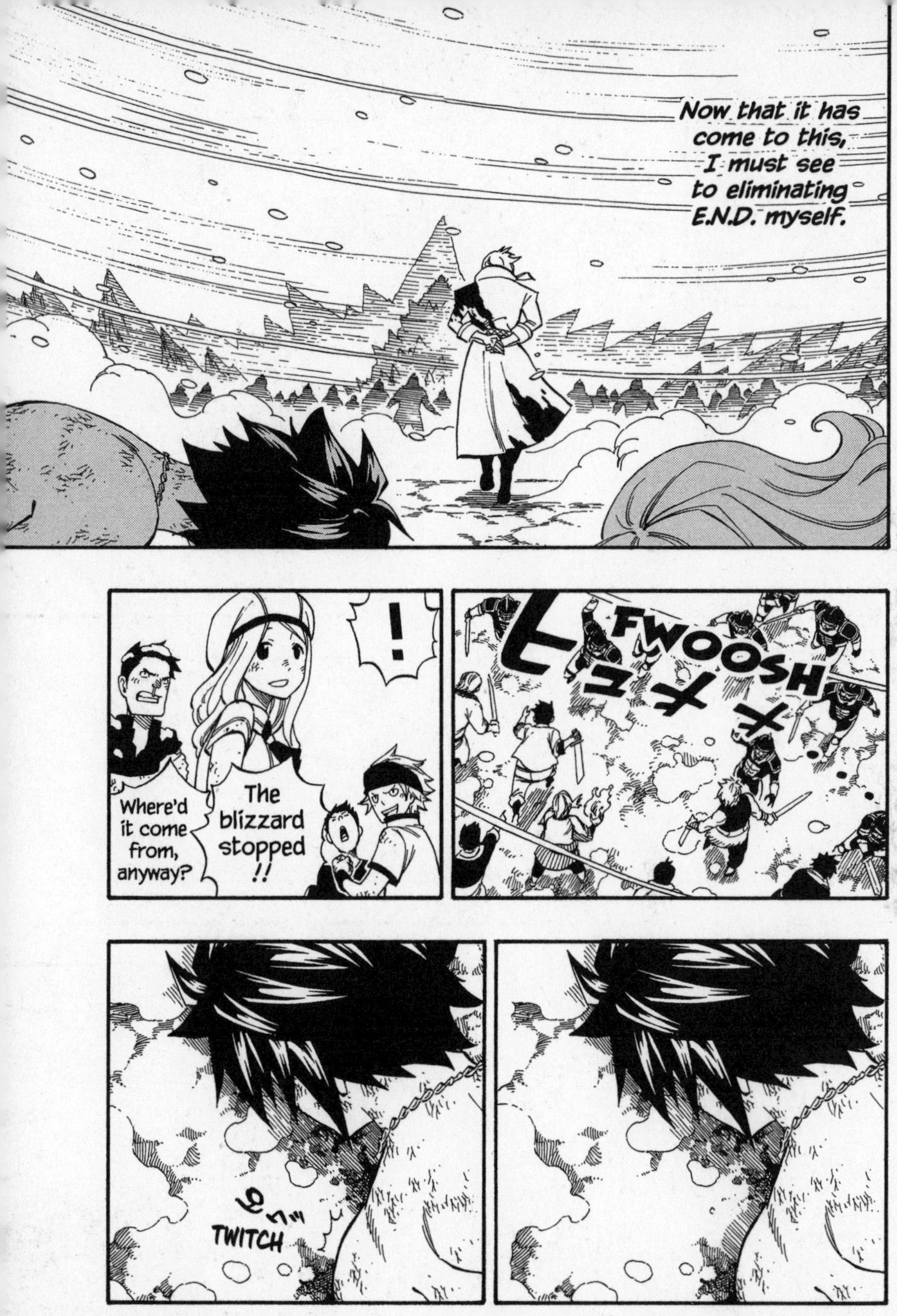
Now that it has come to this, I must see to eliminating E.N.D. myself.
FWOOSH
!
The blizzard stopped !!
Where'd it come from, anyway?
TWITCH

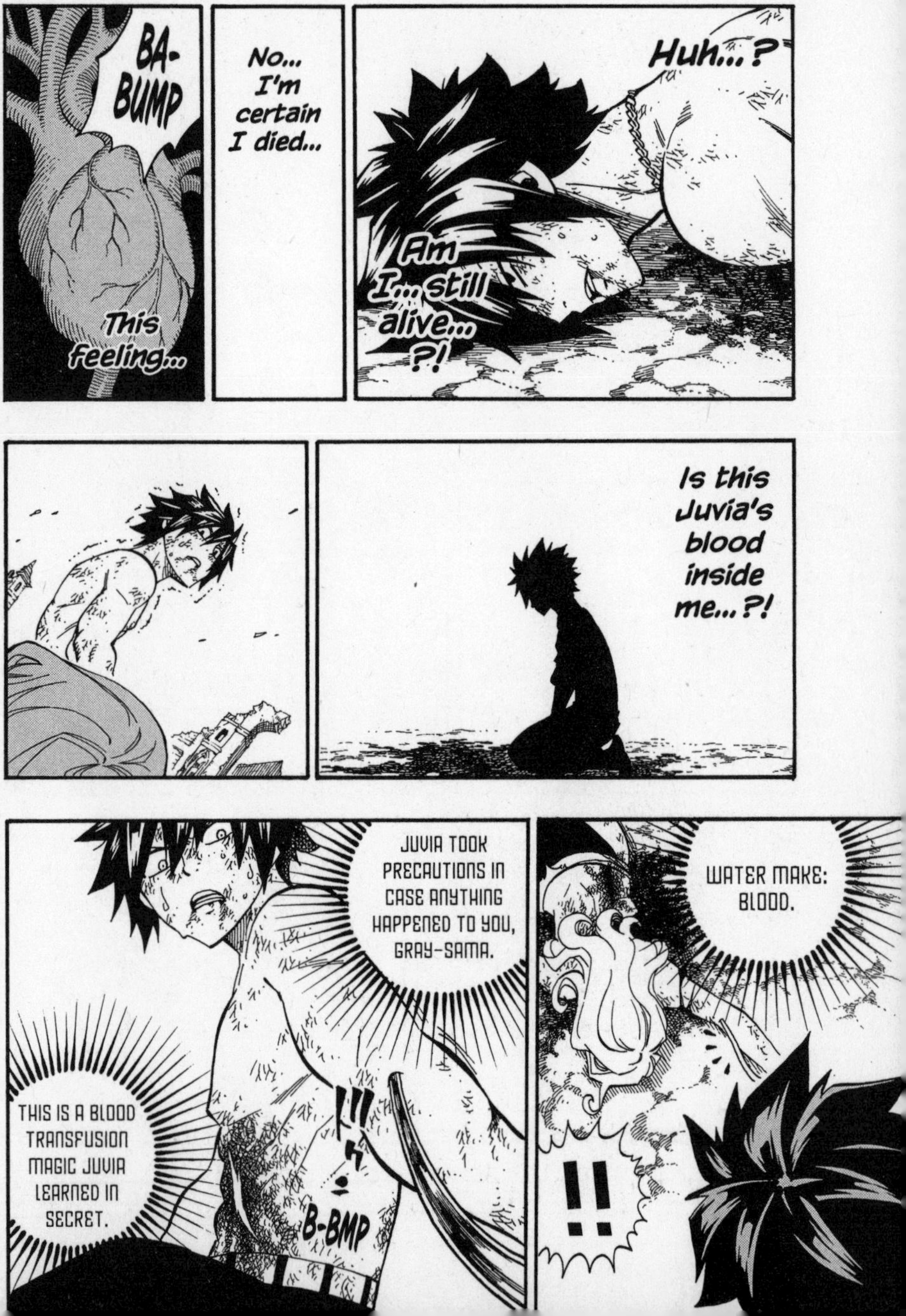
Huh...?
Am I... still alive...?!
No... I'm certain I died...
BA-BUMP
This feeling...
Is this Juvia's blood inside me...?!
WATER MAKE: BLOOD.
!!
JUVIA TOOK PRECAUTIONS IN CASE ANYTHING HAPPENED TO YOU, GRAY-SAMA.
!!
B-BMP
THIS IS A BLOOD TRANSFUSION MAGIC JUVIA LEARNED IN SECRET.

...

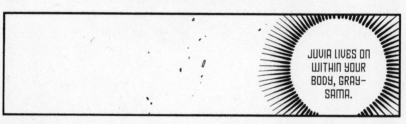

JUVIA LIVES ON WITHIN YOUR BODY, GRAY-SAMA.

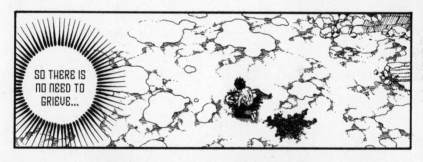

SO THERE IS NO NEED TO GRIEVE...

Juvia...

W...

Wait...

No...

PLIP

PLIP

PLIP

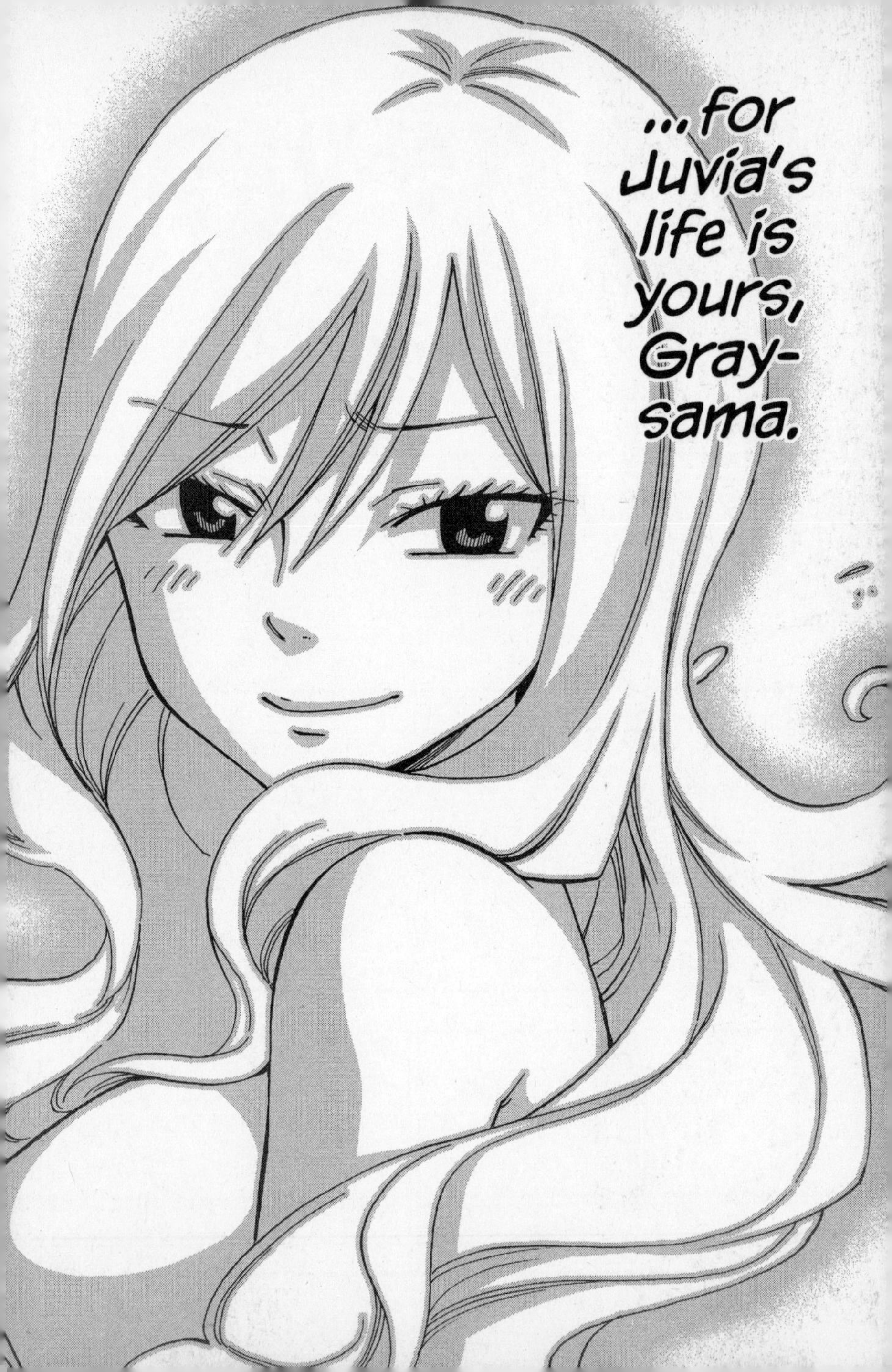
... for Juvia's life is yours, Gray-sama.

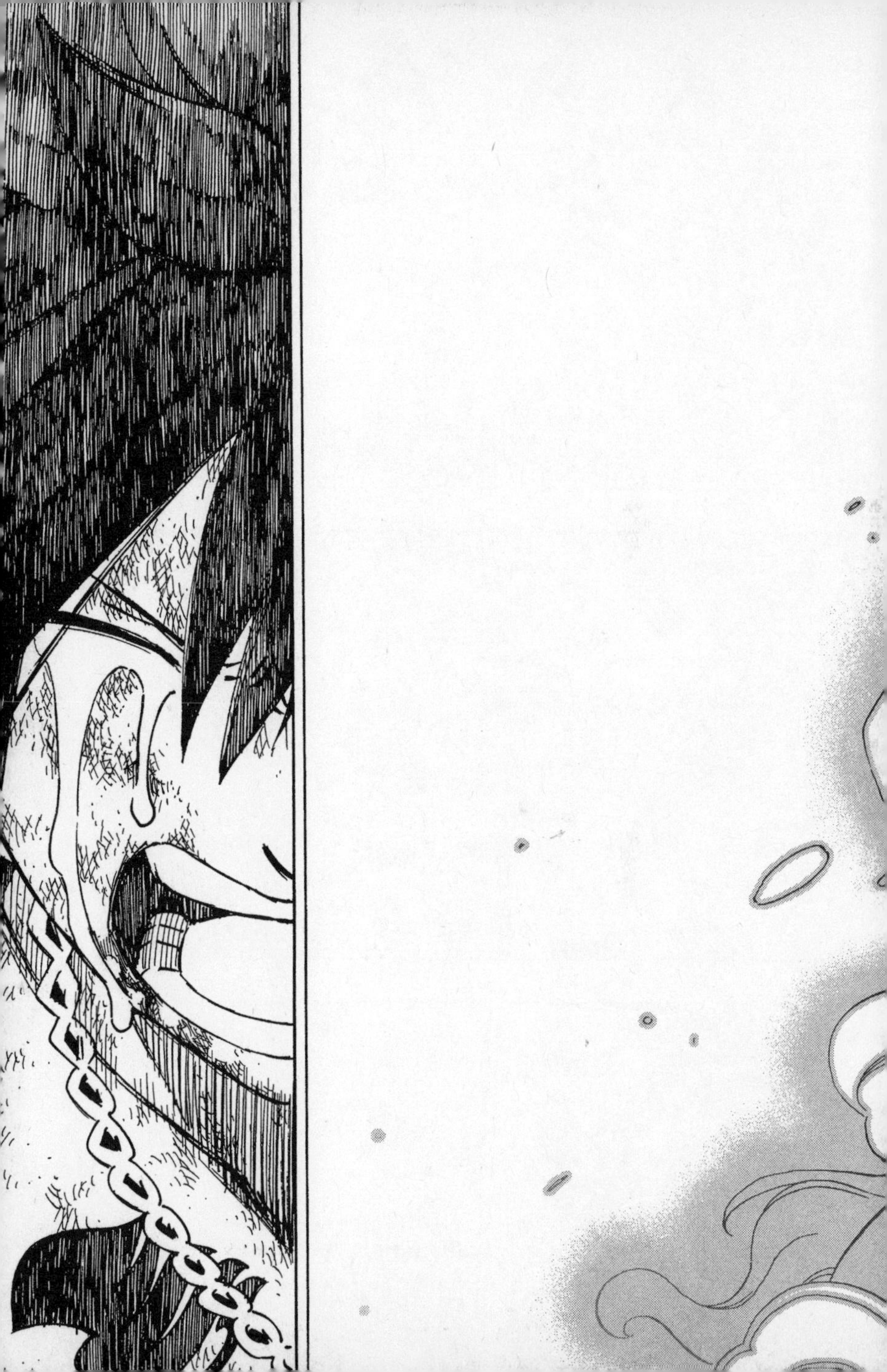

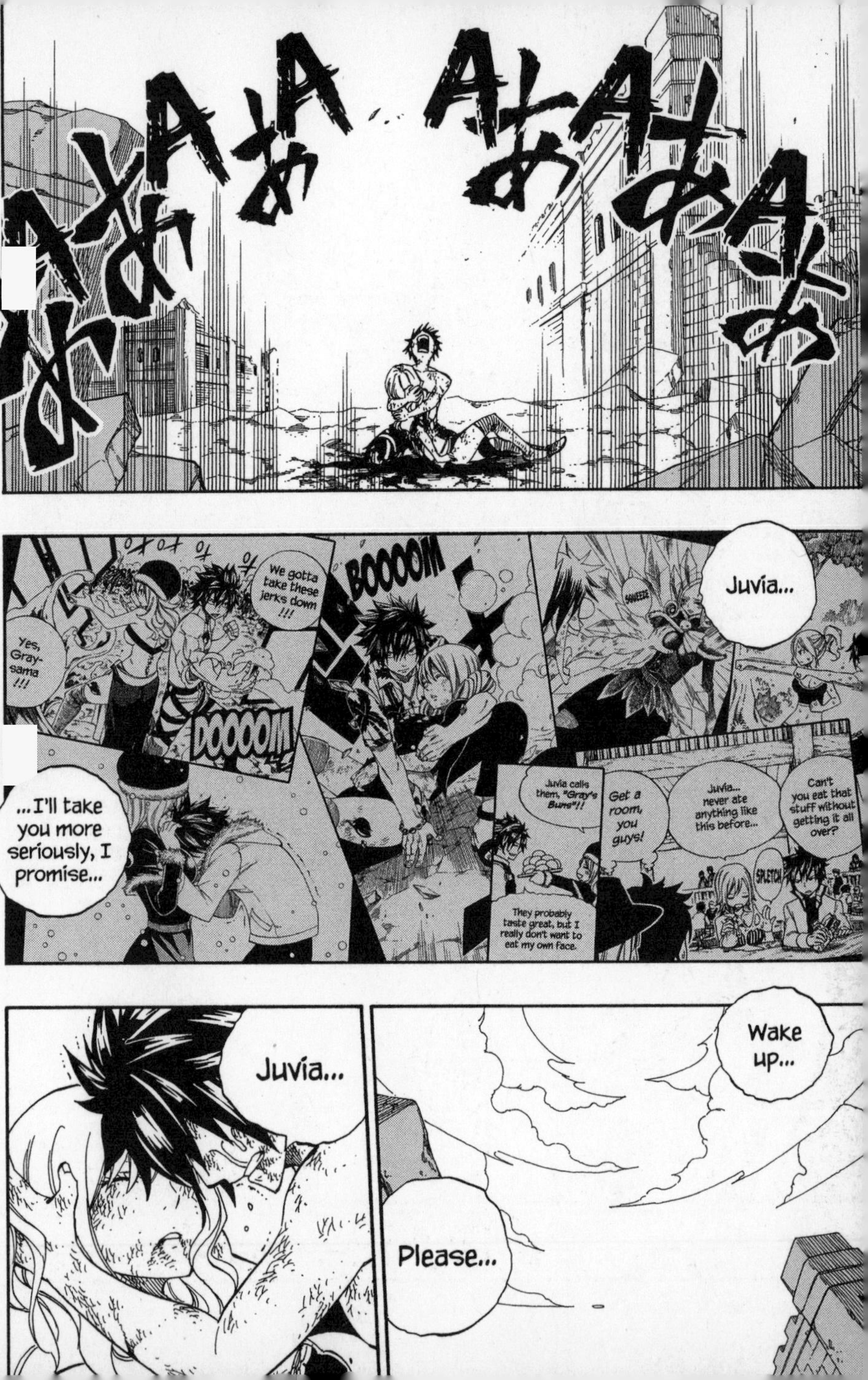

AAAAAA
Juvia...
SQUEEZE
Can't you eat that stuff without getting it all over?
SPLETCH
Juvia... never ate anything like this before...
Get a room, you guys!
Juvia calls them, "Gray's Buns"!!
They probably taste great, but I really don't want to eat my own face.
BOOOOM
We gotta take these jerks down!!!
Yes, Gray-sama!!!
DOOOOM
...I'll take you more seriously, I promise...
Wake up...
Please...
Juvia...

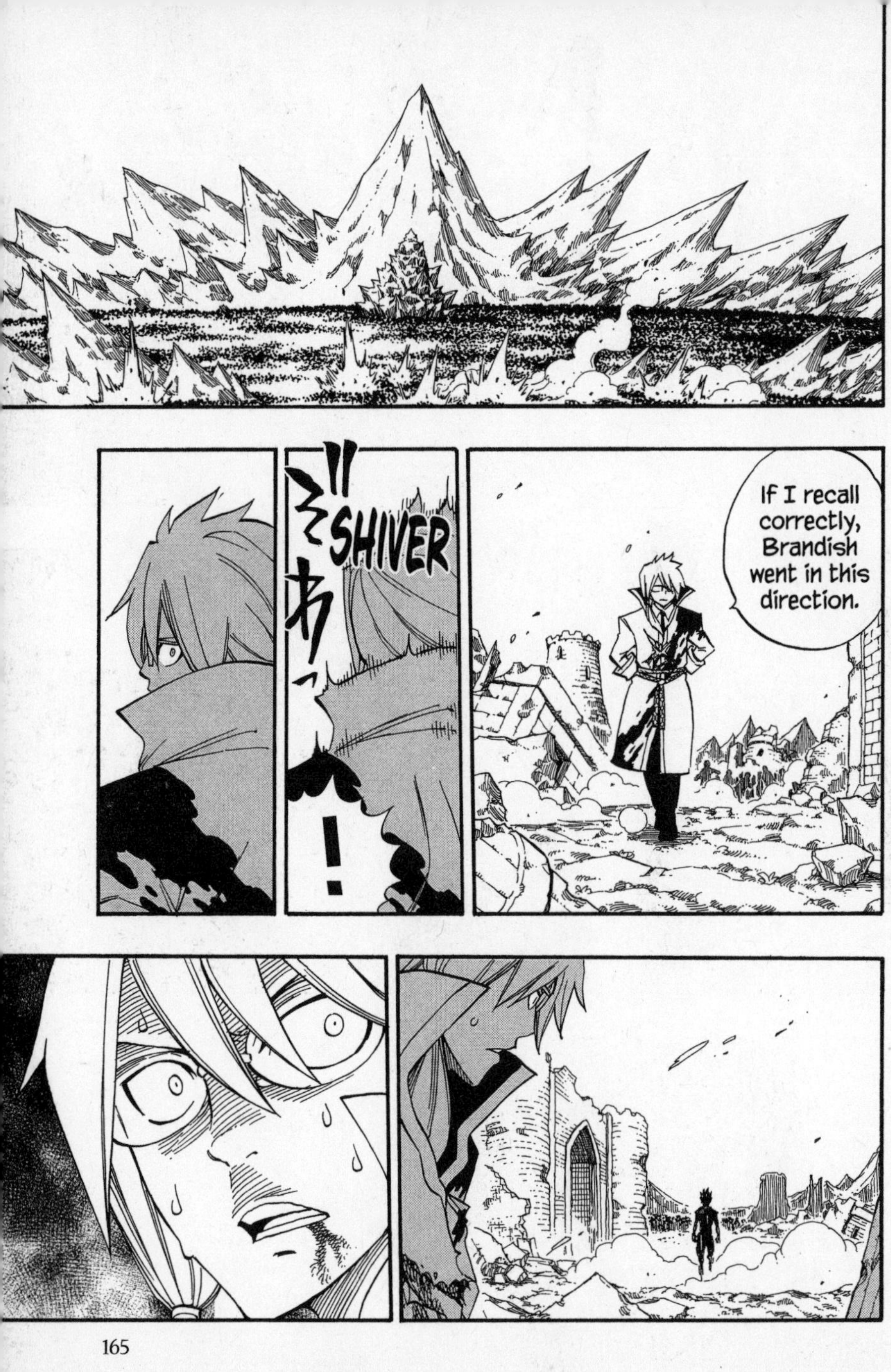
If I recall correctly, Brandish went in this direction.
SHIVER

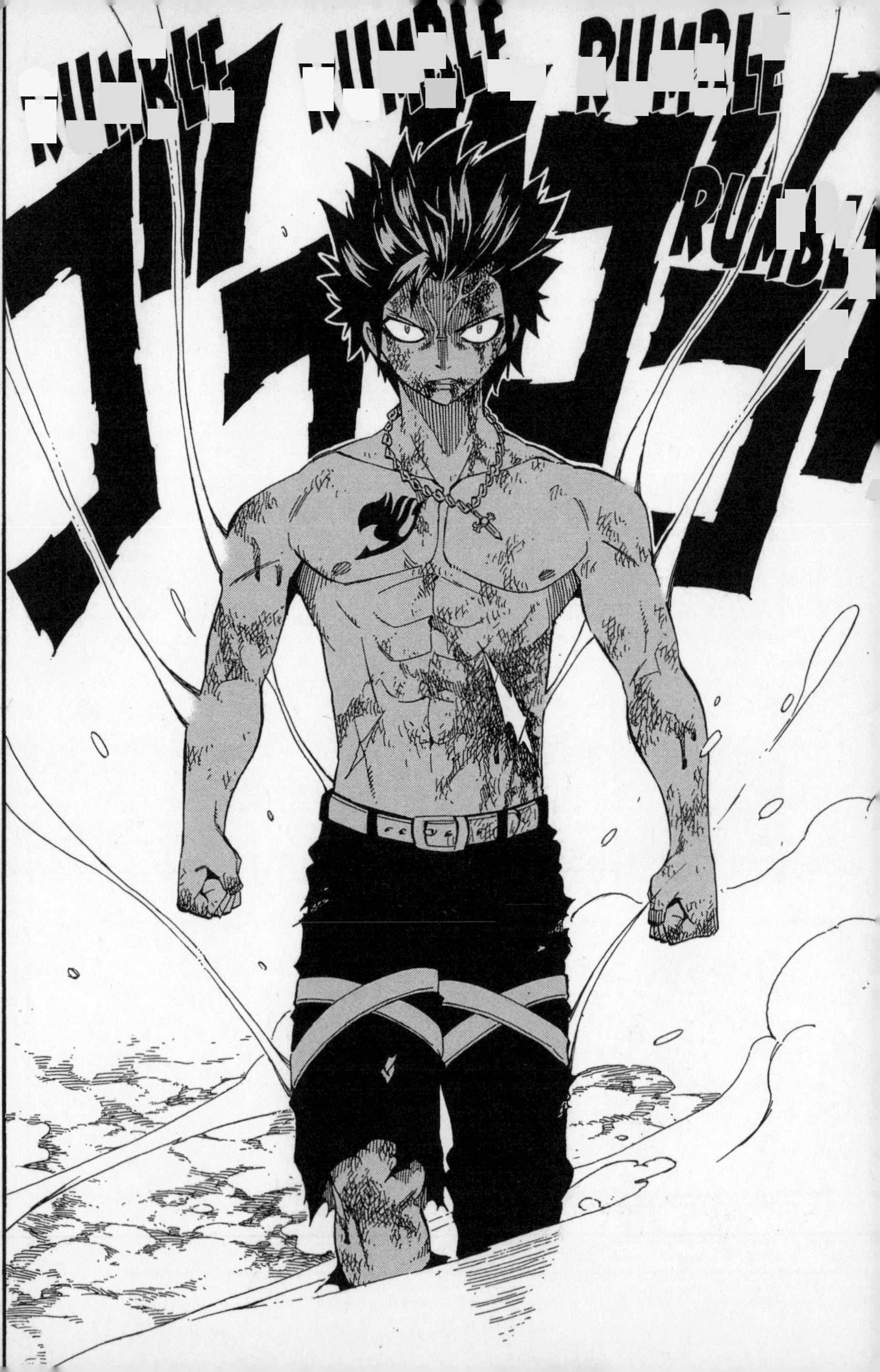
RUMBLE

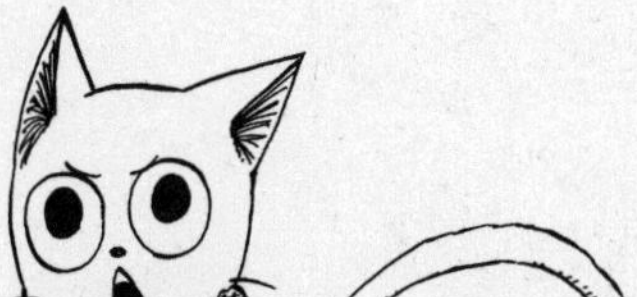

FAIRY TAIL

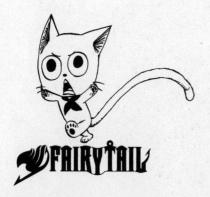

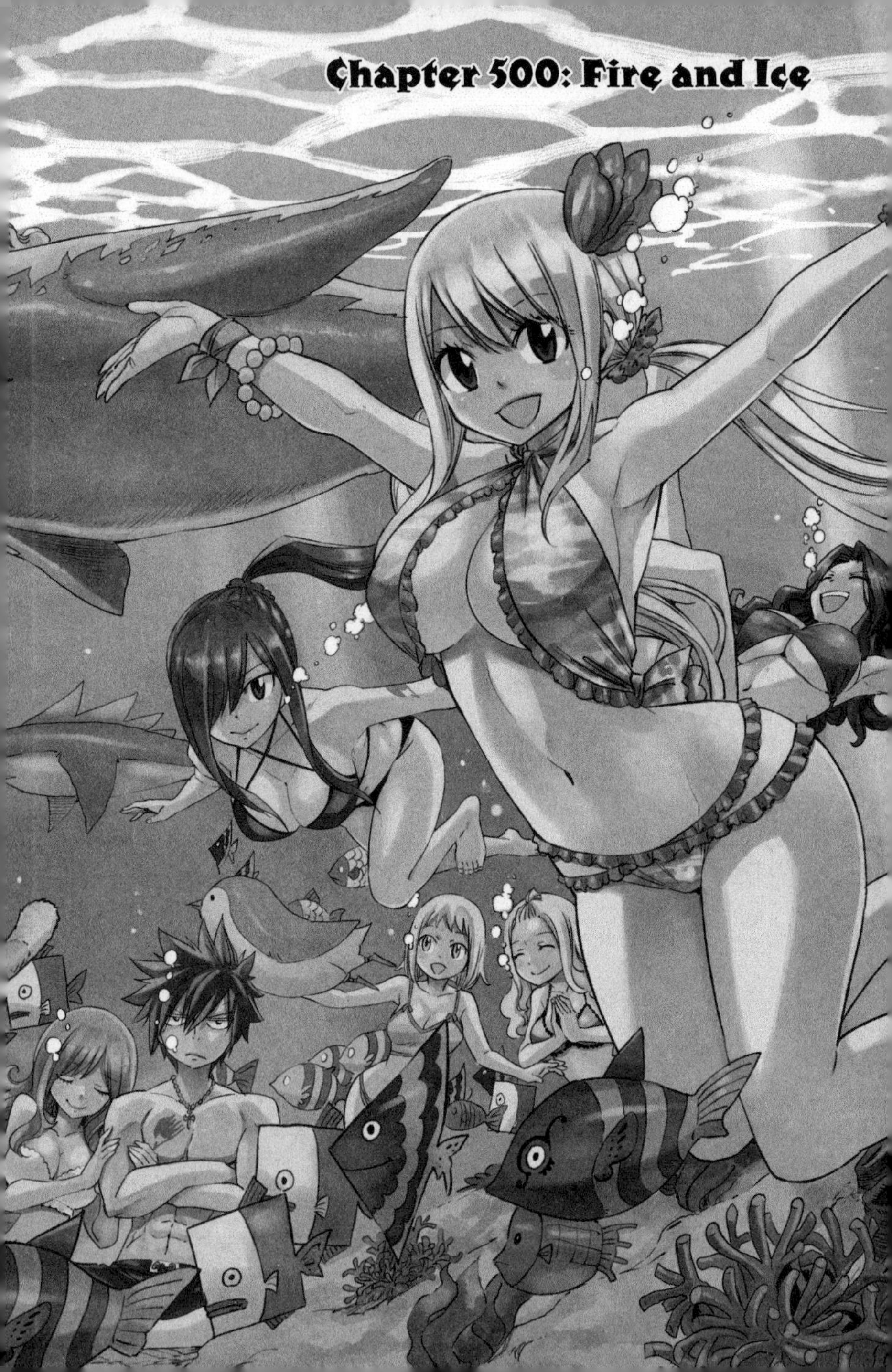
Chapter 500: Fire and Ice

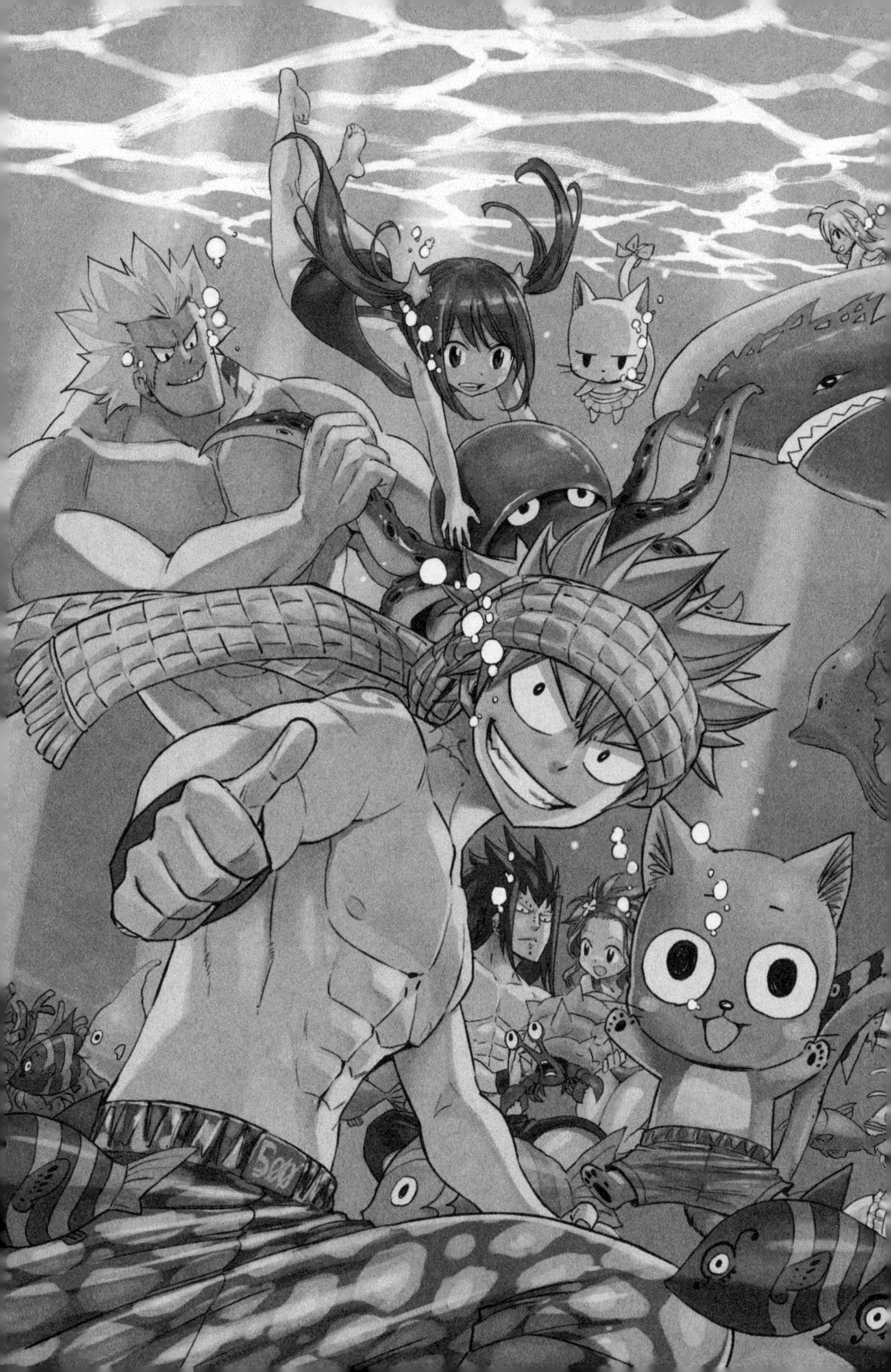

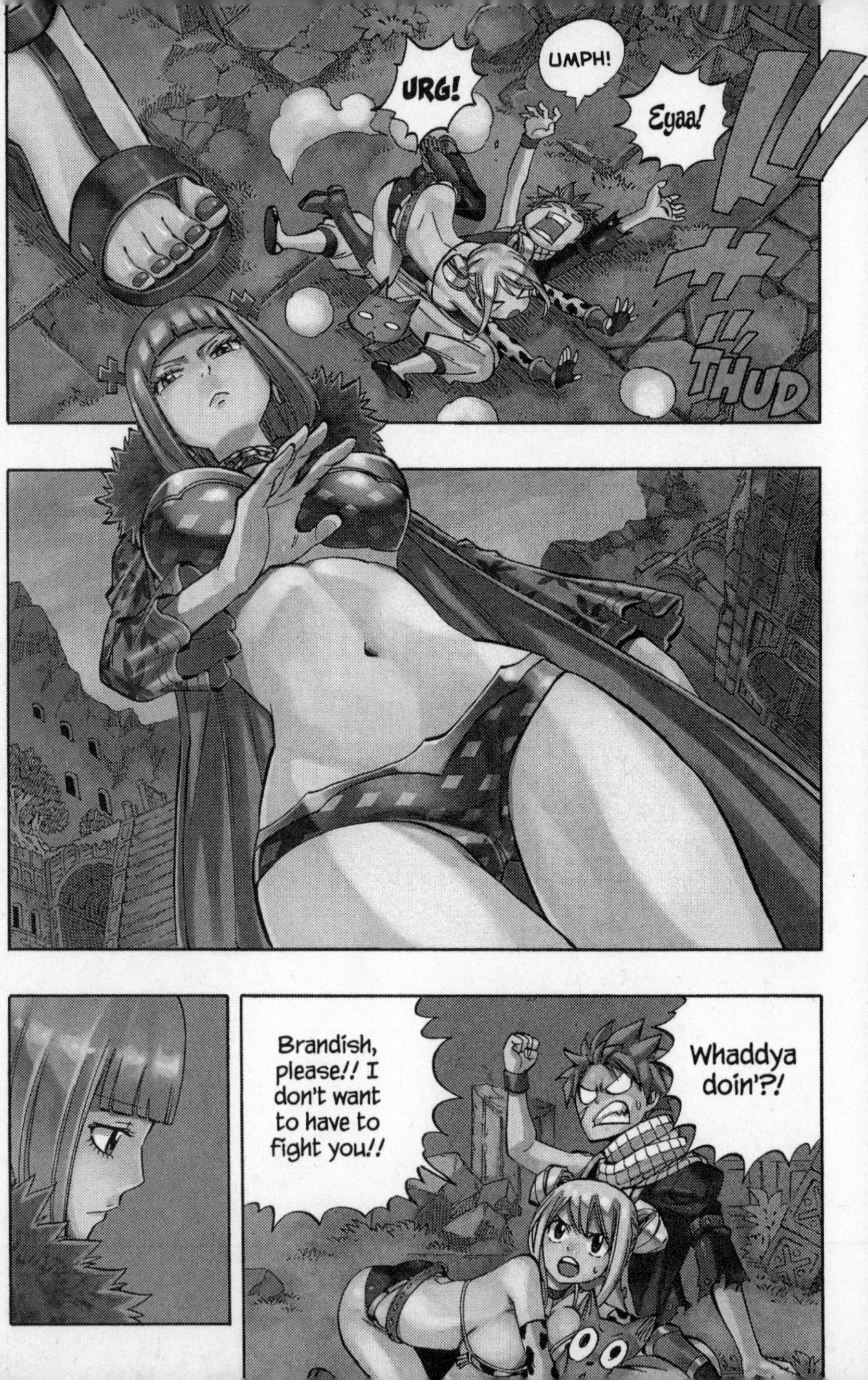
Eyaa!
UMPH!
URG!
THUD
Whaddya doin'?!
Brandish, please!! I don't want to have to fight you!!

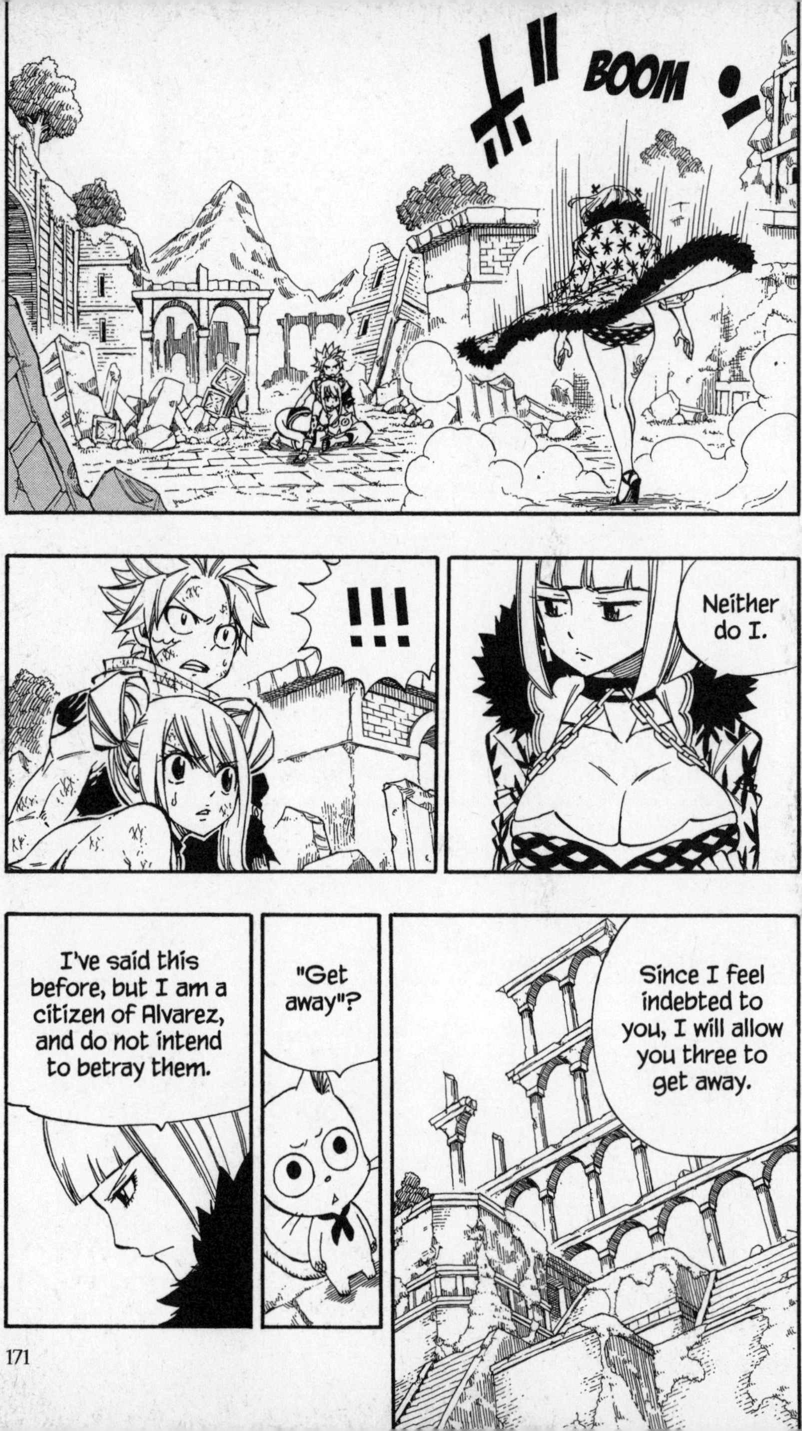
BOOM
Neither do I.
!!!
Since I feel indebted to you, I will allow you three to get away.
"Get away"?
I've said this before, but I am a citizen of Alvarez, and do not intend to betray them.

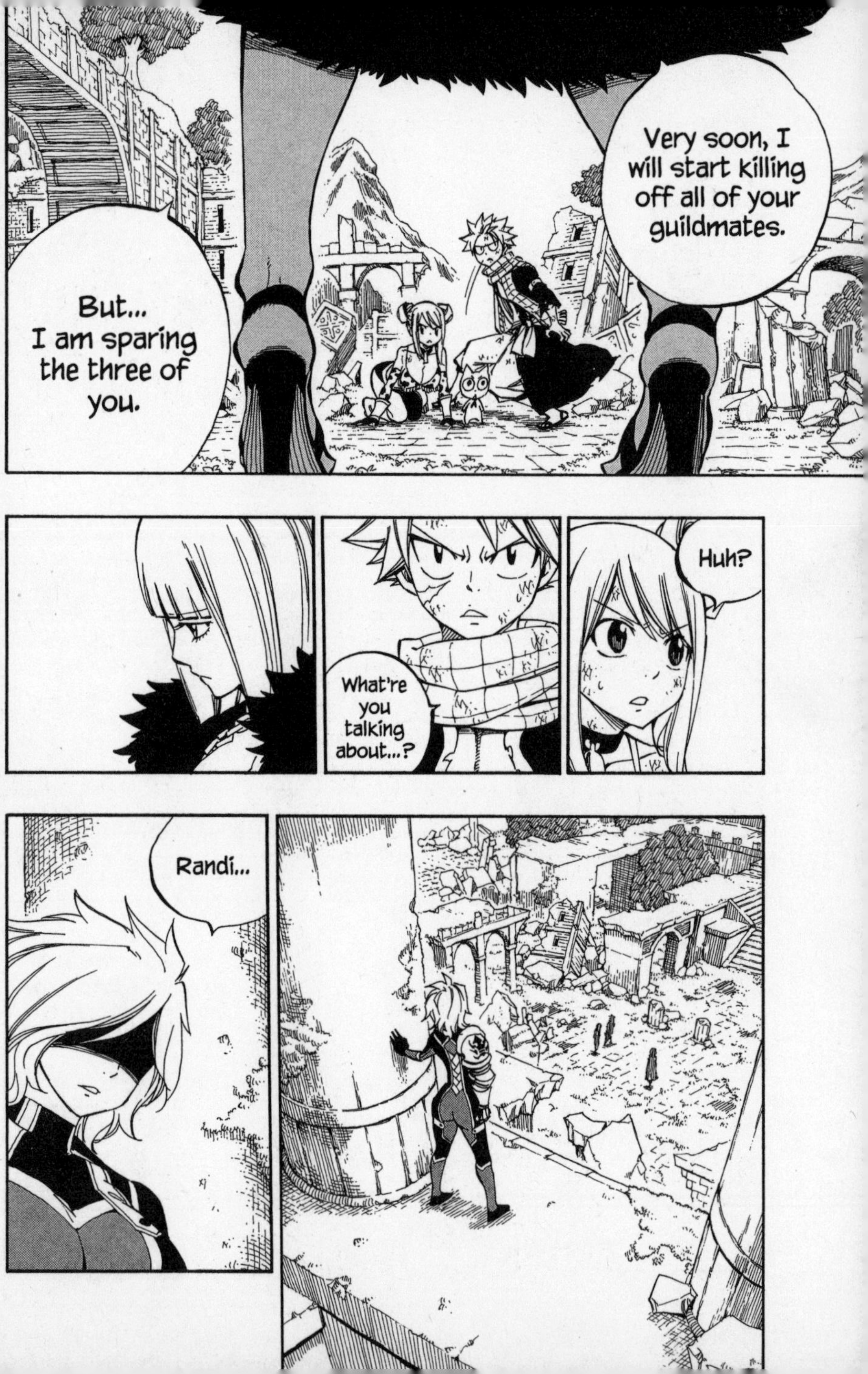
Very soon, I will start killing off all of your guildmates.
But... I am sparing the three of you.
Huh?
What're you talking about...?
Randi...

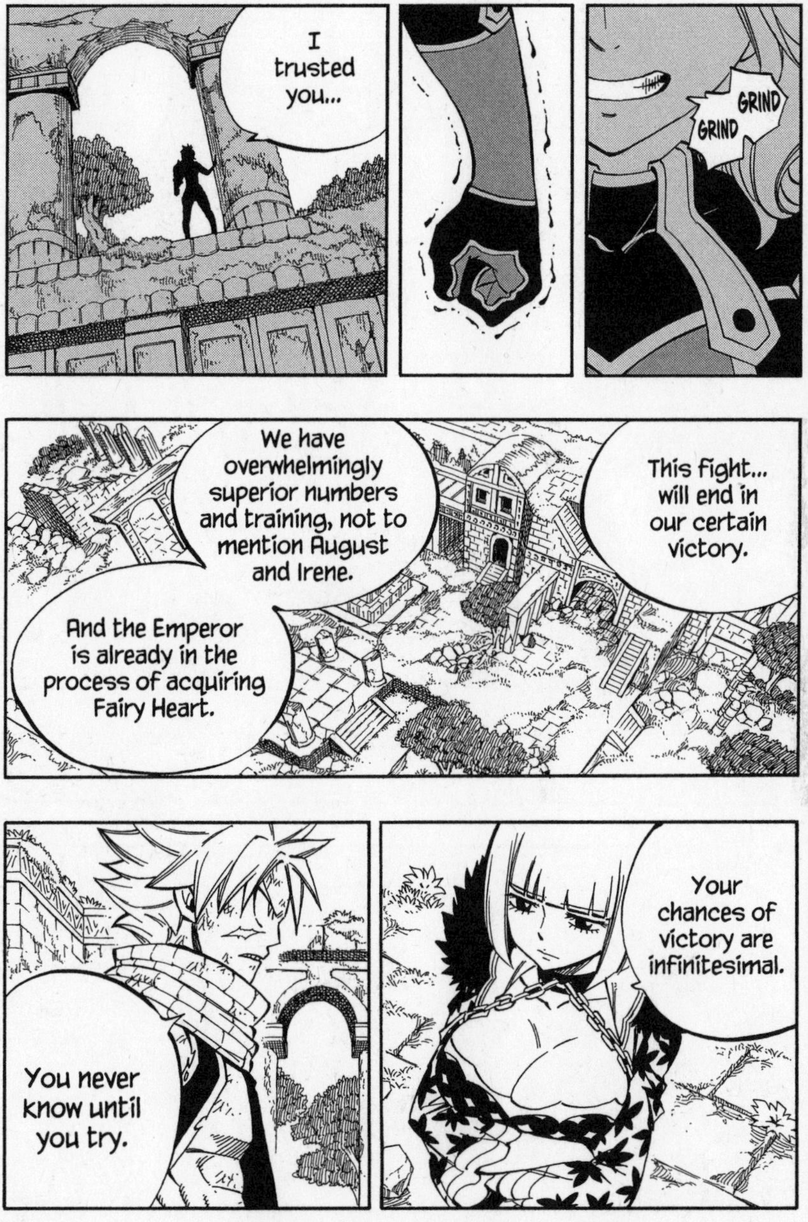
GRIND
GRIND
I trusted you...
This fight... will end in our certain victory.
We have overwhelmingly superior numbers and training, not to mention August and Irene.
And the Emperor is already in the process of acquiring Fairy Heart.
Your chances of victory are infinitesimal.
You never know until you try.

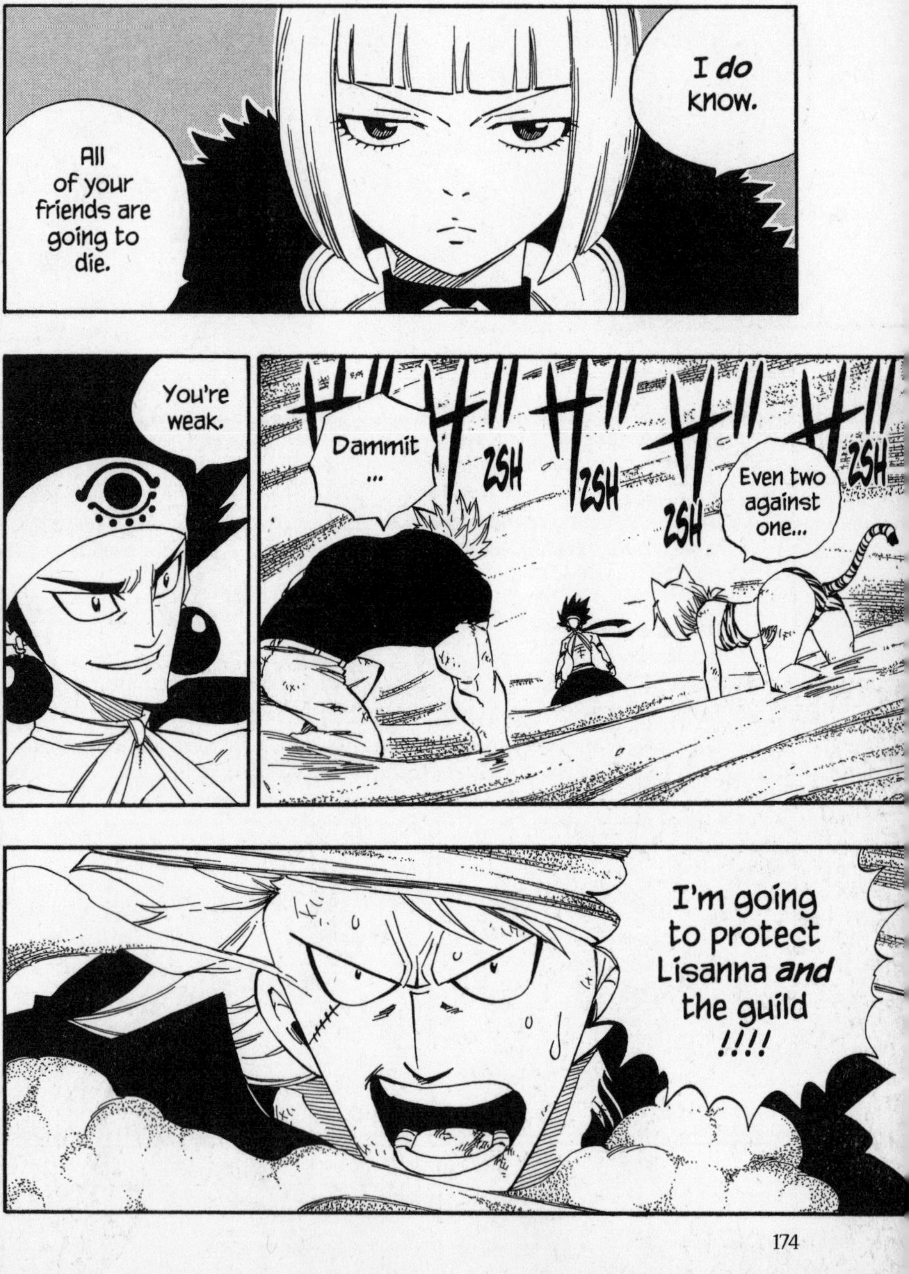
I *do* know.
All of your friends are going to die.
ZSH
Even two against one...
ZSH
ZSH
ZSH
Dammit ...
You're weak.
I'm going to protect Lisanna *and* the guild !!!!

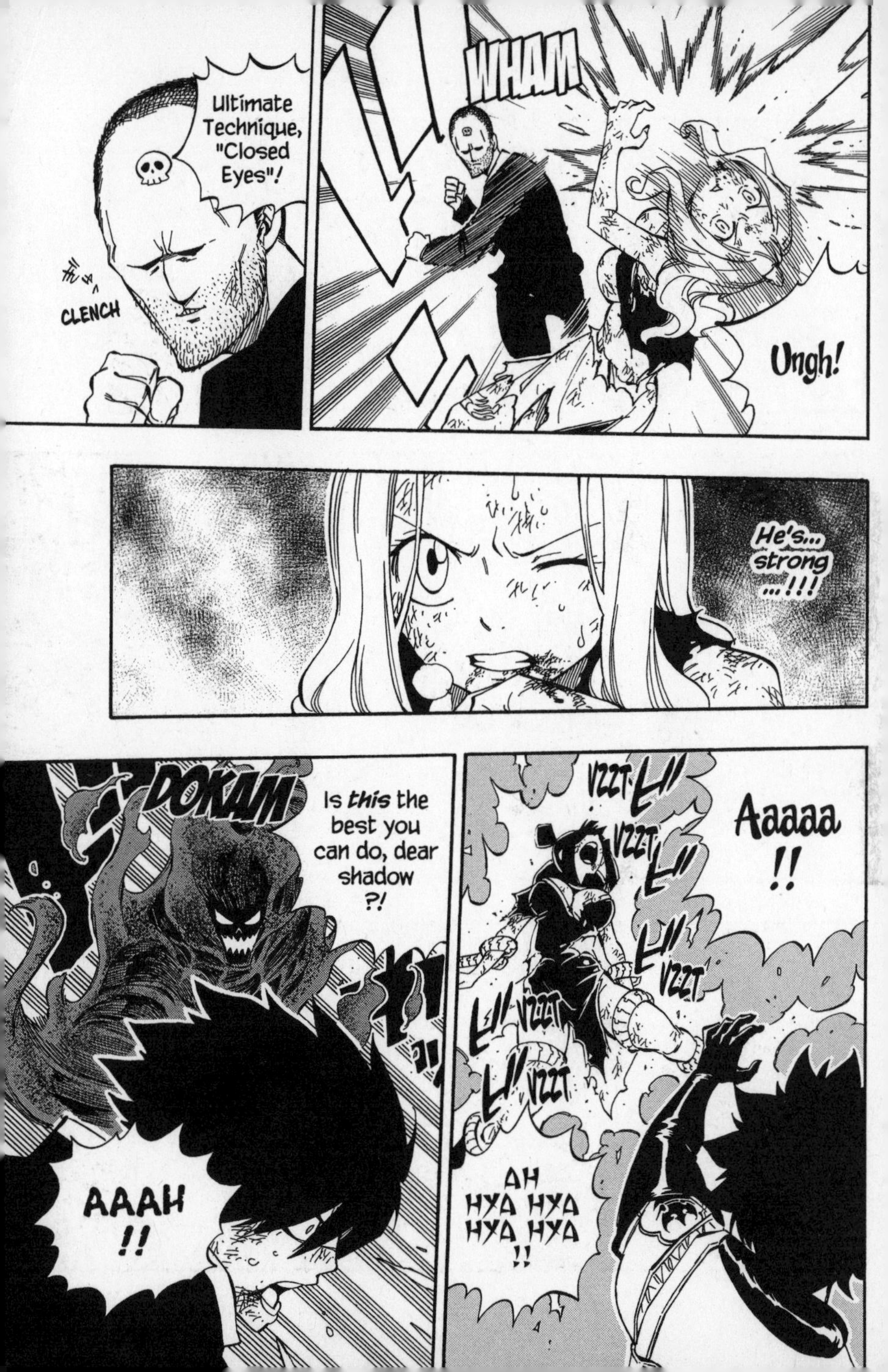
WHAM
Ungh!
Ultimate Technique, "Closed Eyes"!
CLENCH
He's... strong ...!!!
Aaaaa !!
VZZT
VZZT
VZZT
VZZT
VZZT
AH HYA HYA HYA HYA !!
DOKAM
Is this the best you can do, dear shadow ?!
AAAH !!

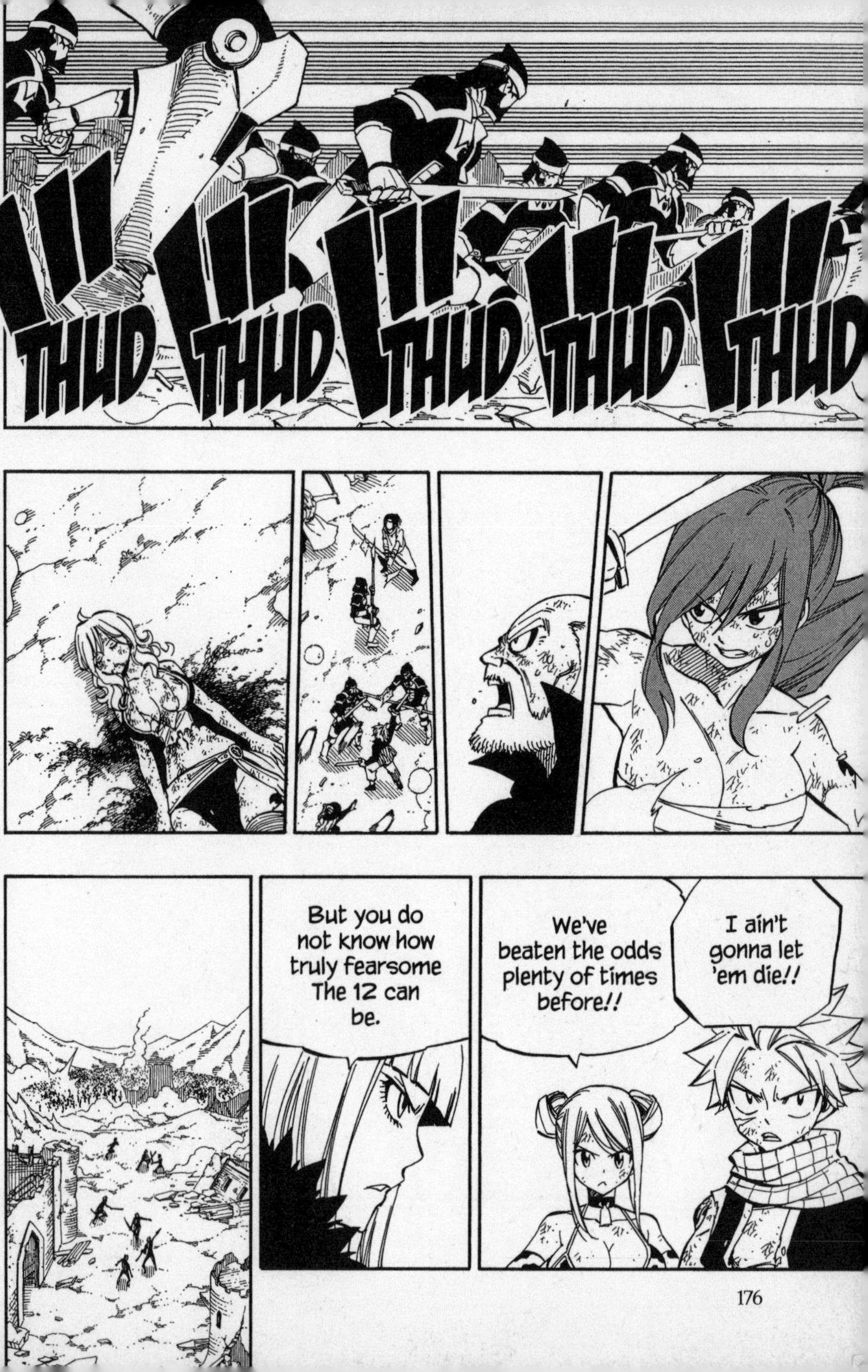
THUD THUD THUD THUD THUD
I ain't gonna let 'em die!!
We've beaten the odds plenty of times before!!
But you do not know how truly fearsome The 12 can be.

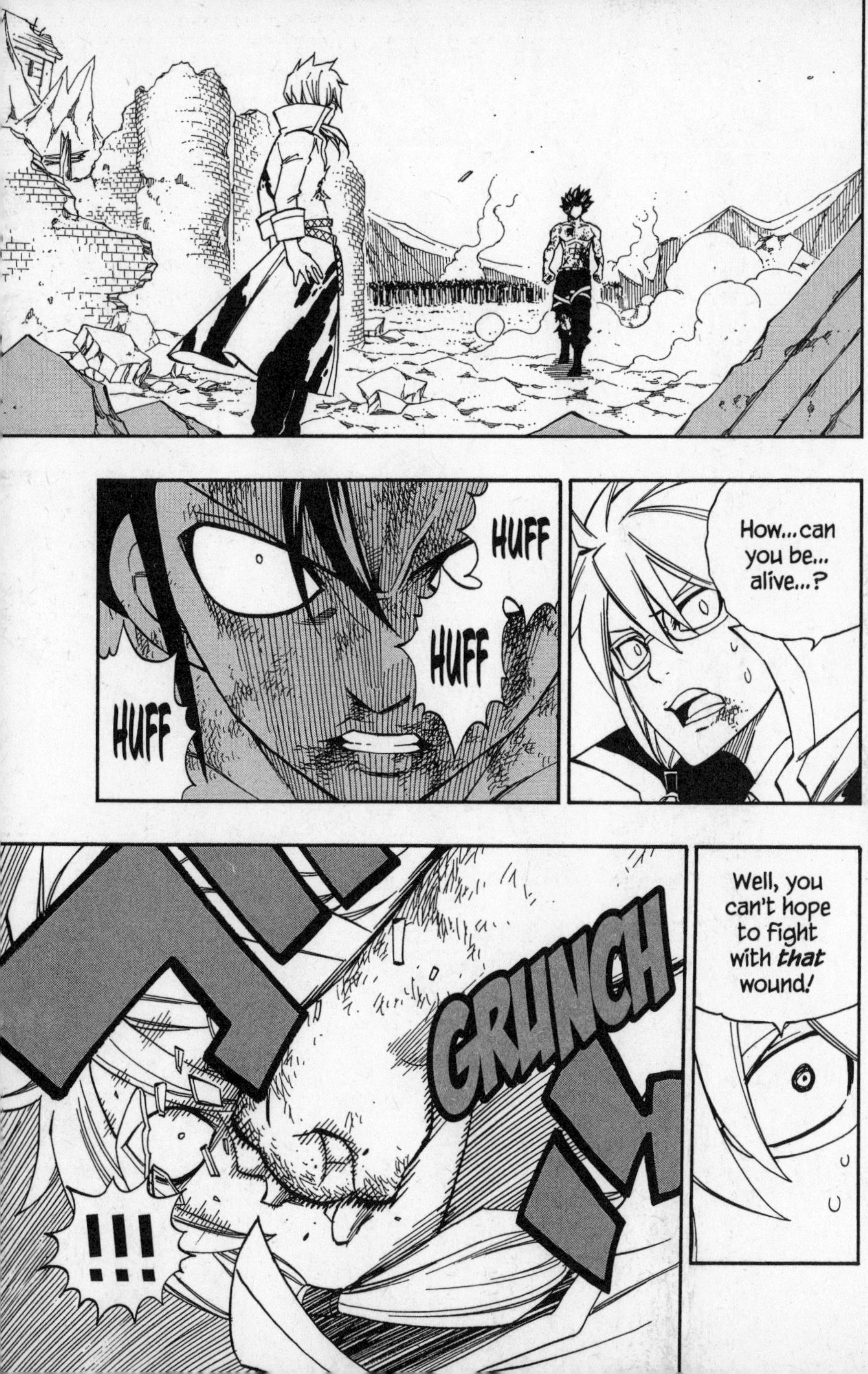
How...can you be... alive...?
HUFF
HUFF
HUFF
Well, you can't hope to fight with *that* wound!
GRUNCH
!!!

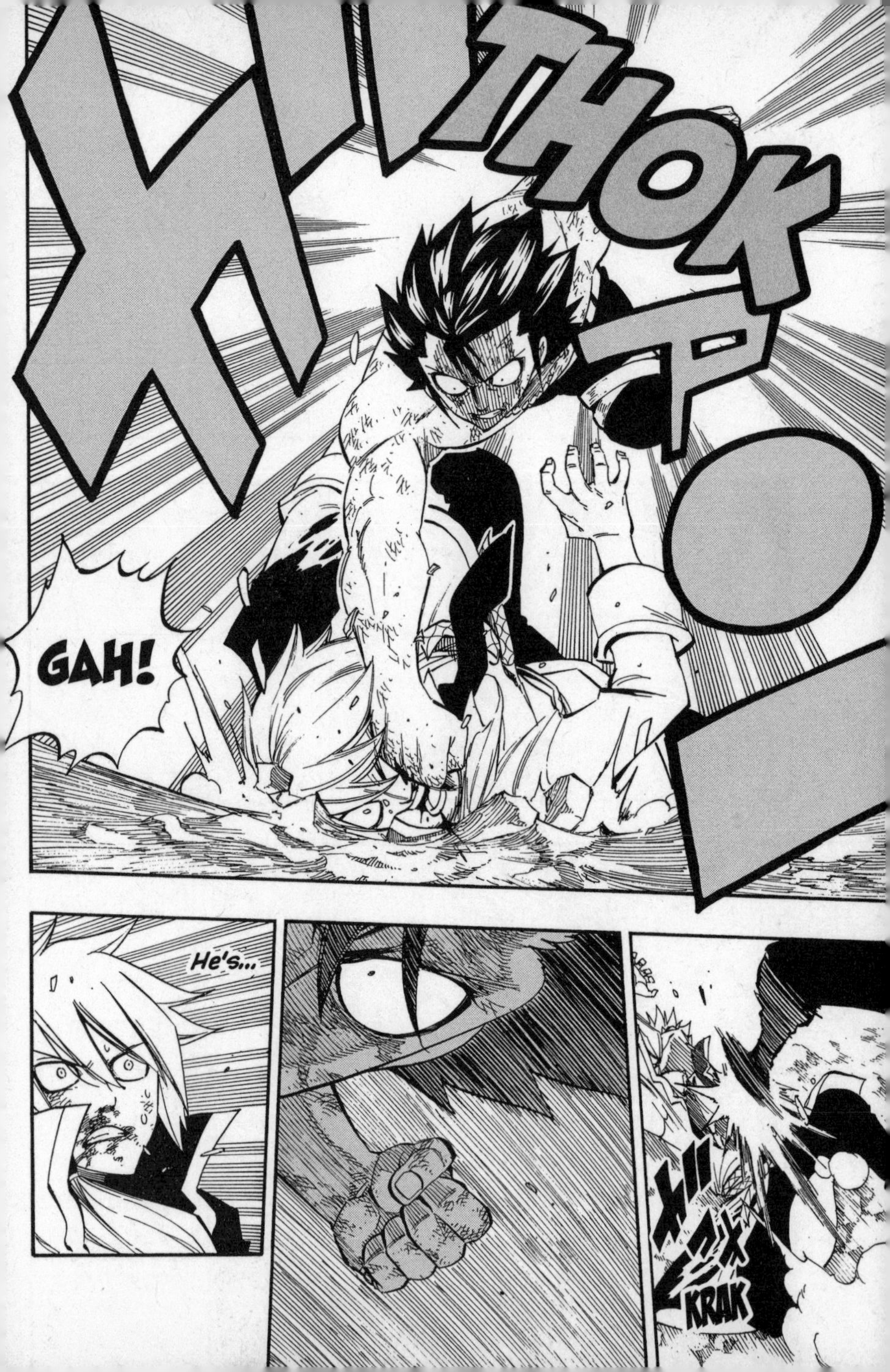
THOK
GAH!
KRAK
He's...

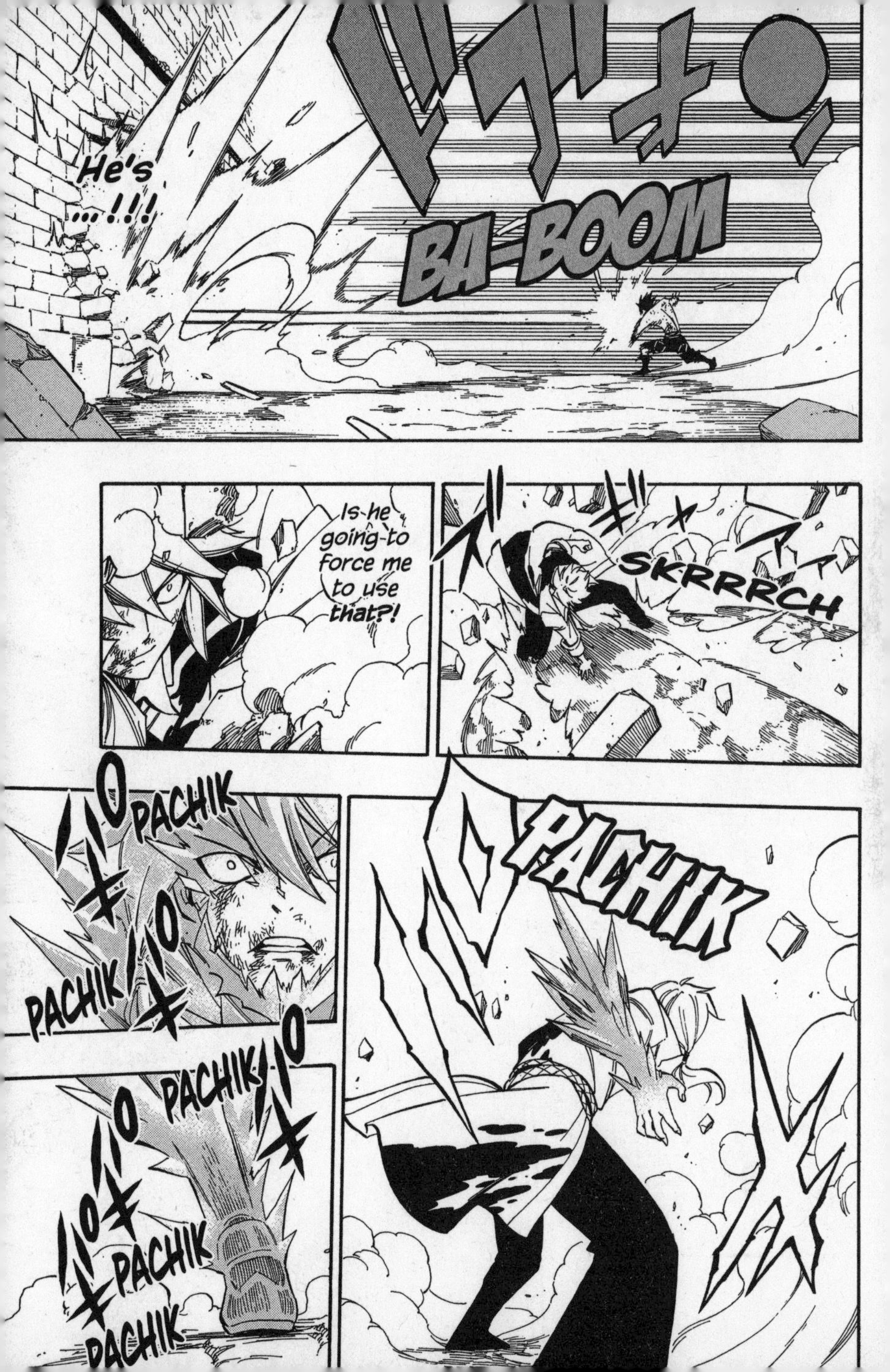
BA-BOOM
He's ...!!!
SKRRRCH
Is he going to force me to use that?!
PACHIK
PACHIK
PACHIK
PACHIK
PACHIK
PACHIK

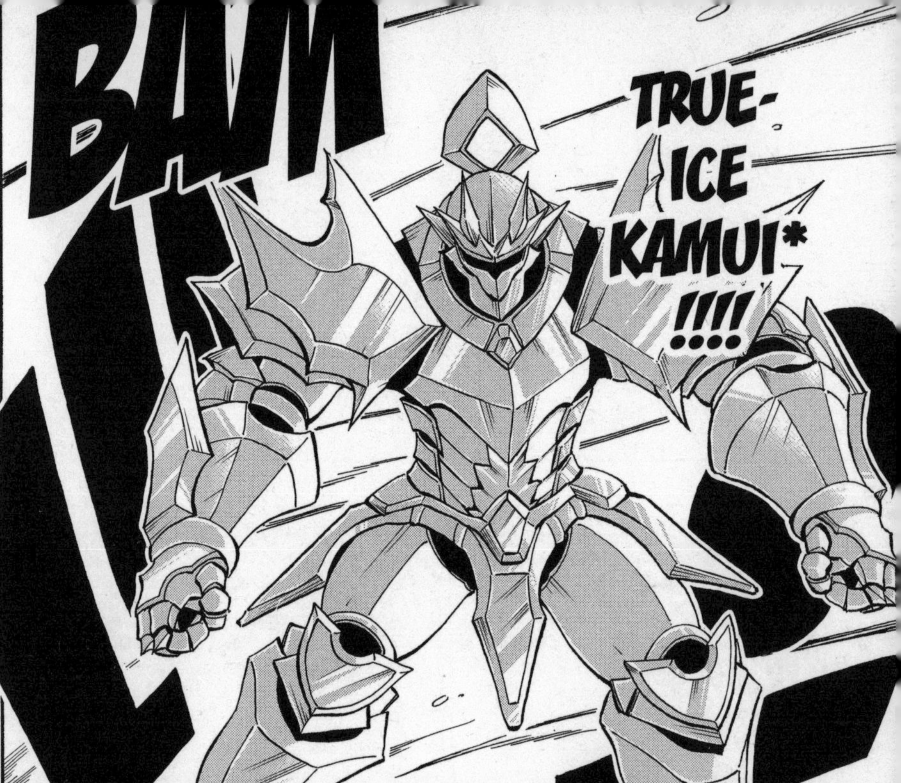
BAM
TRUE-ICE KAMUI*!!!!

*Kamui = Divine raiment

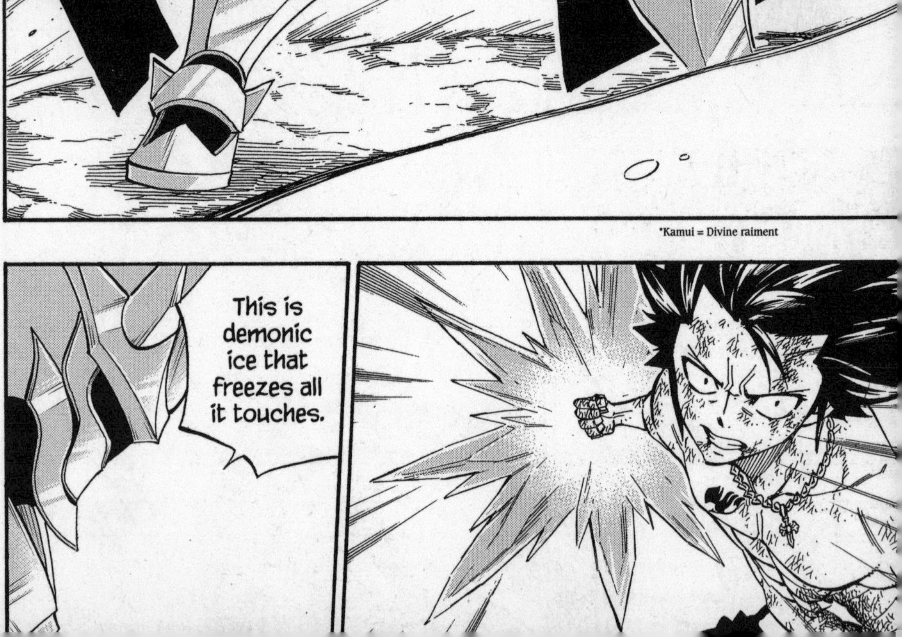
This is demonic ice that freezes all it touches.

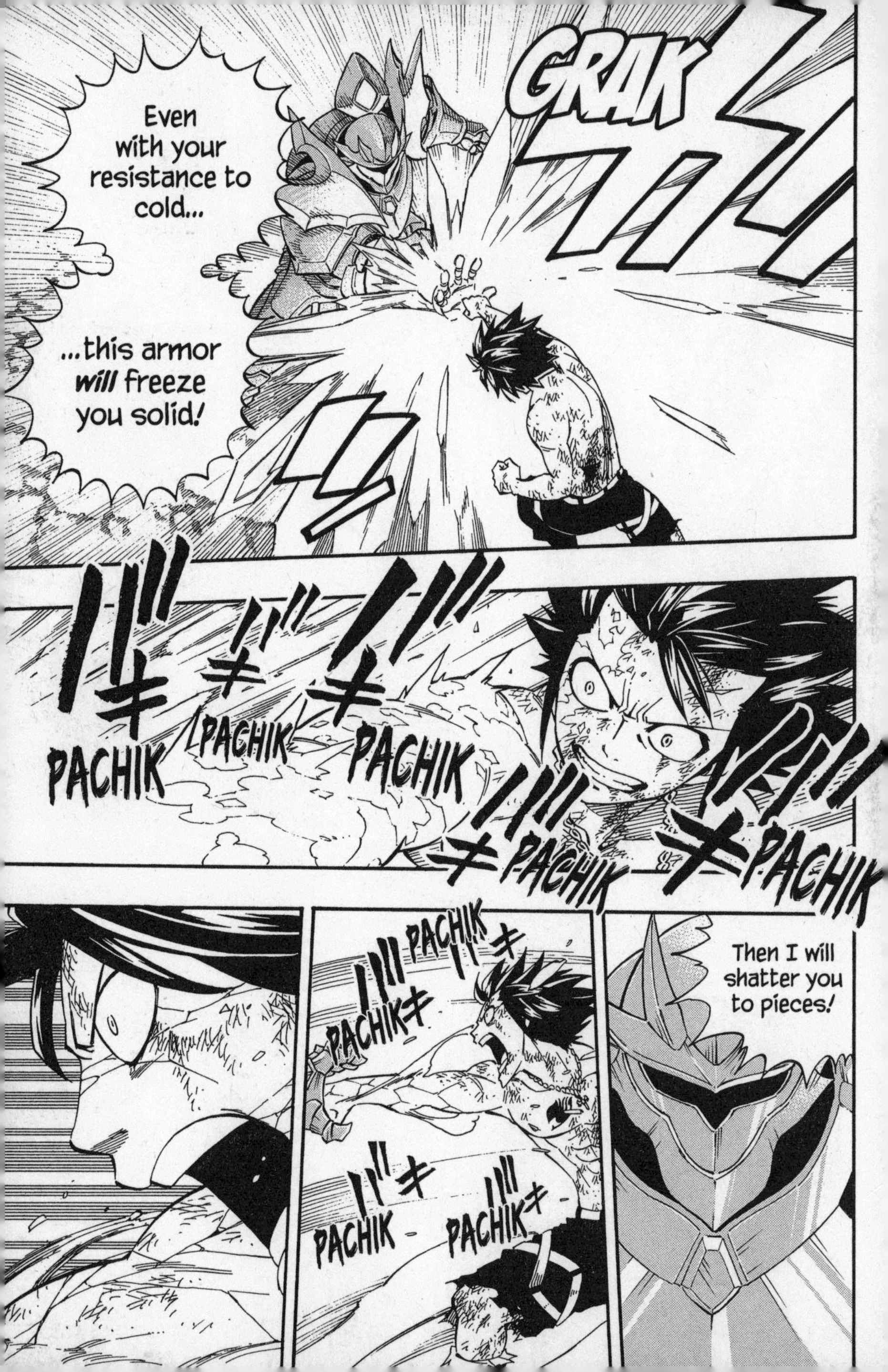
GRAK
Even with your resistance to cold...
...this armor *will* freeze you solid!
PACHIK
PACHIK
PACHIK
PACHIK
PACHIK
Then I will shatter you to pieces!
PACHIK
PACHIK
PACHIK
PACHIK

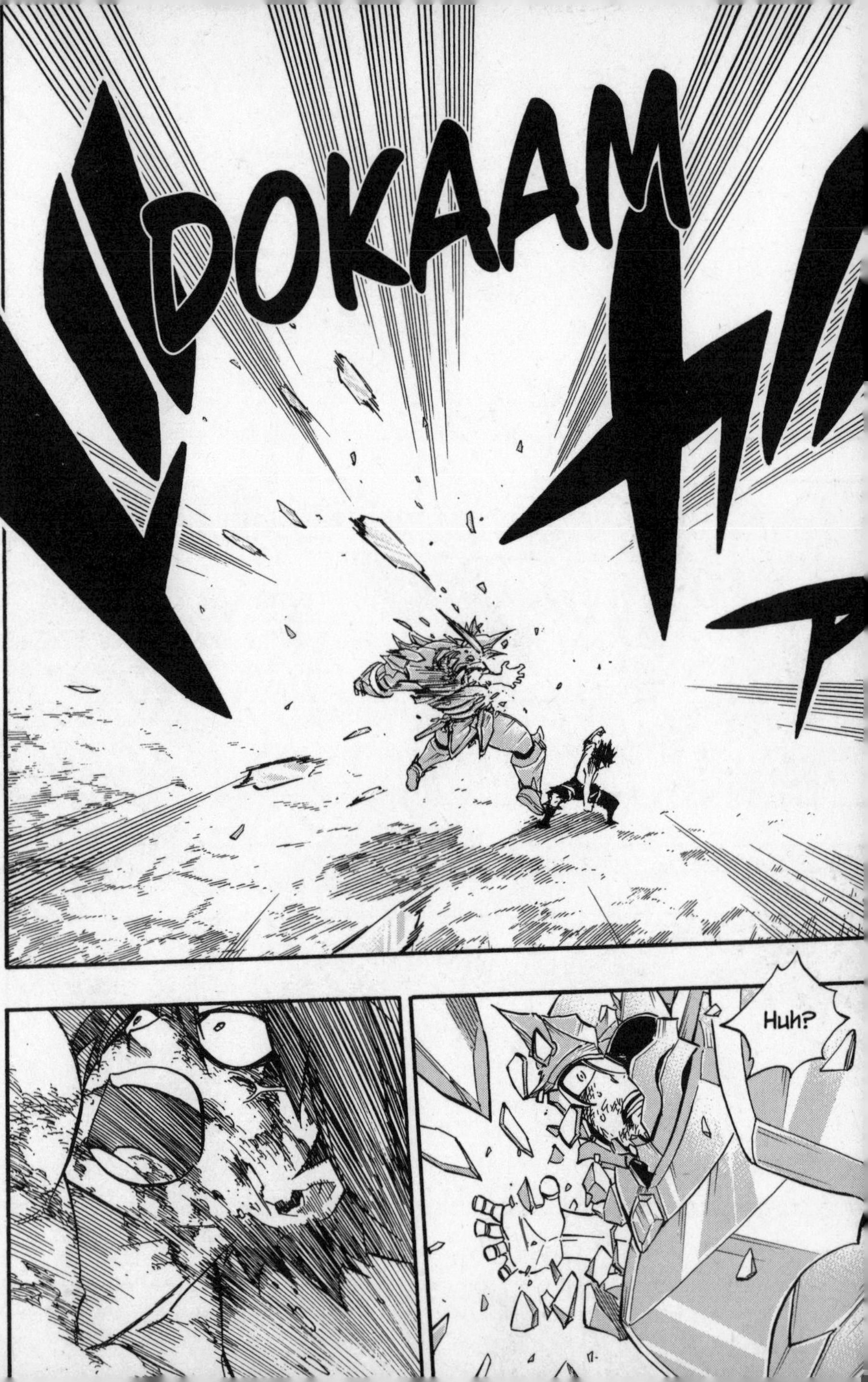
DOKAAM
Huh?

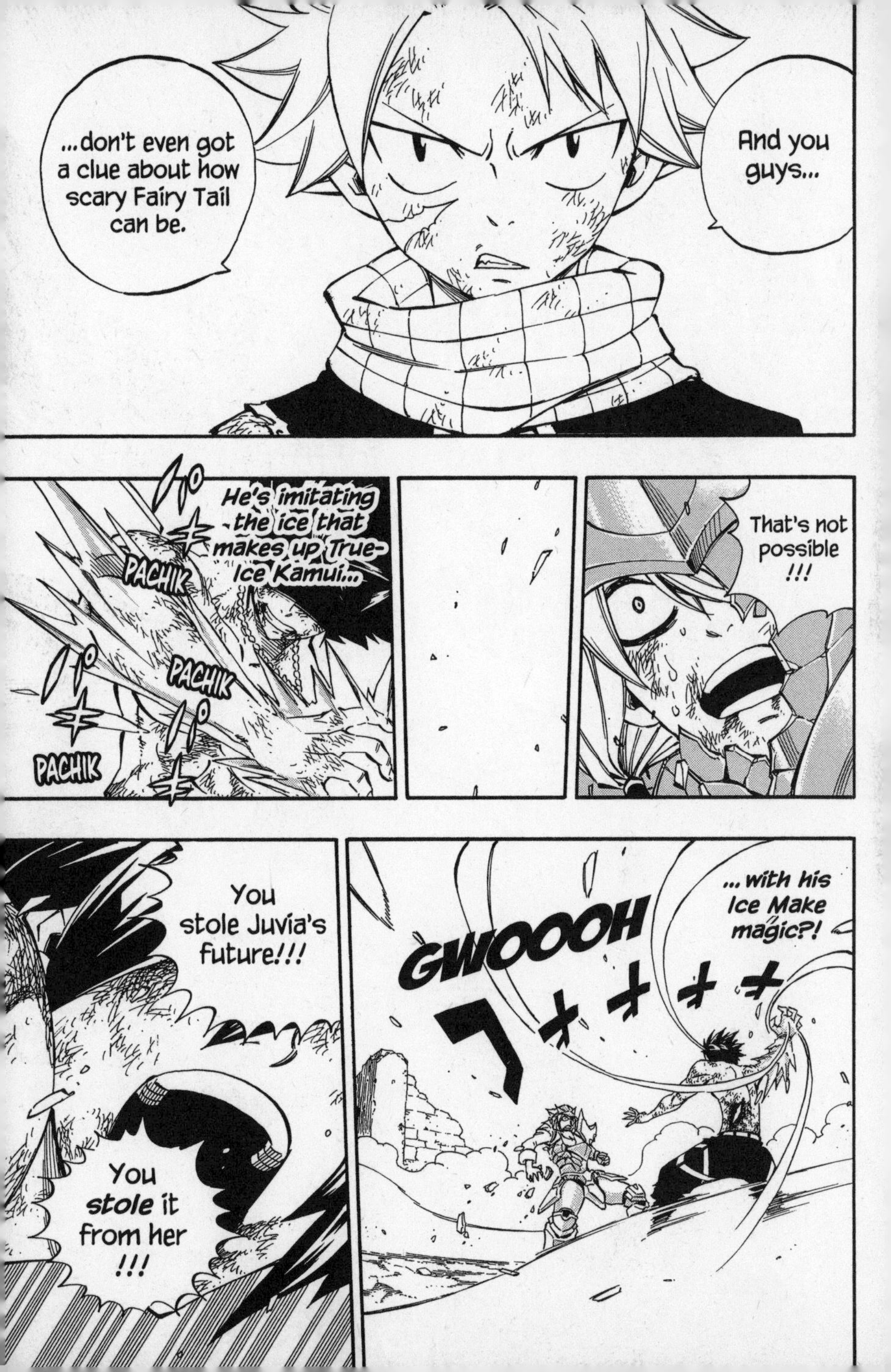

And you guys...
...don't even got a clue about how scary Fairy Tail can be.
That's not possible!!!
He's imitating the ice that makes up True-Ice Kamui...
PACHIK
PACHIK
PACHIK
...with his Ice Make magic?!
GWOOOH
You stole Juvia's future!!!
You *stole* it from her!!!

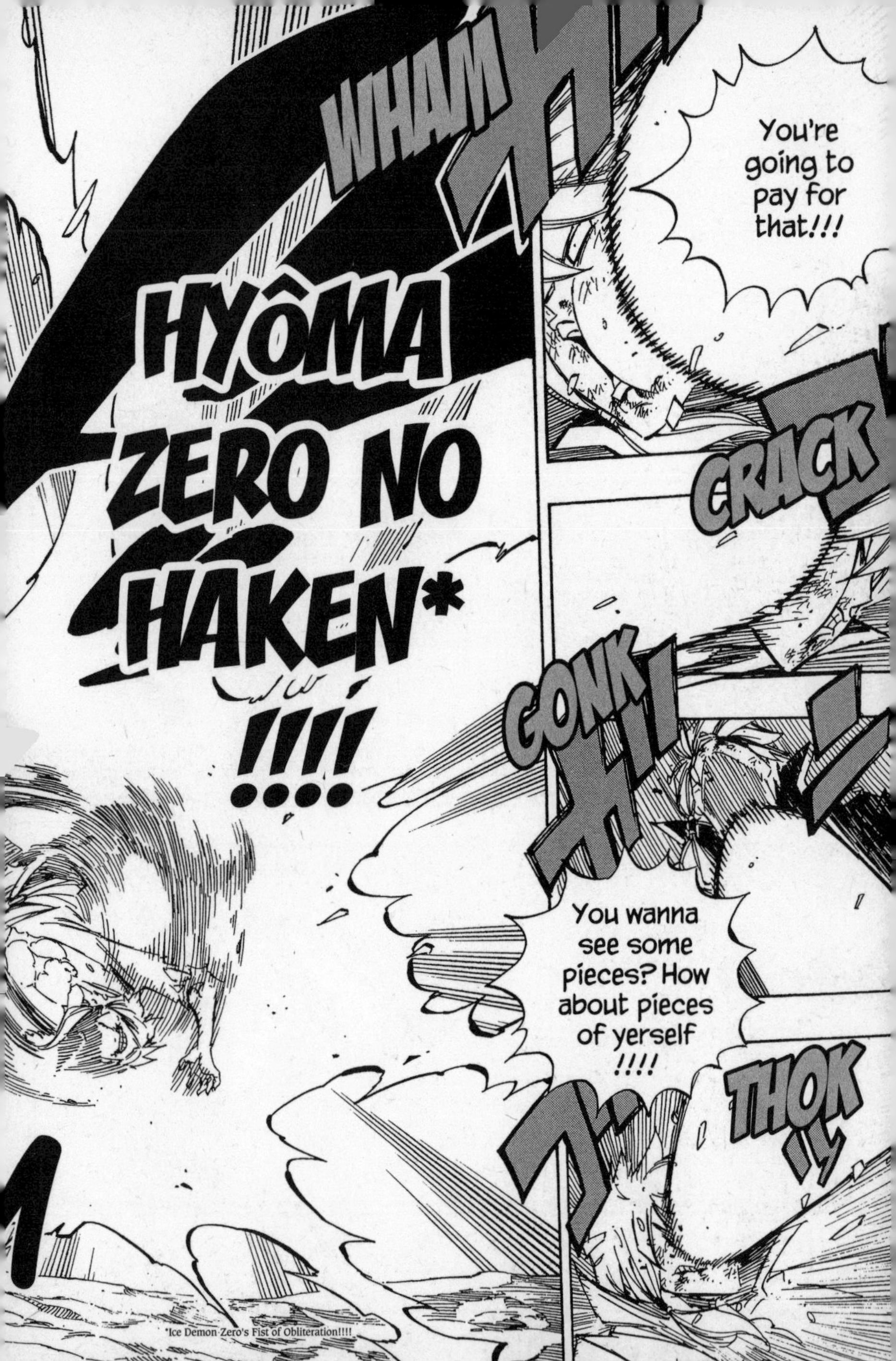
WHAM
You're going to pay for that!!!
CRACK
HYÔMA ZERO NO HAKEN* !!!!
GONK
You wanna see some pieces? How about pieces of yerself !!!!
THOK

*Ice Demon Zero's Fist of Obliteration!!!!

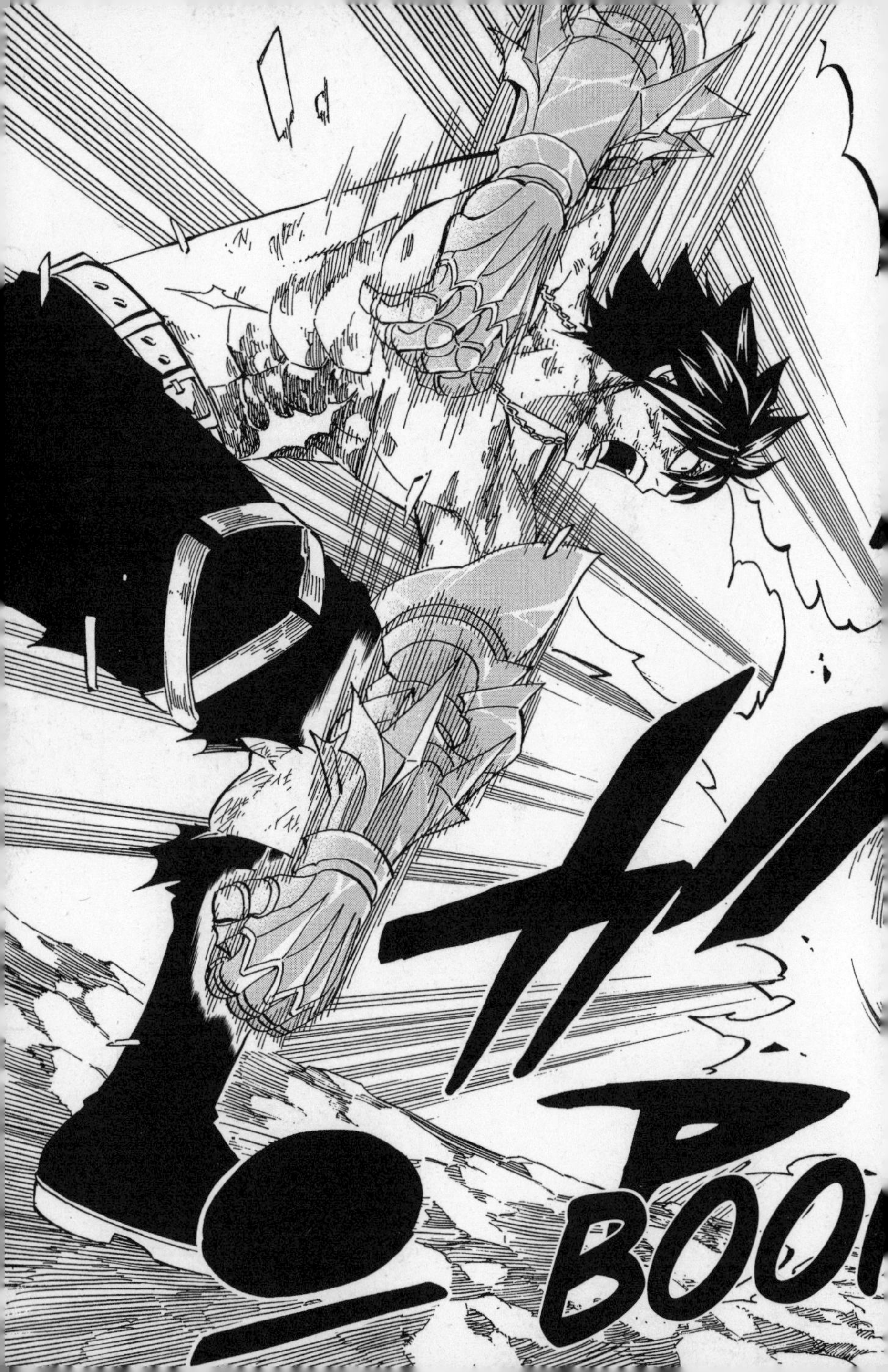
BOO

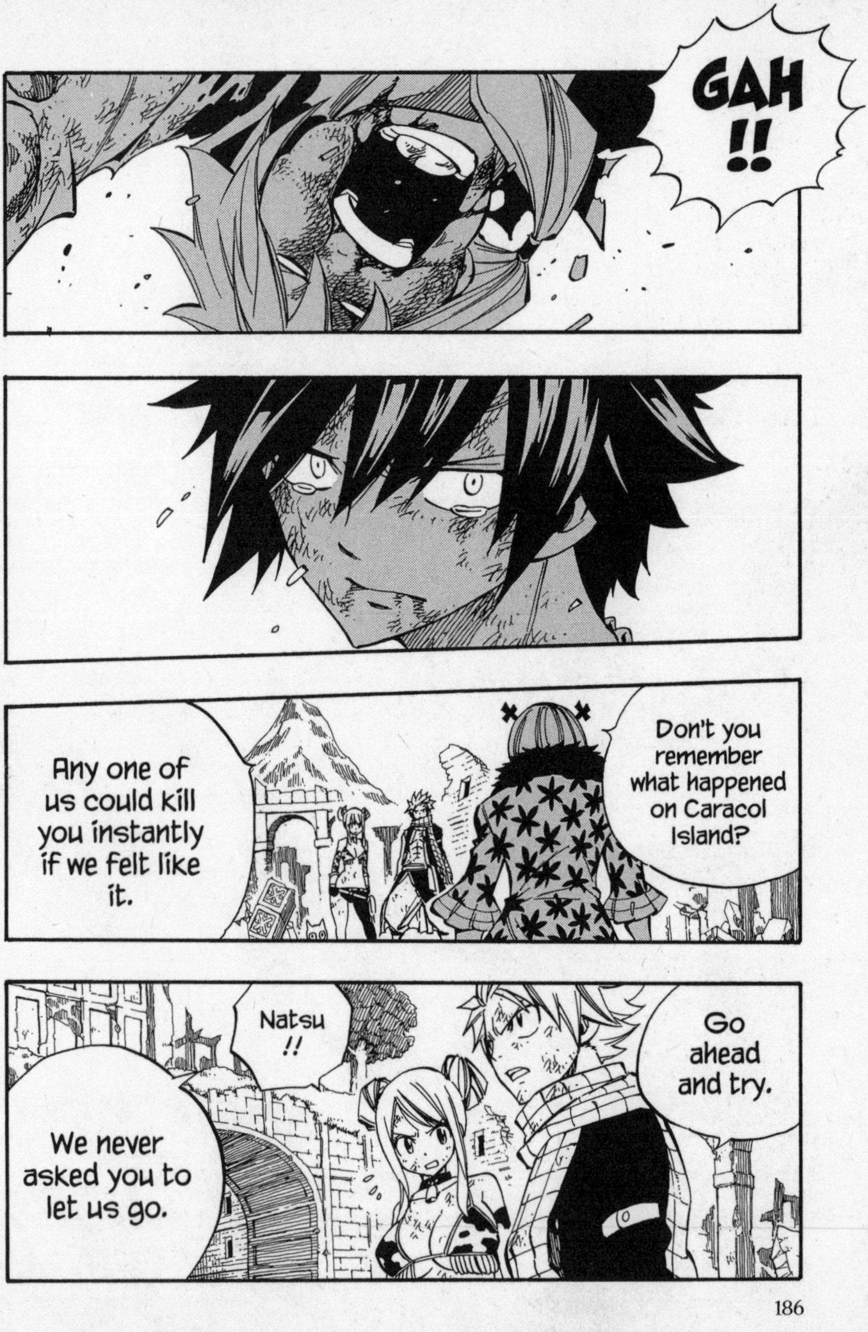
GAH!!
Don't you remember what happened on Caracol Island?
Any one of us could kill you instantly if we felt like it.
Go ahead and try.
Natsu!!
We never asked you to let us go.

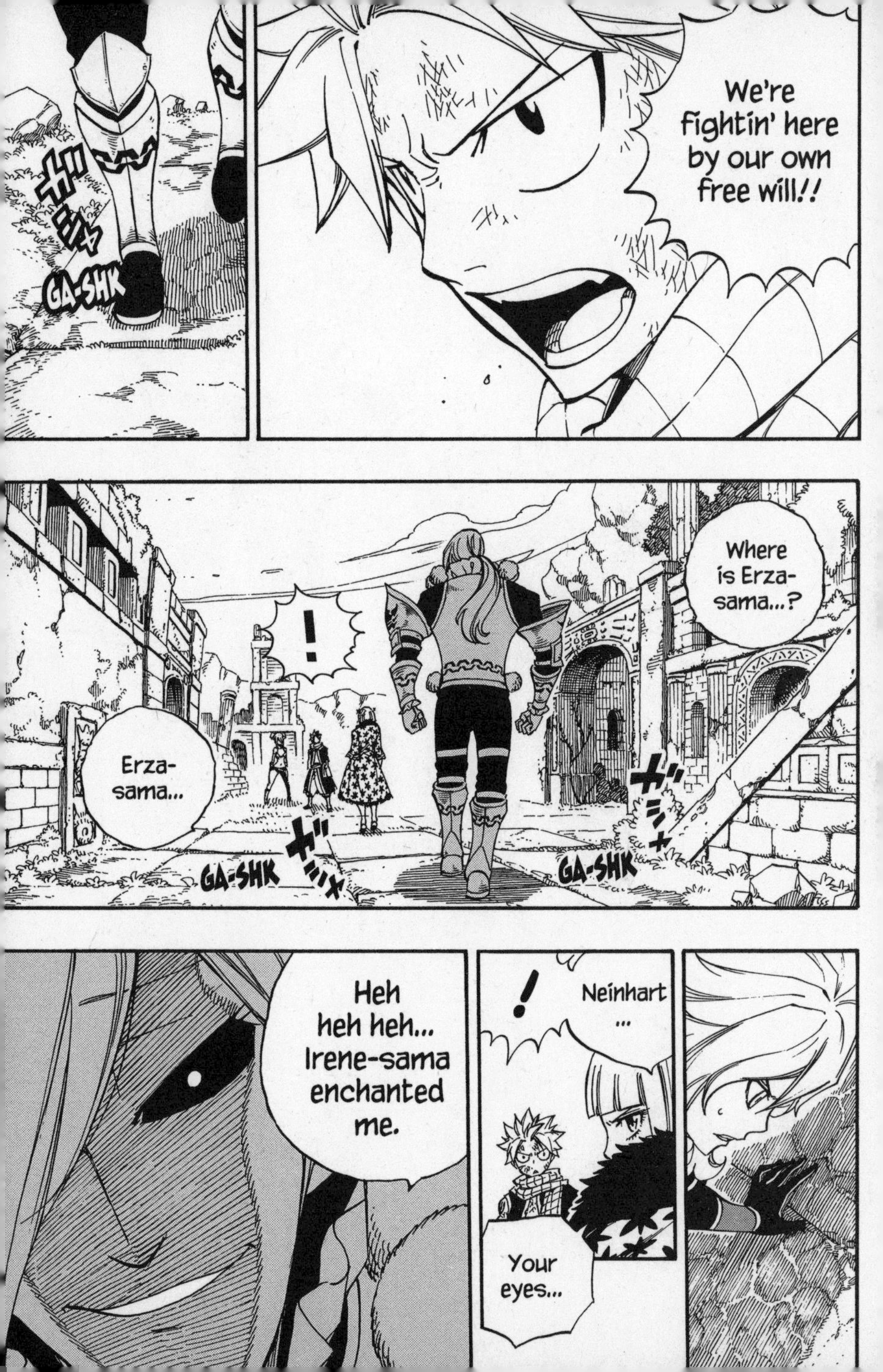
We're fightin' here by our own free will!!
GA-SHK
Where is Erza-sama...?
!
GA-SHK
Erza-sama...
GA-SHK
!
Neinhart ...
Your eyes...
Heh heh heh... Irene-sama enchanted me.

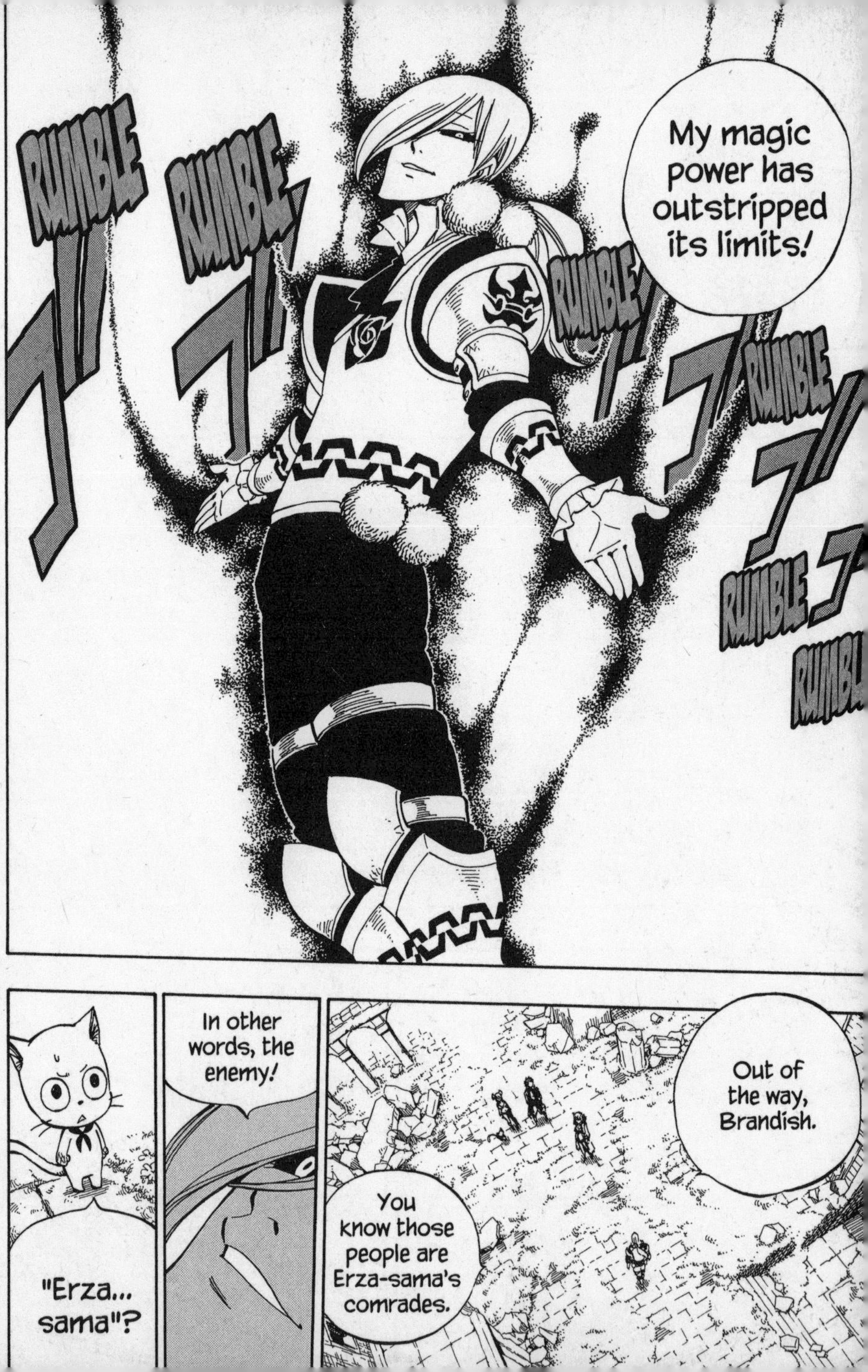

My magic power has outstripped its limits!
RUMBLE
RUMBLE
RUMBLE
RUMBLE
RUMBLE
RUMBLE
Out of the way, Brandish.
You know those people are Erza-sama's comrades.
In other words, the enemy!
"Erza... sama"?

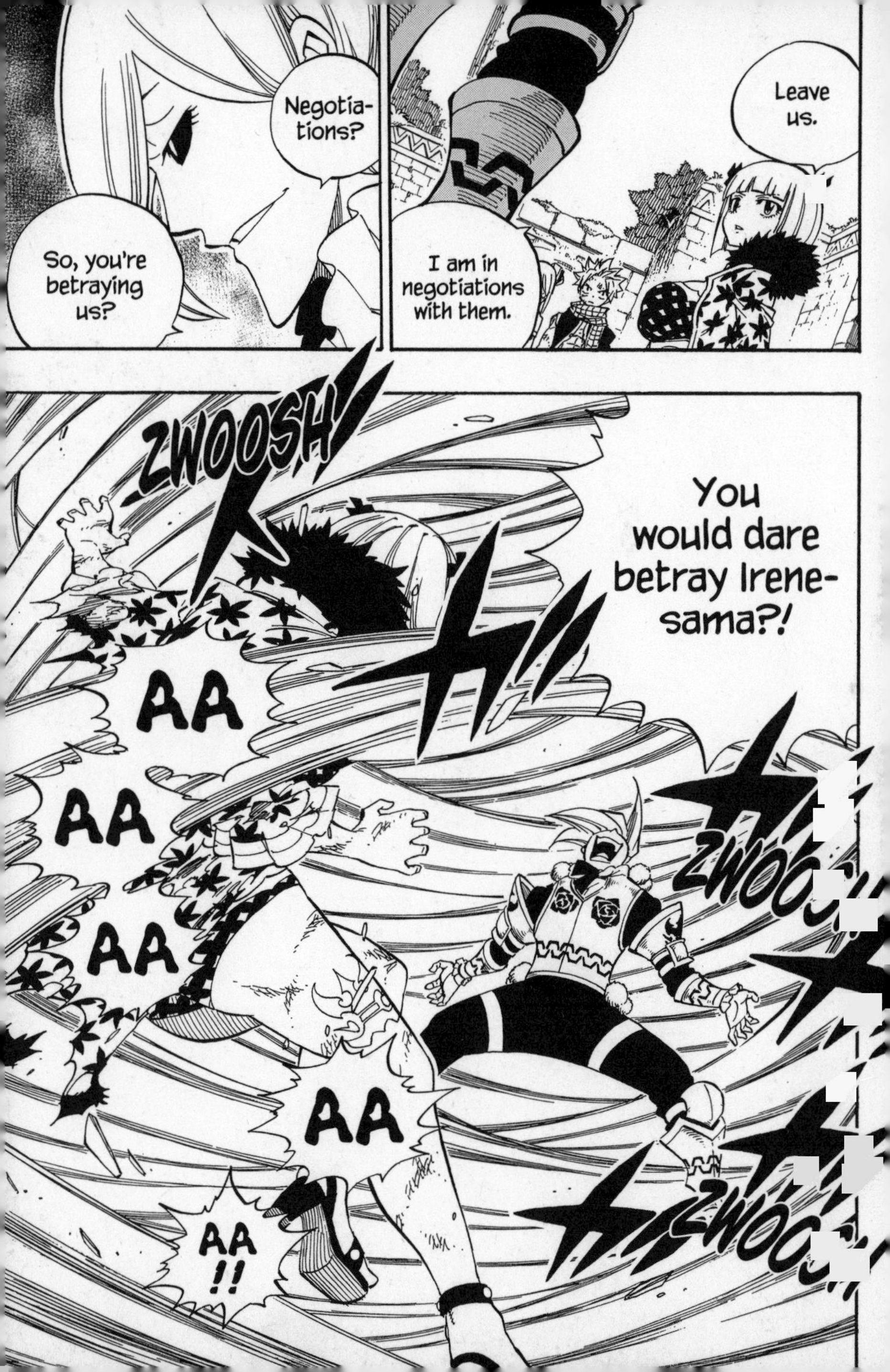

Leave us.
I am in negotiations with them.
Negotia-tions?
So, you're betraying us?
You would dare betray Irene-sama?!
ZWOOSH
AA
AA
AA
AA
AA !!

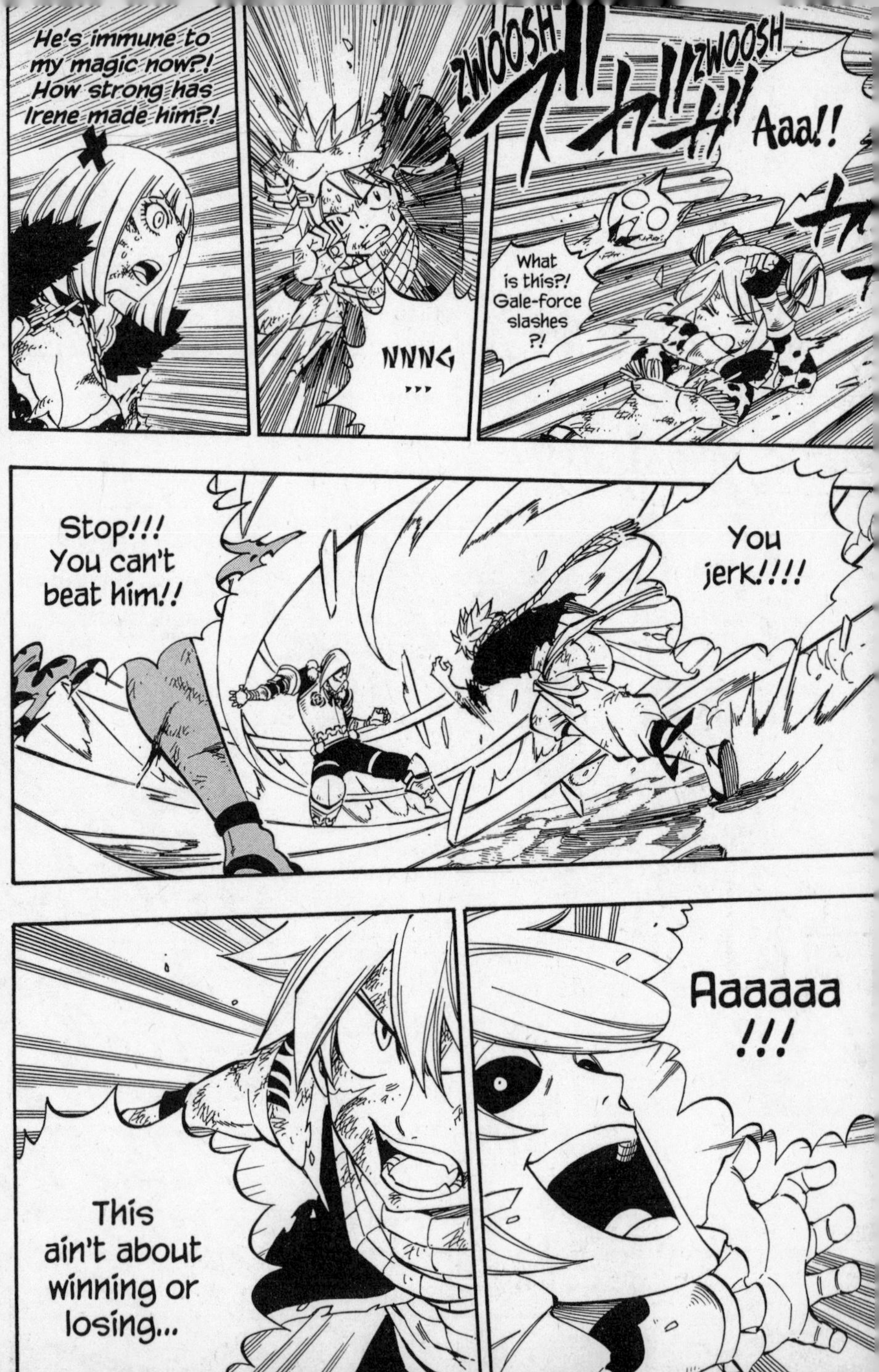
ZWOOSH
ZWOOSH
Aaa!!
What is this?! Gale-force slashes ?!
NNNG ...
He's immune to my magic now?! How strong has Irene made him?!
You jerk!!!!
Stop!!! You can't beat him!!
Aaaaaa !!!
This ain't about winning or losing...

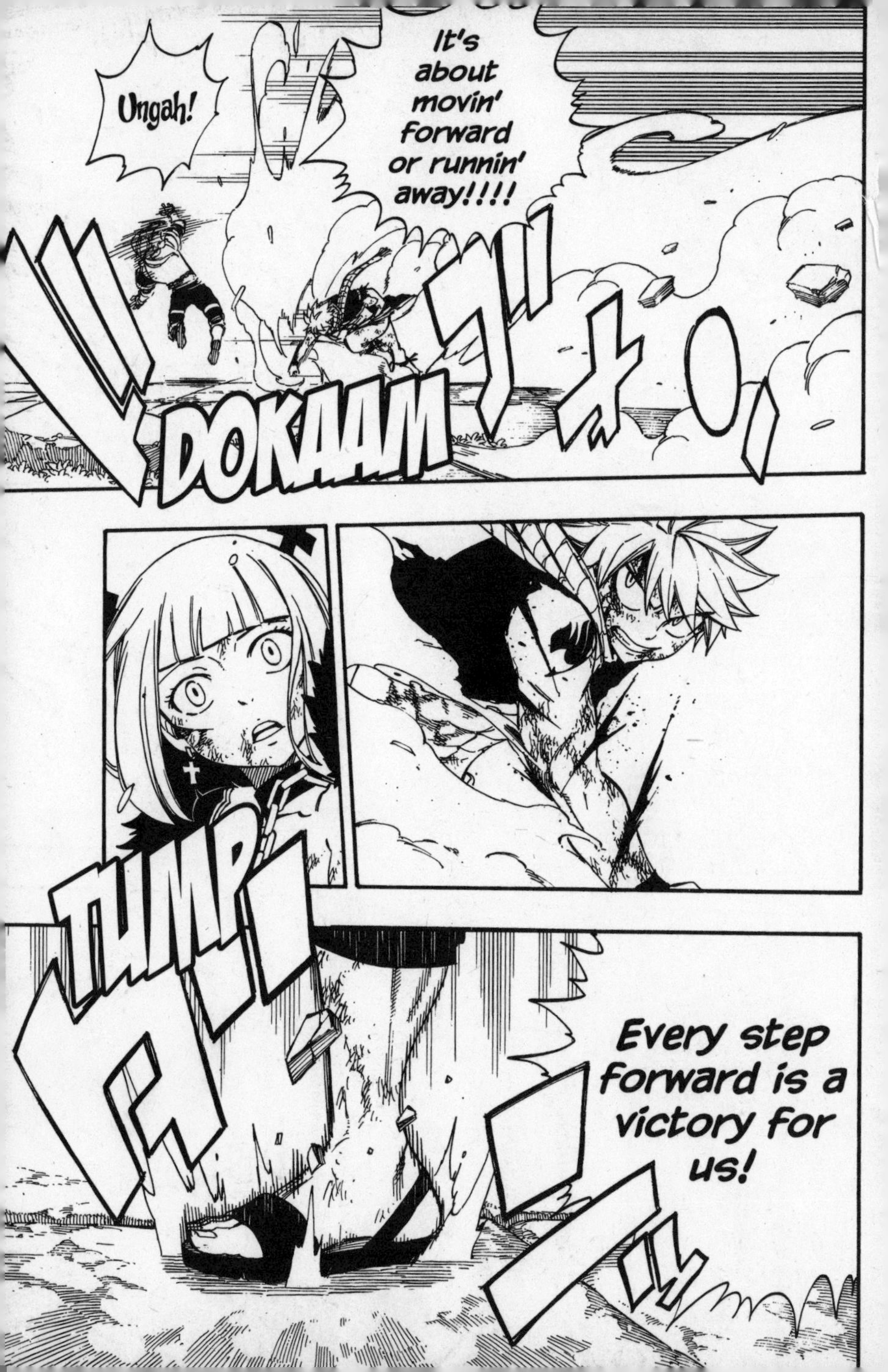
It's about movin' forward or runnin' away!!!!
Ungah!
DOKAAM
TUMP
Every step forward is a victory for us!

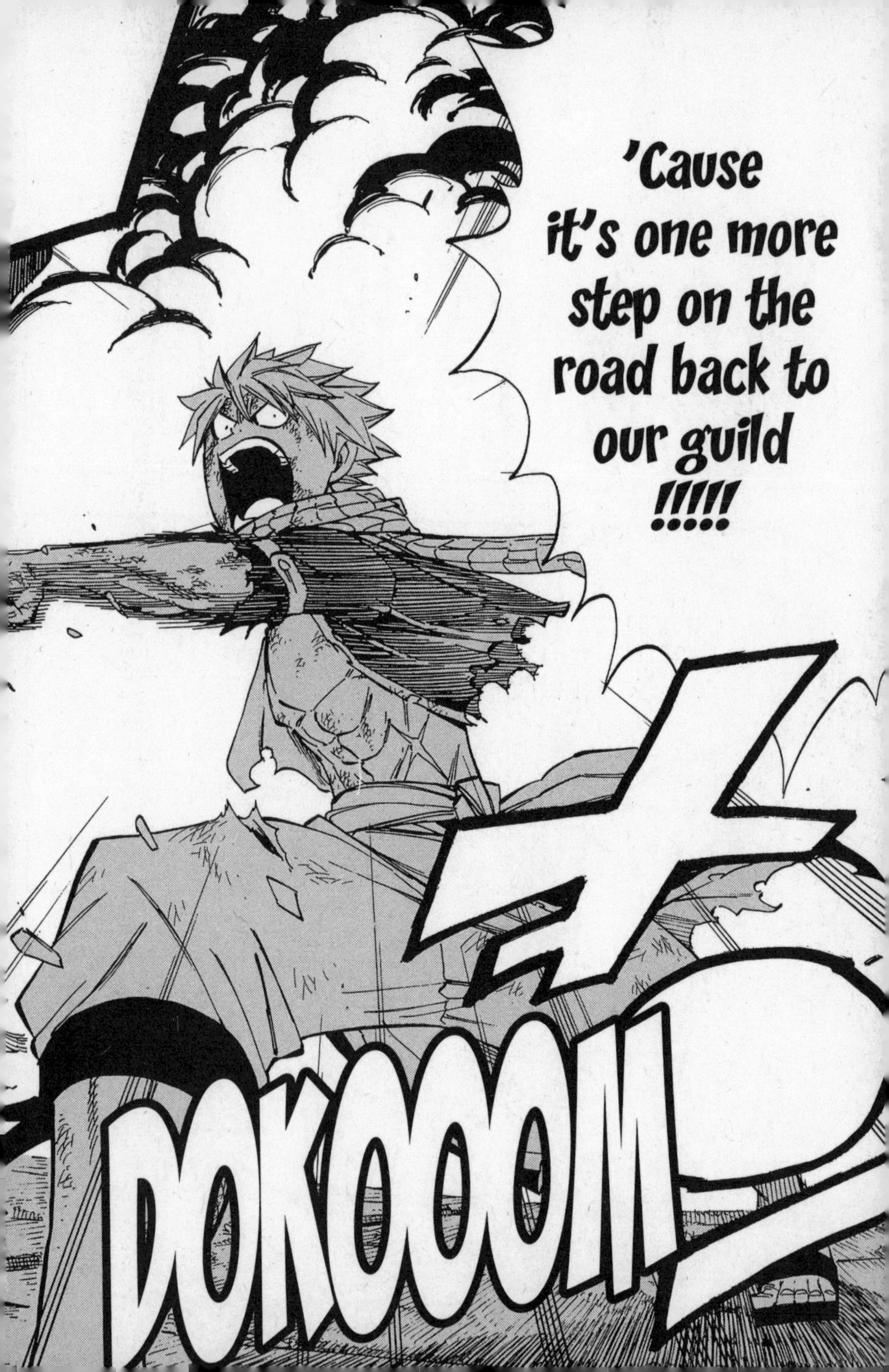
'Cause it's one more step on the road back to our guild !!!!!
DOKOOOM

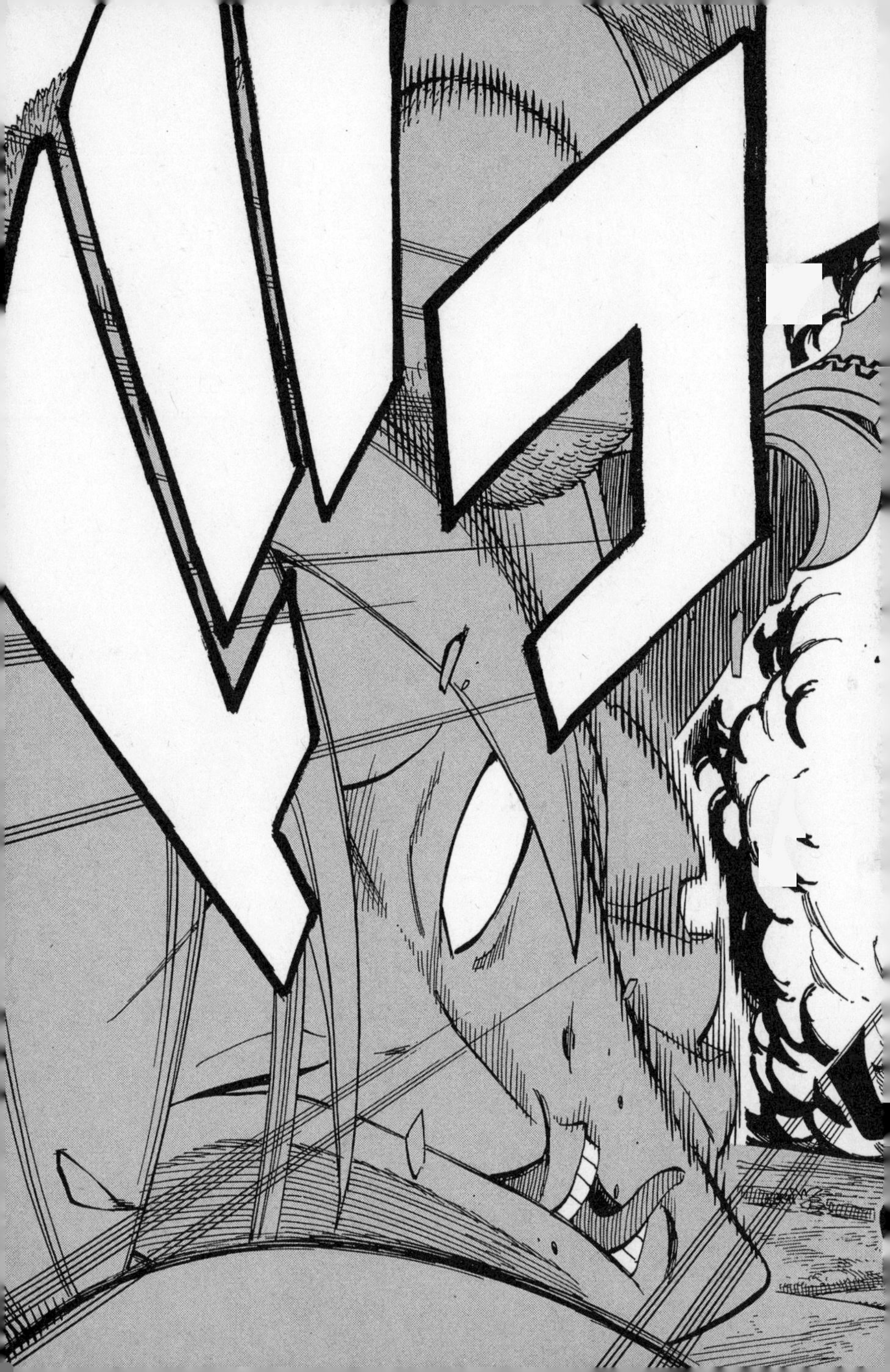

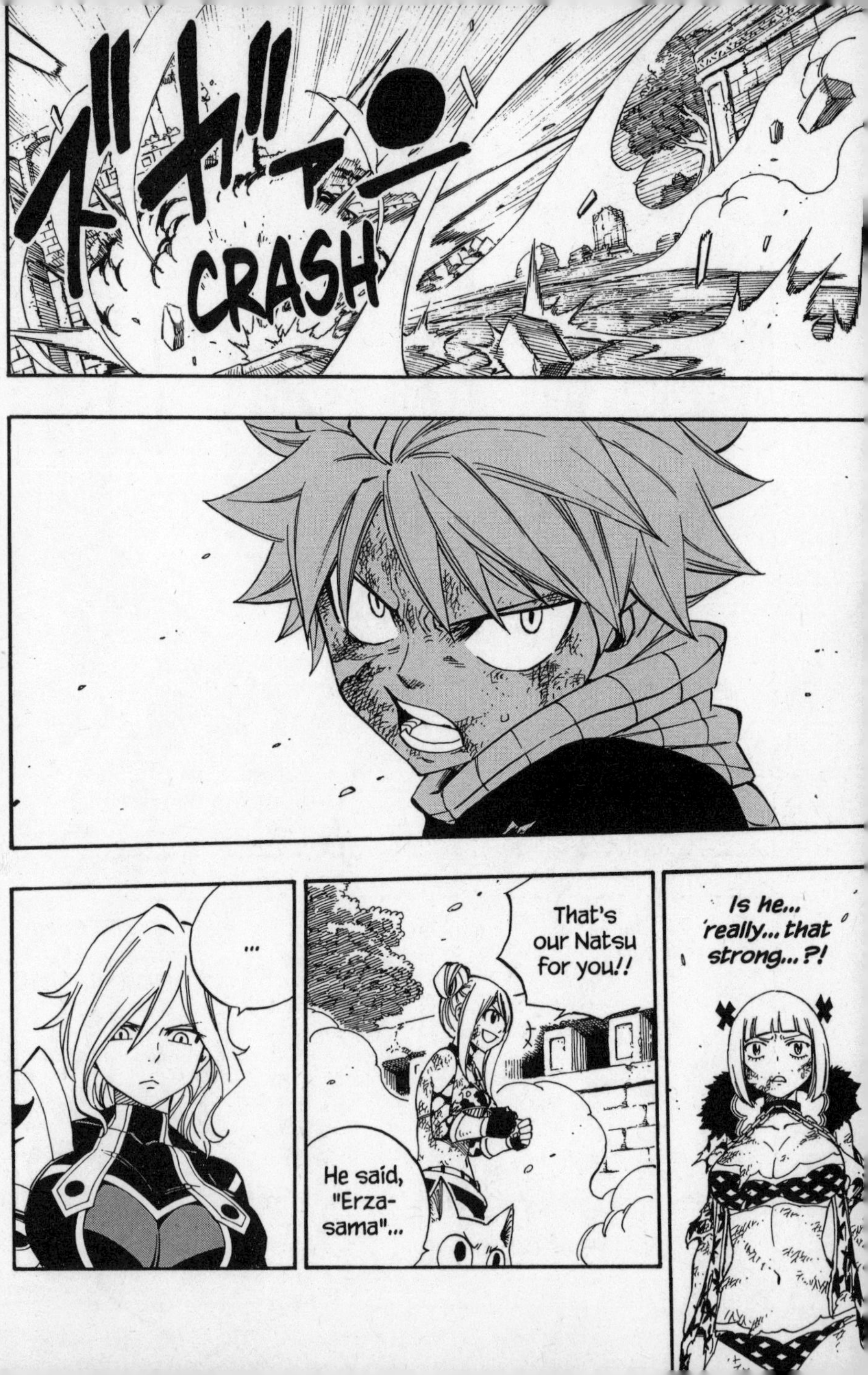
CRASH
Is he... really... that strong...?!
That's our Natsu for you!!
He said, "Erza-sama"...
...

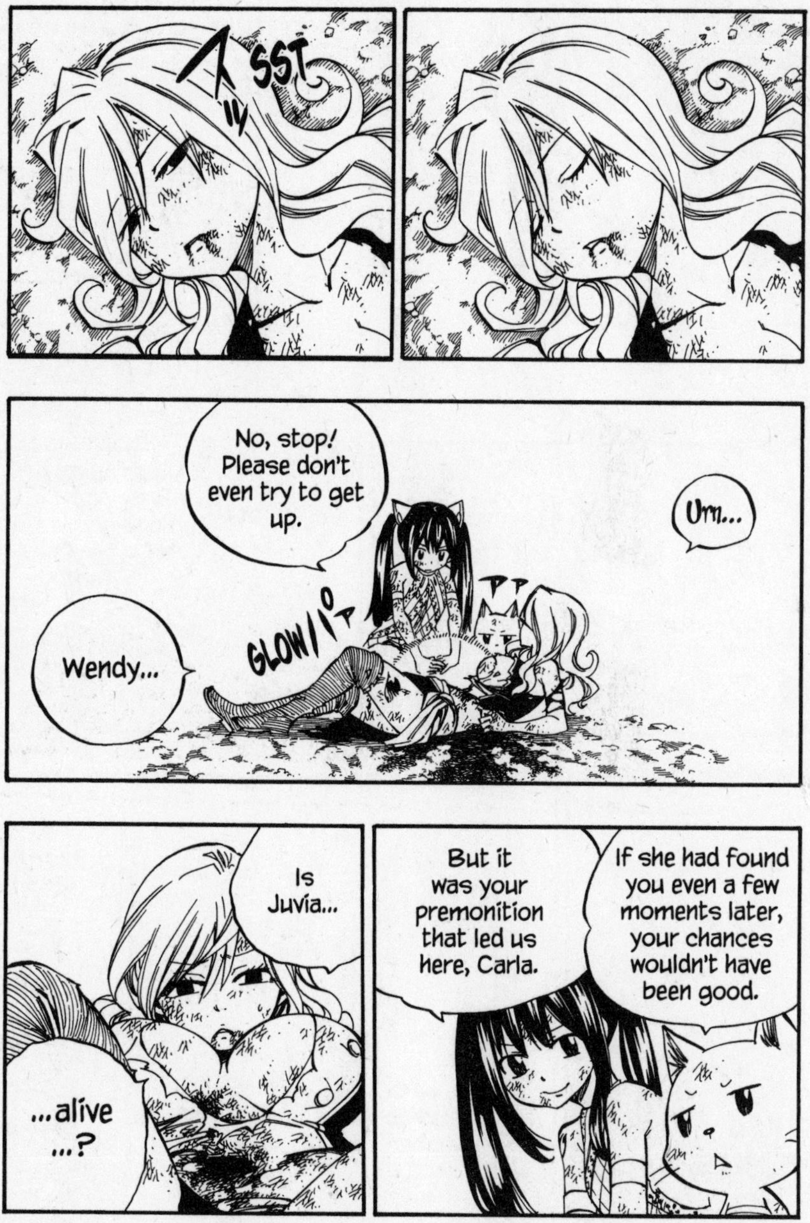

SST
Um...
No, stop! Please don't even try to get up.
GLOW
Wendy...
If she had found you even a few moments later, your chances wouldn't have been good.
But it was your premonition that led us here, Carla.
Is Juvia...
...alive ...?

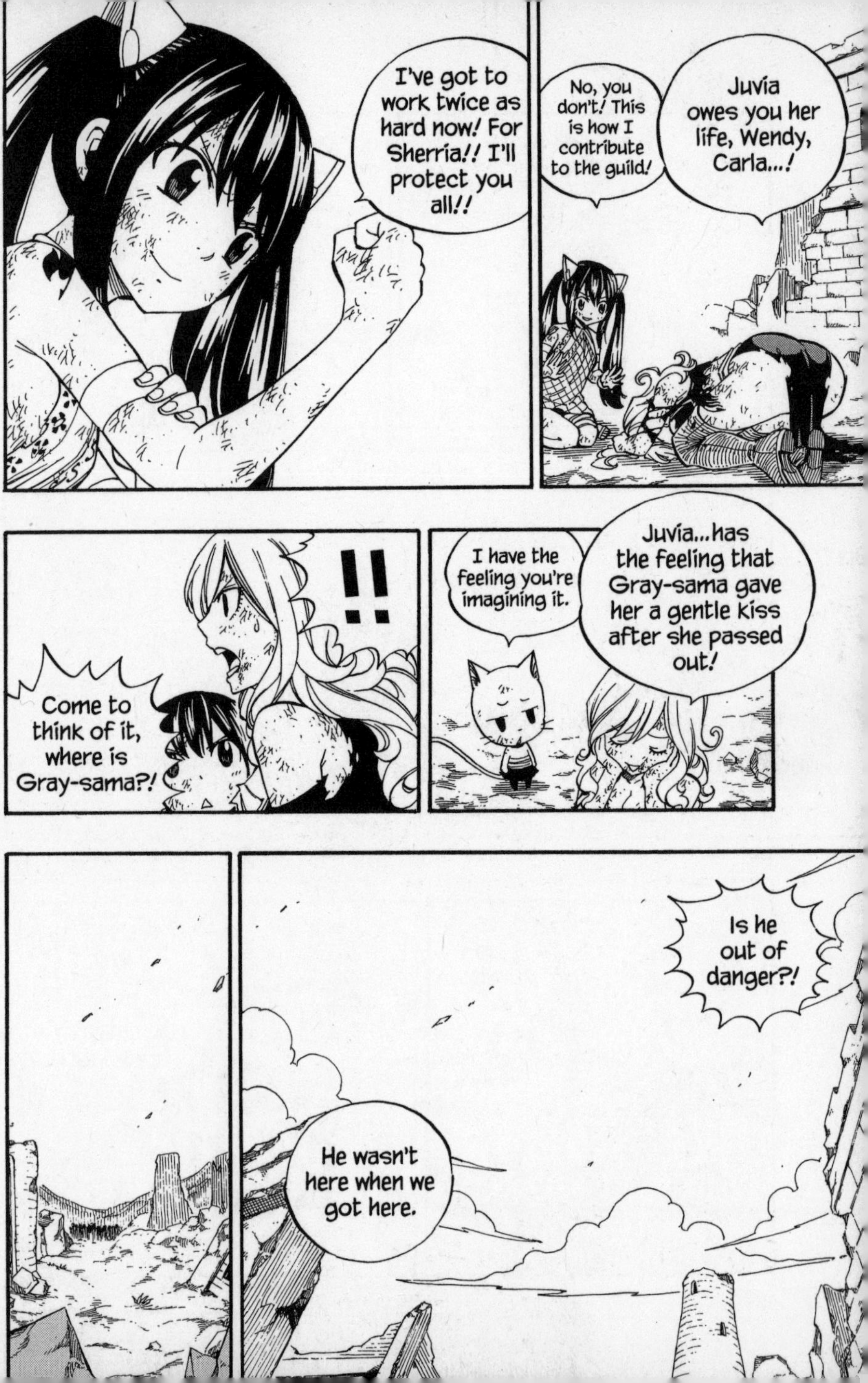
Juvia owes you her life, Wendy, Carla...!
No, you don't! This is how I contribute to the guild!
I've got to work twice as hard now! For Sherria!! I'll protect you all!!
Juvia...has the feeling that Gray-sama gave her a gentle kiss after she passed out!
I have the feeling you're imagining it.
!!
Come to think of it, where is Gray-sama?!
Is he out of danger?!
He wasn't here when we got here.

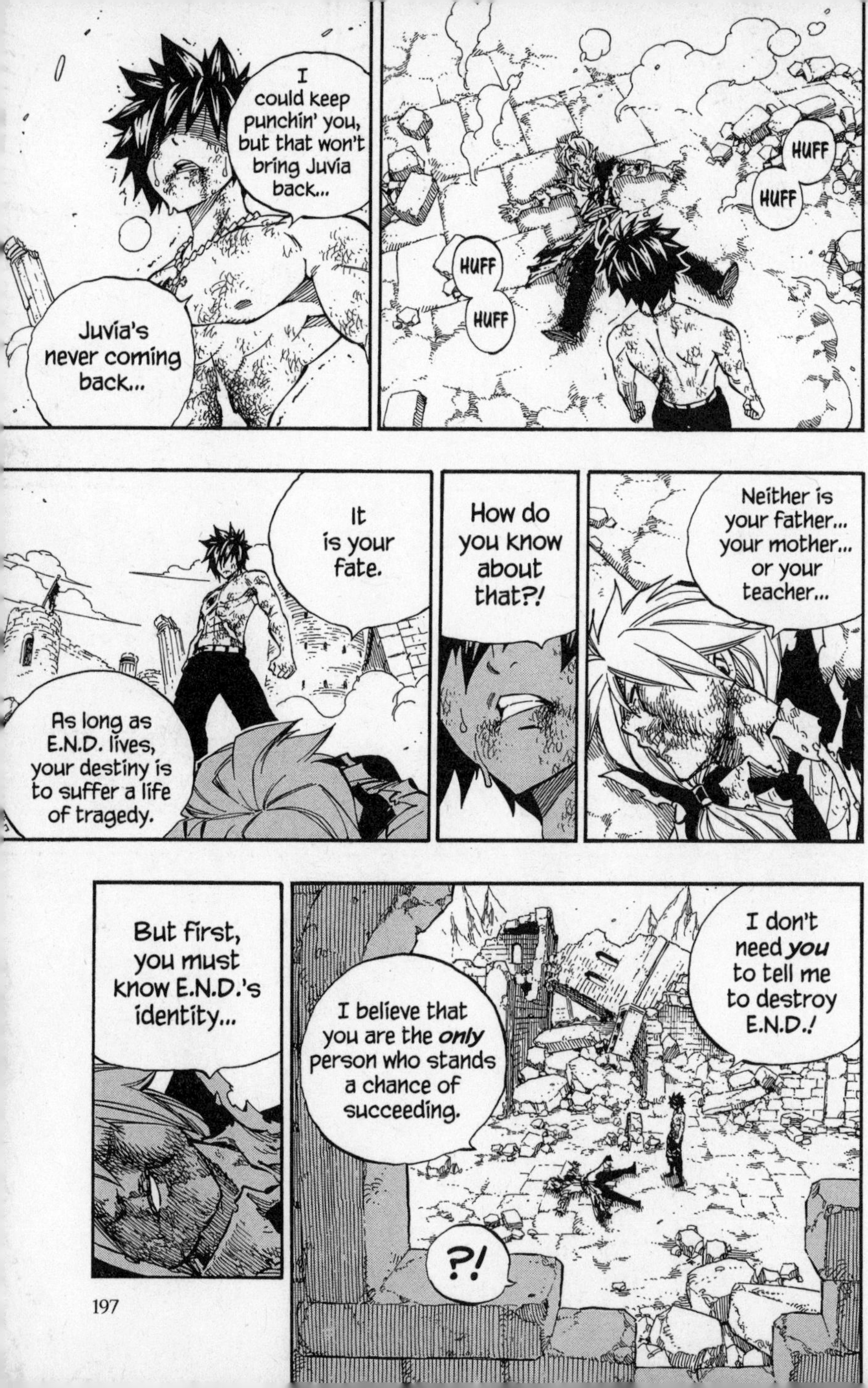
HUFF
HUFF
HUFF
HUFF
I could keep punchin' you, but that won't bring Juvia back...
Juvia's never coming back...
Neither is your father... your mother... or your teacher...
How do you know about that?!
It is your fate.
As long as E.N.D. lives, your destiny is to suffer a life of tragedy.
I don't need *you* to tell me to destroy E.N.D.!
I believe that you are the *only* person who stands a chance of succeeding.
?!
But first, you must know E.N.D.'s identity...

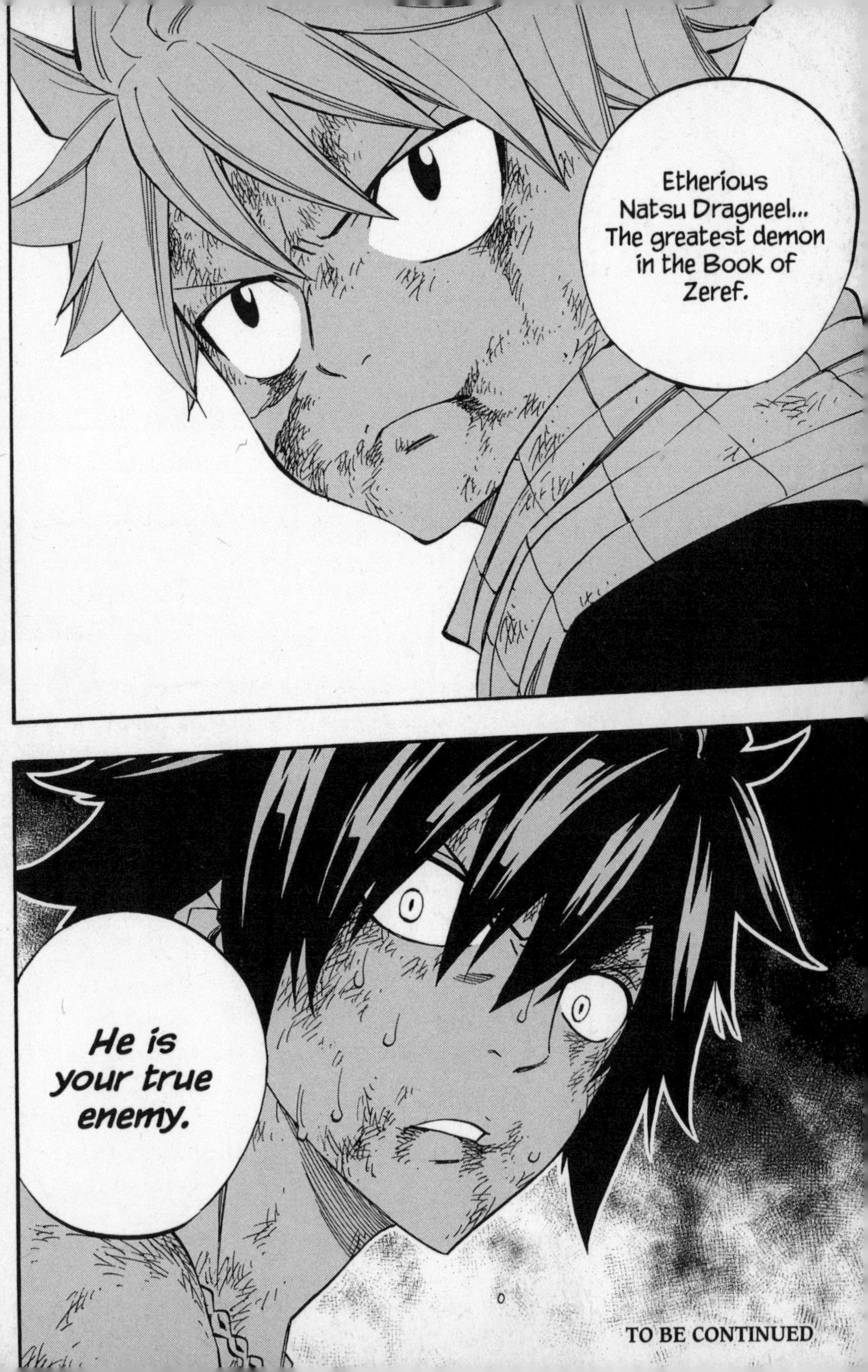
Etherious Natsu Dragneel... The greatest demon in the Book of Zeref.
He is your true enemy.
TO BE CONTINUED

あとがき
Afterword

I'd like to talk a bit about the art exhibition that went up. It went from September 17th, 2016 to September 25th, and it displayed a lot of Fairy Tail original art. Okay, I say "original art," but since a lot of modern manga production takes place in the digital realm, more than half of them were actually reproductions. There was, what you might call, "true" original artwork from the early days, as well as drawings from out of my sketchbooks. I can't tell you how happy I was to see the large numbers of people who visited the exhibition. Actually, I paid a visit myself in secret on the first day. I was disguised so no one would recognize me, and in that way, I got to hear what some of the visitors said.

For example when people said, "I really love this scene!" or, "This Lucy is kinda sexy!" or, "Oh, yeah, that scene. It can still make me cry," you may not have known it, but the author was right behind you at the time (laugh).

But some people saw right through my disguise, and because it was a good opportunity, I started to do sketches. I did quite a few sketches in front of everyone. I'd do a drawing of Gajeel, and someone would say, "Put in Levy next to him," so I'd put in Levy, too. Then, for some reason, I'd sketch Ichiya. I'm so glad that everyone seemed to be having a great time. If there's one thing I regret, it's the gift shop. I had no idea that there'd be so many people who would want so many mementoes, so I'm afraid it was extremely crowded and good items may have been hard to find. So I'll bet it was uncomfortable for quite a few people. I'm really sorry, everybody. I promise to learn from these regrets the next time a chance comes along to have a gift shop.

And so, I find that I'd really like to open another exhibition if the opportunity arises. It would be no fun if it were exactly the same, so my wish is to exhibit recent artwork. I hope I can do it in places where new people can come see it, too.

FROM HIRO MASHIMA

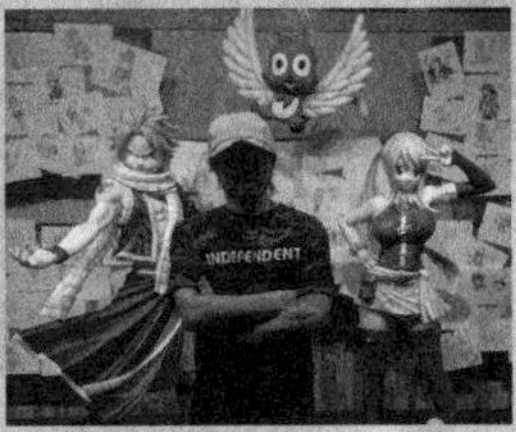
INDEPENDENT

I went to a Fairy Tail exhibition. These are life-sized figures of Natsu, Lucy, and Happy. They are so amazingly well done that even now, I feel like they'll start moving. A lot of guests came to see this, and I want to thank them all from the bottom of my heart!

Original Jacket Design: Hisao Ogawa

FAIRY TAIL 58

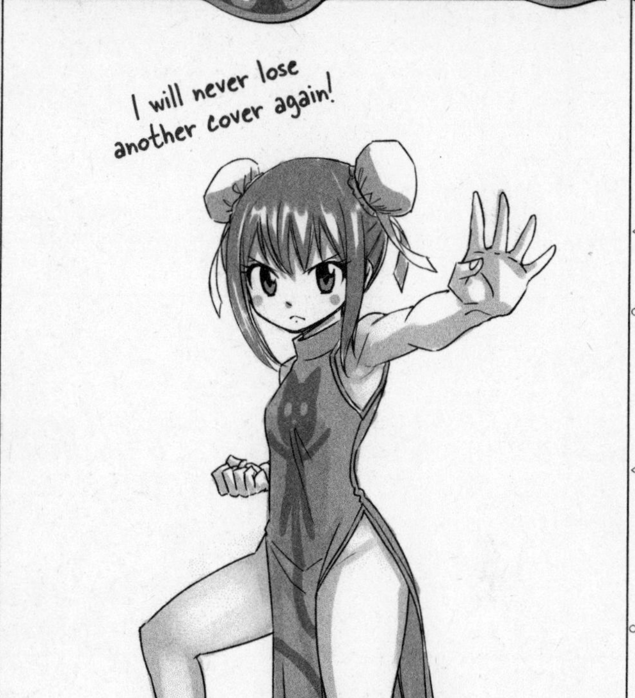
I will never lose another cover again!

HIRO 真島ヒロ MASHIMA

Translation Notes:

Japanese is a difficult language, and translation is often more art than science. For your edification and reading pleasure, here are notes on some of the places where we could have gone in a different direction with our translation of the work, or where a Japanese cultural reference is used.

Page 82, Ginpû-Rôgetsu

This is a Japanese word for which there is no good direct English translation. The meaning refers to the composition and reading of poems that are about sights in the natural world. *Ginpû* is reading poems in gusty winds, and *rôgetsu* means a pleasant night out moon-watching.

Page 100, Haja Kensei

These words in Japanese represent a Buddhist concept of breaking though false doctrines in order to find the true path to enlightenment, and also to protect that true path.

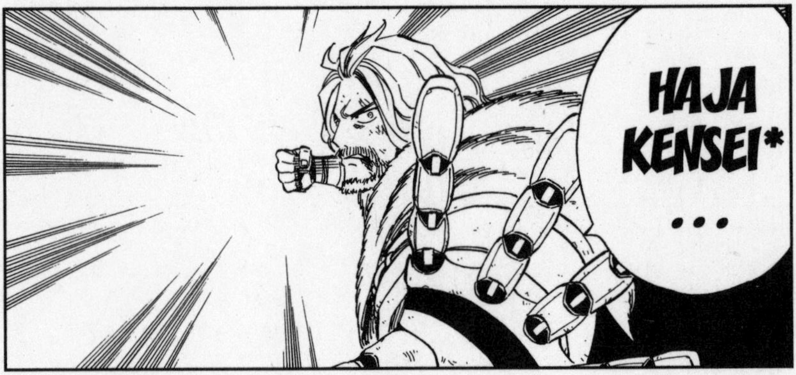
HAJA KENSEI* ...

Page 101, Itten

Itten is the Japanese word for "the entire sky," which in religious works is also called "the firmament." One phrase referencing the Emperor is *Itten no Kimi*, which more literally translates to "the prince under all the skies."

Page 178, Kamui

Kamui, using the *kanji* for "God" and "clothing," is not often used in Japanese. However, it is not completely unheard of. For example, the *kanji* has been used for a Shinto festival, and there is an ancient, legendary Japanese clan that used it. Still, since Invel is using this name for armor, it makes sense that this is a God-like body covering. This should not be confused with the name/legend of Kamui (also called Kamuy) which are the god-like beings in the mythology of the Ainu, an indigenous group located in the far-northern Japanese island of Hokkaido.

Page 188, Gale-Force Slashes

In Japanese, Happy uses the word *kamaitachi* which literally translates to 'weasel scratches.' The term refers to cuts in the skin that one gets from things that aren't visible. For example, from the intense cold of winter or from sharp, strong gale-force winds.

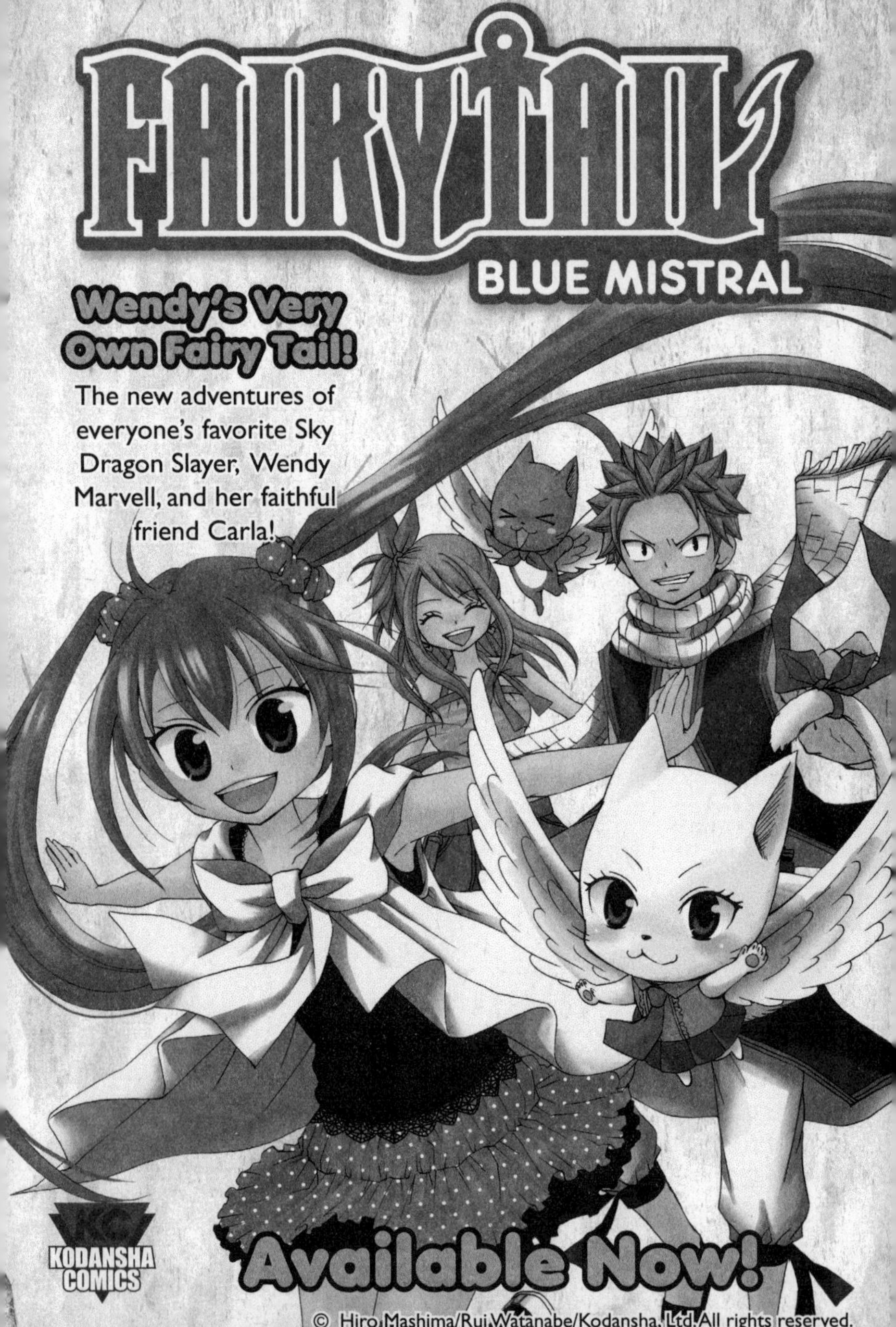
FAIRY TAIL
BLUE MISTRAL
Wendy's Very Own Fairy Tail!
The new adventures of everyone's favorite Sky Dragon Slayer, Wendy Marvell, and her faithful friend Carla!
KC
KODANSHA COMICS
Available Now!
© Hiro Mashima/Rui Watanabe/Kodansha, Ltd. All rights reserved.

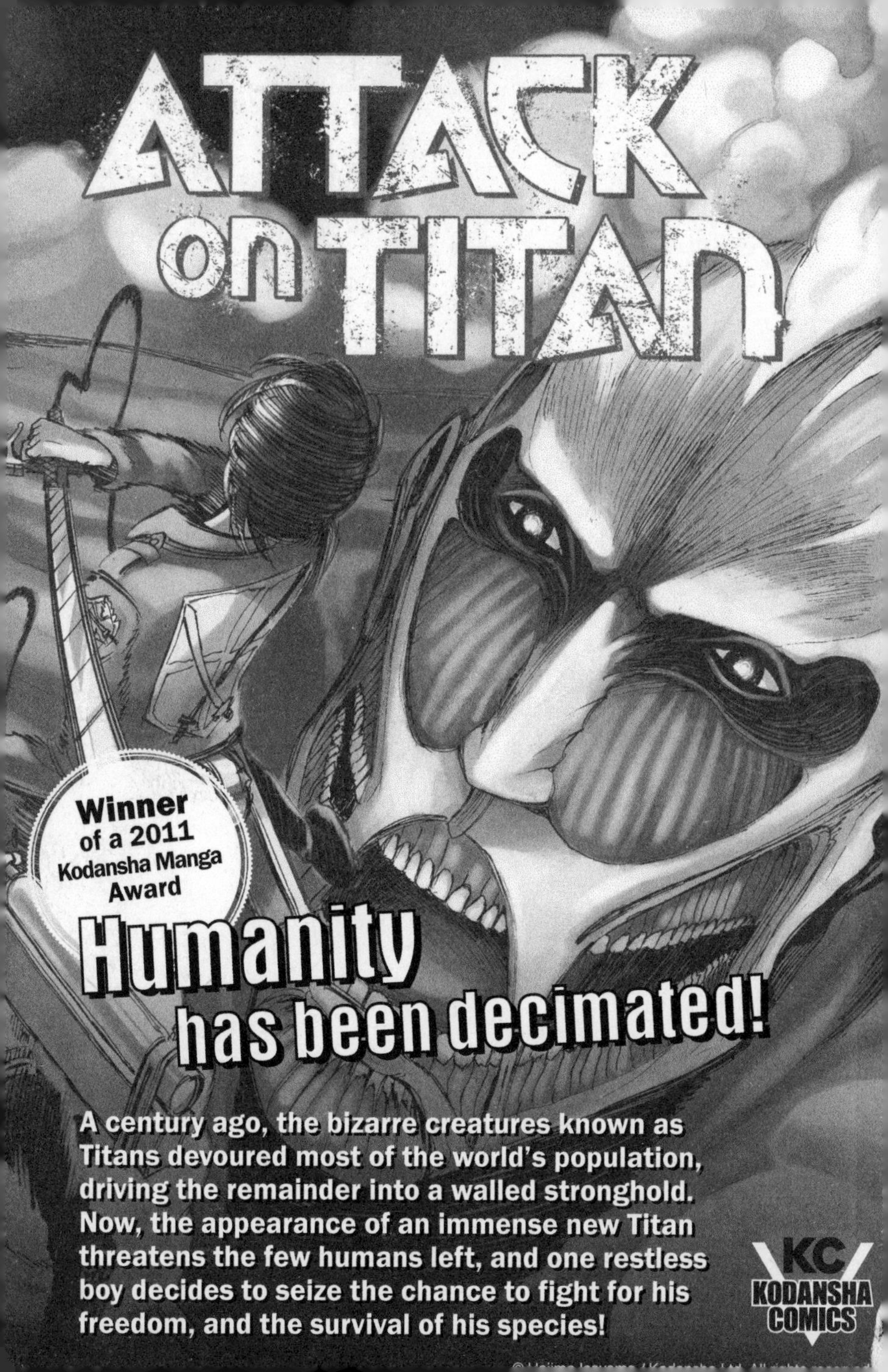
ATTACK on TITAN
Winner of a 2011 Kodansha Manga Award
Humanity has been decimated!
A century ago, the bizarre creatures known as Titans devoured most of the world's population, driving the remainder into a walled stronghold. Now, the appearance of an immense new Titan threatens the few humans left, and one restless boy decides to seize the chance to fight for his freedom, and the survival of his species!
KC KODANSHA COMICS